SURVIVING AND THRIVIN
SECONDARY SCHOOL

G000109749

With an emphasis on developing a reflective, resilient approach that will ensure both effective teaching and teacher well-being, *Surviving and Thriving in the Secondary School* covers key issues that may be encountered in the day-to-day practice of teaching in the secondary school. With evidence-based practice at the forefront, this volume allows new teachers to avoid common pitfalls of teaching and it will help provide a new-found confidence within the classroom.

Including a wide range of tasks that will help guide and demonstrate successful practice, this book covers topics and concerns such as:

- Building relationships within teaching
- Managing and responding to change
- Becoming an inclusive educator
- Working to improve classroom climate and pupil behaviour
- Assessment, homework and marking
- Inclusion of digital technologies and ICT
- Looking after yourself and your professional development

Surviving and Thriving in the Secondary School can be utilised to help support and provide ideas on specific areas of concern, or it can be read as a continuing professional development (CPD) companion, allowing practice to be developed and refined. Written by experts in the field, this volume provides support for all newly qualified teachers and is an essential resource for the first year of teaching and beyond.

Susan Capel is Emeritus Professor (Physical Education) at Brunel University, UK.

Julia Lawrence is Senior Lecturer at the University of Hull, UK.

Marilyn Leask is Chief Editor of the MESH Guides initiative and visiting professor at the University of Winchester and De Montfort University, UK.

Sarah Younie is Professor of Education Innovation at De Montfort University, UK, and Co-Chair of the Education Futures Collaboration charity.

LEARNING TO TEACH SUBJECTS IN THE SECONDARY SCHOOL SERIES

Series Editors: Susan Capel and Marilyn Leask

Designed for all student teachers learning to teach in secondary schools, including those on school-based initial teacher education programmes, the books in this series complement *Learning to Teach in the Secondary School* and its companions, *Starting to Teach in the Secondary School* and this book, *Surviving and Thriving in the Secondary School*. Each book in the series applies underpinning theory and evidence to address practical issues to support student teachers in school and in higher education institutions in learning how to teach a particular subject.

Learning to Teach Art and Design in the Secondary School, 3rd Edition
Edited by Nicholas Addison and Lesley Burgess

Learning to Teach Citizenship in the Secondary School, 3rd Edition
Edited by Liam Gearon

Learning to Teach Design and Technology in the Secondary School, 3rd Edition
Edited by Gwyneth Owen-Jackson

Learning to Teach English in the Secondary School, 5th Edition
Edited by Jon Davison and Caroline Daly

Learning to Teach Foreign Languages in the Secondary School, 4th Edition
Norbert Pachler, Michael Evans, Ana Redondo and Linda Fisher

Learning to Teach Geography in the Secondary School, 3rd Edition
Mary Biddulph, David Lambert and David Balderstone

Learning to Teach History in the Secondary School, 4th Edition
Edited by Terry Haydn, Alison Stephen, James Arthur and Martin Hunt

Learning to Teach ICT in the Secondary School, 3rd Edition
Edited by Marilyn Leask and Norbert Pachler

Learning to Teach Mathematics in the Secondary School, 4th Edition
Edited by Sue Johnston-Wilder, David Pimm and Clare Lee

Learning to Teach Music in the Secondary School, 3rd Edition
Edited by Carolyn Cooke, Keith Evans, Chris Philpott and Gary Spruce

Learning to Teach Physical Education in the Secondary School, 4th Edition
Edited by Susan Capel and Margaret Whitehead

Learning to Teach Religious Education in the Secondary School, 3rd Edition
Edited by L. Philip Barnes

Learning to Teach Science in the Secondary School, 4th Edition
Edited by Rob Toplis

Learning to Teach in the Secondary School, 8th Edition
Edited by Susan Capel, Marilyn Leask and Sarah Younie

Surviving and Thriving in the Secondary School
The NQT's Essential Companion
Edited by Susan Capel, Julia Lawrence, Marilyn Leask and Sarah Younie

SURVIVING AND THRIVING IN THE SECONDARY SCHOOL

The NQT's Essential Companion

Edited by Susan Capel, Julia Lawrence, Marilyn Leask and Sarah Younie

Routledge
Taylor & Francis Group

LONDON AND NEW YORK

First published 2020
by Routledge
2 Park Square, Milton Park, Abingdon, Oxon OX14 4RN

and by Routledge
52 Vanderbilt Avenue, New York, NY 10017

Routledge is an imprint of the Taylor & Francis Group, an informa business

© 2020 selection and editorial matter, Susan Capel, Julia Lawrence, Marilyn Leask and Sarah Younie; individual chapters, the contributors

The right of Susan Capel, Julia Lawrence, Marilyn Leask and Sarah Younie to be identified as the authors of the editorial material, and of the authors for their individual chapters, has been asserted in accordance with sections 77 and 78 of the Copyright, Designs and Patents Act 1988.

All rights reserved. No part of this book may be reprinted or reproduced or utilised in any form or by any electronic, mechanical, or other means, now known or hereafter invented, including photocopying and recording, or in any information storage or retrieval system, without permission in writing from the publishers.

Trademark notice: Product or corporate names may be trademarks or registered trademarks, and are used only for identification and explanation without intent to infringe.

British Library Cataloguing-in-Publication Data
A catalogue record for this book is available from the British Library

Library of Congress Cataloging-in-Publication Data
A catalog record has been requested for this book

ISBN: 978-1-138-48969-1 (hbk)
ISBN: 978-1-138-48970-7 (pbk)
ISBN: 978-1-351-03714-3 (ebk)

Typeset in Interstate
by Deanta Global Publishing Services, Chennai, India

Visit the eResources: www.routledge.com/9781138489707

CONTENTS

Introduction   1

■ Meeting the requirements for newly qualified teacher status
■ Transitioning to beginning teacher ■ How to use this book
■ Continuing professional development (CPD) ■ Terminology used
in this book ■ And finally ■

1 Beyond your initial teacher education: Staying in teaching   6
KATE REYNOLDS

■ The culture and context of your school and learners ■ Building
relationships ■ Building time for yourself – meetings, workload and stress
■ A word about social media and professional associations ■ Inspection,
inspection, inspection ■

2 Managing constant change   13
LIZANA OBERHOLZER

■ Why change and what changes to expect in the education landscape
■ Managing and responding to change ■ Strategies to consider when
faced with change ■

3 Mentoring and being mentored   25
TREVOR WRIGHT

■ Some mentoring challenges ■ Competence, apprenticeship and
reflection ■ The mentoring relationship ■ Focusing observation and
balancing feedback ■ The off-line coach ■

4 Thriving in your subject department   36
STEVEN PUTTICK AND NICK GEE

■ What makes a subject department? ■ Organisational types
■ Departmental cultures ■

ILLUSTRATIONS

Figures

Tables

TASKS

CONTRIBUTORS

Jon Audain is Senior Lecturer in Music and Computing based at the Institute of Education, University of Winchester. He has published in the field of knowledge mobilisation and educational technology and has worked in education for the last 20 years. He is Director of Communications for the MESHGuides initiative, an Apple Distinguished Educator as well as Chair of the Technology, Pedagogy and Education Association.

Nikki Booth is Advisor for Assessment Research and Development at Wolgarston High School, Staffordshire, and PhD researcher at Birmingham City University.

Derek Boyle is the SCITT Director at Bromley Schools' Collegiate, and Fellow of the Chartered College of Teaching.

Natasha Bye-Brooks is Senior Lecturer in Childhood, Youth and Community Studies at the University of Winchester.

Susan Capel is Emeritus Professor (Physical Education) at Brunel University, London.

Helen Cassady is Principal at Cottenham Village College, Cambridgeshire.

Mark Chidler is Senior Lecturer in Geography at Newman University, Birmingham.

Alison Clark-Wilson is Principal Research Lead for the ERDF-funded EDUCATE Project at the UCL Knowledge Lab, UCL Institute of Education (www.educate/london).

Andrew Csizmadia is Senior Lecturer in Computer Science Education at Newman University, Birmingham and Academic Lead for the BCS Certificate in Computer Science Teaching.

Paul Gardner is Senior Lecturer in English/Literacy in the School of Education at Curtin University, Western Australia. He previously worked in the UK and is the UK Literacy Association's Ambassador for Australia.

Jennie Golding is Associate Professor in Mathematics Education at University College London.

Fiona Hall is Senior Lecturer and Award Leader for Education Studies at Staffordshire University and an HLTA Assessor for HLTA North; her research interests relate to the work of teaching assistants.

Barry Harwood is Initial Teacher Education Manager at the University of Winchester.

Terry Haydn is Professor of Education at the School of Education and Lifelong Learning at the University of East Anglia, UK.

Rosalyn Hyde is Principal Teaching Fellow in mathematics education and PGCE mathematics lead at the University of Southampton.

Julia Lawrence is Senior Lecturer at the University of Hull.

Marilyn Leask is visiting Professor of Education at De Montfort and Winchester universities UK, co-chair of the MESHGuide research summaries initiative, and board member of the Council for Subject Associations and the Technology and Pedagogy in Education association.

Brian Matthews ran the PGCE at Goldsmiths, is now part-time at Kings College London and Chair of Fabian Education Policy Group.

Lyn Matthews works as a Primary Consultant with a focus on teaching and learning, coaching and family learning.

Lizana Oberholzer is Senior Lecturer and Programme Lead for the Masters in Leadership in Education, PGCE in Education (Non-QTS) and Postgraduate Teaching Apprenticeships at the University of East London, NASBTT and BAMEed Trustee.

Julia O'Kelly was Head of Secondary PGCE at the University of Chichester for 13 years. She is now retired and is continuing her EdD research into Initial Teacher Education.

Eira Wyn Patterson is Senior Lecturer in Education and Programme Lead for the Masters in Education at the University of Winchester.

Rachel Peckover is Deputy Headteacher at Burbage Junior School and Doctoral Researcher at De Montfort University.

Elizabeth Plummer is Senior Lecturer in Secondary ITE(PE) and Lecturer in Sport and Health at Newman University Birmingham.

Maxine Pountney is Senior and Assessor with HLTA North, one of four Regional Providers of HTLA Assessment, and is former Programme Lead for the HLTA Award based in Sheffield.

Mark Pulsford is a former Primary School Teacher and now Senior Teaching Fellow in the Centre for Education Studies at the University of Warwick.

Steven Puttick is Head of Programmes (Secondary, FE, Research Education) at Bishop Grosseteste University, Lincoln.

Kate Reynolds is Executive Dean and Professor of Education Policy at Bath Spa Institute for Education and Chair of Wellsway multi-academy trust.

Sana Rizvi is Lecturer in Graduate School of Education at University of Exeter.

Chris Shelton is Head of Education at the University of Chichester.

Alexandra Titchmarsh teaches Geography and is Associate Assistant Head (pastoral), including safeguarding at a secondary school in West London.

Trevor Wright was Senior Fellow of the University of Worcester where he led on literacy and English education as well as developing workshops on advanced mentor training, which he presents for ITE providers. He is author and editor of *How to be a Brilliant Mentor*, *How to be a Brilliant Teacher*, *How to be a Brilliant Trainee Teacher* and *How to be a Brilliant English Teacher*.

Sarah Younie is Professor of Education Innovation at De Montfort University, Co-chair of the Education Futures Collaboration charity and is the Editor-in-Chief of *Technology, Pedagogy & Education* journal.

Introduction

The aim of this book is to support you to not only survive, but thrive within your classroom, your tutor time and the school more generally, and to contribute to enhancing pupils' learning, the school and education. The content has been developed to reflect information that you may need during the early period of your teaching career as you develop your effectiveness as a teacher. The contributions in this book come from teacher educators and practitioners with a wide range of experience and research-based knowledge.

Having successfully completed your initial teacher education (ITE), you have developed the knowledge, skills and understanding needed to meet the standards to achieve qualified teacher status (QTS). Although you have qualified, the learning does not stop. Now, you are learning to use these skills across a range of new contexts, embedding and developing further those skills you learnt during your ITE. You are also developing new knowledge, skills and understanding – indeed, this is a career-long process.

In many ways qualifying as a teacher is similar to learning to drive. You learn to pass the test and once you have that certificate/licence you look to apply those skills in actually driving alone and having an increased level of responsibility and accountability. As in driving, when you enter the classroom as a qualified teacher, the support networks you might have experienced in ITE diminish. No one is there on a day-to-day basis to put on the brakes or take over the steering of the lesson – although you have support from a mentor and other staff. During your first year of teaching you are working as hard if not harder than you did during your ITE programme. Understanding how these changes might impact on your work/life balance is therefore important.

Teaching is a complex activity and is both an art and a science. An effective teacher is one who can integrate theory with practice, use evidence to underpin their professional judgement and use structured reflection to improve practice. They are comfortable in the presence of young people and are interested in them as individuals as well as learners. An effective teacher motivates and encourages pupils by planning interesting lessons, and links their teaching to the life experiences of pupils and the world around them. Part of being effective is to respect your pupils and in turn earn their respect, not only through the skills mentioned, but by maintaining firm but fair discipline so that your classroom is one where all expect to learn.

However, there is no one correct way of teaching, no one specific set of skills, techniques and procedures that you must master and apply mechanically. This is, in part, because your pupils are all different and each day brings a new context in which they operate. Also, every teacher is an individual and brings something of their own unique personality to the job and their interactions with pupils. You will however come across quite different approaches to teaching. Although you may come across some school networks where formulaic teaching is required – teachers are given an approach, which all follow: other schools allow more flexibility.

Meeting the requirements for newly qualified teacher status

In the UK, each country has specific requirements that you need to meet for your first year of teaching and what support you can expect in the first, and early, years. Although you should be assigned a member of staff within your school as an induction mentor to support you during the transition from student teacher to beginning teacher, it is also helpful to seek support and guidance from other colleagues. These might be colleagues in your department or faculty or other beginning teachers within your school, local authority or network/Multi Academy Trust. Within your induction period, specialist training should be provided for you to ensure that you have the capacity to complete the specific requirements of your induction in relation to evidencing progress against professional standards or competencies. Whilst this provides you with new networking opportunities, try to maintain your existing professional networks, be they, for example, fellow teachers with whom you went through your ITE programme, or the individuals/ organisations that supported you during your ITE.

Be proactive in seeking advice and guidance, and most importantly don't be afraid to talk about your challenges. Remember you are still learning and continue to do so throughout your teaching career.

Transitioning to beginning teacher

The transition from ITE to starting your first post can be challenging, as you have greater levels of responsibility. You need to get to know not only your pupils, but the wider staff (anyone who contributes to the effective running of the school) and processes. Consider also how relationships might change if you are working in the same school or organisation in which you undertook your ITE – you are no longer a student teacher, so the support you may have been used to is unlikely to still be there.

There is no doubt that the first/early years of teaching are demanding of your time and on you personally as you learn how to manage and motivate adolescents and as you become used to expectations, processes and ways of working that are new to you. But the job does become easier. To return to our analogy of learning to drive a car, where each skill becomes almost habitual, in time many of the ways of managing classrooms and enhancing pupils learning become second nature to you. For example, managing the flow of the lesson becomes instinctive: from setting out the learning goals to the plenary of each lesson where you or the pupils summarise the learning, the work to be done before the next lesson and recap on the longer-term learning outcomes for the pupils in the specific area being taught. However, although it becomes second nature, it should not become routine; you need to continually try to improve in order to enhance pupils' learning – and your enjoyment of being a teacher.

How to use this book

During your ITE you were exposed to a range of knowledge required of a teacher. Indeed, you might have used *Learning to Teach in the Secondary School: A Companion to School Experience* (edited by Capel, Leask and Younie, 2019). Contents included in this text have been selected as those which are particularly relevant to you in your early career. Each chapter within this book is designed to extend the core knowledge covered in ITE and to be read as a stand-alone piece. Where appropriate, links are made to other chapters within this book, to the other texts in the series mentioned below and to additional readings and resources that might support the development of your knowledge.

Whilst there are no discrete sections to the book, the first chapters focus on your transition into the classroom, looking at how aspects might change now that you are teaching full time, and offering support as to how you might manage these changes. Consideration is given to how the way you are mentored might change along with developing your understanding of working in a department and with a wider range of staff supporting learning.

We have also included chapters to encourage you to think about your wider role in supporting the needs of all pupils, with a particular focus on the role of the form tutor as well as your responsibilities in developing pupils' literacy; numeracy; personal, social and health education; and in responding to special education needs and disabilities.

You need to continue to develop your knowledge skills and understanding in relation to teachers' standards and competencies. We have therefore included chapters that focus on developing your skillset in the management of behaviour, transitions, learning environments, as well as assessment and progress.

However, we also acknowledge the stress that teaching can bring, and the final chapters of the book seek to support you in relation to the management of your own workload as well as looking at opportunities for further professional development as you progress within the profession.

This book extends knowledge in the generic, companion text which is designed for student teachers *Learning to Teach in the Secondary School: A Companion to School Experience* (edited by Capel, Leask and Younie, 2019). This book and the generic text are backed up by subject-specific texts in two series (*Learning to Teach (subject) in the Secondary School* and *A Practical Guide to Teaching (subject) in the Secondary School*) (series edited by Capel and Leask) and by *Readings for Learning to Teach in the Secondary School: A Companion to M Level Study* (Capel, Leask and Turner, 2010). This latter text provides extension reading around key areas of professional knowledge underpinning teaching. These books are also supported by *Debates in (subject)* (series edited by Capel). In addition, the MESHGuides (Mapping Education Specialist knowHow) research and evidence summaries (www.meshguides.org) are designed to provide evidence-informed guidance to support you in the early years of your career.

Continuing professional development (CPD)

Opportunities for CPD and ongoing development, which can bring satisfaction as you become more knowledgeable and competent, vary from school to school, region to region and country to country. Try to ensure that you meet regularly with the member of staff with responsibility for your development within the school to discuss opportunities that might become available for you in your overall development and in aspects of work which you might want to pursue in future, e.g. to become a head of year or house or developing a role in teaching and learning. Refer back to targets for development that you might have identified at the end of your ITE programme through your career entry development profile (CEPD) or beginning teacher transition plan. But remember that CPD is not just about going on courses. It might include accessing resources online, joining discussion groups or social media groups, and also observing other teachers in other schools. It also includes using this book to support your development. Throughout we suggest you focus on reflecting on your own areas for development and how your development might be best achieved.

As we have mentioned previously, the standards you have to meet in your first year of teaching depend on the country and school in which you are teaching. Throughout the book, we advise you to check how the advice given can help you to demonstrate that you are meeting the standards for your first (induction) year of teaching.

Terminology used in this book

We call school children *learners* to avoid confusion with *students*, by which we mean people in further and higher education. We refer to those teachers in their first few years of teaching as *beginning teachers* and those learning to teach as *student teachers*.

And finally

Finally, we benefited from advice from experienced teachers when starting our teaching careers and we hope you have this opportunity too. Some examples of how you may benefit include:

- Observing experienced teachers teaching pupils you find challenging. Look at, for example, the pace of the lesson, the way they speak to the pupils, the ways they keep the pupils on task, where the pupils sit, how much attention the teacher pays them, how the teacher engages them in the lesson and the work.
- Role playing the behaviour of pupils you find challenging, consider what it might feel like for the pupil to behave in that way in front of their peer group and then plan different ways that you as the teacher might manage that behaviour.
- Acting on ideas experienced teachers can give you about how to be efficient in keeping up-to-date with marking and paperwork.

■ Getting involved with your subject association (see Appendix 2) and experience the enjoyment of working with others who love their subject; maybe research the teaching of the subject and find out who is exploring how to improve teaching, learning and pupil engagement with the subject, as well as engagement with the world of work.

Do consider how you reflect on your own teaching to ensure that you take time to draw out the positives and areas for development.

Being able to switch off from teaching is important so that you maintain a work/life balance. Protecting leisure time and activities is part of developing this balance. Consider how you can manage your time effectively.

We hope that the text provides the stimulus for you to want to continue to learn and develop throughout your career as a teacher.

Susan Capel, Julia Lawrence, Marilyn Leask and Sarah Younie
January 2019

1 Beyond your initial teacher education

Staying in teaching

Kate Reynolds

Introduction

So, you're a teacher! Welcome to one of the best professions in the world. You have joined tens of thousands of others who have made a personal and professional commitment to making a difference to children and young people. On behalf of all those children and their families we should like to thank you and to wish you a fulfilling career.

This chapter is focused on your early days as a teacher and how you can build the skills and expertise to support your professional development and your long-term career. These days can be confusing and complicated as you come to terms with your new role and your new career. This chapter has been developed using insights from teachers who were one year into their careers. These newly qualified teachers (NQTs) came together as part of Bath Spa Institute for Education's annual NQT research day in the summer of 2017. Various sections of the chapter include quotations from these NQTs to provide insights to help you on your journey as you start out on your career and to give you guidance and advice from those who have already taken the path you have embarked on. (Note: the term 'beginning teacher' is used in this book to include teachers in their first year of teaching and is used in this chapter except where referring specifically to these NQTs.) The insights are intended to help you as you start out on your career and to give you guidance and advice from those who have already taken the path you have chosen. The various sections include quotations from those newly qualified teachers/beginning teachers and are intended to help you on your journey.

OBJECTIVES

By the end of the chapter, you should be able to:

- understand the context in which you work as a beginning teacher;
- prepare to start at your new school;
- build relationships and your resilience;

- professionalise your use of social media;
- manage time and stress.

Check how the information in this chapter enables you to meet the requirements for your first year of teaching.

This chapter also looks at professional associations and trade unions and the roles they play in supporting teachers, particularly in the demanding political and social environment that is now so much a part of being a teacher.

Ultimately, we hope this chapter helps you to enjoy improving your teaching, to avoid career stagnation, to remain positive and to remind you why you went into teaching and the profound and lasting impact you can have on the next generation.

The culture and context of your school and learners

Day one: your new job - you're a teacher! Start at the beginning!

> Forgive yourself for being at the start of your teaching career. You're not supposed to know it all. Be easy on yourself. Try not to be overwhelmed by it all but try one thing at a time.

> *(NQT 1)*

When you start any new job it can be a daunting task to get to know the culture and context of the organisation. This is especially important in teaching where beginning teachers are faced with the dynamic of getting to know new learners, new staff and colleagues and a new working environment. This can be a challenge for the most experienced of us! Task 1.1 is about understanding the school context.

 Task 1.1   Understanding the school context

There is a lot you can do to prepare yourself for the start of your teaching career:

- Get to know the school - each school is different and early research before you join the school is important to help you to understand the culture of the organisation.
- Look at the website.
- Look at inspection reports (on ofsted.gov.uk in England), do your research.
- Take a walk around the community to understand the local context and how people feel about the school. Consider the socio-economic characteristics of the area and consider how they might impact on your role within the school and your teaching? What experiences do your learners bring with them into school?

Be very cautious about what's written in the local media - this can sometimes be a distortion of what's really going on.

Record the information in your professional development portfolio (PDP) (or similar) to refer to and add to later as you learn about the school.

Understanding your new class is equally as important. We know from research that learners come to school with their own understanding, knowledge and perceptions of both the role of education and their place within it. So think about the learners in your own classroom. What do they already know? What experiences have they already had that could influence their approach to learning?

Studies such as those by Berrington et al. (2016) in the UK and Smith and Skrbis (2017) in Australia used large longitudinal datasets to examine the relationships between beliefs about academic success, educational aspirations and educational attainment. Building on Bourdieu's notion of 'habitus' (Bourdieu, 1973), Berrington et al.'s study shows how parental attitudes can have an impact on educational attainment and learners' own aspirations. So we all, teachers and learners, parents and staff, bring to the classroom preconceived notions of what schooling is, its role in our lives and the difference it could make to our future careers and employment. Task 1.2 is about gathering information about your classes so as to understand learners better.

   Task 1.2   Gathering information about your classes

Do your homework before you start your job by gathering the following information:

How many learners are there in your classes?
How many learners are there in your classes with special educational needs?
Do you have learners with English as an additional language – if so what languages do they speak and how can you build this into your teaching?
Do you have any learners who have caring responsibilities? Can you adapt your style so they feel included in your classroom?
Do you have any learners on free school meals? How is the school supporting them? What strategies are already being used in your school that you can adapt to support learners in your classroom?
Are there any instances of bullying or harassment that may have had an impact on your learners?

In the light of this information, what can you do to provide the learners you are responsible for with a supportive inclusive environment that helps them to get the very best from your teaching? See also Chapter 10 for advice on inclusion.
Store the information in your PDP to refer to later as you are planning lessons.

Moreover, in understanding your new classes, it is important to understand the local context in which your learners live and Task 1.1 is designed to help you in this respect. Learners bring these experiences to the classroom and this impacts on your relationships with them. It is useful to understand the local community that your learners come from. What are the demographics of the community? Who are the community leaders? What role do church and faith groups have in supporting your learners' communities?

Building relationships

The lives the learners bring to the classroom can also be a valuable learning tool for the teacher. One of the top tips from the NQTs tells us:

> Building relationships with students is important. Spend some time following students around! You get to know students and then some good strategies and teaching ideas.
>
> (NQT 2)

As well as building strong relationships with your learners, one of the key challenges is to build effective relationships with your headteacher and your colleagues because a school is a community in its own right and a good relationship with your headteacher and other colleagues will support you throughout your teaching career. Headteachers have a daunting task leading schools in complicated social and political environments as well as doing their very best to support their teaching workforce. Get to know your headteacher and understand what motivates them and how you might help them. Leading a school is a complex and very difficult task (witness the numerous books on educational leadership), do what you can to help your headteacher and support them so that they can support you. Make sure you build a strong relationship with your headteacher and other colleagues – it is always useful to touch base away from formal meetings – invite them for a coffee!

Building time for yourself – meetings, workload and stress

So, how can you do this in the early days of your career? When you start any new job, particularly in education, your days quickly become packed with meetings, deadlines, worksheets, action plans and all sorts of administrative activities that help make the organisation run. As a teacher you have an obligation to manage these tasks in the most effective way that you can in order to support your learners, the school and, most importantly, yourself. The NQTs we spoke to emphasised the importance of planning and organisation in order to build resilience in teachers and manage an effective work-life balance. Findon and Johnston-Wilder provide detailed advice in *LTT8* (2019). This means that:

> Although it is great to take every opportunity you can, it is okay to say no. Don't take on extra work if it is going to negatively impact your current responsibilities or more importantly your health.
>
> (NQT 3)

Although, like many professions, teaching can be a stressful job and there is governmental and, indeed, global concern about the numbers of teachers leaving the profession (United Nations Educational, Scientific and Cultural Organization (UNESCO), 2015), some studies are starting to point to the importance of the school in supporting teachers so that they can build resilience, enabling them to continue their career and perform at their very best. As well as the school having an obligation to you, you have an obligation to the school to build resilience amongst your learners and in yourself.

The emotional demands of teaching have been long recognised. For example, teachers were one of the first professional groups in the UK to have government-sponsored guidance written for them about how to prevent and manage stress. However, the evidence ... made it clear that demonstrating resilience by being able to recover everyday as well as expressly challenging difficulties in the workplace, was not an individual responsibility. Rather, shown by the examples (within the next section [of this report]), resilience was a capacity that arose in interactions between people and the practices they inhabited in their workplaces (Day et al., 2011, p. 7).

You could use the chapter from *LTT8* (Findon and Johnston-Wilder, 2019) for suggestions on how you can manage stress, workload and time.

A word about social media and professional associations

As stated in the previous section, supporting yourself in managing the stresses of your new role is important. These days social media is an important part of our working lives. Social media can both be a cause of stress (a 'stressor') and a mechanism for supporting you in your role. Remember it's the same for your learners! Remember to protect yourself and your learners from the worst of social media (online bullying and harassment) by taking simple steps like checking who is the author/person behind the social media and do they have a particular agenda they are pushing. Remember you can always 'block' those people who are bullying you – and of course if a child's safety is at all threatened you must report it, in line with your school's safeguarding policy.

So, there seem to be two schools of thought about social media and the internet. The first is that social media is full of trolls, people showing off, people seeking attention and dodgy websites! The second sees social media and the internet as another source of information, support and advice. That doesn't mean we shouldn't stay critical of sources and where information has come from, in much the same way that we are critical of books, newspapers and magazines. However, for teachers, who can often feel isolated in their own classrooms, the internet can be a source of companionship and wise words. In particular, teachers – both newly qualified and those with more experience – have been quick to use Twitter as a source of sharing advice and information, as well as views on government policy! It is worth taking some time to explore the vast array of bloggers and Twitter users to find those who can support you in your work as a classroom teacher. Websites such as meshguides.org, enable teachers to have access to up-to-date academic research in a way that is easily digestible given their workloads (see also Appendix 3).

Many of the mainstream education newspapers and professional associations now have a digital or internet presence. This helps you as a beginning teacher to keep up-to-date with your subject and with some of the wider policy changes that are a day-to-day part of being a teacher. Publications such as *Schools Weekly*, the *Times Educational Supplement* (now known as *Tes*) and your professional subject association can offer invaluable support to help you to be resilient in your career and to get through the knocks and challenges that face all teachers.

As well as picking up top tips from other teachers on Twitter, the internet can be a valuable source of continuous professional development. Search for your local university where you may find a wide range of activities, public lectures and support, particularly if you intend to go on to postgraduate studies such as a Masters, PhD or an education professional doctorate. Organisations such as Network for Learning (www. networkforlearning.org.uk) provide nationwide opportunities for practising teachers to update their curriculum and their assessment techniques and to keep abreast of changes in classroom policy. Needless to say, you need to be very careful about your digital footprint and to ensure that your digital profile is that of a professional.

To help you start your internet journey, some websites, blogs and Twitter accounts that you might find useful are listed at the end of this chapter as Further resources – use these as a starting point and build your own suite of social media contacts.

Trade unions can also be a valuable source of support for teachers. As well as supporting you in your day-to-day terms and conditions of work, these organisations represent your interests at the local and national level as they seek to influence the development of education policy. You will have heard of many of the unions from your initial teacher education. Unions such as the National Education Union (NEU) and the National Association of Schoolmasters Union of Women Teachers (NASUWT) also provide resources, courses, advice and support that can be very useful as you build your career (see Further resources).

Inspection, inspection, inspection

In England, the inspection agency is the Office for Standards in Education, Children's Services and Skills (Ofsted). In Northern Ireland it is the Education and Training Inspectorate; in Wales it is Estyn; and in Scotland, school inspections come under Education Scotland. These inspection agencies have become synonymous with the actual inspections of schools. In England, the word 'Ofsted' can strike fear into the heart of many an excellent teacher. However, I like to look at inspection in a different way – it is your chance to shine! It is your chance to show how very good you are at teaching. The key to a good inspection is to know your learners and your school, know your data and, in particular, know the progress of learners in your classroom. Again, this is where social media can be a huge support – ask on Twitter for top tips for your inspection, what went well for others, what you can learn from and how you can build this into your day-to-day classroom practice.

SUMMARY AND KEY POINTS

This chapter has focused on some of the key issues you face as you start your new career as a teacher. Specifically it has looked at how to help you:

- understand the context in which you work as a beginning teacher;
- prepare to start at your new school;
- build relationships and build your resilience;
- professionalise your use of social media;
- manage your time and stress.

Teaching is a challenging profession but it is also an incredibly rewarding one! You are joining a profession with hundreds of thousands of people who can support you. Have a long and prosperous career and I wish you all the very best.

Your experience as a teacher is bigger than one difficult placement, mentor, head of department, class or lesson observation. Stick in there! It gets better!

(NQT 4)

Record in your professional development portfolio (PDP), how the information in this chapter enables you to meet the requirements for your first year of teaching.

Further resources

Findon, M. and Johnston-Wilder, S. (2019) 'Developing your resilience: managing stress, workload and time', in S. Capel, M. Leask and S. Younie (eds.), *Learning to Teach in the Secondary School: A Companion to School Experience*, 8th edn, Abingdon: Routledge, pp. 43-59.

 Websites:

https://debrakidd.wordpress.com - Debra's blog has a big following and raises issues of concern to the teaching profession.

www.edcentral.uk - another source of a daily roundup of news for teachers.

www.independentthinking.co.uk - an organisation dedicated to supporting teachers in the classroom to think independently!

www.nasuwt.org.uk - NASUWT

www.neu.org.uk - NEU

www.schoolsimprovement.net - provides a daily roundup of education news via email.

www.schoolsweek.co.uk - a weekly magazine for schools and teachers.

www.teachertoolkit.co.uk -A great place to start and has links to many other websites and tools. Badged as 'the most influential education blog in the UK', it is focused on the United Kingdom - most countries have something similar - and you can do an internet search for 'useful websites for teachers in [your country]'.

www.tes.co.uk - the national newspaper for teachers and teaching - Tes (*Times Educational Supplement*) gives weekly news and reviews.

All of the websites above also have Twitter accounts - so there's lots out there to help you.

Twitter accounts:

@Bathspaeddean - you can follow me if you want!

www.theeducator.com/blog/20-uk-teachers-follow-twitter - a list of 20 teachers to follow on Twitter. Take a look and see who you like.

Appendices 2 and 3 list subject associations, teaching councils and relevant websites.

Books in the *Learning to Teach* series that you may find helpful are as follows:

Capel, S., Leask, M. and Younie, S. (eds.) (2019) *Learning to Teach in the Secondary School: A Companion to School Experience*, 8th edn, Abingdon: Routledge.
This book is designed as a core textbook to support student teachers through their initial teacher education programme.

Capel, S., Leask, M. and Turner, T. (eds.) (2010) *Readings for Learning to Teach in the Secondary School: A Companion to M Level Study*, Abingdon: Routledge.
This book brings together essential readings to support you in your critical engagement with key issues raised in this textbook.

The subject-specific books in the *Learning to Teach* series, the *Practical (subject) Guides*, *Debates in (subject)* and *Mentoring (subject) Teachers* are also very useful.

2 Managing constant change

Lizana Oberholzer

Introduction

Change has become the constant in relation to the wider education landscape. For example, *The Importance of Teaching: The Schools' White Paper* (Department of Education (DfE), 2010) outlined reforms to the National Curriculum in England as well as changes to examinations, teacher education and training and how special education needs and disabilities (SEND) should be approached. Further, developments in the different types of schools being created in England have added to this changing landscape. Despite these challenges, teachers continue to work tirelessly to ensure that pupils make effective progress.

Such changes impact greatly on teacher workload (see Chapter 20; and Findon and Johnson-Wilder (in *LTT8*, 2019), with concerns raised on how changes also impact on teachers' and pupils' well-being. These concerns are being recognised, see for example, DfE (2010) for more information). However, while such publications suggest there is a clear and important need and drive to review the challenges faced by teachers in the workplace, factors including budget constraints and limited funding to support pupils' needs and for the upkeep of premises are evident and impact on workload.

Apart from teachers being challenged by the constant change in the education landscape, the reality for a beginner or novice teacher is that change occurs daily in the classroom and in the school context in which you find yourself. You need to understand the changes taking place and your role within these in order to digest, manage and respond to them. You need to respond to changes in a pragmatic and positive way. It is therefore important to discuss the importance of how to respond to change in a forever changing landscape, both as a front-line member of staff as well as a colleague responding to the national picture. As you start your career, take time to work with your mentor and colleagues to discuss how to engage effectively with this.

OBJECTIVES

At the end of the chapter you should be able to:

■   understand what changes are taking place within education in England;
■   understand what strategies to consider when you need to respond to change;
■   access a range of strategies in your own personal toolkit to enable you to cope
    with change;
■   reflect on the impact of change on your own professional development.

Check how the information in this chapter enables you to meet the requirements for
your first year of teaching.

Why change and what changes to expect in the education landscape

Change is often necessary and important to move us into the right direction. As educationalists we are encouraged to reflect on our practice in response to changing needs. Such needs may be in relation to others around us, economic, national criteria, changing standards and/or learners' needs. Whether in the classroom, school context or in a wider context in regard to the education framework, in order to respond to such changes throughout your career, you need to become an effective, reflective and resilient practitioners.

It is often the case that you observe leaders responding to change in a variety of different ways. You might that observe one might respond to change in a reactive way and another in a reflective, strategic and progressive way. There are many factors and reasons for the way in which leaders respond in the way they do. Often responses are dictated by the situation and the sense of urgency, which is demanded of the school, the department or the individual. As a beginner or novice teacher, you need to learn how to respond to situations and to reflect upon the impact of your actions both in and on practice (Schon, 1983).

It is often the case that change is something that is not favoured by many, and responses by colleagues are often that 'we have always done it like that'. The view is often that if it works well – why change it! However, in a changing landscape that needs to prepare young people for the challenges and changes in an ever-evolving world, change within education is necessary to ensure that we prepare them well.

The White Paper (DfE, 2010) argues that curriculum changes aim to move the education system towards improved world rankings and a world class education for young people to ensure that they are competitive in the changing global economy. However, change is also necessary throughout a teaching career to ensure that you as a practitioner continue to grow, develop and evolve to support pupils in the most effective way.

Being flexible, proactive and responsive to change is a very important quality to develop as a beginning teacher. Being able to think on your feet, to respond immediately to your learners' needs and also to reflect on your practice after lessons is key. The same flexibility is needed when you are dealing with whole school change as well as with national changes.

Reflecting on where you are at and what the next steps are enables you to positively work your way through these changes to enable you to support your school and learners in the best possible way (Gibbs, 1988; Schon, 1983). Being positive about change enables you to think more creatively about the situation. Being solutions-focused enables you to be more proactive in your day-to-day engagement with your role as well as your pupils.

To summarise, as outlined above there are three different layers of changes that you can expect in your role as teacher. These are:

■ National changes – changes that are often driven by political agendas and policies for example, changes to the National Curriculum.

■ Whole school changes – changes that are implemented by your school leadership team, which is rolled out to the entire school, not just a department, with the expectation that the entire school engages with these changes. These changes are often linked to political, policy or national agenda changes (Bleiklie, 2006).

■ Changes and challenges in your classroom – changes you decide to make, or adjustments that you might make in response to how your pupils learn or need to progress, which are often linked to the whole school agenda, but which can also be bespoke and specific to the pupils you are working with.

The benefit of being flexible to change is that it ensures you can proactively and strategically respond to new directions in a creative way to ensure you are able to provide your pupils with the best possible ways forward. Being positive about change ensures you develop a mindset where change is perceived as necessary and important to ensure you provide your pupils with an up-to-date education to equip them well for the next stage of their learning journey. Change forces both teacher and pupil to adopt a life-long learning strategy to ensure they develop successfully. Task 2.1 encourages you to start to reflect on some of the recent changes experienced in education.

 Task 2.1   Reflection of current changes in education

As a beginning teacher, you might be aware of some of the changes regarding the National Curriculum (DfE, 2014a), the *SEND Code of Practice: 0–25 Years* (DfE and Department of Health (DoH), 2015) and various other reports (if you are teaching outside England, access educational documentation relevant to your country).

Reflect on all the changes you are aware of and discuss with an experienced colleague or your mentor:

1. how your school responded to these requirements;
2. how this needs to be translated into the classroom.
3. What are the challenges the school needs to face regarding these changes?
4. How are colleagues also reflecting on and challenging some of these core issues?

Write your reflections in your professional development portfolio (PDP) (or similar), so that you can refer to them at a later date.

Task 2.1 encouraged you to reflect on how a school might respond to national change and how it also might impact on the classroom teacher. The next section aims to help you reflect on how you can respond to change even more effectively on a day-to-day basis in your own practice as a front-line classroom practitioner.

Managing and responding to change

Whole school

Due to national changes, school leaders need to ensure that the strategic response to these policy changes are implemented effectively within your school. This means that a whole school policy will be shared with staff in relation to the next steps that are to be taken. Some of the most recent and dramatic changes are arguably the changes to the curriculum, and each and every subject and department in schools needs to respond to these to ensure that pupils can progress well.

In making changes to the curriculum, school leaders need to ensure that they review any proposed changes. Decisions need to be made regarding the way in which changes are to be addressed in terms of the topic areas to be delivered. Further, decisions in relation to how topics are delivered and assessed also need to be taken into account. For example, changes in how pupils are assessed in primary schools in England and changes to GCSE assessment have both required school leaders to reflect on how attainment and progress are developed and assessed, as well as how targets and aspirational targets are set.

Note: The type of educational system in which you work in, impacts on the school's ability to make change. For example, if your education context is centrally controlled by the government you will mostly be told what to do. If, however, you are based in a less prescriptive context (for example an Academy or a Free school in England), the leadership team may make changes specifically based on the needs of the school. Thus, as a beginner teacher, you should be aware that not all schools function in the same way. However, what is consistent is that all schools are expected to be fully mindful of the requirements and specifications for national examination, as pupil are tested in a standardised way.

Task 2.2 asks you to find out about your school policies and strategies and how you can best respond to these in your own practice.

 Task 2.2   Whole school policies and their impact on you as a teacher

1. Access your school policies. As you read and work through them, annotate each piece to enable you to reflect on what each policy means in relation to your own practice.
2. Make an appointment with your mentor or an experienced colleague to talk these approaches through and check how you need to respond to these in your own practice and within your classroom.

Reflect on what you have learnt and strategies you need to implement and record these in your PDP for you to refer to over a period of time.

Individual change

Whole school change leads to individual change that you need to make within your classroom. You need to execute the approach provided by your school leaders to ensure you support the whole school agenda, which in turn aims to address the national agenda. Examples of these agendas in England include:

■ Systematic Synthetic Phonics (SSP) being taught as a national priority, whatever key stage you are teaching in and across. In secondary education, phonics is mainly used when supporting learners faced with literacy challenges. It is often used during intervention tasks.

■ All teachers being teachers of SEND as outlined by the *SEND Code of Practice: 0-25 Years* (DfE and DoH, 2015). It is important to ensure that you are fully aware of changes occurring nationally to ensure you provide the best possible support for your learners in the classroom.

Attending whole school meetings and professional development events are key to ensure that you keep up-to-date with how the school is moving forward in addressing change (see Chapter 20 of this book for further details on ongoing professional development. Keay (in *LTT8*, 2019) also provides further guidance on developing as a teacher).

You will find that during observations of your lessons school leaders review how you are responding to these requirements in an effective way in line with the school's approach.

Implementing change in your classroom

The reality is that apart from national agendas and whole school agendas, the average classroom teacher needs to respond to change constantly (Bolton, 2010; Gibbs, 1988; Schon, 1983). Change is a regular occurrence in the classroom and, as a teacher, you need to be flexible and responsive to the needs of pupils as they indicate to you what the impact of your delivery is on them and their learning. It is a constant 'dialogue' of how the learning journey is unfolding and you, as the teacher, need to review how to move forward and in which direction to benefit pupils' learning best. In addition, you also find that you are perhaps the only constant in the classroom of 30 pupils where each pupil is a variable. Their home circumstances, situations, the way they feel and how a previous lesson has impacted on them might affect what you do on an hourly and daily basis. Responding to these variables takes real skill, resilience and constant reflection in and on practice (Schon, 1983).

When observing experienced colleagues who have achieved a high degree of mastery in teaching, you often find that they make teaching look easy (Blanchard, Fowler and Hawkins, 2018; Dreyfus and Dreyfus, 1986). For example, the way in which they respond to the needs of learners is different. Pupils might grasp a concept very well in the lesson, which indicates that the teacher needs to progress learning more quickly, or they may need to slow down when a group of pupils are finding the learning more challenging. Experienced teachers seem to seamlessly move from one situation to the next with ease to promote pupils' learning in a thoughtful and reflective way. It is not uncommon for you, as a beginner teacher, to think that teaching looks easy; until you encounter situations where you need to think on your feet, which means that you need to unpack the situation, explore options and consider ways forward. It might take longer to deal with the situation and issues. Your practice has not become automatic yet, compared to your more experienced colleagues, where they are able to respond intuitively. You need to encounter similar situations a number of times, applying a range of strategies until you reach a point where you have layered your knowledge with a bank of experiences to ensure that the decisions you make are effective in relation to the situation. This includes reflecting upon which strategy you need to use to ensure that you are becoming an experienced practitioner working towards mastery (Blanchard et al., 2018; Dreyfus and Dreyfus, 1986). Task 2.3 asks you to reflect on some of what you have seen and how this can be applied within classrooms.

 Task 2.3   Reflecting on others' teaching

Reflecting on your observations of more experienced colleagues:

1.   Consider which lessons were made to look extremely easy, and what it was about the lesson that made it appear to be easy and less complex than it might have been?
2.   How did the teacher respond to all the challenges unfolding?
3.   What did you learn from these observations and how can you transfer your learning into your own practice?

Record your reflection in your PDP. Review these reflections periodically to see if you have changed the way you teach and respond to change.

As a beginner teacher you also need to consider and respond to the individual changes experienced by your learners daily. A classroom teacher needs to respond to every child's needs and every day is different. Working with pupils on a daily basis presents a challenge in regard to the change of dynamics in the classroom. You need to make sure you continue to reflect on what causes the changes and how you are able to respond effectively to these changes.

Consider carefully how the time of day you meet your groups presents different challenges and when those challenges change in regard to the dynamics of the group. Behaviour might be different early in the morning or after lunch. Take time throughout the day to reflect on how you can manage these challenges, and how your planning can address the different needs of the groups you are working with at various times of the day. You might need to plan your lessons to reflect when groups need more chunking and movement in their learning for example, or when a more challenging piece of work requires a more appropriate delivery and how that should best be delivered.

Home circumstances might be an issue too. At times pupils might arrive at school not having eaten breakfast. This will have a profound impact on how they engage in your lessons. Not having breakfast will leave a child hungry and unable to focus on their learning. They might feel vulnerable, struggle to feel safe and consequently lack the readiness to open up to their learning (see Cameron and Green, 2012, who outline how physical motivators can impact on how individuals respond to change).

Find out more about your pupils to enable you to support them and to address these challenges effectively to ensure that you manage these potential changes in expected behaviours, but also to ensure that you can help the child maximise his or her learning.

Learning needs of different pupils and how they respond to some of the ideas or methods you use, can often be unpredictable. It might be that the level of challenge moves them beyond feeling safe and they might challenge your practice through their behaviour. You need to be flexible and able to make necessary changes within your lessons to ensure all your pupils are on board and learn. Pupils respond in different ways to new ideas and stimuli. Do not be surprised when an idea works extremely well for one group but results in chaos when delivering it to another. Continue to reflect on your practice and aim to be flexible. Think of possible backup plans and make sure that you always reflect on how you can move situations forward rather than only reviewing where it went wrong (Ghaye, 2011). Always make sure that you continue to celebrate your success and enjoy what went well too. As teachers, we often emphasise the negative but do not celebrate success with our pupils (Ghaye, 2011).

Workload and changing directions

As mentioned earlier in the chapter, you often need to respond and embed policy and the whole school agenda into your work as a front-line teacher. This might mean that you are faced with additional work (see Chapter 20 for more guidance on looking after yourself). For example, in recent years curriculum changes (particularly in England) have resulted in a number of changes in the classroom. The national curriculum (DfE, 2014a) requires a stronger focus on systematic synthetic phonics (SSP) and grammar, which requires schools to evaluate and consider where it needs to be embedded in the curriculum and how it needs to be delivered (see Chapter 7 for more details on how English can be developed within your own subject area).

Changes in approaches to tracking of pupil progress (see Chapter 14 for more detail) and assessment – most notably Progress 8 and Attainment 8 (DfE, 2014b) have also been implemented (Chapter 15 provides more details on Progress 8 and Attainment 8).

Normally, changes are implemented at the start of an academic year and you are able to work with your teams on these to ensure that your year group, department or subject respond to these in the appropriate way (Durrant and Holden, 2006). Working collaboratively with a team of colleagues on how to interpret and address these changes is key and helps you to develop a clear understanding of how to absorb both the requirements and the impact of these changes.

You need to respond efficiently to the changes, in regard to your year or phase or department's development targets and agenda as well as the whole school development targets, to ensure that you are meeting the needs of your learners in an appropriate way. By collaborating, you may notice that your workload is managed more effectively. Working with more experienced colleagues through the different changes enables you to become more confident and you learn how to respond to change in future when you are faced with similar alterations to the curriculum or other aspects of your role.

Staff can respond to change in many different ways. Cameron and Green (2012) highlight that teams can respond physically to change. Reactions might manifest themselves in individuals feeling unsafe or withdrawing from engaging with the changes. Ideally, individuals embrace the change and continue to work collaboratively with others on how to understand what the change means. To help you look at how you can address change and your own workload challenges look at the DfE (2018b) *Workload Reduction Toolkit*. This provides you with a supportive outline by which you can reflect on reducing your own workload to ensure that you are able to optimise your time in the classroom. Now complete Task 2.4.

M

  Task 2.4   Managing change

Discuss with your mentor or another experienced colleague how changes have been managed and approached in regard to the National Agendas in the country in which you are teaching – for example, the use of Progress 8, data tracking, changes to national policy in England. Focus particularly on how the work was shared and how the team managed the workload aspect of these changes. Access relevant research literature to review the effectiveness of the implementation of the new approach and develop an action plan to focus on how you would work differently next time.

Discuss your reflections with your mentor and store them in your PDP for future reference.

Strategies to consider when faced with change

Throughout this chapter a number of strategies have been introduced. In the next section, some of the key points are emphasised in more detail. Change is often a great opportunity to review practice, and responding to change in a positive way is always far more productive than to react to it in an obstructive or negative way (Durrant and Holden, 2006). As a beginner teacher, the key is to reflect carefully on what is proposed and how you can be of help and support to move these changes forward in your own practice.

Always strive to be flexible and be mindful that change is inevitable in an environment, such as a school, where you are faced with so many variables. It is impossible not to encounter change. Always aim to reflect on practice to enable you to respond to change immediately if necessary, in particular in your classroom. However, it is also important to reflect on practice to ensure that you are able to evaluate how you can continue to improve and move matters forward. Change inevitably disrupts the status quo.

Two common responses to change are anxiety and disorientation. People frequently respond to change in different stages:

Adaption – by responding to change in a creative way and moving forward creatively by embedding it into their practice.
Shock – by responding at times with anger, refusal to engage.
Acceptance – by recognising that change is necessary and that it needs to be moved forward.
Defence – by defending previous practices and approaches. There may be comments, frequently heard such as, 'we have always done it like this'.

(Gateshead Council, 2009)

Cameron and Green (2012) develop this further, arguing that responses to change can be exhibited with shock, followed by denial, anger, blame, bargaining, apathy, acceptance, exploration, understanding, and integration. Once the integration point is reached the change is sustainable.

As a practitioner, it is important to recognise your response to change to enable you to move through the different phases more effectively to reach a creative point, where you can tackle what is required with a creative and positive approach. It is important to be mindful of your own reactions and responses to change to ensure that you are able to build in effective mechanisms to cope with the various aspects of change. You might be an individual who accepts change with ease and moves it forward without worrying too much, or you might be shocked by change, you might enjoy being habitual and having routines. You may find that your own reaction to change might vary, depending on the change. It is therefore important to have a good understanding of how you personally might react to change (Cameron and Green, 2012). In addition, remind yourself of the fact that change is inevitable, and in schools you need to adapt to change on a regular basis. Now complete Task 2.5.

 Task 2.5   Evaluating your response to change

Evaluate your own response to change. What is your initial reaction to change? How does change make you feel when it is introduced? How do you work through the different stages identified above? Evaluate what you need to do to ensure, in future, that you can work around these views to enable you to respond in a positive way.

Discuss your reflections with your mentor and store them in your PDP for future reference.

Working with your mentor and other members of your team in a positive and collaborative way enables you to cope with the new requirements more effectively. When you are working in a team you need to be self-aware to enable you to work well with others. When change is introduced in your context, colleagues are likely to respond to change in a variety of different ways, some might be advocates and others might block change completely. Colleagues might move through the different stages of change at different times, depending on the individual, the circumstances and the amount of change they need to manage (Cameron and Green, 2012). This might even be a reaction to ideas and views you might propose. It is important to learn early on in your career how you can respond to these different issues more effectively. Reflect on how you personally can turn the negative into a positive, how can you take small incremental steps to become an advocate for a new initiative? For example, with regard to curriculum change, you might try a few new ideas out or look at an example of how it could work and share it with a few experienced colleagues to get the conversation going. If it is a new strategy your school wants to embed, try out a few small activities and review how it impacts on pupils' learning and outcomes. Share your practice and ideas with your mentor or an experienced colleague and refine what you do. You will soon find that your positive attitude to these changes, turns into creative opportunities where you can share ideas with like-minded colleagues. This in turn will have a positive influence on others.

Nolan (2007) highlights five basic principles for change in schools:

- Focus on developing an understanding of the initiative (more than ownership); seek to understand and take initiative to embrace the change.
- 'Think big, start small', aim to embed the new changes with small incremental steps to ensure that you are able to manage it effectively.
- Focus your commitment on what matters most in your practice, for example, to ensure that learners progress and learn. Then consider how you can use the change implemented to ensure that your learners flourish.
- Interrogate the status quo first, evaluate key messages and current practice, explore how the change helps to develop and improve things.
- Use resisters to your advantage (resisters are always great people to discuss new approaches with). Explore and analyse what they think and say and think outside the box to ensure that you are able to consider all angles, to move forward in the best way possible.

When working with colleagues who block situations, it is often useful to ask them to help and support you in developing your new ideas. They often start off in a negative way, but they soon see the benefits of what you are doing. Keep working with others to strengthen your practice.

Change can be a dividing force in many contexts; however, addressing it in a proactive way ensures that it becomes a creative process (Cameron and Green, 2012). You will find that some colleagues focus on activities and tasks to address the change and others collaborate more. The most helpful thing for a beginner teacher to do is to work with others on how to address change and learn from others how they approach the different demands of the changes they need to face and address. Make sure you contribute positively and ask as many questions as possible to ensure that you are able to learn and develop your own skill set effectively to support your learners too (Blanchard et al., 2018).

We are often told that 'the only thing that is constant is change.' If you are able to embrace change and think through the changes positively, you are able to progress this more effectively as a beginner teacher and beyond. Embedding these strategies early on in your career enables you to become open to change and this also helps you when you need to lead change in future – when you have reached a point where you need to work with your own teams. However, if change (and in particular strategies regarding marking or planning change) increases your workload to a level that is not manageable, make sure you discuss your experiences and concerns as soon as possible with your mentor or an experienced colleague. It is vital to ensure that you continue to manage your workload positively to enable you to continue to make a difference in your school. If you are not able to engage with your mentor, you can also look at the Workload Reduction Toolkit (DfE, 2018b) to reflect on how you can address your practice. Now complete Task 2.6.

 Task 2.6   Reflecting on change

Reflect on the changes you have encountered so far in your teaching career. How did you respond to these changes and what opportunities arose from them? How did you use the opportunities to enable your pupils to progress and move forward in their learning? How did you become a positive force for change? Store your responses in your PDP for future reference.

SUMMARY AND KEY POINTS

In the ever-changing landscape of education, change is the constant all teachers need to work with, whether it is responding to policy or national changes, national agendas, whole school agendas or changes in the classroom. Change offers the opportunity for teachers to ensure that pupils gain an up-to-date education to prepare them well for their future role in the world around them.

Therefore, as a beginner teacher you should continue to:

■ review and reflect upon the changes that are taking place within education;
■ develop an understanding of the range of strategies you can use when considering your response to a change;
■ consider what strategies are most effective in supporting you to cope with change;
■ continue to reflect on the impact of change on your own professional development.

Record in your PDP how the information in this chapter enables you to meet the requirements for your first year of teaching.

Further resources

Websites:

The following website links provide guidance for teachers in relation to the effective management of aspects of their teaching and associated tasks.

DfE (Department for Education) (2018a) *Reducing Teacher Workload.* **Available from: www.gov. uk/government/publications/reducing-teachers-workload/reducing-teachers-workload (accessed 1 December 2018).**

DfE (Department for Education) (2018b) *Workload Reduction Toolkit.* **Available from: www.gov. uk/government/collections/workload-reduction-toolkit (accessed 11 November 2018).**

Appendices 2 and 3 list subject associations, teaching councils and relevant websites.

Books in the *Learning to Teach* series that you may find helpful are as follows:

Capel, S., Leask, M. and Younie, S. (eds.) (2019) *Learning to Teach in the Secondary School: A Companion to School Experience,* **8th edn, Abingdon: Routledge.**
This book is designed as a core textbook to support student teachers through their initial teacher education programme.

Capel, S., Leask, M. and Turner, T. (eds.) (2010) *Readings for Learning to Teach in the Secondary School: A Companion to M Level Study,* **Abingdon: Routledge.**
This book brings together essential readings to support you in your critical engagement with key issues raised in this textbook.

The subject-specific books in the *Learning to Teach* series, the *Practical (subject) Guides, Debates in (subject)* and *Mentoring (subject) Teachers* are also very useful.

3　Mentoring and being mentored

Trevor Wright

Introduction

All of the chapters in this book suggest the many complex challenges and opportunities that await you in enhancing a professional but authentic version of yourself as a beginning teacher. In every part of this process, your developing relationship with your induction mentor is crucial. However, it's a challenging relationship. This chapter seeks to identify some of its complexities and, more importantly, to offer practical solutions.

> ### OBJECTIVES
>
> At the end of this chapter you should be able to:
>
> - identify some challenges of working with your induction mentor;
> - understand different models of mentoring and why a reflective model is appropriate for your current stage of development;
> - consider the complexity of the mentoring relationship;
> - understand the importance of balanced feedback on your teaching;
> - consider the value of having an off-line coach in addition to your mentor.
>
> Check how the information in this chapter enables you to meet the requirements for your first year of teaching.

Some mentoring challenges

Of course, you already know about mentoring. It has been a significant part of your initial teacher education (ITE). You have probably experienced its positive strengths in developing, for example, subject pedagogy, supporting behaviour management, encouraging professionalism, offering emotional support and so on. Nevertheless, you might at this point be wondering why it has to continue. You have passed your 'driving test', but now apparently you have to wear a set of 'P' plates for at least another year.

It's vital that you welcome the continuation of mentoring in your induction year rather than resenting it. The support of a mentor through your early career stages is part of a set of provisions required by the Department for Education (DfE) for newly qualified teachers in state schools in England (though they are not compulsory in independent schools, academies or free schools). Similar provisions exist in Northern Ireland, Scotland and Wales. Such provisions should work entirely to your advantage. They should make you the envy of teachers who don't have them. They include a reduced teaching timetable, reasonable and systematic teaching demands and regular observation and feedback. And, centrally, they include the appointment of a mentor to oversee these provisions and your well-being and development.

You are likely to have arrived at your first school with a completed Career Entry and Development Profile (CEDP). As Cuerden (2018) says, your CEDP should be a detailed account of your qualifications and experiences and include your own perceptions of your strengths as a teacher and your development needs at this stage. One function of your early meetings with your mentor must be to ascertain whether the objectives in your CEDP are still relevant and applicable with regard to your new post and its particular demands. They need interpreting in terms of your new timetable. These early discussions help you to establish a sound, purposeful relationship with your mentor. You need to prepare for these meetings, showing a professional commitment to developing your practice as you move from ITE into your first post. Task 3.1 asks you to arrange a meeting with your mentor to check objectives in your CPD.

 Task 3.1   Checking objectives in your CEDP

In an early meeting with your mentor, discuss your CEDP, in particular whether the objectives are still relevant to your current situation. Identify which developmental needs you are going to address first. Identify activities you are going to undertake to develop these and how you are going to measure progress (the rest of the chapter should help you with this part of the meeting).

Record your progress in addressing your development needs in your professional development portfolio (PDP) (or similar), to refer to later and inform future discussions with your mentor.

Competence, apprenticeship and reflection

You may have already discovered that mentors vary in their attitudes and approaches to the job. Maynard and Furlong (1995), for example, observed three *models* of mentoring – competence, apprenticeship and reflection – and certainly mentors mix these components differently, sometimes as chronological stages. A mentor often favours one above the others. Some focus on the development of a fixed set of *competences*, e.g. the Teachers' Standards in England (DfE, 2011) and develop a programme of support based on the achievement and the monitoring of these skills. Others may favour a predominantly *apprenticeship* model, where the mentoring relationship is designed to help you develop through the modelling of good practice by trusted professionals. The *reflective* mentor encourages a dynamic and complex set of inputs leading to discussion, comparison and synthesis. Now complete Task 3.2. The next section will look in more detail at what each approach means.

 Task 3.2   Your mentor's views of competency, apprenticeship and reflection, and their approaches to mentoring

Discovering your mentor's views about these three mentoring models – competency, apprenticeship and reflection – is one useful early activity in defining and developing your relationship. You may want to bring these three mentoring models to a meeting and discuss explicitly what your mentor thinks of them. As a qualified teacher, not a student teacher, you should be clear with your mentor about the support that you now need as you move forward in your career. It is important to come to an agreement about this. Regular discussions with your induction mentor are a requirement of provision in your first year of teaching and these conversations should include a shared understanding of the mentor's approach. This understanding is enhanced by analysis of the various activities that the mentor organises for you.

Recording your thoughts on the approaches and your mentor's view of them in your PDP should help you to maximise the support from your mentor (and may help you in any mentoring role you might undertake in the future).

Equipped with a growing and shared understanding of your mentor's approach, you should take as much control as you can of the mentoring process. You should be involved in setting targets for development; you should ask for specific focuses on, for example, lesson observations; you should request meetings with and observations of other staff for specific development purposes. Of course you should do this with tact and professionalism; you and your mentor should both see your induction as a collaboration. To survive and thrive, you have to work with your mentor to set the agendas for your induction. Observations, discussions, feedback sessions and decisions about your progress should be shared activities, instigated by both of you.

Competence model

In a competence approach to mentoring you will probably focus on the Teachers' Standards (DfE, 2011) in England. This is of course important, but your ITE programme has probably already confirmed that you've met these Standards. As you move through your induction year, nevertheless, you should use them as a conversation focus, revisiting them and re-interpreting them at a more advanced level. For example, your understanding of learning management should be developing from basic, extrinsic systems such as rewards and sanctions towards a more sophisticated understanding of intrinsic management where pupils' motivation is increasingly generated by the work itself. During your ITE programme you have probably already begun this journey. You should be inviting your mentor to observe your teaching in connection with particular Standards that you want to concentrate on in order to further this sophistication, and you should remember that these focuses need not always be deficit focuses.

You may have agreed with your mentor that you need to develop a particular Standard and you may invite her to observe a particular lesson with a view to generating a feedback conversation that will carry you forward with new suggestions. This process – of targets based on perceived weaknesses that need improvement – is one that you've almost certainly experienced as a student teacher. It may well reflect some of your own approaches to assessing pupils' work. Less common, but equally important, especially now that you're a qualified teacher, is the converse target-setting model of developing your strengths and talents. You and your mentor see a particular strength in your teaching. You discuss ways of developing this yet further. As a qualified teacher, you have a mission not only to get better at what you're not so good at, but also to develop your existing strengths and talents absolutely as far as you can. This positive model of target setting is how you define yourself as an effective professional. This is considered in Task 3.3.

 Task 3.3 Targets for development

Examine the targets you have agreed with your mentor. Answer the following questions. You may want to discuss these questions and answers with your mentor.

1. Are the targets based on Teachers' Standards or other competences?
2. Are the targets collaborative? Do you both agree on them?
3. Are the targets accompanied by advice and other inputs (such as the observation of other colleagues) to help you to achieve them?
4. Are the targets monitored? Does your mentor systematically comment on your performance against these targets in subsequent observation and feedback?
5. Do the targets include the development of perceived existing *talents* as well as the remedying of perceived *weaknesses*?

Store your thoughts on the responses and any discussions in your PDP to use to enhance the use of targets in developing your teaching.

Apprenticeship model

Of course, your mentor knows more about teaching than you do. It would be odd if she didn't. In fact, as a beginning teacher you are surrounded by expert professionals. The notion that you can learn the job by watching, listening and copying is common among student teachers and among mentors. It is obviously powerful to draw on all of this rich expertise; but it's constricting if it becomes set into an apprenticeship approach to mentoring. Teaching is a profession, not a trade. You need to continue to define yourself as a teacher and this means that you need to be involved in a rich, dynamic reflective process.

One problem with the apprenticeship model of teacher development is that you are almost invisible in the process. You watch somebody - your mentor, or another colleague - as they teach. They have skills, confidence and effectiveness. If you are simply invited to replicate them - to watch and copy - you have no opportunity to question, understand and develop. If your lesson beginnings are poor, for example (and lesson beginnings, as you know, are crucial), your mentor may ask you to observe a colleague whose lessons are famously orderly and whose lesson beginnings never fail. She lines Year 8 up in the corridor and tells them in no uncertain terms what's expected of them when they enter the classroom. She reminds them to observe the seating plan. They have silent settler activities already on the tables. Nothing bad happens.

If the mentoring process is simply an apprenticeship then you will be invited to begin your next lesson in the same way. It may work for you (if it does, it's a matter of luck) but it may not. There are various reasons why what works for one teacher (or class) may not work for another, and understanding these reasons is part of your development.

You have almost certainly worked through such processes as a student teacher. If, as a beginning teacher, you find that your mentor is still operating an apprenticeship model, you need to discuss this. You need to move beyond it. To develop as a professional you need something more complex and nuanced in which you are an active, not a passive, observer. Your mentor, who may be an experienced mentor of student teachers, may need to consider the different mentoring needs of qualified teachers. You may need to work with her to establish this.

Dynamic reflection - inputs and outputs

Maynard and Furlong's (1995) research was focused on student teachers and, as a beginning teacher, you should be experiencing the third model of mentoring they identified - mentoring that is reflective. You should be moving beyond simple mentoring models based on competences and apprenticeship. You need a sophisticated, active and collaborative form of mentoring.

Your experiences, as arranged between you and your mentor, offer various inputs. She provides feedback on your work, she arranges for you to make observations of colleagues, she offers you formal and informal training. These inputs into your practice and development need to be digested when they arrive and before they can be used; this is the process of reflection. This reflection needs not to be passive but to build into a systematic, shared, active and targeted process. We could call this *dynamic reflection*.

A central component of this reflection is *synthesis*. You may find many contradictions in the advice you receive and the observations you make. You have to draw the inputs together and make sense of them. For example, one colleague will tell you never to talk while children are talking - always demand and wait for silence; another colleague will point out that some lessons would never get started at all if such advice were followed. Which is the right way? Is there a right way? To whom should you listen?

Of course, if you only received one piece of advice, there would be no confusion; but there would be little stimulus for reflection. The discussion of *two or more* pieces of advice takes you towards an understanding of the complexity and variety of teaching. In this sense, you need multiple inputs so that you can understand and define your own outcomes.

Let's return to the example of lesson beginnings. You and your mentor have agreed that they need work. This judgement would be made, perhaps, during her observation of your teaching and would begin a process of dynamic reflection. Among other reflective inputs, your mentor might decide that you need to watch some effective lesson openings. As we've seen, watching only *one* effective teacher, managing *one* effective lesson beginning, offers little ground for reflection and synthesis, however impressive the exemplar may be. At best this is apprenticeship mentoring.

Some simple rules apply here. The observation of a skilled colleague, for example, is not a random activity, but a *focused*, thematic observation. The activity is pointless and perhaps even destructive if it isn't *targeted* (on a development area) and if it doesn't yield material for *reflection*. Furthermore, you need *plurality*. You need to watch *two or more* colleagues who begin their lessons effectively but differently. Finally, you need opportunities for discussion and comparison – either with your mentor or with the observed teachers. *Reflection often begins with discussion.*

Plurality is vital to this reflective process. Watching at least two lesson beginnings – the lady with the corridor line-up, a man with an apparently entirely contrasting, informal approach –forces you to think about what's going on underneath. Why do they both work? Is one better than the other? Why do you prefer one of them? Are there actually fundamentals to these lesson openings that make them less different than they appear to be?

In summary, we are saying that the input–output model for your mentoring must be complex if it is to be effective. A simple input–output model is based on replication. Good practice is observed and copied. This is a two-stage process in which you yourself are almost non-existent. It can have no long- or medium-term benefit; if it works in the short term, it is a matter of good fortune. It may be helpful as scaffolding but, like all scaffolding, it is temporary. The complex model, a three-stage process, places dynamic reflection between the input and the output. Discussion, synthesis, comparison, contrast, selection and personal evaluation transform the inputs into original, crafted and premeditated outputs.

Such dynamic reflection needs to exist as a habit, which you must manage. If necessary, you do this by asking your mentor to extend your inputs to include a range of focused experiences, and also by structuring the reflection in your formal and informal meetings. You need to discuss those observations, issues and targets with your mentor, in order to make meaningful decisions about what you're going to do. In other words, you need to be functioning at three stages of the process – with a range of inputs, with structured reflection and with focused, consequent future planning. Task 3.4 asks you to reflect on inputs into your development.

Task 3.4   Reflecting on inputs into your development

List the inputs that have been generated between you and your mentor in the last month. These may include, for example, lesson feedback, training and development conversations, readings, meetings with colleagues, observations of other teachers, visits to other schools, auditing of subject knowledge, auditing of Teachers' Standards. Consider the following questions with regard to these inputs. You may want to discuss the questions and answers with your mentor.

1   Did these inputs allow for *comparisons* with regards to selected themes? (Themes may include, for example, lesson beginnings, differentiation, inclusion, questioning techniques, literacy, constructivism, teacher language, planning, task setting and so on).
2   Did you discuss the purpose and focus of activities before undertaking them?
3   Were you able to draw together various activities into focused, thematic conversations with your mentor?
4   What decisions have you been able to make recently about your own development as a result of these mentoring inputs?

Make notes on the answers in your PDP to help improve the value of inputs to your development as a teacher.

The mentoring relationship

Mentoring relationships are complex. One reason for this is that the relationship between mentor and mentee is usually asymmetrical. That is to say that, on your side, this relationship may carry a weight of significance, sometimes even of emotional significance, that the mentor probably doesn't share. As a student teacher, you may remember this intensity. Student teachers in the early stages often use emotional language ('love', for example) when talking of their mentors. Your mentor is committed to you, of course, but she has many other working priorities. And then, the fact that your mentor is there to support you but also in some sense to judge your competence can lead to further imbalances.

One of the processes that you have already worked through as a student teacher is the balancing of this relationship and, as you work with your new induction mentor, you have to re-address this calibration. When properly run, on both sides, this relationship can be enormously beneficial.

Focusing observation and balancing feedback

Professional exchange lies at the heart of the mentoring relationship, and mentor feedback on observed lessons is a significant part of these conversations. It can be a microcosm of the relationship as a whole. The ways in which the relationship thrives or falters may be reflected in feedback sessions. Sometimes, the success of the relationship depends on the success of these feedback conversations.

Lesson observations are often very significant events in your induction programme. In many schools they are formally timetabled and may be carried out by senior staff other than the mentor. Successful outcomes may matter very much to formal judgements made about your development. It isn't easy to offer advice on how to be confident in such situations. It goes without saying that you should be well prepared, with full lesson plans (in line with your school's planning protocols); that you should anticipate questions that you may be asked; that you probably shouldn't be over-ambitious in terms of resources; and that pupil learning not teacher performance should be at the heart of these lessons. You should be able to answer these three age-old questions: What were the pupils meant to learn? Did they learn it? How do you know? Remember to draw reference to your plan as well as to the lesson itself.

These quite intimidating events may be a little mitigated if they exist within a programme of regular and less formal observations by your mentor and other departmental staff. These observations should be less about judgement and more about development. The feedback that follows these observations should have the clear purpose of enhancing your practice and your understanding of it. 'For best results, mentoring should … be removed from all formal performance management' (Coskeran, 2013). Such purely developmental mentoring may be hard to come by in the intense, judgemental atmosphere of your induction, but, certainly, one key aspect of feedback balance is a shared understanding of how these two purposes – summative judgement and formative development – combine and separate in your observation programme, both across the weeks and months and within each individual feedback conversation. If your mentor's approach is principally based on what Hobson and Malderez (2013) call 'judgementoring', you need to discuss this as part of your early, agenda-setting mentor meetings.

Explicit, agreed and proactive arrangements for mentoring are vital to the well-being of the mentoring relationship, and nowhere is this more true than in the matter of lesson feedback. I remember in my early days as a mentor giving a very great deal of detailed advice to a student teacher. I told her of many things that could have improved the lesson that I had just watched. I thought she would be grateful, and would prosper as a result of my input, but I soon discovered that she had in fact been intimidated to the point of distress.

The point here is that my mentoring intentions were good. My only wish was to offer support. I thought she was a strong student teacher, but, as you know, a mentee can only process so much advice. Your mentor needs to understand that developmental points may be seen as criticisms. You need to feel that criticism is balanced with compliment. There are still many mentors who, despite their entirely honourable intentions, appear to offer a predominance of negatives when giving feedback, and this may well happen when the mentor sees much promise in the mentee and seeks to develop it. Over a period of time this can lead to a deterioration in the overall relationship.

Of course you can talk to your mentor if you feel that this is happening; she may be quite unaware of it. But you can also avoid it by establishing feedback protocols. In the first weeks, you and your mentor should work together to establish a regular feedback system, and you should stick to this until, by agreement, you evaluate and modify it. The protocol varies according to individuals, but (as an example only), you and your mentor may agree at an early stage that each lesson feedback will be based on agreements such as those outlined in the following list:

- three positive points;
- two developmental targets;
- explicit comment on progress regarding previously agreed targets;
- always begin with your opinion of the lesson;
- always conclude positively;
- always define future targets (SMART – specific, measurable, achievable, realistic, timed), probably using Teachers' Standards;
- lesson summatively graded once per month;
- discus this agenda itself and whether it needs to change.

In particular, the use of numbers (only two development targets), though mechanistic, is crucial. It is a focusing discipline for your mentor, it ensures that you have material outcomes that you can handle and it provides a balance in the conversation. The numbers may also remove emotion from the feedback; the 'negatives' (actually development points, becoming targets) are not unexpected because they are a requirement of the system that you have both already agreed to. If, as time goes on, you find the conversations still too negative, or (alternatively) too unchallenging, you can return to the numbers and change them. Crucially, the relationship between summative and formative purposes is established and agreed. Task 3.5 looks at establishing a protocol for feedback on your lessons.

 Task 3.5   Establishing a protocol for feedback on your lessons with your mentor

Early in your induction year, read the example protocol for feedback listed as bullet-points above and discuss these points with your mentor. Set out a written, agreed system for lesson feedback, discussing each point, including the numbers that you have agreed on. Agree a meeting date in the not-too-distant future in which you re-evaluate and possibly change aspects of this protocol to suit your individual and developing needs.

Store the agreed protocol in your PDP and return to it if it is not adhered to, is not working or is not supporting your development.

The off-line coach

We are seeing the complexity of your relationship with your mentor in terms of a range of purposes and contexts for mentoring. In particular, we are seeing that the mentor has dual roles in enhancing your practice but also judging it. At times these roles may seem confused and self-contradictory and settling this muddle matters to your progress and well-being. We have suggested that clear sets of protocols in advance of mentoring events help with this. For example, formal 'observations' by senior staff may be agreed as largely summative, assessive events, whereas informal, regular observations from your mentor may be regarded as predominantly formative. Or perhaps you agree on a mixture of formative and summative feedbacks across (for example) a month, with one mentor observation out of four providing a summative judgement of your teaching. A highly skilled mentor may seamlessly offer both functions in one feedback, but you must both be clear in advance that this is happening and in what proportions. It is your responsibility to ensure protocols are clear and support your development.

We are trying to suggest arrangements that clarify the various purposes of mentoring and ensure positivity. One further role in this connection is that of coach. Hughes (2018) talks about the difference between coach and mentor. As terms they are often confused, frequently regarded as synonyms, but one useful distinction can be inferred from the world of professional sport. The coach of a world-class tennis player may not be as great a player as his charge. His role is not that of the mentor, who knows more than his mentee, but that of supporter and observer. It is this distinction that is of use here. In school, the establishment of an off-line coach for your induction can be hugely beneficial. A coach, perhaps a member of your department, and an addition to your official induction mentor, may observe you, offer feedback and arrange other inputs. In other words, she may carry out a range of mentoring activities. But there is one crucial difference between her (perhaps quite informal) role and that of your mentor – she will never be asked for or offer an opinion on your standing with regard to passing or failing induction, and you both know this from the outset. Hughes (2018, p.129) says of a coach, 'this is someone who has no formal part in the assessment process but can coach the trainee in a safe environment'. Such an arrangement can provide a liberating, professional and developmental relationship that supplements your crucial relationship with your induction mentor. You may be offered a coach, but if not, it is your responsibility to ask for one.

SUMMARY AND KEY POINTS

In this chapter we have covered:

- the positive value of mentoring as part of induction arrangements;
- the use of your Career Entry and Development Profile;
- the competence, apprenticeship and reflective models of mentoring;
- the importance of collaboration with your mentor;
- feedback and the setting of targets;
- balancing your relationship;
- mentoring inputs and outputs;
- establishing mentoring and feedback protocols;
- the off-line coach.

Record in your PDP, how the information in this chapter enables you to meet the requirements for your first year of teaching.

Further resources

Coskeran, S. (2013) *Effective Teacher Mentoring*. Available from: www.sec-ed.co.uk/best-practice/effective-teacher-mentoring (accessed 25 November 2018).
This is a useful account of attitudes for mentoring, covering a range of research papers, and considering why mentoring in schools doesn't always reach its potential.

Cuerden, J. (2018) 'Mentoring the newly qualified teacher', in T. Wright (ed.) *How to be a Brilliant Mentor: Developing Outstanding Teachers*, 2nd edn, Abingdon: Routledge, pp.147-161.
This is a useful chapter within a book that covers many contexts for mentoring in UK schools.

Hobson, A.J. and Malderez, A. (2013) 'Judgementoring and other threats to realizing the potential of school-based mentoring in teacher education', *International Journal of Mentoring and Coaching in Education*, 2 (2), 89-108.
This paper suggests that what its authors call 'judgementoring' may be a growing phenomenon, and that this may be an institutional trend.

Hughes, S. (2018) 'Mentoring and coaching; the helping relationship', in T. Wright (ed.) *How to be a Brilliant Mentor: Developing Outstanding Teachers*, 2nd edn, Abingdon: Routledge, pp.120-135.
The chapter looks at the similarities and differences between mentoring and coaching and what they can each offer teachers.

Maynard, T. and Furlong, J. (1995) *Mentoring Student Teachers: The Growth of Professional Knowledge*, London: Routledge.
Although this book focuses on student teachers, it remains a seminal text that examines mentoring focuses, systems and attitudes.

Appendices 2 and 3 list subject associations, teaching councils and relevant websites.

Books in the *Learning to Teach* series that you may find helpful are as follows:

Capel, S., Leask, M. and Younie, S. (eds.) (2019) *Learning to Teach in the Secondary School: A Companion to School Experience*, 8th edn, Abingdon: Routledge.
This book is designed as a core textbook to support student teachers through their initial teacher education programme.

Capel, S., Leask, M. and Turner, T. (eds.) (2010) *Readings for Learning to Teach in the Secondary School: A Companion to M Level Study*, Abingdon: Routledge.
This book brings together essential readings to support you in your critical engagement with key issues raised in this textbook.

The subject-specific books in the *Learning to Teach* series, the *Practical (subject) Guides*, *Debates in (subject)* and *Mentoring (subject) Teachers* are also very useful.

4 Thriving in your subject department

Steven Puttick and Nick Gee

Introduction

There is greater variation in 'performance' and 'culture' within schools – that is, between departments in the same school – than between schools (Ko, Hallinger and Walker, 2015; Strand, 2016): subject departments are an important unit of analysis that is more significant than 'the school' for a wide range of factors, including pupils' outcomes, interpretation and implementation of policy, teacher development and teachers' experiences (Puttick, 2018, p. 26). An effective department is greater than the sum of the individuals, yet it can take work to create a cohesive, collaborative department in which everyone thrives. This chapter provides an introduction to the growing body of research on departments, helping you to critically reflect on your department and identify opportunities for making a positive contribution to your department.

You may be fortunate enough to work in an amazing department that feels encouraging and 'safe' so that you can express your opinions honestly, be challenged and flourish. This chapter aims to make explicit some of the aspects contributing to these kinds of departments. If you work in a department with scope to develop, this chapter aims to introduce you to some of the research to better understand departments and provide you with tools to improve your department. The chapter equips you with practical suggestions drawn from research on school subject departments and the wider field of organisational effectiveness to make a positive contribution to your departmental culture. In particular, the chapter introduces the concept of 'psychological safety', and gives you suggestions for ways in which you can help to develop your department into one that is more creative, more constructively critical and 'psychologically safer' – a department that is educationally inspiring for both pupils and teachers.

OBJECTIVES

At the end of this chapter you should be able to:

■ describe different types of departments and identify distinctive characteristics of your department;
■ critically reflect on the development and reproduction of departmental cultures;
■ foster more constructively critical and 'psychologically safe' departmental cultures.

Check how the information in this chapter enables you to meet the requirements for your first year of teaching.

What makes a subject department?

Let us start by reflecting on your own experiences of subject departments. Task 4.1 provides a format for doing this.

 Task 4.1   School subject departments

I wonder what you think a department is? What comes to mind when we discuss subject departments?

Take a large (A3) sheet of paper and draw a concept map for subject departments. This might be at an abstract level or you might want to work up from the specific example of your own department. The following prompts might be of use in starting your concept map:

■ Where is the department?
■ What things are important to – or 'make up' – a department?
■ Who uses, or is involved with, the department? In what ways might these different people 'see' the department differently?
■ What is the purpose of the department? Who decides this?
■ What kinds of spaces are constructed by the department?
■ What influences (internal/external/advisory/statutory) affect the department's work?
■ What role does 'culture' play in the life of the department?

Record your thoughts in your professional development portfolio (PDP) (or similar) to refer to later.

Organisational types

When you think about your department you might think about physical areas and spaces – classrooms, corridors and offices – or it might bring to mind associations with particular colleagues, teachers, teaching assistants and others who all share responsibility for your subject. In this chapter, we include all of these aspects; departments as social groups and physical areas within schools brought together through a focus on a particular subject or subjects. Research on departments suggests that shared areas to collaborate and discuss are important (Childs, Burn and McNicholl, 2013). However, it is unlikely that the physical structure of the department is under your control, and so while the built environment – the physical bricks and mortar – of a department is important, we devote more space to the social construction of departments, beginning with their organisational types. Differences between organisational types are related to differential access to resources, spaces, staffing and autonomy. For example, while Childs et al. (2013) chose to only observe departments with a shared departmental office – concluding that these spaces can be very important – many departments either do not have such spaces, or share these spaces across subjects. Normally this is because of the different sizes of departments; one factor contributing to the differences across the departmental typology shown in Table 4.1.

Different organisational structures present different challenges and opportunities (Fenwick, Minty and Priestley, 2013; Gunter, 2001; Hannay and Ross, 1999; Siskin, 1994). These challenges and opportunities are related to the varying numbers of subject colleagues, levels of autonomy, strength of subject identity and the particular, highly

Table 4.1 Department typologies (Busher and Harris, 1999; Puttick, 2016)

Type of department	Description
Federate	Several subjects that may work closely together, as their subjects are sometimes seen as having similar approaches towards knowledge. For example, a humanities department including history, geography and religious education.
Confederate	Several subjects grouped together with shared management and possibly space, but with little in common between the subjects. For example, a department including citizenship, business studies and music.
Unitary	A single subject department with its own head of department and space, neither affiliated to nor managed by a larger faculty.
Impacted	The same as 'unitary', but smaller. Busher and Harris (1999) include geography departments as an example of this group, having only two or three designated rooms, with two or three full time teachers.
Diffuse	One subject area, with a designated Head of Department (HoD) but without an identifiable base. For example, Personal, Social and Health Education (PSHE) may be taught across the school by teachers for whom PSHE is not part of their job title/description and only constitutes a minor part of their timetable.

situated ways in which these work out in school micro-politics. Take a moment to consider the kind of department you work in and other departments in your school. Task 4.2 provides some guidance to do this.

 Task 4.2   Departmental classifications

1) Devise your own typology, or adapt from the example above to create a categorisation of your department.
2) Reflect on the characteristics of your department and its effectiveness.
3) In what ways might these characteristics differ from those of an 'ideal' department?
4) What strengths does this highlight about your department?

Discuss these with other beginning teachers to see what characteristics they have identified. Store this information in your PDP.

Departmental cultures

Culture is used here to mean the

> beliefs, values, habits and assumed ways of doing things among communities of teachers who have to deal with similar demands and constraints over many years. Culture carries the community's historically generated and collectively shared solutions to its new and inexperienced membership.
>
> *(Hargreaves, 1994, p. 165)*

Including 'beliefs, values, habits and assumed ways of doing things' makes culture all pervasive: like the air you breathe in the department. And, like air, the quality of the culture affects the flourishing – or not – of those inhabiting it. Research on departmental cultures is often 'highly evaluative' (Puttick, 2016, p. 137): positive characteristics include high levels of collaboration, openness to new members and a 'making-explicit' of the basis on which decisions are made (Burn, 2007). The most positive departments are summarised by McNicholl, Childs and Burn (2013) as being ones in which 'teacher collaboration was facilitated by an ethos that signalled it was safe and even a professional expectation to air and share problems' (p. 268). The 'safety' of great departments is discussed further below through the lens of psychological safety.

One example of a negative department culture is analysed by Sirna, Tinning and Rossi (2008) in relation to physical education. The spaces of the physical education offices in their study are experienced by beginning teachers as unsafe, being highly gendered and 'toxic'. They describe student teachers being socialised into accepting problematic attitudes including sexist jokes and a 'laid-back' approach towards teaching, for example, by acting as if no one actually plans lessons. Asking questions about subject knowledge was seen as being overly keen and/or exposing oneself as having weak subject knowledge: teachers 'sacrificed asking questions … because they feared that it might make them seem incompetent or otherwise negatively affect their evaluation' (Sirna et al., 2008, p. 296). Sirna et al. (2008), found a range of different responses to these departmental cultures. Most student teachers complied, either passively by nodding/laughing/not challenging, or actively, for example, by contributing their own highly gendered, sexist jokes. Over time 'normalising' processes happen, and 'certain practices, which were once disturbing, come to seem reasonable or "natural"' (p.297). One consequence is that questions and contributions are inhibited because 'in addition to seeming out of sync with the group, asking questions might lead to perceptions of incompetence or being over conscientious' (p. 294). The concept of psychological safety offers an alternative, presented here as one way of making explicit the kinds of dispositions and values that enable departments to thrive as open, safe environments that welcome questioning, uncertainty and professional dialogue.

Psychologically safe departments

Imagine a nurse on a night shift concerned about the dosage a patient is receiving. Wanting to phone the doctor at home to check, they recall the disparaging comments made about their abilities in the past, and decide against calling. Far away, a young pilot in a military training flight notices that the senior officer might have made a crucial mistake. But, not wanting to speak up, they also let the moment go by. Finally, a senior executive, new to the team and feeling like an outsider, has grave reservations about a planned takeover. Everyone else seems so enthusiastic, so again they opt to go along with it rather than raise their concerns.

These three scenarios are used by Edmondson and Lei (2014) to introduce the concept of psychological safety. Psychological safety 'describes people's perceptions of the consequences of taking interpersonal risks in a particular context such as a workplace' (Edmondson and Lei 2014, p. 24). It means 'ensuring that no one is penalized if they ask for help or admit a mistake' (Edmondson, 2008, p.xx). She argues that no one wakes up in the morning wanting to be seen as being ignorant, incompetent, intrusive or negative! We might similarly imagine the teachers described in Sirna et al.'s (2008) study not wanting to go into their departmental office to reveal their discomfort with the kinds of 'joking' they encountered. In a more commonplace example, we might imagine a student teacher listening to a discussion about a particular aspect of subject knowledge – which they have never encountered before – and not wanting to reveal their lack of knowledge. These scenarios create tensions. In the face of such a dilemma one strategy is to just not say anything. To supress genuine concerns or doubts and continue as if everything is fine so that you are not judged as incompetent. The aim of building 'psychological safety' is to find creative and productive ways to, individually and collectively, work with these tensions; creating openness so that there is a supportive departmental culture in which reasons for acting are made explicit, questions about contestable issues are rigorously explored, and lack of knowledge about areas provides great opportunities to learn and teach one another.

There is something about education that makes these kinds of situations – characterised by uncertainty or contestable positions – possibly more likely than the examples from medicine, the military and business because education is inherently contestable (Pring, 2004). It is also highly complex, and questions about education are based on value judgements that rely on whole belief systems. When you discuss ideas around the curriculum or the aims of your subject, you are unavoidably entering into some big questions: What is good education (Biesta, 2009)? What does it mean to be an educated 19 year old in this day and age (Pring et al., 2009)? What are schools for (Young, 2009; White, 2007)? Even at a slightly lower level of analysis, the following questions start to indicate some of the complexities:

■ Is the subject primarily defined by formal curricula (such as a National Curriculum, Examination Specifications, Governmental Subject Content), or by its 'parent' academic discipline?
■ Does subject knowledge come primarily from the most recent awarding body-approved textbooks or peer-reviewed journal articles? Which should be most authoritative for the teacher of an examination class when they conflict?
■ How should we assess pupils?

While there might be broad agreement on a very basic level about differences between formative and summative assessment, recent experiences in educational assessment reveal significant challenges and points of substantial disagreement around assessment. For example:

■ Should assessment be judged by norm or criterion referenced standards?
■ Should marking and assessment use descriptors or comparative judgement?

In their review of marking accuracy, The Office of Qualifications and Examinations Regulation (Ofqual) (2016) found that nearly 50% of English Literature pupils - marked by trained assessors - did not receive the 'correct grade' on a particular paper. Are some differences based on the subjective nature of some of this material?

■ How should conflicts between markers' judgements be managed?
■ How might we create space for reasonable disagreement without unfairly judging others as not-knowing, or being unable to assess in their subject?

The highly complex nature of teaching and education makes it inevitable that teachers have differing beliefs - and varying levels of understanding - about the assumptions underpinning schooling and the ends towards which they are working. Psychologically safe departments are spaces for holding, expressing, robustly critiquing and refining these (and other) perspectives. There are obvious ways in which the physical education departments described above (Sirna et al., 2008) are psychologically unsafe. There is a low bar over what constitutes 'risk' because even refusing to participate in highly gendered, sexist joking might be - particularly for the beginning teacher - a risk. There is also a high level of interpersonal consequence for these risks: there seems to be significant pressure to participate in these negative practices, and not doing so risks alienation and a lack of inclusion in the department. Edmondson (2008) categorises

Table 4.2 Issues associated with a lack of psychological safety (adapted from Edmondson, 2008)

Issue	Summary
Critical information and ideas fail to rise to the top	'When people get the message that speed, efficiency, and results are what matter, they become exceedingly reluctant to risk taking up managers' time with any but the most certain and positive of inputs. They don't offer ideas, concerns or even questions'.
People do not have enough time to learn	'[S]witching to a new approach can lower performance in the short run ... overemphasis[ing] results can subtly discourage technologies, skills or practices that make new approaches viable'.
Unhealthy internal competition arises	'To motivate people to execute well, companies often reward those divisions or plants with the best performance. This can make people reluctant to share ideas or best practices with their colleagues in other groups'.

problems faced by organisations that are not psychologically safe into three main areas. These are illustrated in Table 4.2.

Now complete Task 4.3.

   Task 4.3   Developing psychological safety

For each negative above, identify positive examples to show either what is working well in your department, or other concrete ideas about what a positive example would look like. What responses might you and your department have to these areas? In what ways can you maximise opportunities to develop 'safer' departmental cultures? This might include specific action within your control. For example: new ways to openly raise questions in the department that are welcomed and encouraged; revising how summative assessments are reported to create more collective and less individual responsibility.

Discuss your findings with your mentor (or someone else) and store the outcomes of your discussions in your PDP to refer to later.

In making her argument about these categorisations, Edmondson (2008) uses a distinction between 'execution-as-efficiency' and 'execution-as-learning'. In the former, delivering to targets is rewarded, and so doing the set process as efficiently as possibly is the focus. In the latter, critically reflecting on the process and aims, so that teachers learn, is the focus. Returning to the argument made about the inherently contestable nature of education, there are good reasons to suggest that there is pressure on school subject departments to operate in an efficient way, rather than in a way that maximises learning. One implication of fostering psychological safety is that disagreeing with or raising questions about practices – even if they are widely shared across the profession – should be well received. These questions will not be dismissed, and particularly not with a roll of the eyes and any variations on the phrase 'but *everyone* knows that ...'. To use an extreme example, it was once widely believed that the earth was flat ... What kinds of assumptions are shared within your department? How might you collectively uncover and make explicit what these beliefs are? Are there good reasons for believing and doing these things? What kinds of language do people use to disagree with ideas within the department? Now complete Task 4.4.

M

> ### ✎ Task 4.4   Analysing departmental discourse
>
> Reflect on your observations and analysis of your department carefully, and use these questions to compare and contrast with the experiences of departments that others in your private professional network have. For example: What do you notice about the ways in which agreement is reached? What happens when disagreement takes place? How is this resolved? With what kinds of language are questions or concerns responded to? What about these exchanges might be said to foster psychological safety? What aspects could be further developed? What changes to format/organisation/language might help?
>
> Discuss your findings with your mentor (or another colleague). Store your reflections in your PDP so that you can review them at a later date.

Making departments psychologically safer – or trying to effect any kind of cultural change within organisations – is a challenge, contextually specific, and depends on the kinds of relationships you build. In their work on organisational effectiveness, the 're:Work' team at Google use the following headings to give practical suggestions for developing psychological safety, adapted here for the context of school subject departments:

■ *Demonstrate engagement*: Be 'present' in conversations, show you are listening, respond verbally and make eye contact. Do you have your smart phone or tablet open during meetings?!

■ *Show understanding*: During meetings and conversations, acknowledge areas of agreement and disagreement, be open to questions, avoid locating blame and focus on solutions, think about facial expressions. How do you react when someone admits they are not familiar with a particular area of subject knowledge? What is your response when a colleague disagrees with your approach towards behaviour management?

■ *Be inclusive in interpersonal settings*: Be available and approachable, step in if colleagues talk negatively about other colleagues, build rapport.

■ *Be inclusive in decision-making*: Ask for input, opinions and feedback, explain the reasoning behind decisions, acknowledge input from others.

■ *Show confidence and conviction without appearing inflexible*: Invite challenge to your perspectives, model vulnerability by sharing your weaknesses and failures with colleagues and by not trying to hide struggles with behaviour management, particular classes or areas of subject knowledge. What opportunities could you build for colleagues to share areas of subject knowledge expertise?

SUMMARY AND KEY POINTS

■ Research on departmental cultures offers evidence of a range of experiences: some highly negative or 'toxic', whereas others are highly supportive and collaborative. The departmental level has been shown to be the key to school effectiveness. Therefore, making all departments as positive as possible should be seen as a vital task for all teachers and leadership teams.

■ Education is 'inherently contestable' and involves high levels of complexity. Therefore, making reasoning explicit is important, as is constructing departments that are open to discussion.

■ Developing 'psychologically safe' departments offers a useful approach for reflecting on the types of departments we construct, and the degree of openness that exists for colleagues to raise questions and contribute without being dismissed or ridiculed. We are constantly creating and re-creating departmental 'cultures', and there are lots of small concrete steps that you can take to make departments more psychologically safe.

Record in your PDP how the information in this chapter enables you to meet the requirements for your first year of teaching.

 Further resources

Edmondson, A. (2008) 'The competitive imperative of learning', *Harvard Business Review*, 86 (7-8), 60-67. Available from: https://hbr.org/2008/07/the-competitive-imperative-of-learning (accessed 1 December 2018).
An accessible summary of Edmondson's work on developing psychological safety in organisations.

Edmondson, A. (2004) 'Building a psychologically safe workplace'. Amy Edmondson at TEDxHGSE. Available from: www.youtube.com/watch?v=LhoLuui9gX8 (accessed 1 December 2018).
A video of a talk from a TEDx event on psychological safety, including further analysis of illustrations discussed in this chapter.

Google re:Work resources. Available from: https://rework.withgoogle.com
A regularly updated resource, synthesising a wide range of materials with a very practical focus, and a number of interesting case studies all framed around the ideal of 'making work better'.

Pring, R. (2004) *Philosophy of Education: Aims, Theory, Common Sense and Research*, London: Continuum.
Analysis of a number of significant issues and questions about education, including the aims of education, and arguments for the inherently contestable nature of education.

Puttick, S. (2017) '"You'll see that everywhere": institutional isomorphism in secondary school subject departments', *School Leadership and Management*, 37 (1-2), 61-79.
An example of empirical research on departments, including some detailed comparative analysis between departments.

Appendices 2 and 3 list subject associations, teaching councils and relevant websites.

Books in the *Learning to Teach* series that you may find helpful are as follows:

Capel, S., Leask, M. and Younie, S. (eds.) (2019) *Learning to Teach in the Secondary School: A Companion to School Experience*, **8th edn, Abingdon: Routledge.**
This book is designed as a core textbook to support student teachers through their initial teacher education programme.

Capel, S., Leask, M. and Turner, T. (eds.) (2010) *Readings for Learning to Teach in the Secondary School: A Companion to M Level Study*, **Abingdon: Routledge.**
This book brings together essential readings to support you in your critical engagement with key issues raised in this textbook.

The subject-specific books in the *Learning to Teach* series, the *Practical (subject) Guides*, *Debates in (subject)* and *Mentoring (subject) Teachers* are also very useful.

Working with teaching assistants and other adults in the classroom to support subject teaching

Fiona Hall and Maxine Pountney

Introduction

As a newly qualified teacher, it can be quite daunting to find yourself working with and managing the work of support staff. Although the Senior Leadership Team is responsible for their deployment within the school, it is often the teacher that has 'the day to day responsibility' (Sharples, Webster and Blatchford, 2015, p. 7) for directing and deploying the support in class. You may find a range of additional adults support your work in the classroom from Teaching Assistants (TAs) or someone with a similar role such as Learning Support Assistants (LSAs) to technicians and those involved in pupil welfare for example learning mentors (Blatchford et al., 2009). Given the diversity of titles used in schools in England to identify support staff roles it is important for teaching staff to identify what these roles involve in terms of the support individuals provide in the classroom. For clarity, throughout this chapter, the term TA is used when referring to all additional adults working directly with you in the classroom and who are there predominantly to directly support pupils' learning and the term support staff is used when referring to all those who may offer a supporting role in the classroom including technicians and learning mentors.

Many studies have been carried out that indicate successful teaching depends on the effective deployment and collaboration between professionals, but it is not without its challenges; teachers and TAs are already time-pressured and opportunities for them to meet have been in short supply (Russell, Webster and Blatchford, 2016). Knowing the strengths of your TAs is crucial, good communication is fundamental and valuing their contribution is essential in order to establish a positive working relationship alongside the rationale of how you are going to work together. Teaching Assistants are often experienced practitioners showing resourcefulness, imagination and patience (Packer, 2017). They are able to offer support to the teacher as well as supporting teaching and learning (Sharples et al., 2015).

This chapter draws on recommendations made from recent research that outlines effective practice in schools relating to TA deployment and how teachers and TAs can work together effectively. By beginning to understand the diversity, strengths and experience of the support staff in your school and the ways in which you can develop the potential of what they can offer (Teaching and Development Agency (TDA), 2008), they can be deployed according to their skills, knowledge and understanding and become an integral part of your teaching.

OBJECTIVES

At the end of this chapter you should be able to:

■ have a better understanding of the range and diversity of support staff roles in school;

■ develop some strategies for working more effectively with your support staff in the classroom;

■ recognise the 'educational landscape' is changing and there is a need to respond to that change proactively.

Check how the information in this chapter enables you to meet the requirements for your first year of teaching.

Support staff - defining their role

Raising Standards and Tackling Workload: A National Agreement (Department for Education and Skills (DfES), 2003a) resulted in increased responsibility for support staff in schools in England. In today's schools, support staff cover a range of roles: working with individuals, groups and whole classes to support and lead teaching and learning activities both in and out of the classroom as well as providing specialist support within a particular subject or across the curriculum in Special Educational Needs and Disability (SEND) roles. Many support staff also take on additional roles such as midday supervisors, pupil welfare officers, administrative positions, facilities staff or site staff (Blatchford, Russell and Webster, 2012).

Why the diversity of roles? In 2003, the DfES attempted to 'tackle the workload' of teachers by implementing a *National Agreement* (DfES, 2003a) to reduce the administrative tasks undertaken by teachers, reduce the expectation to cover for absent colleagues and establish a protocol for Planning, Preparation and Assessment (PPA) time. This led to the introduction of new support roles in the form of Cover Supervisors to provide cover for absent colleagues and Higher-Level Teaching Assistants (HLTAs) to provide in-class support for pupils and teachers, which included targeted interventions and PPA cover. Although it was initially envisaged that most TAs would take on more clerical and administrative tasks as well as their traditional role of in-classroom support, which they have done, in reality their role has grown and developed significantly and substantially to include many of the activities originally assigned to cover supervisors and HLTAs.

Since 2003, the 'role' of the TA in school has broadened considerably and many TAs have developed specialist roles according to the needs of the school and their own personal skills and expertise. Their generic roles and responsibilities are still to support teaching and learning but their specific role in any given school is not always easily defined. Butt and Lance (2009) reported 'a trend for TAs' roles to be morphing from those of helper to associate teacher, leading to a blurring of boundaries between those who teach and those who support teaching' (Butt and Lance, 2009, p. 227), which has been reiterated in later research by Warhurst et al. (2014). The successful HLTA Programme supports this trend. Many TAs now working in school in England have been assessed against 33 Professional Standards and awarded HLTA status. The figure currently stands at around 56,000 in England (HLTA National Assessment Partnership (HNAP), 2018). Sharples et al. (2015) suggest there are around 15% of TAs who have HLTA status, although many do not actually use this title for the roles they perform (Graves and Williams, 2017). All this can make it even more difficult for a beginning teacher to understand exactly what people do in school. Now complete Task 5.1.

✎ Task 5.1   How well do you know your support staff?

How well do you know your support staff?
What qualifications, specialism or expertise do they have?
What training have they attended?
What do they see their role to be?
How long have they been in this role?
What can they offer to complement your role in providing teaching and learning
   opportunities and support for pupils?

Ask, listen, respect and acknowledge what they say – using this information helps you to deploy your TAs more effectively and helps you to build a constructive and professional relationship in the classroom.

Store the information in your professional development portfolio (PDP) (or similar) to refer to later.

TA numbers in England have increased significantly since 2003 and are now in the region of 266,000 (Department for Education (DfE), 2016a). The ratio is roughly one TA to every three teachers, so there is a very good chance in most schools that you are working with another adult in your classroom for at least part of the day. The rise in numbers sparked a great deal of research into the role of support staff in schools, with one of the most significant pieces of research being the Deployment and Impact of Support Staff (DISS, 2003-2009). The study examined the characteristics of TAs, their training, their roles, pay and conditions as well as the impact they had had in classrooms in relation to their deployment, preparedness and practice (Blatchford et al., 2012). In the final report Blatchford et al. (2009) concluded that although TAs were often highly regarded by teachers, their impact on learner achievement was questionable through no fault of their own. However there has been much training and development in relation to TAs' pedagogical role in more recent years; UNISON (2013) indicated a clearer understanding in schools in relation to TA deployment and TAs are now routinely involved in whole school training. Several Education Endowment Foundation (EEF) supported projects have provided resources and guidance and have shown that effective training of TAs has led to increased achievement for pupils, (EEF Projects and Evaluation, 2018). Many schools are also using the DFE's revised professional standards for teaching assistants, promoted by a number of organisations to help clarify TA roles and to set expectations in relation to performance management (UNISON, National Association of Head Teachers and Senior Leaders (NAHT), National Education Trust (NET), Maximising the Impact of TAs (MITA) and Redhill teaching School Alliance (RTSA), 2016). Though non mandatory and non statutory these standards will help you understand your TA's role.

Qualifications, training and experience of TAs

All local authorities, schools and academy trusts in England now require TAs to have level 2 qualifications in Maths and English and often ask for or expect TAs to have recognised qualifications in Supporting Teaching and Learning or an equivalent, at NVQ levels 2 or 3. It is worth recognising that some TAs have been in school for several years and though they possess few formal qualifications, they may have considerable experience in supporting teaching and learning, as well as life experience from former careers. Although these are now the minimum requirements to be considered for a TA post, many TAs have gained higher level and degree qualifications (UNISON, 2013). In addition, and partly as a result of the growth in routes into teaching, there has been an increase in the number of graduates working as TAs, often to gain experience of working in the classroom whilst considering the next step in their career.

Although TAs are not a homogenous group in terms of their academic levels, continuing professional development (CPD) training is now seen as integral to their roles so that the support they provide for the teacher is underpinned by a greater depth of knowledge and understanding. Richards (2017), writing for the *Times Educational Supplement* (TES) suggests research by the EEF and Maximising the Impact of Teaching Assistants (MITA) has shown that TAs who are 'well deployed with high quality support and training can make a significant impact' in the classroom. Specific examples can be accessed on the EEF website at: https://educationendowmentfoundation.org.uk/ and MITA can be found at: http://maximisingtas.co.uk/. All TAs have to attend in-service training in school to meet statutory requirements in line with national frameworks for health and well-being, such as safeguarding, and many TAs undertake additional training to deliver specific intervention programmes such as maths or literacy or generic training, for example behaviour management, to underpin their practice. Goldsmith (2018) suggests that any training offered should not just be 'an add-on to a process developed and deployed for teaching colleagues' but needs to acknowledge that 'support staff are experts in their own fields, made up of discrete specialist teams' and that their training needs to be 'just as precise, tailored and targeted as that offered to teachers'. However, time and finance continue to be constraints in many schools and although programmes and websites have been developed to support TAs' CPD, keeping up to date with the latest developments in education and providing effective support for teachers and pupils requires classroom teachers and TAs to work together to share knowledge and develop strategies. Remember a TA may be picking up subject knowledge by working closely with you and from observing good teaching practice.

Deployment, preparedness and practice

Deployment

TAs in secondary schools can be deployed in a number of ways. Some secondary schools have TAs assigned to departments, working under the head of department whilst others may deploy them as part of the Special Educational Needs and Disability (SEND) department under the direction of the SEND Coordinator (SENDCo). However, how you deploy TAs and volunteers in the classroom is down to you and is one of the Teachers' Standards in England (DfE, 2011) – and one that if addressed successfully can have an effect on many of the other standards.

The EEF report (Sharples et al., 2015, p.17) made a number of recommendations and suggested strategies for 'maximising the use of TAs in everyday classroom contexts', stating that TAs should:

- 'add value to what teachers do, not replace them;
- help pupils develop independent learning skills and manage their own learning' (Sharples et al., 2015, p.4).

This indicates a need for collaborative working with teachers to 'ensure TAs are fully prepared for their role in the classroom' and not used 'as an informal teaching resource for low-attaining pupils' (Sharples et al., 2015, p. 4) but this does have an impact on a teacher's time. The report acknowledges that finding 'extra time' within a busy school timetable to plan with your TA cannot be underestimated, but also accepts it is difficult to achieve any of the recommendations above without some form of 'out-of-class liaison'. The report (Sharples et al., 2015, p.20) suggests some strategies to support collaborative working though some of these recommendations are beyond the remit of the class teacher to action. The report has, however, identified some strategies aimed more pertinently at class teachers, including the need to share planning in advance so that TAs are aware of 'concepts/information being taught, intended learning outcomes, skills to be learned and expected/required feedback' (Sharples et al., 2015, p.4).

The DISS study found that low attaining pupils and pupils with SEND were routinely supported by TAs often away from the class resulting in segregation from their classes and teachers (Blatchford et al., 2012). As a follow up to the DISS study, Webster and Blatchford's 'Making a Statement Project' (2013) in relation to the experiences of pupils with SEND indicated that TAs are often responsible for planning for pupils with SEND, either working with them away from class or are called upon to differentiate tasks at the point of delivery. Further research from the 'Special Educational Needs in Secondary Education' study indicated that pupils with SEND are often taught in smaller classes alongside low attaining peers (Webster and Blatchford, 2017). All the studies showed that pupils with SEND obtained most of their teaching from the TAs rather than teachers and that in some cases TAs were doing too much for the pupils leading to a lack of independent learning. The SEND code of practice has definitely placed more responsibility and accountability on teachers for pupils with SEND in their classrooms (DfE and Department of Health (DoH), 2015). Teachers need to make sure they differentiate appropriately, considering all the children in the class. Even if a TA is present to support a specific learner, it is good practice for them to provide support to the learner as part of a group as well as moving away entirely to encourage greater independence.

Ultimately you need to think how your TA adds value in your classroom and what your TA can do to help keep your classroom running smoothly. One key suggestion is in relation to classroom management; which is that TAs are really useful in dealing with low-level disruption that can impact on the fluidity of a lesson.

Preparedness

Russell et al. (2016) have key recommendations for schools to aid TA preparedness. These include:

■ create time for teachers and TAs to meet;
■ make adjustments to TAs working hours to facilitate this;
■ be creative with timetables in order to create time;
■ formalise how teachers plan and share lesson information;
■ set a standard expected in plans that are for TAs covering lessons.

Clearly, much of this is at whole school level so on a practical level in class you need to plan how you are going to utilise your TA and how you are going to communicate this to them. To accommodate time constraints many secondary staff now rely on email contact to share planning, discuss ideas, identify the TAs role and give feedback on learner progress. A little more detail on a lesson plan is invaluable for TAs, as is prior access to it. You may also find that a few minutes can be spared in a lesson when pupils are working in order to discuss progress and next steps. Although it is your job to plan for all the children, if TAs are well briefed beforehand they may have additional ideas that can help support children in the class. In particular if they are there to help support children with SEND, they may have some specific ideas in relation to a child's particular needs but can only use these to best advantage if they are aware of the lesson's intentions. In addition, if they are responsible for delivering specific intervention, effective liaison between you and your TA can help them make the explicit connections between classroom learning and structured interventions for the learner (Sharples et al., 2015). Prior liaison of some description eliminates the need for TAs to 'tune in' to the lesson alongside pupils when the lesson starts and they can therefore be of greater support to you. If you share thorough planning with your TA, they will know their role and what strategies to use and what learning you want children to achieve; the TA also knows what else you may require of them for the lesson if you share this beforehand. This really helps if your TA has to unexpectedly cover part of a lesson for you, the more details you can give them; the more successful the lesson will be. Now undertake Task 5.2.

Task 5.2   Reflecting on your practice in working with a TA

Think about your lessons over the course of a week where you have TA support.

How much do your TAs know about each lesson?

How much prior discussion with TAs do you have?

Do you invite their contribution to planning and preparation of resources and activities?

Which pupils do you ask them to support?

How much direction do you give to your TAs on how to support learning?

Do you take into account their experience, knowledge and understanding when deploying them in the classroom?

How do you get feedback from the TA regarding pupils' learning?

How do you support pupils with SEND in your classes so they can be included in the learning activity?

What strategies have or can you you use to make communication between you more effective (including email, whats app etc)?

Store the information in your PDP to refer to later.

Following the EEF Report (2014) and advice from MITA (Russell et al., 2016), training packages are now being offered by training companies or inhouse to enable TAs to develop their practice and skills but the first point of learning and development for many TAs is in the classroom and guidance from teachers can be invaluable in helping to improve practice, especially for new and inexperienced TAs. It is strongly recommended that you read 'Making Best Use of Teaching Assistants: Guidance Report' (Sharples, Webster and Blatchford, 2015) for more information and guidance and that you ensure you work with all the pupils in your class, including those with SEND, to allow all pupils to benefit from your knowledge and skills.

Finally some sound practical advice for in the classroom comes from Packer (2017) who looks at how teachers can 'make effective use of one of the most valuable resources in their classroom – teaching assistants', stressing the importance of communication: 'Even if you can only manage a two minute conversation just prior to the lesson, it's better than nothing!' It helps you to reflect on your practice and consider how to work in partnership with your TAs to support all pupils in the class, not just those with SEND.

Practice

What TAs do in lessons is down to you and the more direction you can give them to help support learners the better they can do it. Questioning is an area where support may be needed. In order to develop quality questioning to enable TAs to promote pupils' thinking, as a teacher you may need to be specific and proactive by providing key questions or examples of what you want to see being used. Resources such as 'questions and key words for critical thinking' (Russell et al., 2016, appendix 4) are now readily available online (MITA, 2018) to encourage TAs to consider the type of questions they use with pupils. A printable poster (MITA, 2018) summarises Webster's (2017) 'Five step teaching assistant model to increase pupil independence':

1) self-scaffolding - TAs observe, allowing pupils time and space to process and try the task before intervention;
2) prompting - TAs intervene/'nudge' the pupils with an appropriate question;
3) clueing - TAs drip feed clues to prompt;
4) modelling - TAs model new or misunderstood skill or strategy;
5) correcting - answers provided (should be avoided).

Now undertake Task 5.3.

 Task 5.3   Increasing learner independence

Download the poster from the MITA website (http://maximisingtas.co.uk/resources/making-best-use-oftas-eef-guidance) and share it with your TA.
Ask them to reflect on the model, and ask them where they think they use aspects of the model.
Aim to encourage self-scaffolding strategies at some stage in the lesson.
Store the information in your PDP to refer to later.

If you have TA support for a lesson it is likely that at some stage interventions are taking place in your classroom or elsewhere in groups, pairs or with individuals. Specific intervention programmes are often prescriptive and should be followed as intended to be most effective but make sure you know what is being taught and give any guidance if needed. Make sure TAs understand what they are being asked to deliver in the context of your lesson and your expectations in terms of learning. In addition make sure they are clear about any assessment that is needed. Ensure you monitor pupils' progress alongside your TA and bring any learning from the intervention into the main lesson where possible. Research shows interventions are more effective if the TA has had some specific training (Alboraz et al., 2009) so check if your TA has received the training for the interventions they deliver and if not support an application for training. Show an interest in the interventions carried out by monitoring the learning outcomes and discussing the methods used as a good way to share your knowledge and understanding of an individual's needs and progress. Share your expectations for the learner in order to inform future joint planning.

Classroom leadership and relationships with other adults

Schools are all about working in teams and as a teacher, when working with pupils, colleagues and parents or carers, you have a role and a purpose when working within that team. However, the teamwork in your classroom is very personal to you and your TAs and a key component to the success of that team is to work in partnership. Morgan and Ashbaker (2011) reported that teachers were not managing the additional adults in their classrooms to best effect and UNISON (2013) also indicated a need to develop teachers' management of TAs. A recent newly qualified teacher (NQT) survey in England, identified that only 54% of beginning teachers felt their initial teacher education providers had prepared them well in how to effectively deploy support staff (National College for Teaching and Leadership (NCTL), 2016). Realising there is a team in your classroom with an understanding that you need to lead it is important.

Developing cohesion in the classroom built on trust and respect enables a greater exchange of ideas between teachers and TAs (Chopra and Uitto, 2015) and good classroom relationships with other adults has also been shown to enhance learner achievement (Cremin, Thoman and Vincett, 2005). Hall et al. (2015) suggest communication is key to success and a good team is one that encourages communication between all necessary parties for the benefit of pupils; a failure to communicate effectively impacts negatively on pupils' learning. Ultimately to 'develop effective professional relationships with colleagues' (DfE, 2011, p.13) is one of the Teachers' Standards in England. It is therefore vital that you are able to establish clear boundaries and expectations regarding your own role and that of your TA as well as behaviour management and class routines (Packer, 2017). Find out if there is a policy in school and familiarise yourself with it if there is. Be clear to discuss roles, responsibilities and expectations with your TAs. Now undertake Task 5.4.

 Task 5.4   Effective working

What examples do you have of working effectively as part of a team?
What made it successful?
Think of when you have shared knowledge, training or information with colleagues
   in school. How did you manage this? Positives? Constraints?
What would you do differently?

Discuss this information with your mentor (or someone else) and store the information in your PDP to refer to later.

Burnage (2017) offers the following strategies to enable support staff team leaders to develop successful and highly motivated teams. These are transferrable to the role of the teacher as a leader of support staff within the classroom and implemented through communication and team working.

■   Motivation - make support staff feel valued, secure and safe with the leadership offered.
■   Ownership - ownership of actions and decisions by support staff within the guidelines set by the teacher.
■   Communicate effectively - use praise, personalised support and set clear targets.
■   Know yourself as a leader - what style do you adopt/what style is needed? For example coach, mentor, dictator.
■   Lead your team members as individuals - according to their capability and commitment, making use of an appropriate leadership style.

Relationships within teams are crucial and managing people is not easy, especially managing others who you perceive to have much more experience than you. Russell et al. (2016) offer some good advice:

- Communication: be clear and specific - don't assume your TA knows what you want them to do.
- Class interaction: empower your TA to be active in lessons; acknowledge their experience.
- Decision making: allow your TA to make decisions in line with your ground rules for behaviour - very empowering.
- Build on your TAs strengths: get to know them and build on these, including hobbies and experiences they can bring to the learning in the classroom.
- Feedback: provide constructive feedback.

Now undertake Task 5.5.

M

 Task 5.5   How confident are you in working with your TA?

Packer (2017) makes suggestions in relation to working with your TA. These have been made into a task for you to consider.

How confident are you in preparing/directing the work of/collaborating with your TA?

Pick a lesson and work through the checklist below.

Planning

Aim to have a direct conversation with your TA before the session (even if it is only brief at the beginning) so you know they understand what you want them to do, e.g. modelling the task, helping to keep learner(s) focussed, scribing, rewording instructions, using additional resources or making assessment and observational notes. Questions to consider:

- Do I have the same TA support each week for specific lessons? If not, how do I manage this? Have I allowed flexibility to modify the plan if need be?
- Have I taken into account my TA's role/contribution/strengths (if I know them) when planning the lesson and is this clear on the plan?
- Have I provided my TA with a copy of the lesson plan/notes in advance/or at the start of the lesson with as much detail as they need to be able to do an effective job?
- Are the learning objectives clear on the lesson plan/differentiated if relevant?
- Have I identified the strategies I would like them to use for learning/managing behaviour/my expectations, including use of key questions and words to encourage learning?

During the lesson you might ask your TA to:

- aid access to learning such as modifying resources;
- pre-teach concepts, such as reiterating key vocabulary that is needed, or give structure to enable pupils to begin the task;
- remodel the task;
- scaffold the task;
- scribe;
- reinforce instructions;
- help pupils use equipment;
- encourage participation and discussion;
- question;
- assess;
- make links – ask pupils to apply knowledge.

After the lesson

Make sure you get feedback from your TA as this helps inform your future planning. Arrange with them how you are going to do this – use of sticky notes, email, tick sheet, feedback on work.

Discuss this information with your mentor (or someone else) and store the information in your PDP to refer to later.

Good organisation, a clear focus, clarity of direction and hard work can help to establish effective team processes such as communication pathways and decision making. Once established it benefits everyone – teachers, TAs and pupils – to work in a positive classroom environment where learning is the priority.

SUMMARY AND KEY POINTS

- The adults supporting you in the classroom are often well qualified, experienced and skilled individuals and can add enormous value to your classroom, enabling pupils to be involved in your lessons and make good progress.
- For the above to happen you need to take responsibility and make sure TAs are clear on what is expected from them and ensure they are well prepared for what they need to do. This takes time and investment from you both; and establishing good relationships makes this more likely.
- Having respect for and valuing your TA's contribution enhances pupils' learning and outcomes and ensures a positive working environment for everyone.

Record in your PDP, how the information in this chapter enables you to meet the requirements for your first year of teaching.

Further resources

Russell, A., Webster, R. and Blatchford, P. (2016) *Maximising the Impact of Teaching Assistants*, 2nd edn, London: Routledge.
This book offers key advice on how a school can audit and develop their use of TAs.

Sharples, J., Webster, R. and Blatchford, P. (2015) *Making Best Use of Teaching Assistants*, London: Education Endowment Foundation. Available from: www.educationendowmentfoundation. org.uk (accessed 26 August 2019).
The report draws on a number of research reports that make recommendations for TA deployment.

Websites:

https://educationendowmentfoundation.org.uk – Education Endowment Foundation.

The website gives access to a range of research projects that have been conducted in schools as well as requests for schools to get involved in research. By signing up to alerts you can have the very latest research in your areas of interest.

www.maximisingtas.co.uk – Maximising the Impact of Teaching Assistants (MITA).

This website has numerous practical reports on how to best use the additional adults in your classroom including a useful guide to online resources at http://maximisingtas.co.uk/assets/ llsmaximise-ta-doc.pdf

www.sec-ed.co.uk – SECEd.

This magazine and its accompanying website haveall the latest news in relation to secondary education as well as reports in relation to additional adults in the classroom.

www.skillsforschools.otg.uk – Skills for Schools.

This is an online guide to careers, training and development for support staff in schools, managed by UNISON.

www.TES.com – *Times Educational Supplement.*

This magazine and accompanying website contain the latest news in relation to education and regularly run features relating to teaching assistants.

www.hlta.org.uk - *Higher Level Teaching Assistants National Assessment Partnership.*

This provides an overview of the HLTA Award and HLTA status including information about the 33 professional standards.

Appendices 2 and 3 list subject associations, teaching councils and relevant websites.

Books in the *Learning to Teach* series that you may find helpful are as follows:

Capel, S., Leask, M. and Younie, S. (eds.) (2019) *Learning to Teach in the Secondary School: A Companion to School Experience*, 8th edn, Abingdon: Routledge.
This book is designed as a core textbook to support student teachers through their initial teacher education programme.

Capel, S., Leask, M. and Turner, T. (eds.) (2010) *Readings for Learning to Teach in the Secondary School: A Companion to M Level Study*, Abingdon: Routledge.
This book brings together essential readings to support you in your critical engagement with key issues raised in this textbook.

The subject-specific books in the *Learning to Teach* series, the *Practical (subject) Guides*, *Debates in (subject)* and *Mentoring (subject) Teachers* are also very useful.

6 Role of the form tutor

Alexandra Titchmarsh

Introduction

Pastoral care means all provision made in a school for assuring pupils' well-being and for supporting pupils in their personal and social development, as well as their overall academic development, for the time that they are in the school.

As a subject teacher, you have a duty of pastoral care to pupils in your classes. Indeed, '[a]ll teachers have a role in pupils' pastoral care, as the pupils' emotional state influences how secure and safe they feel in the learning situation, which impacts upon their motivation and hence on their achievement' (Heilbronn, 2004, p. 49). However, as well as your subject teaching, a majority of teachers also have responsibility for a form (or house) group (see below). Being a form tutor is not an 'add-on' to your role as a subject teacher; rather it is a critically important core role that contributes to teaching and learning. Pastoral care provided by the form tutor is equally as important as the care provided by the subject teacher. It is one of the key aspects by which, in England, the Office for Standards in Education, Children's Services and Skills (Ofsted, 2012a) measure the quality of a school and the all-round education that a school provides for its pupils.

There is a significant overlap between the role of a classroom teacher and the role of a form tutor. Both have the academic progress, personal and social development, mental and physical well-being and safeguarding of pupils at the heart of their responsibilities. However, as a classroom teacher you are more focussed on academic development within your specific subject area. As a form tutor, you

> might liaise with parents about a pupil's performance across all subject areas in the school curriculum. [however] form tutors tend to have primary, though not exclusive, responsibility for the emotional, spiritual, cultural and social in addition to the academic well-being of pupils in their group.
>
> *(Fletcher, 1997, p. 46)*

This aligns with the thoughts of Marland and Rogers (2004, p. 38) who said, 'A form tutor is a teacher whose subject is the pupil'. Recently, Baggaley (2018) of the Personal, Social, Health and Economic (PSHE) Education Association has said that it is important that we are 'guaranteeing young people an education that supports their physical and mental health, wellbeing and relationships'. This may well become more of a focus for the form tutor as PSHE education becomes mandatory in all schools in 2020 (Chapter 9 focuses on PSHE education).

OBJECTIVES

At the end of this chapter you should be able to understand:

■ how pupils might be grouped for pastoral care;
■ the importance of the form tutor to the pupils;
■ the role of the form tutor and what you might do as a form tutor on a weekly basis, as well as on a less frequent basis, e.g. termly and/or when necessary;
■ the importance of safeguarding pupils;
■ the importance of preparing for tutor time;
■ the attributes and skills of a good form tutor.

Check how the information in this chapter enables you to meet the requirements for your first year of teaching.

Grouping pupils for pastoral care

There are different ways of grouping pupils for pastoral care, in either forms or houses.

Often pupils are grouped in forms by school year, each with a form tutor e.g. all pupils in, say, form 9A are in Year 9. In these age-related tutor groupings, pupils' pastoral well-being is overseen by a head of year. In some schools, pupils are grouped in houses as opposed to year groups each with a house tutor. In these house groupings, pupils' pastoral well-being is overseen by a head of house. Some schools have vertical tutor groups, where pupils range from Years 7-11, or even Year 13, with four or five pupils from each year group in one form each with a tutor. Oversight of pupils' pastoral well-being of vertical groups varies according to the school. It could be a head of year, or where the vertical grouping is by house, a head of house, or another member of staff. Throughout the rest of this chapter we refer to form tutor, tutor group and head of year. However, if your school groups pupils by house or by vertical groups, then substitute the terms used in your school, e.g. house tutor or head of house.

Often pupils in a tutor group are only grouped together for form time and possibly PSHE lessons, but taught in other groupings for subjects (see Titchmarsh in *LTT8* (2019) for further information about pupil grouping). Now complete Task 6.1.

Task 6.1   Pastoral groupings in your school

Make sure you are clear about how pupils are grouped for pastoral care in your
  school.
Try to find out why this particular form of grouping is in place. Has it always been
  like this or has it changed? Why? Are the pupils only together for form time or
  are they taught as a form for some subjects? Talk to the head of year for the
  year for which you are a form tutor about the strengths of the system as well
  as any weaknesses.

Record the information with your reflections in your professional development
portfolio (PDP) (or similar) and review and add to your ideas as you become more
experienced as a form tutor.

The role of a form tutor

The role of a form tutor is pivotal in the day-to-day running of a school and the well-being
of pupils within the school. The role is complex as it is such a multifaceted position.

As a form tutor, you influence how an individual or a whole group of pupils start their
school day. This is key when trying to get the best out of your pupils.

A form tutor's role is to look after each pupil as a whole. Crucially, the role includes
caring for pupils in your tutor group, monitoring and supporting their progress personally,
socially and academically. It also includes encouraging participation and involvement in
activities on a day-to-day basis, as well as events such as sports day, and relaying high
expectations of standards of presentation, uniform, behaviour, work and attainment. In
essence, a good form tutor gathers knowledge of each pupil within their tutor group,
forms strong and positive relationships with each pupil and their parent(s)/guardian(s)
and builds a cohesive and supportive team ethos within the tutor group.

As a form tutor, you model good behaviour and habits (such as time keeping and social
skills). You are expected to be punctual to tutor time as this is part of setting the standard
and high expectations for pupils. This also helps to prepare pupils as fully as possible for
day-to-day life outside of school and for challenging situations as adults so that they can
take them in their stride when they occur (Purdy, 2013).

A form tutor is often seen as a confidant to pupils. In this role, it is not the big things that
make a difference but the ability to listen, offer advice and be a friendly face that make a
successful form tutor. Ultimately, the role is about showing the pupils you care and that you
are willing to 'go the extra mile' for them. Think about how you would want your own child
or sibling to feel – supported, so that they can do their very best each day.

As a form tutor, you should be aware of friendship groups, familial relationships and
pupil/staff relationships of pupils in your tutor group. Changes in these could explain
changes in behaviour or attainment. If you have any concerns about these discuss these
with your head of year or safeguarding officer/lead. Often pupils will have conversations

within your earshot that they don't realise you can hear. These conversations often provide good insight as to what events are happening with particular pupils or groups of pupils.

Now complete Task 6.2.

 Task 6.2   Roles of a form tutor in your school

Obtain a list of the requirements you are expected to fill in your role as a form tutor. Make sure you are clear what each of these requirements entails. Ask your head of year if you are not clear.

Record the information in your PDP, along with ideas about how you might meet the requirements. Reflect on this and your developing practice periodically and build a portfolio of resources, ideas and successful activities.

What does a form tutor do?

One of the first things you need to do with your tutor group is to start the process of bonding with them. You may well be a form tutor for a brand new Year 7 tutor group or for an established older tutor group (or vertical tutor group). There are many different activities you can do with your tutor group to break the ice and bond with them. Some examples can be found on the *Times Educational Supplement* website (www.tes.com).

On a daily basis, as a form tutor you are normally expected to take registration for the school day. This should be a priority every morning. You may also have to take the register at an afternoon registration; otherwise the register taken in the first lesson after lunch forms the second registration of the day. A register is a legal document that must be kept accurately. Amongst other legal requirements, the register provides the basis for truancy calls to be sent out. It is expected that the form tutor will identify patterns of lateness and/or absence and will liaise with the appropriate staff (most commonly the head of year and attendance officer) to highlight issues. Form tutors who go 'above and beyond', take time to rectify problems with punctuality and absence of members of their form if it is within their ability to do so. This may include, for example, a letter or phone call home, punctuality/absence report or other solutions.

There may be other roles you are required to undertake; check with your head of year or mentor for the expectations of a form tutor in your school.

What does a form tutor do on a weekly basis?

Your weekly checklist as a form tutor may look something like the list below.

> *Conversations about behaviour*, both positive and negative. Many heads of year run a behaviour and achievement points log for tutor groups in their year to be completed on a weekly basis. This is something you can also do yourself; ask your head of year or mentor to show you how to do this as different schools use different systems. The advantage of having behaviour/achievement logs on a weekly basis

is that you can have personalised conversations with pupils who have either done well or appear to be struggling. The better you know your pupils the better the response from a pupil will be. It can become very easy to fixate on negatives, so always remember to make a conscious effort to praise positives as well.

Conversations about attendance. As a form tutor you see your tutor group every day (in some schools, twice a day). You are therefore the first port of call to pick up any patterns of either absence or lateness. For example, you may well notice that pupil X is frequently absent on a Wednesday. It may well be that a particular subject is taught on Wednesday and that pupil X does not like/ enjoy the subject for some reason. As a form tutor, it is your role to get to the bottom of identifying patterns of absence and lateness and finding out the reasons behind them. The better you know your pupils, the easier it is to identify problems and have those conversations. It is important to remember that if you have any concerns related to the safeguarding of a young person you must disclose these to your designated safeguarding officer immediately (see below).

Equipment and uniform checks. It is important that all pupils arrive at school ready to learn. As the form tutor is the first teacher the tutor group sees each day, it is important that you set them up for the day. You may want to do equipment checks once a week; this ensures that all pupils have the tools for learning available to them. If a pupil does not have the right equipment, you may want to send them to buy equipment if there is a stationery store in school. Otherwise, if you have a pen that you can lend them for the day, then maybe do this – just remember to get it back at the end of the day or else you will lose pens frequently! You should be checking uniforms each day in line with the school uniform policy. Some schools issue warnings the first time the correct uniform is not worn, whilst other schools send pupils home. Ask your mentor for advice on this as it is important that you are following school policy and doing the same as other staff. Remember to follow up concerns about equipment and uniform with a phone call or email home and then do a re-check the next day.

Conversations with parent(s)/guardian(s). These conversations could be instigated by either yourself or the parent(s)/guardian(s). In many schools the form tutor is the first line of contact with home and parent(s)/guardian(s) automatically contact you if they have a concern about their child. If you feel the conversation may be a difficult topic, you could always write a 'script' of what you want to say and show this to your head of year or mentor. They may well support you with the first few phone calls.

Homework planner monitoring/checking/signing. If your school has homework planners, it is important to monitor/check/sign these regularly. Some schools now use online homework systems as an alternative to traditional planners. Schools have slightly different policies as to how often they should be checked by both the tutor and parent(s)/guardian(s), so make sure you ask your mentor about this. Checking the homework planner means that you have regular contact with parent(s)/guardian(s). Often parent(s)/guardian(s) use the planner as a form of communication and write notes for you in there. You can also do the same. In addition, as you monitor homework you can link up missing homework with any possible behaviour issues. If a pupil is not writing their homework down, they are unlikely to complete it as they will have forgotten it before they even get home!

Leading PSHE lessons within tutor time (although often more 'challenging' topics are delivered by external providers) and planning or implementing activities which are relevant to the pastoral plan in place at your school. Your head of year may have organised a weekly timetable of activities. These are likely to be based on a theme, either a new one each week or a rolling theme for, say, half a term. You may well be asked to contribute to planning and preparing the activities for a particular session (PSHE is covered in Chapter 9).

Assembly. You may be required to deliver assemblies on a rota with your tutor group. Even if you are not leading an assembly, you will be expected to take your tutor group to assembly and supervise them. Different schools have different assembly rotas and you may find there are several assemblies a week (e.g. there may be a whole school assembly on a Monday and a year group or house assembly on a Wednesday). Often assemblies provide you with themes to follow up on during the week during tutor time.

Now complete Task 6.3.

 Task 6.3   Meeting parent(s)/guardian(s)

Observe an experienced form tutor or head of year holding a meeting with a parent(s)/guardian(s). Before you observe the meeting, have a conversation with the experienced tutor/head of year about what you would expect to see from them. During the meeting, write down your observations briefly (this may include phrases that you can use when you hold meetings with parent(s)/guardian(s)). Afterwards, have a debrief with the tutor/head of year and see what they thought went well and how they would change it in future meetings.

Record the information in your PDP. Reflect on this advice in light of your experiences with parent(s)/guardian(s) and add notes about what approaches work well for later use.

What does a form tutor do less frequently, on a termly basis?

Your checklist for termly activities might look something like the list below:

Discuss tracker results and set SMART (specific, measurable, achievable, relevant and time-bound) targets for pupils in order to support academic progress. As the form tutor you have an overview of how each pupil is doing. This will guide you in conversations about important topics such as revision, options of subjects and interventions. You need to be as honest, but supportive as possible with pupils, offering practical guidance on how to improve.

Liaise with parent(s)/guardian(s) regarding positive points or concerns about academic progress and/or behaviour. It may well be school policy that there is an academic review day. Here you are expected to discuss the overall progress of pupils with parent(s)/guardian(s) and collectively set SMART targets.

What does a form tutor do less frequently, as and when needed/appropriate?

Safeguarding: The safeguarding of pupils is a key role as a form tutor.

Referral: Your head of year is always your first point of contact regarding pupils you are concerned about. If you need help or advice on anything related to your tutor group, they should be the member of staff you speak to first. You will regularly have meetings as a tutor team and these may provide an opportunity to raise any concerns. However, if your concerns are more urgent, arrange an early time to speak with your head of year. You may sometimes have urgent concerns that are to do with the safeguarding of a pupil. These must go through your designated safeguarding officer; this is often a member of the senior leadership team. As part of your induction process you should be trained in safeguarding, should be made aware of the schools' referral system and the appropriate safeguarding officers and receive refresher training every year to remind you.

Disclosures: As a form tutor you may well take on the role of a confidant. As a result, you may find that pupils disclose information to you that they are not comfortable disclosing to other adults. It is important that you do not tell a pupil that you will ensure confidentiality of any information they share with you. Never ask a pupil leading questions when they are disclosing to you. Where possible, just listen and take on board what they are saying. Try not to add your own experiences as this may well alter their account. When responding to the pupil do not use phrases such as 'that must be awful'.

After a disclosure, write down immediately and accurately the information about the disclosure. Each school has a slightly different form on which to record disclosures. Make sure you are familiar with both the form and its location. In some schools it is online and in others it is kept as a blank paper copy somewhere central such as the front office or staffroom. Once you have completed the form, you need to pass it on to the designated safeguarding officer immediately.

You may well make observations about a pupil as opposed to them disclosing information to you. Although at the time, something may not seem like a big problem, e.g. an unwashed uniform or a pupil's behaviour has changed, this still needs to be passed on. It may well be that other members of staff also have concerns or have also noticed changes. When concerns are pieced together, they can show up bigger issues.

You might find that pupils disclose information about other pupils to you. This again must be handled sensitively and the origin and natures of the disclosure must be considered carefully. Again, this needs to be recorded (as above) and escalated to your safeguarding officer. If in doubt, always contact one of your safeguarding officers. It is better to be over cautious than not cautious enough on.

If you are ever unsure whether something is safeguarding (information you have received or your own observation), consult the designated safeguarding lead in your school.

Liaising with other professionals: The pupils in your tutor group see you as their champion. As a good form tutor you want the very best for your tutor group and liaise with other staff to gain this in an appropriate manner. As a form tutor you are expected to liaise with other professionals. The staff you most often liaise with are your head of year and subject teachers. In addition to this you may well be asked to complete information for other staff members such as information about statutory annual reviews for pupils with special educational needs and disabilities (SEND) or for other professionals such as the school counsellor. Often the forms guide you through the process, but if you are unsure seek guidance from your head of year or the member of staff that sent you the form.

Now complete Task 6.4.

 Task 6.4   Safeguarding procedures in your school

Make sure you know who the safeguarding officer is in your school and you are clear about safeguarding procedures. Either ask the safeguarding officer any questions you have about safeguarding procedures or ask them to brief you about the procedures that operate within the school, depending on whether or not you have attended safeguarding training in your school. (Note: your induction should include safeguarding training.)

Record these procedures in your PDP for future reference.

Preparation and organisation for, and running of, your form time

Teaching is a demanding and busy job and there are many demands on your time. You therefore prioritise what you do with your time. Unfortunately, if you are not pastorally minded, the preparation for form time is often overlooked. However, it is important to prepare for tutorial periods as you would prepare for a lesson. To ensure that preparation for tutor time is not overlooked, it is worth setting aside a specific time (e.g. one specific period) each week to prepare for your tutor group lessons and any administration relating to your tutor group. This allows you to be clear and organised for the following week. However, teaching is a dynamic profession, where every day is different. The nature of pastoral work is that frequently you cannot plan for changes that happen each day, but at least if you have prepared as much as you can for the week, that gives you a head start. (Findon and Johnston-Wilder in *LTT8* (2019) provide advice about time management and managing stress.)

In some schools there is a tutor board. It is worth bearing in mind that each school may have compulsory guidance about what must be included on the tutor board. This must be adhered to, so if you are not clear of your school's requirements for the tutor board, ask your head of year or mentor what they are. This should not mean that you cannot go beyond that to add a personal touch and develop the tutor board as you see appropriate for your tutor group. You may, for example, prioritise pupils taking ownership of the board and allow the tutor board to be maintained by the tutor group. Beyond the expectations of the school they can add, for example, pictures of school trips they have been on, events, birthdays, stars of the week as voted by the tutor group or by the form tutor. Some of the best tutor groups follow a theme such as Harry Potter or Mr. Men. It is unlikely that a themed board will work with older tutor groups, but it may work well with younger or vertical tutor groups. You could put this to a class vote.

Attributes and skills of a good form tutor

Form tutoring is a role that requires diplomacy and genuineness, among many other skills, but it is also one that offers the potential for immense reward at work.

Carnell and Lodge (2002a) identified the following attributes that make a good form tutor, from the perspective of a pupil.

> The Good Tutor ... Listens to you. Is not judgemental. Does not raise issues about things you have done in the past. Is someone you can relate to. Listens to the troubles you are having with your subject teachers. Organizes a way of sorting out your differences with the subject teacher. Is someone who will listen but will also advise. Can advise on different aspects of life (not just school things). Supports you. Gives you reassurance. Is knowing they are there and will help you.
>
> (Carnell and Lodge, 2002a, p.13)

The best form tutors are there to guide and advise pupils about how to develop in all aspects without passing judgement.

Other attributes include:

■ Being consistent, fair and acting as a mediator for pupils in the group, if necessary.
■ Being able to establish, encourage and maintain positive pupil-pupil and pupil-teacher relationships.
■ Being able to create a positive ethos/attitude within the tutor group as well as a tutor group identity and cohesion.
■ Having high expectations of every individual in the tutor group, regarding quality of work, behaviour and uniform.
■ Looking to reward achievements positively and implement, where necessary, appropriate sanctions and liaising with the head of year over referred behavioural problems where necessary (see above).

Carnell and Lodge (2002b) also identified some top tips for tutoring, many of which, as you can see, are attributes of a good form tutor:

■ Demonstrate traits such as punctuality and preparedness.
■ Show equality and approachability in order to develop trust.
■ Keep a sense of humour; you may well have your tutor group for 5 years, so you need to develop a good relationship.
■ Celebrate important events (e.g. birthdays) and achievements (these do not necessarily have to be school-based).
■ Be reflective about the strengths and weaknesses of the members and dynamics of your tutor group - be proactive about working on these.
■ Always remain professional with your tutor group - avoid negative comments or gossip about other members of staff.
■ Use your tutor group as a form of pupil voice - pupils are often very open about the strengths and weaknesses of a school.

- Encourage your tutees to say thank you to staff who have gone above and beyond, or run extra-curricular activities etc. (This could, for example, become a half-termly activity where you ask your tutees to write a thank you note to a member of staff that has helped them that half term.)
- You may want to introduce inspirational quotes either daily or weekly.
- Always be prepared. You should be as prepared for tutor time as you are for lessons.
- Be prepared to communicate with parent(s)/guardian(s). If you can build these links well it helps the all-round development and well-being of pupils.

Task 6.5 asks you to consider what attributes and skills you need to be a good form tutor.

 Task 6.5   Attributes and skills of a good form tutor

From what you have read so far, you should be able to identify at least some of the attributes and skills of a good form tutor from the various roles you are required to undertake. Write a list of what you think the attributes and skills are. Next to each attribute or skill identify whether you think it is a strength of yours or an area for development. Consider, and talk to your mentor as appropriate, how you can develop those attributes and skills you identify as areas for development and improve further those you identify as strengths.

Keep a record in your PDP and review your practice against this as you become more experienced.

SUMMARY AND KEY POINTS

- This chapter has focussed on your role as a form tutor, which, in many schools, runs alongside your role as a subject teacher. It has stressed the importance of the multi-faceted role of a form tutor in assuring pupils' well-being and for supporting them in their personal, social and academic development. Thus, your role as a form tutor is as important as your role as a subject teacher to the pupils.
- There are key requirements for you as a form tutor on a daily, weekly, termly and when necessary basis, which this chapter has identified.
- The role of safeguarding is a key aspect of the role and you should be clear about safeguarding in relation to pupils in your tutor group – as well as subject classes and the school as a whole.
- In order to use tutor time to best effect and to be as effective as possible in your role as a form tutor, you need to prepare for tutor time and need a range of attributes and skills, some of which you may need to develop.

The role of a form tutor can be very demanding, but it can also be very rewarding. It can provide career development opportunities through the pastoral system, e.g. head of year, assistant head for behaviour. We are sure you will find the role rewarding.

Record in your professional development portfolio (PDP), how the information in this chapter enables you to meet the requirements for your first year of teaching.

Further resources

Heilbronn, R. (2004) 'Tutoring and personal, social and health education', in S. Capel, R. Heilbronn, M. Leask and T. Turner (eds.) *Starting to Teach in the Secondary School: A Companion for the Newly Qualified Teacher*, London: RoutlegdeFalmer, pp. 45-59.

Niemtus, Z. (2015) 'Six basic steps to becoming a brilliant form tutor', *The Guardian*, 26 August 2015. Available from: www.theguardian.com/teacher-network/2015/aug/26/six-basic-steps-brilliant-form-tutor (accessed 18 August 2019).

Watson-Davis, R. (2005) *The Form Tutor's Pocketbook*, Alresford, Hants: Teachers' Pocketbooks.

 Websites:

    www.pshe-association.org.uk – the PSHE Association.

    This supplies safeguarding resources for members via the association's online library.

    www.teachertoolkit.co.uk/2018/06/12/effective-form-tutor/ – *Times Educational Supplement* teacher toolkit.

    @teachertoolkit – *Times Educational Supplement* teacher toolkit, Twitter handle.

    @UKPastoralChat – Twitter handle.

    This provides lots of ideas for pastoral leaders including form tutors.

Appendices 2 and 3 list subject associations, teaching councils and relevant websites.

Books in the *Learning to Teach* series that you may find helpful are as follows:

Capel, S., Leask, M. and Younie, S. (eds.) (2019) *Learning to Teach in the Secondary School: A Companion to School Experience*, 8th edn, Abingdon: Routledge.
This book is designed as a core textbook to support student teachers through their initial teacher education programme.

Capel, S., Leask, M. and Turner, T. (eds.) (2010) *Readings for Learning to Teach in the Secondary School: A Companion to M Level Study*, Abingdon: Routledge.
This book brings together essential readings to support you in your critical engagement with key issues raised in this textbook.

The subject-specific books in the *Learning to Teach* series, the *Practical (subject) Guides*, *Debates in (subject)* and *Mentoring (subject) Teachers* are also very useful.

7 Every teacher is a teacher of English

Paul Gardner

Introduction

The idea that all teachers, irrespective of their subject specialism, are teachers of English can be traced back to the 'Language Across the Curriculum Movement' that began in London in 1966 (Parker, 1985). Almost a decade later, the influential 'Bullock Report' reiterated the importance of developing language across the curriculum (Department of Education and Science (DES), 1975, p. 514). English for cross-curricular purposes was also one of five models of English devised by Brian Cox (1991), who chaired the English working party for the first iteration of the National Curriculum in England (DES, 1988). In Australia, the genre theorists (Martin and Rothery, 1993), influenced by the functional grammatics of Michael Halliday (1978), drew attention to the relationship between the social purposes of different text types and their internal textual structures, syntax (grammar) and vocabulary.

The pedagogy of functional literacy involves teachers explicitly teaching the specific linguistic and textual features of different texts to learners as a means of empowering them to become effective readers and writers.

All of these educationalists have one thing in common: the realisation that *each curriculum subject organises language in specific ways and that full access to the curriculum will be denied to learners, unless they are taught how to unlock and manipulate subject-specific language.* Indeed, the matter of teaching subject-specific language is also a matter of equity (Beacco et al., 2015, p.13) and it is best taught by subject specialists who understand the way language and thought are organised in their discipline (Henderson and Exeley, 2019, p.23).

OBJECTIVES

By the end of this chapter you should be able to:

- understand reasons why subject specialist teachers need to teach the aspects of literacy that are relevant to their subject;
- have a range of strategies designed to assist learners to access the curriculum whilst also learning to use subject-specific language;

■   have an overview of the linguistic skills learners may have acquired by ages 7 to 11 years and 11 to 14 years (Key Stages 2 and 3 (KS2 and KS3) in England);

■   understand the ways in which subject-specific language is different from the everyday language of spoken English.

Check how the information in this chapter enables you to meet the requirements for your first year of teaching.

Text types in your subject

The responsibility for teaching the full range of text types that learners will encounter across the curriculum, at the level required, is beyond the scope of English specialists. Hence, in addition to teaching subject-specific knowledge, skills and concepts, subject specialists also need to assist learners to master the language of the subject. However, the language of the subject means more than simply teaching subject-specific vocabulary; it also requires subject specialists to explicitly scaffold: learners' discussions of concepts; their comprehension of subject-specific texts; and their writing of the text types that are typical in the discipline. Vollmer (2006, p.5) points out that different subjects use different thematic patterns and rhetorical devices that are distinct from everyday language use. This necessitates that subject teachers consider the conceptual literacy and discourse competence required to access their discipline.

Before leaving the point about the construction of subject-specific texts, it is important to note that many subjects use multimodal texts; that is, a combination of meaning-making systems (semiotic systems) in a single text. Charts, graphs, diagrams and maps are examples of texts that often integrate linguistic, numeric and visual symbols. Full understanding of such texts requires the reader to comprehend the inter-relationship of these symbols and how they operate in the mutual construction of meaning. Some learners may be encountering these multimodal texts for the first time in the secondary classroom, so they need guidance on how to use the different symbols employed by the text in order to unlock the text's overall meaning.

The scope of English is broadened further when we consider the increasing importance of digital literacy in the 21st century. In fact, some educationalists no longer refer to 'literacy' in its singular form, but to 'literacies' (Kalantzis et al., 2016) in acknowledgement both of the plurality of semiotic systems within texts and also the skills required to read different types of text. So, in teaching the subject it is imperative that subject specialist teachers reflect on how knowledge and concepts are represented in their subject because learners' access to the subject may be impeded by the language of the subject. Now complete Task 7.1.

   Task 7.1   What are the typical text types in your subject?

Before reading on, reflect on the key points in the introduction and particularly consider the types of text that are typical in your subject. Are all of these written texts, or are some multimodal? If a learner has never or has rarely seen the text types typical of your subject, how might you scaffold their navigation of these texts in order to understand them?

Make notes in answer to the questions above and discuss the points with others teaching your subject. Keep the notes in your professional development portfolio (PDP) (or similar) for use when planning lessons.

English to be expected of learners at Key Stage 2

In England, the National Curriculum Programme of Study in English establishes the expected learner achievements in KS2 (Department for Education (DfE), 2013a) and KS3 (DfE, 2013b). An overview of these expectations is set-out in Table 7.1.

More broadly, the relevant curriculum document for KS2 states:

> By the end of Year 6, pupils' reading and writing should be sufficiently fluent and effortless for them to manage the general demands of the curriculum in Year 7, across all subjects and not just in English, but there will continue to be a need for pupils to learn subject-specific vocabulary.
>
> *(DfE, 2013a, p. 31)*

Although this statement recognises the scope of the cross-curricular dimension of English, it implies curriculum access will occur if subject-specific vocabulary is acquired by learners. Although vocabulary is essential to developing learners' understanding of a subject, it is not sufficient in itself. Currently literacy teaching in English primary schools is dominated by the Simple View of Reading (Gough and Tunmer, 1986; Hoover and Gough, 1990). According to this view, fluent reading is achieved when good word decoding skills and good spoken language comprehension skills are combined. Whilst good decoding skills and good language comprehension skills assist readers, Norris and Phillips (2003) assert they are insufficient to enable learners to fully access meanings across all the text types found in subject disciplines. One reason for this is that written language is not the same as spoken language. In addition, the grammatical and textual structures of subject-specific texts become more demanding as learners' progress through KS3 and KS4. It is likely learners will encounter subjects, or aspects of subjects, not covered in the primary curriculum. Across all subjects, learners may also be encountering concepts and ideas that require them to talk, read and write in ways not expected of them previously.

No matter what is stated in Programmes of Study, we have to recognise that learners develop at different rates in different ways and that learning can be influenced by factors beyond the boundaries of school. As Stephen Ball (2018b, p. 208) notes, many English schools are influenced by '... performance management derived from business practices rather than educational principles ...'. According to Ball, it is a situation that has led to disarray in the education system in England. Therefore, we cannot expect that when learners arrive at secondary school, they will have had common experiences of primary education. We also need to recognise that an increasing number of learners are growing up in poverty; some learners may have had periods of absence from school because they have had to care

Table 7.1 English in the National Curriculum at KS2 and KS2

English KS2	English KS3
Reading	**Reading**
■ morphological and etymological knowledge of words such as: see English Appendix 1. ■ texts for a range of purposes ■ making comparisons within and between texts ■ exploring meanings of words in context ■ summarising main ideas across several paragraphs ■ justifying answers by drawing on evidence from the text ■ identifying how language, structure and presentation influence meaning ■ distinguish between fact and opinion ■ retrieve, record and present information from non-fiction texts ■ explain and discuss what has been read showing understanding ■ building on their own and others' ideas and challenging ideas, giving justifications for their views ■ knowledge of how to use reference books, including contents and index pages	■ learning new vocabulary, relating it explicitly to known vocabulary and understanding it with the help of context and dictionaries ■ making inferences and referring to evidence in the text ■ knowing the purpose, audience for and context of the writing and drawing on this knowledge to support comprehension ■ checking their understanding to make sure that what they have read makes sense Read critically through: ■ knowing how language, including figurative language, vocabulary choice, grammar, text structure and organisational features, presents meaning ■ making critical comparisons across texts
Writing	**Writing**
■ Plan writing for specific audiences and different purposes, using similar texts as models for their own ■ Noting and developing ideas, drawing on reading and research where necessary ■ Select appropriate grammar and vocabulary with an understanding of how choices can change and enhance meaning ■ Précising long texts ■ Using discourse connectors to build cohesion within and across paragraphs ■ Use appropriate presentational devices such as headings, sub-headings, bullet/dot points; ■ Edit their own and others' writing by ■ Evaluating its effectiveness, proposing changes to vocabulary, grammar and punctuation to enhance and clarify meaning ■ Ensure the consistent use of tense through-out the text ■ Ensure correct subject-verb agreements (e.g. when using singular and plural forms. ■ Using the appropriate register and grammatical structures (e.g. between speech and writing)	writing for a wide range of purposes and audiences, including: ■ well-structured formal expository and narrative essays ■ notes and polished scripts for talks and presentations ■ a range of other narrative and non-narrative texts, including arguments, and personal and formal letters ■ summarising and organising material, and supporting ideas and arguments with any necessary factual detail ■ applying their growing knowledge of vocabulary, grammar and text structure to their writing and selecting the appropriate form ■ drawing on knowledge of literary and rhetorical devices from their reading and listening to enhance the impact of their writing ■ plan, draft, edit and proof-read through: ■ considering how their writing reflects the audiences and purposes for which it was intended ■ amending the vocabulary, grammar and structure of their writing to improve its coherence and overall effectiveness ■ paying attention to accurate grammar, punctuation and spelling; applying the spelling patterns and rules set out in English Appendix to the key stage 1 and 2 programmes of study for English

Grammar and vocabulary	Grammar and vocabulary
■ Recognise vocabulary and structures appropriate to form, including subjunctive forms ■ Know how to use passive verbs ■ Use perfect form of verbs to mark relationships of time and cause ■ Use expanded noun phrases to convey complicated information concisely ■ Use modal verbs or adverbs to indicate degrees of possibility ■ Use relative clauses beginning with who, which, where, when, whose, that or with an implied relative pronoun; ■ Use grammatical and other features such as: ■ Use commas to clarify meaning, avoid ambiguity or indicate parenthesis ■ Use semi-colons, colons or dashes to mark boundaries between independent clauses ■ Use colons to introduce a list ■ Use hyphens to avoid ambiguity ■ Punctuate bullet points consistently	■ extend and apply the grammatical knowledge set out in English Appendix 2 to the key stage 1 and 2 programmes of study to analyse more challenging texts ■ study the effectiveness and impact of the grammatical features of the texts they read ■ draw on new vocabulary and grammatical constructions from their reading and listening, and using these consciously in their writing and speech to achieve particular effects ■ know and understand the differences between spoken and written language, including differences associated with formal and informal registers, and between Standard English and other varieties of English ■ use Standard English confidently in their own writing and speech discussing reading, writing and spoken language with precise and confident use of linguistic and literary terminology
Speaking and listening	**Speaking and listening**
■ listen and respond appropriately to adults and their peers ■ ask relevant questions to extend their understanding and knowledge ■ use relevant strategies to build their vocabulary ■ articulate and justify answers, arguments and opinions ■ give well-structured descriptions, explanations and narratives for different purposes, including for expressing feelings ■ maintain attention and participate actively in collaborative conversations, staying on topic and initiating and responding to comments ■ use spoken language to develop understanding through speculating, hypothesising, imagining and exploring ideas ■ speak audibly and fluently with an increasing command of Standard English ■ participate in discussions, presentations, performances, role play, improvisations and debates ■ gain, maintain and monitor the interest of the listener(s) ■ consider and evaluate different viewpoints, attending to and building on the contributions of others ■ select and use appropriate registers for effective communication.	■ Use Standard English confidently in a range of formal and informal contexts, including classroom discussion ■ give short speeches and presentations, expressing their own ideas and keeping to the point ■ participate in formal debates and structured discussions, summarising and/or building on what has been said

for parents or siblings; some learners may have experienced trauma due to conflict and migration and for others English may be their second, third or even fourth language. Some learners, on the other hand, may have parents who have an adept command of academic English; some of these parents may even be experts in your subject specialism. These learners are likely to seem 'brighter' than the first group and 'sail' through the subject. Society is not a level playing field and often a learner's real ability can be masked by a still-emerging command of the kind of language required for academic success. As teachers, we have a shared duty to ensure that all learners are given the necessary skills, knowledge and concepts to be successful at school and that includes the linguistic skills necessary to access concepts, ideas and theories in different subject specialisms. So, it is important that you find out as much as you can about the learners you teach and even more important is that you demonstrate that you value them as individuals. Now complete Task 7.2.

 Task 7.2   Survey the linguistic resources of your learners

Given the point that your learners are likely to have had different experiences of language use and exposure to a variety of texts, undertake a survey of new learners to identify their familiarity with the grammatical and textual structures, as well as non-linguistic symbols that frequently occur in your subject.

However, you can only do this if you have firstly consciously considered the conventional grammatical structures and text types of your subject. It may be necessary to explore these before devising a survey. Table 7.2 below may provide a starting point if your subject is listed.

Record your notes in your PDP for use when planning lessons.

Describing language

We can look at language at a number of levels, from the smallest unit of spoken language, the phoneme, and the smallest unit of written language, the grapheme, to the largest unit, the text. There are many ways to describe language but for the purpose of this chapter, the following descriptors have been identified. Each of these descriptors is described below, together with explanations of their implications for your teaching:

- phonology – the sound patterns of language
- lexis – words
- syntax – grammar
- semantics – meaning
- text

Language is a semiotic system, that is – it is a system of socially agreed signs that can be manipulated to create and communicate meaning. However, it is not the only semiotic system learners need to be able to navigate. Anstey and Bull (2018a) for example identify five semiotic systems: *linguistic, visual, spatial, gestural* and *audio*. These are

Table 7.2 Text types across the curriculum (adapted from OECD, 2014)

Subject/ Genre	Explanation	Information reports	Recount	Narrative	Description	Investigative reports	Evaluations	Data displays	Procedure	Persuasion	Argument	Analysis	Discussion	Inquiry
Maths	Y	Y	Y			Y	Y	Y						
Science	Y (causal)	Y				Y			Y	Y	Y		Y	
History	Y		Y	Y	Y					Y			Y	
Geography	Y				Y		Y	Y		Y			Y	Y
Citizenship	Y										Y			
Economics -business		Y						Y			Y			
Arts					Y		Y					Y		
Design and Technology					Y		Y							
Physical Education			Y			Y	Y							

increasingly present in 21st-century texts. They highlight the need for teachers to be aware of how these systems function in education and propose a pedagogy in which teaching these multiliteracies are embedded in the planning and delivery of learning (Anstey and Bull, 2018b).

Phonology (sounds)

Phonology involves knowledge of the sounds that comprise a language. As we know English has stressed and unstressed syllables, which can change when the word form changes, e.g. pronounce – pronunciation; syllable – syllabic.

Units of sound below the level of the syllable are called phonemes. These correspond to individual letters, or combinations of letters that make a single sound, which are known as graphemes. Letter-sound relationships are known as grapho-phonic correspondence, a term that will be familiar to learners in England, as one that they will have learned in primary school. So, grapho-phonic correspondences can be individual letters, such as b, d, t, etc., but also include the following:

- digraphs – e.g. 'sh', 'ch', 'ph', 'ss'
- trigraphs – e.g. 'igh'
- quadgraphs – e.g. 'ough' as in 'rough' and 'through'.

In this latter example, we see the difference between the pronunciation of 'ough' in 'rough' and 'through', which demonstrates the inconsistency of English phonology. So, as a subject specialist, it is important that learners hear you repeatedly read and correctly pronounce subject-specialist vocabulary. It is also important that they see the word as you read and pronounce it.

English is not a phonetic language, that is, as discussed above, it can have inconsistent letter-sound correspondences. As an aside, it is possible to create unique nonsense words by splicing together letter-sound correspondences. A well-known example used by linguists to demonstrate this point is the word 'ghoti', which is pronounced 'fish' by taking the 'gh' from 'enough', the 'o' from 'women' and the 'ti' from 'condition'.

On a more practical level, when introducing new words to learners it is useful to bear in mind both the phonological and morphemic components (morphemes are explained) below of English and to consider what learners may already know about the new words they encounter in your subject. If we take the word 'photosynthesis' as an example, almost all learners will recognise the prefix 'photo'. So, the emphasis can shift to decoding what may be unknown. It is possible to 'chunk' the remainder syllabically, as follows – 'syn-the-sis' and then blend the syllables with 'photo' to read the whole word. This approach should also help them remember how to spell the word.

Lexis (words)

In addition to the phonological aspect of new subject-specific vocabulary, Figure 7.1 identifies four further dimensions of words to be considered by subject specialists. These are orthography, morphology, semantics and etymology. It is suggested these inter-related dimensions of the word should be taught so that pupils acquire a comprehensive

Five dimensions of the word

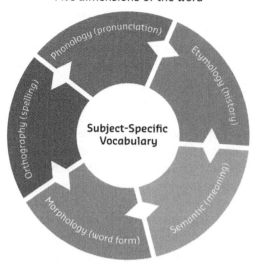

Figure 7.1 Five dimensions of the word

knowledge of specialist language in a particular subject. For example, the word 'aerobic' is listed in the Assessment of Qualifications Alliance (AQA) – GCSE Physical Education subject-specific vocabulary. Some pupils may already know and use the word. However, many pupils will not know its meaning or what it looks like and, therefore, will not be able to use it appropriately in classroom talk or read and spell it, unless they are explicitly taught to do so. As with all learning, we should build on what learners already know. The prefix 'aero' is likely to be familiar to pupils because it is the name of a well-known chocolate bar and is also the prefix of aeroplane. Although many pupils may be more familiar with the variation 'airplane'. We might ask what creates the bubbles in the chocolate bar. Once learners have made the connection between 'aero' and 'air', it is then possible to extend understanding to the more specific meaning pertaining to oxygen and then the relationship between exercise, heartbeat and the effective supply of oxygen to the muscles. 'Aero' is a familiar sight word and, for this reason, learners may already know how to spell it. In which case, it is relatively simple to teach the suffix 'bic'. So far then you will have taught the morphology of the word, aero – bic, as well as its spelling and pronunciation. In addition, by affirming the meaning of the prefix, you are teaching a semantic that can be generalised to all other words with the same prefix and thereby you equip learners with a means of decoding and understanding those words, when they are met by the learner for the first time. Finally, you may deem it appropriate to refer to the history of the word (etymology), which was first used in its current form and meaning in 1968 by the American physician, Kenneth H. Cooper but is derived from the French word 'aerobie' and was used by Louis Pasteur in 1863. The word has its roots in Ancient Greek and derives from the morphemes 'aero' (air) and 'bio' (life).

Spelling (orthography)

Grapho-phonic inconsistency is the reason English is described as having a deep orthography, or complex spelling system. Another reason is that English is a 'multicultural' language, drawing its vocabulary from many other languages. Most people are familiar with its roots in Greek and Latin. History specialists will know that after the Norman Invasion of 1066, French became the official language of England. Words such a beef (boeuf) and mutton (mouton) were used by the elite, whilst servants spoke Saxon. Today certain words of French derivation have retained their French spelling and pronunciation, of which - rendezvous and rapport - are examples. Other reasons for some of English's unique spellings include:

- some of the first printers in England were Dutch who drew on their own language to spell certain words - the use of the letter 'h' in 'ghost' and 'ghastly' are examples;
- the payment to printers in the 15th century was for each line of print, which resulted in letters being added to words to create more print (an example being 'frend' - 'friend');
- the printing of the Bible in English was still forbidden in the 16th century, so it had to be printed in English abroad and then smuggled into England, however foreign printers would have made up some English spellings;
- the inclusion from Shakespeare's work of approximately 2,000 new words to English at a time when there were no rules for spelling;
- the first dictionaries were based on the most commonly used spellings of words rather than orthographic consistency.

There are numerous words in English that are difficult to pronounce when first seen and difficult to spell when first heard. So, giving learners explicit exposure to both the aural and visual components of subject-specific words is important. One simple example is the word, 'islet', which may occur in Geography. If learners apply a phonic approach to decoding the word, they are likely to say is-let, rather than 'eye'-let. If they only hear the word, without seeing it written, it is unlikely they will spell it correctly when they need to write.

Morphemes

Morphemes are units of meaning. English has a morphemic system consisting of two elements: root words and affixes, of which there are two forms - prefixes and suffixes. Affixes alter the meaning of the root word, e.g. the root word 'help' is altered by the suffix -less, or by adding the prefix un-, combined with the suffix -ful.

Many subject-specific affixes derive from English's Greek and Latin roots. It is useful to teach learners the meanings and the origins of affixes, so they can be applied to new words that are read independently. For further information about common affixes derived from Greek and Latin see McEwan (2008) in the Further resources section at the end of this chapter. Teaching the morphemic structure of words assists learners' development of spelling (Bryant and Nunes, 2004), decoding and meaning.

Etymology

Words have histories. Many of them have travelled through time, changing or retaining their original meanings as they passed from one culture to another, or simply evolved.

Learning the history of a word can be fascinating and helps learners to understand its meaning in the context of modern usage. As well as teaching the derivation and meaning of affixes, teaching the origins of subject-specific vocabulary contributes to the broadening of knowledge, as well as a general awareness that our knowledge comes from many cultures. For example, the words, 'algebra' and 'zero' can be traced back to Arabic roots, although the latter is believed to have originated in India.

Teaching the meaning of subject-specific words (the semantics) and their origins not only helps learners to understand the texts they read, but it also demonstrates the interdependence of human cultures and thereby avoids knowledge seeming ethnocentric. Now complete Task 7.3.

 Task 7.3   Using the five dimensions of the word, plan the development of subject-specific vocabulary

List six key words in your subject with which learners may be unfamiliar. Plan how you would introduce this subject-specific language to pupils using the five dimensions model in Figure 7.1. You can use the example of 'aerobic' above.

Record your notes in your PDP for use when planning lessons.

Grammar (syntax)

The idea that grammar should be taught explicitly almost as a subject in its own right is contested while research suggests teaching grammar in the context of texts that learners read and write has positive outcomes for able learners (Jones, Myhill and Bailey, 2013). Halliday (1978) suggests a socio-cultural approach to linguistics, which posits that language use is influenced by three inter-related factors: subject matter and context, or 'field'; relationship of participants, or 'tenor'; and the means by which communication occurs, or 'mode'. Although Halliday's (1978) work was mainly located in spoken language, his ideas were adopted by educationalists who saw an application to written language. The genre theorists (Martin and Rothery, 1993) proposed that learners should receive explicit teaching in relation to the grammar and textual organisation of different texts, based on their social function. For example, Knapp (1992, p.13 cited in Knapp and Watkins, 2005, p. 27) identifies that narrative writing, explanations and instructions involve the organisational process of sequencing. However, whereas in narrative sequencing people and events appear in time and space, in explanations phenomena are organised in terms of time and causal relationship. The logical sequencing of action or behaviour is what influences the textual structure of instructions. Arguments, on the other hand, initiate a proposition, which is followed by persuasive devices to encourage acceptance of a particular point of view.

The function of each text type influences the way the text is organised, which in turn shapes the kind of grammar required. Informational texts, which are the kinds of texts learners encounter across the curriculum, tend to be written in the passive voice, which means the object of the sentence is placed in the position of the subject. In the example below, the subject has been italicised in the first sentence and then re-written to show the active voice in the second sentence.

'The town was flooded by *a storm*.'
'*A storm* flooded the town.'

Another feature of information texts is nominalisation, which involves turning a verb into a noun. In the example below, the verbs '(to) distribute' and '(to) indicate' have been nominalised.

'The unequal *distribution* of wealth in Britain is an *indicator* of the country's lack of egalitarianism'.

Other features of information texts are their heavy information load and grammatical complexity. Take the following two sentences from a History text as an example:

Passed by a conservative-dominated Parliament in 1815 and 1828, the Corn Laws had imposed a sliding tariff on imported wheat (then known as 'corn'). When the price of wheat produced in Britain fell below a certain level, import duties would keep out cheaper foreign grain.

(Merriman, 2004, p.666)

In order to understand this short piece of text, learners have to process the following information:

Sentence 1 – conservative, parliament, 1815, 1818, *Corn* Laws, sliding tariff, imported, *wheat*;
Sentence 2 – price, *wheat*, Britain, import duties, cheaper foreign *grain*.

Even if learners know the meaning of each term, they have to retain each piece of information as they process the meaning of the whole sentence. However, words with which they are unfamiliar are likely to impede the processing of meaning. In one instance, the writer has assisted learners. The italicised words all belong to the same lexical set and although the reader is informed that *corn* and *wheat* are the same thing, the same is not true for *grain*. So, the reader must deduce this connection. The text is further complicated by the fact the subject in each sentence does not appear until approximately halfway through. In the first sentence the subject is 'the Corn Laws' and in the second it is 'import duties'. In each case, the main clause is preceded by a relatively long subordinate clause.

Taken together these grammatical features make most informational texts very formal in tone and quite distinct from the spoken language of most learners. For this reason, schooling literacy can seem alien to many learners and may hinder their access to knowledge and concepts. However, by supporting learners to unlock the codes and structures of language in your subject you are adding to their linguistic repertoire and ultimately equipping them to be more empowered citizens. It is said that 'knowledge is power', but language is the means by which knowledge is conveyed. If learners acquire both knowledge and the skills to articulate that knowledge, they are then able to construct powerful arguments to 'get things done'. This is one aspect of the social purpose of language.

Semantic

The most obvious example of semantics in language is the definition of a specific word. However, meanings exist at other levels of language, e.g. phrases, clauses, sentences, idioms, proverbs, metaphors, texts etc. In addition, multimodal texts provide additional levels of meaning making in the form of shape, colour, spatial relationships, symbols, icons, sounds etc. Each subject utilises different semiotic systems to construct meanings and the subject specialist needs to be aware of how these systems operate because subject content is inextricably linked to the language of the subject. Since content understanding is accessed through language, it follows that to teach the subject also necessitates teaching the language of the subject.

Another factor to consider is how the meanings of commonly used words can change in subject-specific contexts and how meanings of the same word can change between subjects. For example, the word 'plane' in everyday spoken language is an ellipsis for aeroplane, but in Mathematics it refers to a flat, two-dimensional line. The word 'scale' has one meaning in Geography but quite a different meaning in Music. For further information about subject-specific language see the Further resources section at the end of the chapter. In Task 7.4 you are asked to identify common words with different meanings in your subject.

 Task 7.4   Common words with different meanings in your subject

Identify words in your subject that have a common usage but have a different meaning specific to your discipline. Some examples are provided below:

Mathematics – reflection – translation
Science – reaction – stress
Music – register – scale (also Maths and Geography)
Dance – elevation – execution.

The presence of commonly used words in subjects can be a source of conceptual confusion for learners. So, it is necessary to explicitly teach the subject-specific meanings of these words.

Make a list of words in your subject and record this in your PDP for use when planning lessons.

Text

Texts synthesise all the above elements, i.e. words, syntax and semantics, but they do so for specific purposes and functions. The specific function or purpose of a text influences its design, which includes overall structure, syntax and word choices. Textual structure not only refers to the format of the text but also to discourse connectors that feature in its organisation (i.e. text appropriate words and phrases that give the text cohesion and coherence). As learners progress through schooling, the nature of texts are increasingly less like spoken language and become more formal and academic, making them more technical and abstract. The genres learners are likely to encounter across the secondary curriculum are represented in Table 7.2. The information is based on a summary of text types to be found in the Australian National Curriculum in which literacy is identified as a cross-curricular capability (Australian Curriculum, Assessment and Reporting Authority (ACARA), 2016).

The importance of oral language

Well planned and adeptly structured classroom talk is essential for effective development of subject knowledge. In his seminal work on the subject, Douglas Barnes (1976) drew attention to the relationship between peer talk, thinking and learning. Talk is especially effective when tasks are designed to elicit explanatory, evaluative and hypothetical thinking. By means of structured collaborative talk, learners are able to make their thinking 'material' and available for reflection. Mercer (2000), who built on the work of Barnes, refers to the 'interthinking' that occurs when learners engage in exploratory talk, which involves them: having to present ideas supported by evidence; asking challenging questions of one another; and elaborating on answers and generally scaffolding thinking and learning by means of the dialogic process. Along similar lines, Alexander (2005) refers to 'dialogic teaching' as the means by which teachers model the effective use of classroom talk using questions designed to elicit and probe learners' thinking. Dialogic teaching also has the advantage of allowing teachers to monitor learners' metacognition and thereby gain insights into their level of understanding and any misconceptions they might have. For example, a teacher might ask learners if they can explain how a tree grows. Let us suppose they say the roots take in water and nutrients from the soil, which feed the tree. They may also know a tree needs 'light'. These answers signify a misconception that may be a result of information learners have previously been given. However, misconceptions inform us about where to 'target' our teaching. These learners need to know that the sun is the vital 'fuel' and that through the process of photosynthesis green plants create their own food in the leaves, not the roots. However, the learners' answers also reveal their awareness that water and nutrients, transported by the roots, contribute, along with carbon dioxide, which is missing from their answers. The other missing factor is chlorophyll, which assists photosynthesis. These elements and processes cause the production of sugar and oxygen. The latter is released into air, whilst the sugar feeds the tree's growth. This navigation of meaning through talk belongs to the socio-cultural theory of language and learning that emanates from Vygotskian theory (Lyle, 2008). However, the development of talk, through group work, needs to be carefully scaffolded and will be ineffective if learners are not provided with purposeful learning tasks. We shall return to this point when discussing directed activities related to texts (DARTs) at the end of the next section. In the meantime, the complexity of what causes tree growth might be 'tackled' by creating a 'recipe' in which ingredients are listed and processes are explained. Now complete Task 7.5.

 Task 7.5   Organising talk for learning

The types of talk that occur in classrooms underpin the quality of language and thought that is made possible. In many classrooms teachers dominate talk, employing a discourse strategy known by the acronym IRF. This discourse pattern is typified by the teacher initiating talk (I) by means of a question; a learner usually responding (R) with an answer and the teacher then giving feedback (F) with a response that usually informs the learner whether the given answer was correct or not. Many of the questions teachers ask are pseudo questions; that is, questions to which they already know the answer. Learners are required to identify the answer that is in the teacher's head. In addition, many of these questions are knowledge based, requiring low level cognition. Alexander, Mercer and others propose strategies that foster purposeful talk that can engender deep-level thinking. Further explore the relationship of talk and learning by accessing the Mapping Educational Specialist knowHow (MESH) Guide Classroom Dialogue and Learning http://meshguides.org/guides/node/1148. After reading these consider how you would encourage purposeful talk in your subject for different year groups.

Make notes and record these in your PDP for use when planning lessons.

Reading

It would be something of a truism to say that reading is a complex process; more complex than is suggested by Gough and Tunmer (1986) 'simple model of reading' referred to in the discussion of KS2 English above. A more detailed view can be found in Freebody and Luke's (1990) four resources model of reading, which involves the reader as a 'code-breaker', 'text participant', 'text user' and 'text analyser'. This model requires a reconceptualisation of what readers do as they read, which involves more than decoding words to reach the embedded meaning of the text, as is implied by the conventional use of the word 'comprehension'. Although the model was originally devised for print based texts, it has since been modified by Serafini (2012) to acknowledge the increasingly multi-modal nature of modern-day texts. In extending Freebody and Luke's work, Serafini begins from the premise that readers must be 'navigators', 'interpreters', 'designers' and 'interrogators' of texts that often integrate several semiotic systems. As 'navigators' readers need to be able to 'break the code' of print but must also understand the visual architecture of design, the visual grammar of images and be able to find their way through texts that are not necessarily organised sequentially. In 'interpreting' texts, Serafini acknowledges the contribution of reader response theory (Rosenblatt, 1978), which challenges the idea that a text has a single unified meaning. In reader response theory readers are positioned as active agents, creatively engaging with the text to construct meaning. Each time we read a text we may derive different or additional meanings. Meaning involves a transaction between the writer's intended meaning and the reader's interpretive resources, which include: personal experiences, knowledge of other texts, cultural perspectives etc. This idea is further extended by the concept of the 'reader as designer'. Multimodal texts tend not to be linear, which means the reader can choose their own pathway through the text, alternating between semiotic modes of representation. In this sense the reader 'designs' the experience of reading the text. The fourth dimension, the 'reader as interrogator' closely resembles Freebody and Luke's 'text analyser', which involves critically analysing the text.

Language is value laden and texts, therefore, are not neutral entities. They are written in particular cultural, socio-historical and ideological spaces and are read by readers who may occupy different cultural, socio-historical and ideological spaces.

Schleppergrell, Greer and Taylor (2008, p. 176) make the point that writers make particular choices when creating historical texts and that readers need to interrogate what has been excluded from the text as well as what has been included; who has not been represented in the text and what point of view of past events is being constructed. Hence, they need to critically analyse how language is being used to represent the past. The reader as critical interrogator applies to all subjects in which particular points of view; perspectives and rhetorical or persuasive devices are embedded aspects of texts.

It is especially important for you, as a subject specialist, to consider all aspects of reading in your discipline, and how you can scaffold learners' access to the way meanings are constructed through texts. One means of doing this is by modelling how to read subject-specific texts. Modelled reading is when the teacher reads a text, but in doing so demonstrates the meta-cognitive strategies they use to understand the text. This may mean showing learners that main clauses in sentences convey the substantive information, with additional information provided by subordinate clauses. Reading strategies can also be emphasised, such as re-reading, pausing to reflect on meaning, highlighting specific words/phrases that need to be defined etc. Extending the above discussion around talk for learning, collaborative learning strategies that combine talk with directed activities related to texts (DARTs) provide a purposeful way of both organising group work and assisting pupils to comprehend subject knowledge. DARTs emerged from the work of Lunzer and Gardner (1979) who saw traditional comprehension as a passive process and explored alternative ways to actively engage readers with texts. See Shaw (in *LTT8*, 2019) for some DARTS activities. DARTs strategies include the sequencing of parts of text, labelling diagrams based on information provided, converting text from one genre to another, graphic organisers, jigsaw activities etc. The Collaborative Learning Project (see the Further resources section) is a useful repository of teacher produced cross-curricular DARTs resources. Now complete Task 7.6.

 Task 7.6   What types of readers do learners need to be in your subject?

This task requires you to extend the thinking elicited in Task 7.2 by reconsidering the types of texts in your subject and the kind of reader the learner needs to be. Use Serafini's four classifications: 'navigator', 'interpreter', 'designer' and 'interrogator' to identify how learners need to engage with texts. You may find learners are required to use all four roles of the reader at different times for different purposes and outcomes.

Make notes and record these in your PDP for use when planning lessons.

Writing

There is a strong tendency in education to use writing as a means of assessing learners' knowledge and understanding. In addition, learners may be used to receiving teacher feedback on their writing that has emphasised transcriptional error (e.g. spelling, punctuation, capitalisation, handwriting and syntax) with very little reference to the quality of their ideas and thinking. For this reason, many learners internalise the idea that writing is less about content and more about technical accuracy. These two factors, writing as assessment and the emphasis on technical accuracy, have been found to have a long-lasting negative impact on the individual's confidence with writing, even at under-graduate level (Gardner, 2014). The consideration you have already given to the types of text commonly found in your subject help you to guide learners as writers in the discipline. Explicitly teaching learners the syntax and textual grammars typical in the subject can begin by reading with them to identify these features. Following this identification stage, you can work with learners collectively to create shared texts in which you model the process of writing and its allied metacognitive processes. Gradually allow learners to become more and more autonomous as writers, after they have worked collaboratively. It is possible to integrate joint writing activities in the DARTs tasks, referred to above. Finally, writing is an iterative process of drafting, reviewing and revising. So, it is not always realistic to expect learners to execute a perfect text in 'one sitting'. Therefore, build in opportunities for your learners to review and redraft their writing to ensure clarity and coherence. One way of doing this is to pair pupils as 'critical friends' who use a checklist of key points relevant to genre and subject content, as a means of evaluating one another's writing prior to revisions and final submission to be reviewed by you, the teacher. Now complete Task 7.7.

Task 7.7   Planning language and learning in your subject

Review what you have read in this chapter and plan a sequence of lessons on a specific content area in your subject with a view to not only teaching knowledge, skills and concepts but also the relevant components of language, including new vocabulary, grammar and textual features. Consider how you will organise talk for learning; how you will scaffold writing tasks; and how you might employ group learning by devising a DARTs activity that will engage learners in collaborative engagement towards a joint outcome.

Evaluate the success of your strategies once you have taught the lessons, perhaps asking for feedback from your learners. Record the outcomes in your PDP.

SUMMARY AND KEY POINTS

■ Language is organised differently across the curriculum, which means that all teachers need to scaffold learners' development of subject-specific language, alongside their acquisition of subject-specific knowledge and concepts.

■ Texts are increasingly multi-modal and the reading and writing of texts require an adept command of the integration of semiotic systems and how meanings are encoded in the interaction of these systems.

- ■ It cannot be assumed that learners will have encountered, in their primary schooling, the text types found across the secondary curriculum and, therefore, teaching the language of the subject is a matter of social equity, as much as it is about scaffolding the learning of individual learners.
- ■ Five levels of language are described; these are phonology, lexis, syntax, semantics and text.
- ■ The five dimensions model can be used as a prompt for introducing pupils to subject-specific vocabulary.
- ■ Semantics functions at multiple levels of language: words, phrases, clauses, sentences and texts. All levels of language need to be considered when teaching subject-specific language.
- ■ Dialogic and exploratory talk are essential to learners' development of subject-specific language, thought and understanding.
- ■ Reading is an active process of meaning-making, involving readers as navigators, interpreters, designers and interrogators.
- ■ The writing of subject-specific genres needs to be scaffolded by subject specialists.
- ■ Writing is a means of learning and should not be considered solely as a means of assessing learners' knowledge.

Record in your professional development portfolio (PDP), how the information in this chapter enables you to meet the requirements for your first year of teaching.

 ## Further resources

Greek and Latin affixes

McEwan, E.K. (2008) *The Reading Puzzle: Word Analysis*, Thousand Oaks, CA: Corwin Press. Available from: www.readingrockets.org/article/root-words-roots-and-affixes (accessed 14 November 2018).

Gill, N.S. (2018) *Greek and Latin Roots*, ThoughtCo. Available from: www.thoughtco.com/greek-latin-roots-stems-prefixes-affixes-4070803 (accessed 14 November 2018). Group work/DARTs

Collaborative Learning Project. Available from: www.collaborativelearning.org/ (accessed 14 November 2018).

Gardner, P. (2002) *Strategies and Resources for Teaching and Learning in Inclusive Classrooms*, London: David Fulton Publishers.

Language and education

Hornberger, N. (ed.) (2008) *The Encyclopaedia of Language and Education*, Switzerland: Springer. Available from: https://link.springer.com/referenceworkentry/10.1007/978-0-387-30424-3_84 (accessed 14 November 2018).
The *Encyclopaedia of Language and Education* provides useful extension to many of the areas covered in this chapter.

Subject-specific language

Art

AQA Subject-specific vocabulary. Available from: www.aqa.org.uk/resources/art-and-design/gcse/art-and-design/teach/subject-specific-vocabulary (accessed 14 November 2018).

Design and Technology

AQA Subject-specific vocabulary. Available from: www.aqa.org.uk/resources/design-and-technology/gcse/design-and-technology/teach/subject-specific-vocabulary (accessed 14 November 2018).

Penyrheol Comprehensive School (2016) Glossary of D and T terms. Available from: http://penyrheol-comp.net/technology/glossary/ (accessed 14 November 2018).

Geography

GeogSpace (n.d.) *Teaching Literacy in Geography*, Australian Geography Teachers Association. Available from: www.geogspace.edu.au/support-units/language-of-geography/log-illustration1.html (accessed 14 November 2018).

Cambridge English (n.d.) Teaching Geography through English: A CLIL approach. University of Cambridge. Available from: www.unifg.it/sites/default/files/allegatiparagrafo/21-01-2014/teaching_geography_through_clil.pdf (accessed 14 November 2018).

History

Schleppergrell, M.J., Greer, S. and Taylor, S. (2008) 'Literacy in history: language and meaning', *Australian Journal of Language and Literacy*, 31 (2), 174-187.

Mathematics

Meiers, M. (2010) 'Language in the Mathematics Classroom', *The Digest*, NSWIT. Available from: www.nswteachers.nsw.edu.au (accessed 14 November 2018).

Physical Education

AQA Subject-specific vocabulary - GCSE. Available from: https://filestore.aqa.org.uk/resources/pe/AQA-8582-VOCAB.PDF (accessed 14 November 2018).

Religious Education

AQA Subject-specific vocabulary - GCSE. Available from: www.aqa.org.uk/resources/religious-studies/gcse/religious-studies-a/teach/subject-specific-vocabulary (accessed 14 November 2018).

San Jose State University - Basic Religious Studies Vocabulary. Available from: www.sjsu.edu/people/jennifer.rycenga/courses/gsr/s1/Vocabulary_Sheets_GSR07.pdf (accessed 14 November 2018).

Science

AQA (n.d.) *Subject Specific Vocabulary (Science)*. Available from: https://filestore.aqa.org.uk/resources/science/AQA-SCIENCE-GCSE-SUBJECT-VOCAB.PDF (accessed 14 November 2018).

Assessment Resource Banks (2018) *Language of Science*, Wellington, New Zealand: Ministry of Education for New Zealand. Available from: https://arbs.nzcer.org.nz/language-science-specialised-language (accessed 14 November 2018).

Victoria State Government (2018) *Introducing Scientific Language*, Melbourne, VIC: State Government of Victoria. Available from: www.education.vic.gov.au/school/teachers/teaching resources/discipline/science/continuum/Pages/scilang.aspx (accessed 14 November 2018).

Appendices 2 and 3 list subject associations, teaching councils and relevant websites.

Books in the *Learning to Teach* series that you may find helpful are as follows:

Capel, S., Leask, M. and Younie, S. (eds.) (2019) *Learning to Teach in the Secondary School: A Companion to School Experience*, 8th edn, Abingdon: Routledge.
This book is designed as a core textbook to support student teachers through their initial teacher education programme.

Capel, S., Leask, M. and Turner, T. (eds.) (2010) *Readings for Learning to Teach in the Secondary School: A Companion to M Level Study*, Abingdon: Routledge.
This book brings together essential readings to support you in your critical engagement with key issues raised in this textbook.

The subject-specific books in the *Learning to Teach* series, the *Practical (subject) Guides*, *Debates in (subject)* and *Mentoring (subject) Teachers* are also very useful.

8 Every learner counts

Learning mathematics across the curriculum

Jennie Golding, Rosalyn Hyde and Alison Clark-Wilson

Introduction

In the 21st century, mathematical confidence and functionality are considered to be of crucial importance to individuals and to national economies, which is reflected in national policies, as well as in the status of international performance comparisons such as the Programme for International Student Assessment (PISA) (Organisation for Economic Cooperation and Development (OECD), 2009) and Trends in International Mathematics and Science Study (TIMSS) (International Association for the Evaluation of Educational Achievement (IAEEA), n.d.), which compare educational systems and outcomes for participating countries. However, as a subject specialist in another subject, you might well think you simply can't afford the teaching time to deliberately embed mathematics in your lesson. In this chapter we try to show how, by being aware of how your subject harnesses mathematical thinking, even if only in low-key ways, you can support learners in making confident and informed use of that – but we also encourage you to keep talking to the teachers of mathematics in your school, so that they become more aware of what your learners are meeting and when. That way, learners can begin to make meaningful connections across the curriculum, and enhance their grasp of, and interest in, your own subject.

In England the National Curriculum describes the centrality of mathematics in the curriculum as follows:

> Mathematics is a creative and highly interconnected discipline that has been developed over centuries, providing the solution to some of history's most intriguing problems. It is essential to everyday life, critical to science, technology and engineering, and necessary for financial literacy and most forms of employment. A high-quality mathematics education therefore provides a foundation for understanding the world, the ability to reason mathematically, an appreciation of the beauty and power of mathematics, and a sense of enjoyment and curiosity about the subject.
>
> *(Department for Education (DfE), 2014c, p. 3)*

Numeracy, including statistical literacy, is a part of effective mathematical functioning and can be defined as the 'ability to use mathematics in everyday life' (National Numeracy, 2017). The digital world for which learners are now being prepared requires high levels of engagement with many varied tools and resources unknown to earlier generations and so, as teachers, you have a responsibility to support learners to engage with those new demands and opportunities, including working in mathematical ways wherever there is a need to do so.

Because mathematics is so pervasive across the curriculum and beyond, all teachers need a fundamental knowledge of both how to teach mathematical ideas within their subject area, and how learners learn them. Teaching mathematics is, like all teaching, a highly skilled undertaking, but specialist and non-specialist teachers alike can take up a wide range of support and advice available to them to support this endeavour: see the Further resources at the end of the chapter.

OBJECTIVES

By the end of this chapter, you should be able to:

■ understand how to help learners grasp core mathematical concepts;
■ analyse the opportunities for developing learners' mathematics skills, knowledge and understanding in your subject;
■ recognise the value and roles of mathematics and mathematical thinking in multiple contexts, subjects and everyday life;
■ understand some ways of developing positive attitudes to mathematics in learners.

Check how the information in this chapter enables you to meet the requirements for your first year of teaching.

The nature of mathematics

Learners have a variety of views about what mathematics is, and of their relationship with it. We take the view that learning and teaching mathematics is fundamentally about recognising pattern and structure (sometimes in abstract forms) and working with this recognition in reasoned ways that both stem from, and are applied to, the world around us: that includes other curriculum areas!

Mathematics helps us to make sense of the world and provides ways of thinking about and solving both practical and abstract problems. It is not 'magic' that appears out of nowhere nor is it disconnected from anything else. So a priority for learners engaging with mathematical ideas is that mathematics should be approached in ways that 'make sense'. Users of mathematics in other subjects might not be confident about the underlying reasons for something, for example, the form that 'standard deviation' of a set of data takes – but it is important to communicate to learners that there *is* good reason – perhaps that they could ask a mathematics teacher about – and that, for applications, what is most important is understanding and interpreting the information that measure gives.

Not all teachers are mathematically fluent or confident – and, unfortunately, some have had negative experiences of learning mathematics themselves. It would be very sad if those negative experiences were also projected onto future generations of learners, so as a teacher, it is important to try to model positive attitudes to mathematics and to demonstrate how to approach situations where you are mathematically challenged: Has anyone met this idea before? What does it mean? If you *are* faced with questions about the mathematics that you cannot answer, tell learners you will talk with colleagues and then come back to them.

Ideally, a school will have policies that make it clear in your schemes of work where learners are meeting mathematical ideas for the first time in your subject and where they have already met them in their mathematics curriculum. It is helpful for learners, if they have met ideas elsewhere, if you know *how* those have been approached, and find this out from learners; if this is the first time that they have met a mathematical idea, that's fine. In either case, talk with a mathematics teacher if it is not clear to you how best to approach the idea, ideally in advance of working with a mathematical concept in class.

For example, in Geography, learners might well be meeting the mathematical representations such as stacked bar charts or choropleths that show area as proportional to number for the first time. Support learners to make sense of them. In other cases, learners might have met underlying ideas but perhaps in a different guise. For instance, by KS4, graphs arising from experimental data are treated differently in each of Biology, Chemistry and Physics, because of the nature of the data represented. However, in mathematics lessons learners are more usually dealing with continuous functions that require representation with a smooth curve. In another example, 'lines of best fit' in Mathematics GCSE only relate to directly proportional relationships, but in Business or Science or History the 'best fit' from a limited number of data points might well be a curve. Such issues of interpolation and extrapolation occur across the curriculum and learners can benefit from talking about their experiences in other parts of the curriculum. Further, there is symbiosis here: practical work in any subject that requires measuring or recording or representation of data.

One area that can often challenge learners is the use of formulae. Try to help them make sense of the underlying *meaning* of the formula, ask them to estimate values for the quantities involved, use learners to explain to the class the approach they prefer to use, listening for the vocabulary and sense-making they are drawing on, so that you build support rather than cause further confusion.

And always, if in doubt, talk with mathematics colleagues, and don't feel guilty about doing so: your conversation also helps them to appreciate learners' needs beyond the mathematics classroom, which they in turn can draw upon in their own teaching. That way, everyone benefits: you will be more confident about how you are working mathematically with learners; your colleagues teaching mathematics will also develop their repertoire of where else in the curriculum learners are engaging with mathematical ideas. Your colleagues can also enrich learners' experiences and support them to link their learning across the curriculum, which is key to working confidently with mathematics.

The curriculum in mathematics

It is helpful for teachers who use mathematics in their subjects to have some familiarity with learners' prior mathematical experiences. The Mathematics National Curriculum (DfE, 2014c, p.3) aims to ensure that all learners:

- become fluent in the fundamentals of mathematics, including through varied and frequent practice with increasingly complex problems over time, so that learners develop conceptual understanding and the ability to recall and apply knowledge rapidly and accurately;
- reason mathematically by following a line of enquiry, conjecturing relationships and generalisations, and developing an argument, justification or proof using mathematical language;
- can solve problems by applying their mathematics to a variety of routine and non-routine problems with increasing sophistication, including breaking down problems into a series of simpler steps and persevering in seeking solutions.

Note this goes well beyond 'doing the mathematics'. When learners are *fluent* in mathematics they are able to recognise when to use their mathematical knowledge, can use it flexibly and efficiently, and apply it to a range of situations and problems. Allied with this, of course, is a familiarity with an increasing range of mathematical facts, procedures and concepts. By the time they arrive at secondary school, most learners are reasonably confident with the four operations (+, -, ×, ÷) for whole numbers of any size, for many decimals, and for some fractions. They have met a range of measures and statistical representations and worked with 2-D and 3-D shapes. But they won't necessarily be confident in working with all those in new situations.

In mathematics, learners need both 'procedural fluency' and 'conceptual understanding'. This is because it is not sufficient only to be able to recall the procedure for carrying out a calculation: often when solving a problem or applying that knowledge the learner needs a deeper understanding in order to recognise and apply mathematics appropriately. Cross-curricular teaching such that learners can really understand the mathematics they are using helps learners to develop robust procedures and build confidence.

Importantly for teachers of other subjects, the second and third aims of the Mathematics National Curriculum encapsulate the kinds of mathematics-related skills learners need for the development of statistical literacy. For example, learners can engage in analyses of fair-trade issues, of global neonatal mortality rates, of athletics records. ... In your subject areas, learners might be engaged in problems related to how something changes, or has changed, with time, what quantities are interdependent and in what way, whether we can formulate relationships in such as a way as to be able to predict. ... In order to support learners in becoming able to function mathematically within your subject, you need to have some understanding of where it fits within their mathematics curriculum trajectory.

Now complete Task 8.1.

 Task 8.1   Identifying the mathematics required in your subject

Look at the curriculum for one of your teaching groups and identify the parts where your learners might need to use mathematical skills and knowledge. Use the Mathematics National Curriculum (www.gov.uk/government/publications/national-curriculum-in-england-mathematics-programmes-of-study) to help you to identify when they meet those criteria in their mathematics lessons: Have they met them at primary school? Or in KS3?

Now meet with someone who teaches your, or similar, learners' mathematics to discuss how the identified skills and knowledge are addressed. Curriculum mismatches, whether in timing or approach, need not matter if they are understood. If your learners' first encounter with a mathematical concept, tool or skill is in your lessons, both you and their mathematics teacher need to be aware of that. Similarly, if there are reasons for a variety of approaches, it is helpful to learners if those are understood by all the teachers who are working with that material. For example, is the plotting of a set of experimental points on a graph to be followed by joining them with straight line segments, or a curve, or a line of best fit, or ...? And why? Make a note of any outstanding tensions.

Discuss this information with your mentor and store the information in your professional development portfolio (PDP) (or similar) to refer to as you plan your lessons.

As with any teaching, your knowledge does need to be secure with respect to your own subject knowledge, including its mathematical aspects. However, even this is not sufficient; you also need 'Pedagogical Content Knowledge' (PCK) (Shulman, 1987). This is the knowledge that makes the discipline accessible to learners. It is one thing, for example, to know how to calculate, for instance, a percentage decrease in population during the Black Death (which is content knowledge); it is quite another to be able to explain this to learners in a way that makes sense to them, using appropriate examples and diagrams and in a way that draws on appropriate prior learning.

Pedagogical content knowledge for teaching mathematical aspects of the curriculum in school includes an understanding of an appropriate subset of:

- conceptions and common misconceptions in mathematics;
- progression in learning mathematics, including some familiarity with the mathematics curriculum that enables appropriate approaches in other areas;
- use of multiple appropriate representations, common models, concrete-pictorial-abstract approaches to developing concepts;
- appropriate and meaningful use of mathematical digital technologies, and a variety of other tools, for teaching and learning using mathematics;

■ importance of meaningful, progressive and rigorous language in learning mathematics: the language, including symbolism, of mathematics is a very compact and precise one, and that precision needs to be learnt over time in order to communicate mathematics effectively. Much of that can be done via teacher modelling, and the building up of learners' experiences accompanied by appropriate teacher expectations. For example, 'sums' are a particular sort of calculation that uses addition: if another sort of process is indicated, or it is not yet decided, it is helpful to refer to that as purely a 'calculation'.

■ knowledge of how learners interact with mathematics, their typical progression, ways of thinking, acting and being with mathematical aspects of your subject, and their affective needs as they do so.

We now discuss these different types of pedagogical knowledge briefly, using examples that should be familiar and applicable to those whose main role is teaching other subjects in the curriculum.

Conceptions and misconceptions in mathematics

Estimating, and considering whether one's answer makes sense, are important skills for calculating. Some learners think that 'multiplying makes things bigger', or 'to multiply by 10 all I need to do is add a zero on the end of a number'. This is not surprising given that their first experiences are with numbers greater than one, where this is true. This is an example of a *partial conception*, where the learner is seeking to generalise from their experience but does not yet have sufficient experience to understand that they are incorrect in their assumption. Other misconceptions may emerge because the learner misunderstands the mathematics. For example, learners might interpret a distance-time graph comprising straight-line segments as a journey that goes up and down hills. Alternatively, misconceptions might arise where learners have experienced poor, or limited, explanation on the part of the teacher.

Far from setting out to be troublesome, learners try to make sense of mathematical ideas. However, given their much more limited life experience, it is not surprising that the sense they make is often initially different from that made by adults, and particularly mathematically confident adults. Processes of 'cognitive conflict' whereby learners come to see their present understanding is not fit for purpose in wider context, can often underpin changes in conception – important knowledge for the wider adult (mathematical) community as it is not always clear why learners misunderstand some ideas. Finding this out can often be achieved by providing opportunities to work in situations where the learner has already developed sense-making – perhaps here, with money – and provoking that cognitive conflict. In the case of multiplying by ten, for example, it is clear that the price of ten £4.99 DVDs is not £4.990!

Progression in learning mathematics

Topics in mathematics are deeply connected, and new learning almost always relies on previous learning within the same and other topics. For example, drawing a graph from data in science requires an understanding of the number line. It draws on: skills learnt plotting points using ordered pairs; calculations using a variety of small, large, integer and decimal numbers; multiplication facts; a need to recognise patterns; and an understanding that a graph is a representation of an infinite number of two-dimensional points whose coordinates have a particular relationship. Producing a histogram in Business Studies draws on some of these skills, but also further requires an understanding of the difference between discrete and continuous data and a recognition of the differences and similarities between graphical representations and the ways in which graphs are used in both algebra and statistics. Work across the school curriculum draws on different aspects of learners' graphing skills and the need to recognise and apply these skills appropriately.

Representing mathematics

One of the most powerful tools in mathematics is the ability to represent a mathematical situation in different forms in order either to solve it or to explore and explain its different features. Using the previous example of a scientific relationship, the specific case of the mathematical function $2x + 3$ can be expressed algebraically as $y = 2x + 3$ and learners at Key Stage 3 might be expected to have worked with such functions in mathematics lessons. We can also say that 'the y value is double the value of x and 3 more', to make sense of it. We can form a table of some of the pairs of points satisfying this relationship and we can plot them on a graph shown in Figure 8.1 using, for example, a free graph-plotting tool such as Desmos (www.desmos.com). But in physics, a very similar relationship exists between a temperature F measured in degrees Fahrenheit, and a temperature C measured in degrees Celsius: $F = 1.6C + 32$. In both examples, these letters represent algebraic variables, an important mathematical idea that all learners are required to understand by the end of Key Stage 4. Learners need support to build their confidence so that they can deal with different letters but the same underlying ideas. Ideally that support is provided in both mathematics and physics lessons.

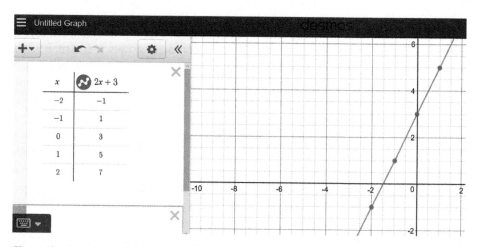

Figure 8.1 Graph and table for $y = 2x + 3$ (image produced with permission using Desmos www.desmos.com/)

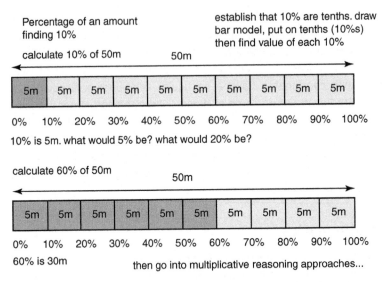

Percentage of an amount
finding 10%

establish that 10% are tenths. draw
bar model, put on tenths (10%s)
then find value of each 10%

calculate 10% of 50m   50m

| 5m | 5m | 5m | 5m | 5m | 5m | 5m | 5m | 5m | 5m |

0%   10%   20%   30%   40%   50%   60%   70%   80%   90%   100%

10% is 5m. what would 5% be? what would 20% be?

calculate 60% of 50m   50m

| 5m | 5m | 5m | 5m | 5m | 5m | 5m | 5m | 5m | 5m |

0%   10%   20%   30%   40%   50%   60%   70%   80%   90%   100%

60% is 30m   then go into multiplicative reasoning approaches...

Figure 8.2 Using bar modelling to find 60% of 50m (screenshot from www.greatmathematicsteachingideas.com)

Using such a tool produces a quick and accurate graph – but also the opportunity to gain a deeper understanding of the relationship, and importantly, the links between the geometric features of the graph and its algebraic or tabular forms.

Another powerful visual representation in mathematics is the use of a bar model, which requires proportional reasoning. The example in Figure 8.2 demonstrates how to find 60% of 50m using bar modelling. If you ask learners how they would approach such a calculation, they might well draw on such a representation.

Concrete – visual – abstract pedagogy

Primary schools and, increasingly, secondary schools, commonly use a *concrete – visual – abstract* approach to mathematics (this is based on Jerome Bruner's conception of the *enactive, iconic and symbolic* (Bruner, 1966)). In this approach learners spend time using physical objects to explore the structure of mathematics problems before moving on to use images as a 'bridge' to learning how to manipulate situations symbolically. For example, learners might use Dienes blocks (place value apparatus), counters, straws, rods or cards before moving on to using a diagrammatic or digital resource, and finally to a confident grasp of the underpinning abstract concepts. That process cannot be rushed if learners are to develop robust conceptual understanding – and you will often see advanced level mathematics learners using diagrams to give them access to the mathematics underpinning a situation in a way that the written or physical situation does not afford: the diagram absorbs some of the mental attention needed to grasp the whole, and so allows freer and more productive use of remaining brainpower. It is therefore important that learners do not think they should have 'grown out of' using diagrams or other representations, but instead be encouraged to recognise them, when appropriate, as valuable tools for thinking.

Learners can also draw their own informal representations, for example: when the situation calls for sharing a quantity in a given ratio, or dealing with the mathematics of a mechanical or technical situation. The evidence is that all learners, not just lower attainers, need time with both concrete materials and visual representations to explore and model problems before working on the mathematics more abstractly. Some other subject areas use quite demanding ideas of, for example, ratio and proportion: it is helpful to learners to allow them to work with these in their preferred way. So if learners appear to have difficulty grasping the mathematical ideas you're using, it might be that using a more visual approach makes links with what they *can* grasp. What you would like to achieve is meaning making in your subject area!

Appropriate and meaningful use of digital technologies

There is an overwhelming choice of digital resources available for teachers (and learners) to use in and with mathematics and it is sometimes challenging to determine if and when they are worthwhile. We have pointed above to Desmos, if you need to produce graphs, and both Excel or Geogebra (www.geogebra.com) can be harnessed to represent and analyse data. Learners require a scientific calculator for GCSE Mathematics, and it is reasonable to expect them to have that available for use in other subject areas as well. If you are dealing with comparatively complex formulae, e.g. calculating the radius needed for a choropleth, learners might need support in using their calculator appropriately, but again, try to help them make sense of what they are doing and then they will retain that.

Language for learning mathematics

Learning and teaching mathematics uses language in a highly specialised manner. When considering the vocabulary of mathematics there are technical words that are used only in mathematics, and there are words that have different meanings in mathematics than they do in everyday life. For example, when two shapes are 'similar' in mathematics we mean that they have a specific defined relationship, with the same shape but possibly different size, not that they are 'a bit the same'. Some aspects of grammar, such as 'and', 'or' also operate differently and usually more rigorously in mathematics, and that rigour has to be developed and maintained if the concision of mathematical language is to retain its usefulness, but don't be afraid to use mathematically related vocabulary particular to your subject as well: for example, learners in their mathematics lessons will have had limited experience of using experimental data, but in context, the notions of 'dependent' and 'independent' variable are powerful and precise. Explaining mathematics-related tools therefore requires careful use of precise language by both teachers and learners.

Now undertake Task 8.2.

Task 8.2   Analysing the mathematics in learners' subject work

Pick a topic from the scheme of work for your subject where learners need to use some mathematics, no matter how basic. After you have taught the topic, choose the written work of some learners to analyse in more detail:

■   What mathematics did learners use in the topic?
■   What evidence do you have that they understood it?
■   What difficulties did they have? Did they reveal any misconceptions about the mathematics?
■   Use some of the ideas in the previous parts of this chapter to help you to think about how you could improve the teaching of this topic in the future.

You might like to refer to the work you did in Task 8.1 to help you.
Discuss this information with your mentor and store the information in your PDP to refer to as you plan your lessons.

In terms of the mathematical skills and processes learners are likely to use across the curriculum, being efficient in carrying out aspects of mathematical calculations is only part of the picture. As already mentioned, it is insufficient for learners to develop knowledge of facts if they don't also have a conceptual understanding of what they are doing. Within calculations, the mathematics curriculum sets out to ensure that for each of the four arithmetic processes (+, -, ×, ÷) learners have a standard method they can apply efficiently and reliably with a variety of numbers, including fractions. However, the curriculum also encourages estimation and mental methods as a first resort, and teachers of other parts of the curriculum have a key role to play here, in modelling their own adult ways of dealing with numbers, and the discipline-specific ways they have of checking that answers to calculations make sense. In so doing, they are supporting learners in developing powerful ways of harnessing mathematical thinking in a variety of situations – in becoming genuine *users* of mathematics.

Mathematical reasoning underpins mathematical problem solving – including the application of learners' mathematical knowledge in other areas. Their reasoning can be built up from asking for straightforward explanations towards the eventual achievement of sustained chains of fairly formal deductive reasoning, but underpinning all of those are consistent questioning of the mathematical thinking learners are engaging in: 'Tell us how you sorted that out'; 'Can you explain why you did that?'; 'How do you know?'; 'What information did you use to come to that answer?'. And importantly, engaging in such questioning whether or not the solution is a valid one, so that over time, learners themselves come to question their chain of thinking at every stage.

Once learners are confident to work in such ways informally and orally, they are then in a position to begin to communicate that thinking in writing. And here we come to another central aim of the overall curriculum – that learners should come to be able to *communicate*, in this case mathematically, in a variety of ways: orally, diagrammatically, graphically, algebraically and via formal written deductive reasoning, among others. Mathematical communication in its most efficient form is very concise – but in order to maintain rigour, that concision needs precise use, and careful development of learners' mathematical communication, often employing standard English terminology in parallel with technical words ('the gradient, or amount of slope of the graph, tells us that ...'; 'How would you explain that in English?') so that learners begin to make the cognitive links between technical descriptions and meaning.

It is fine for learners to experience *challenge* within the range of their mathematical experiences, and learn how more experienced others, notably their teachers, cope with that, by sharing and critiquing their ideas so far, by revisiting possible related facts and processes, by going away and 'thinking about it', and by harnessing the support of others with perhaps different viewpoints or knowledge. *Use errors positively* – as an opportunity to learn – and if one learner has a misconception, you can be fairly sure they are not the only one: be sure to value that opportunity overtly, so that learners come to see how it can be harnessed for positive ends. Sometimes learners think best when they are quiet and on their own, but often a combination of individual thought and cooperative or *collaborative* approaches is the most fruitful, and the range of teachers working with learners in such ways can all contribute to a growing appreciation of that.

SUMMARY AND KEY POINTS

- For non-specialists in particular, this can all seem rather daunting, but positive approaches that emphasise conceptual understanding and working together to make sense of the mathematics, making links within and beyond mathematics, embracing the opportunities offered by misconceptions and by getting stuck, can build up both teacher and learner confidence over time. That way, your consciousness of the mathematical needs of your subject area enhances your teaching, and your learners' confidence and interest in it.

- For those who use mathematics in the curriculum, there are high-quality, evidence-based websites that support such approaches; the mathematics subject professional associations also offer a range of subject-specific support and resources (see below).

- Finally, learners benefit from having teachers who ask more knowledgeable others if they are stuck, reflect with colleagues on their teaching of mathematics-linked parts of their curriculum, and know the subject, their learners and the resources available, harnessing them in positive ways to enjoy working mathematically themselves. It is amazing how those beginner teachers, who come to use mathematics in the classroom with some trepidation, can build up their own enjoyment and confidence by working in these ways, and everyone benefits.

Record in your PDP how the information in this chapter enables you to meet the requirements for your first year of teaching.

Further resources

www.atm.org.uk – The Association of Teachers of Mathematics and www.m-a.rg.uk – The Mathematical Association jointly publish *Primary Mathematics*, as well as a range of other classroom-focused periodicals and other resources.

www.ncetm.org.uk – The National Centre for Excellence in the Teaching of Mathematics is government-funded to support evidence-based good practice in schools, and especially to coordinate high quality teacher development for that.

www.nrich.mathematics.org – NRICH provides challenging and engaging activities at all levels 5-18 to develop mathematical thinking and problem-solving skills that show rich mathematics in meaningful contexts.

Appendices 2 and 3 list subject associations, teaching councils and relevant websites.

Books in the *Learning to Teach* series that you may find helpful are as follows:

Capel, S., Leask, M. and Younie, S. (eds.) (2019) *Learning to Teach in the Secondary School: A Companion to School Experience*, **8th edn, Abingdon: Routledge.**
This book is designed as a core textbook to support student teachers through their initial teacher education programme.

Capel, S., Leask, M. and Turner, T. (eds.) (2010) *Readings for Learning to Teach in the Secondary School: A Companion to M Level Study*, **Abingdon: Routledge.**
This book brings together essential readings to support you in your critical engagement with key issues raised in this textbook.

The subject-specific books in the *Learning to Teach* series, the *Practical (subject) Guides, Debates in (subject)* and *Mentoring (subject) Teachers* are also very useful.

9 Personal, Social, Health and Economic (PSHE) education

Natasha Bye-Brooks

Introduction

Personal, Social, Health and Economic (PSHE) education contributes to and underpins a broad view of the purpose of education. At its best, it:

- supports the development of young people's physical, emotional and social health;
- supports the development of essential employability skills for the 21st century;
- reduces or removes barriers to learning.

Teaching PSHE education can be a daunting prospect for a beginning teacher (tackling issues such as mental health and well-being and sex and relationships education), but it can also be hugely rewarding. This chapter makes no assumption of any prior understanding of PSHE and is intended to be an introduction to the subject. As very few initial teacher education (ITE) programmes offer any substantial coverage of PSHE (Dewhirst et al., 2014), you are encouraged to access the further resources recommended and signposted throughout this chapter. You may also consider becoming a member of the PSHE Association (www.pshe-association.org.uk) and should take any opportunities to increase your knowledge, understanding and experience of PSHE. Whether you end up teaching PSHE or not, the skills and strategies that you gain from an understanding of PSHE will support you as a teacher, whatever your subject area.

OBJECTIVES

At the end of this chapter you should be able to:

- understand what PSHE education is and its importance;
- understand how PSHE education contributes to the wider curriculum aims of creating successful learners, confident individuals and responsible citizens;
- understand who is responsible for the delivery of PSHE education and how PSHE could be organised in schools;

- understand what is expected of you as a beginning teacher and understand where you can go for support in delivering PSHE education;
- understand the broad pedagogical principles that underpin effective practice in PSHE education.

Check how the information in this chapter enables you to meet the requirements for your first year of teaching.

What is PSHE education and why is it important?

Your experience of PSHE education as a young person will vary depending on when you were a pupil, where you went to school and whether you were taught by teachers who had an enthusiasm or passion for the subject (Office for Standards in Education, Children's Services and Skills (Ofsted), 2013a; Dewhirst et al., 2014). Task 9.1 encourages you to consider what you currently understand PSHE education to be.

 Task 9.1   My current understanding of PSHE education

- What are your memories of PSHE education?
- What did PSHE education mean to you as a pupil? Did you receive any?
- Who taught it?
- What was it called?
- Was it a discrete lesson within the curriculum, taught by PSHE education specialists or a rushed worksheet that you completed in tutor time?
- What does PSHE education mean to you now as a beginning teacher?

Record your responses in your professional development portfolio (PDP) (or similar) and refer back to them as you read through the chapter.

PSHE education covers many topic areas, such as drug and alcohol education, relationships and sex education, economic well-being, personal safety, healthy eating and mental health and emotional well-being. However, it is not just about the transmission of information and knowledge about key areas. PSHE education identifies a set of core skills and values alongside these topic areas. The PSHE Association define it as:

> a planned, developmental programme of learning through which children and young people acquire the knowledge, understanding and skills they need to manage their lives now and in the future. As part of a whole-school approach, PSHE develops the qualities and attributes pupils need to thrive as individuals, family members and members of society.
>
> *(PSHE Association, 2017, p.3)*

Effective PSHE education should therefore provide opportunities that enable pupils to:

■ explore attitudes, beliefs and values that influence individuals and their relationships with others and the wider world;
■ respond to their present lives and prepare them for the next stages of their lives, both personally and in the world of work;
■ develop skills relating to practical activities, decision making and problem solving, communication, inter-personal skills and learning through experience and provide relevant and appropriate ways in which these skills may be developed;
■ reflect upon their learning in a safe learning environment.

The 'personal' in PSHE education

PSHE education is all about what is 'personal' and it is this element of PSHE education that can be the most off-putting aspect of the subject for a beginning teacher. 'Personal' in terms of PSHE education is what is relevant to each pupil (McWhirter, Boddington and Barksfield, 2017). This means starting from where the pupil is. The aim is to make even the most sensitive issues appropriate and relevant to the pupils you are teaching at that moment. What might have been appropriate and relevant one year, or for one cohort of pupils, may not be the following year/lesson or a different group within that year. PSHE education and the 'personal' aspect is all about allowing young people the space and opportunity to explore their own developing identities (Coleman, 2011).

The secondary school years are a crucial period in the development of young people, in terms of their physical, emotional, mental and sexual selves. This period of transition is a time of many changes, including changes in the brain affecting reasoning and thinking, puberty, growth spurts and sexual maturation. Teaching PSHE education gives you the privileged position of being there to guide and support young people through this transformation. Effective PSHE education also supports young people in developing the *intra-personal skills* and attributes required to be resilient to the challenges and opportunities that life will bring. These include active listening, empathy, communication skills, team working, negotiation skills and the identification of and using strategies for managing pressure.

What about the 'social' bit of PSHE education?

The 'social' aspect of PSHE education is fundamentally about relationships. Relationships with family, friends and peers can influence health and well-being throughout life in both positive and negative ways. PSHE education can support young people to develop the attitudes, understanding and *inter-personal skills* to help them to enjoy the opportunities as well as deal with the challenges of life.

The 'health' aspect of PSHE education

The definition of health within PSHE education fits the holistic model of health, including: physical health, mental health, emotional health, social health, spiritual health and societal health. All aspects of health are interrelated and interdependent. Sexual well-being for example depends on physical and emotional well-being alongside effective social skills to build healthy relationships. Naidoo and Wills (2016, pp. 3–4) offer some useful insights into the 'dimensions of health and well-being'. It is important that you as a teacher of PSHE spend time exploring what you understand as 'health'.

PSHE education should encourage young people to appreciate that 'health' is more than just being free of disease or illness; it is about reaching their full potential in physical, mental, emotional and social terms. It is also important that your pupils understand the many influences on health: biological, environmental, mental, emotional, as well as social and financial. Angela Scriven's book, *Promoting Health* (2010), has a useful and accessible chapter that looks at the factors affecting health (see Task 9.2 for reflection).

M

🖉   Task 9.2   What does health mean to you? (adapted from Naidoo and Wills, 2016, p. 4)

How would you answer the following?

- I feel healthy when …
- I feel unhealthy when …
- I am healthy because …
- To stay healthy I need …
- … is responsible for my health
- Consider how many of your responses are related to 'physical' aspects of health and well-being and how many are related to 'emotional' or 'mental' aspects of health and well-being?
- Reflect on the PSHE education provision in your placement schools/current school. Does it reflect the physical and emotional dimensions of health and well-being?

Record your responses in your PDP and refer back to them as you read through the chapter.

The 'economic' aspect of PSHE education

PSHE education is often used interchangeably with 'Health Education', or 'Personal Development'. The 'Economic' aspect of PSHE education is a relative newcomer; in 2007 an 'Economic well-being and financial capability' component was added to the English National Curriculum non-statutory programme of study for PSHE. In 2013 the revised National Curriculum (Department for Education (DfE), 2013c) brought personal finance education into both Maths and Citizenship, whilst PSHE education held on to the 'E – Economic well-being'. The link between economic education and well-being are as important as the link between emotional well-being and sexual health and relationships education. Money issues and financial difficulties can be key stress factors for many adults that put pressure on relationships and emotional well-being (Young Men's Christian Association (YMCA), 2016). This research looked at the impact of lifestyle factors on people's well-being and found that financial confidence was the factor that has the most impact on well-being (YMCA, 2016). The skills and attributes young people need to manage decisions related to money and budgeting are often very similar to those needed to navigate other life decisions. The PSHE Association suggests that financial awareness should be addressed directly through one of its core themes – 'living in the wider world'. Pupils are encouraged to understand where money comes from and how to manage it effectively. Economic and Financial Capability education taught within the framework of PSHE education allows pupils the opportunity to develop an understanding of behaviours around money such as peer influence and social media pressure that could influence their financial decisions and attitude to risk. The increase in gambling in the 11–16-year-old age group is a growing concern, with 12% of this age group reporting that they have spent their own money on gambling in the last week (Gambling Commission, 2017).

What does the programme of study look like for PSHE education?

The 2013 Ofsted Report (Ofsted, 2013b), *Not Yet Good Enough: Personal, Social, Health and Economic Education in Schools*, recognised the need to improve the quality of PSHE education provision. In response to this report, the PSHE Association worked with schools to produce a new programme of study for PSHE education. This programme of study identified the key concepts, skills and attributes that are developed through PSHE education from KS1 to KS5 (ages 4–18). The DfE signposts schools to this programme of study and you are strongly advised to use it as your basis for your own PSHE education planning.

It includes three core themes:

■ Health and well-being
■ Relationships
■ Living in the wider world

The PSHE Association has made the programme of study available (www.pshe-association.org.uk/curriculum-and-resources/resources/programme-study-pshe-education-key-stages-).

The programme is not intended to be a definitive or prescriptive approach. Schools are encouraged to develop what is known as a 'spiral curriculum' where prior learning is revisited, reinforced and extended in an age-appropriate context.

PSHE education's contribution to the wider curriculum aims of creating successful learners, confident individuals and responsible citizens

PSHE education is currently not a statutory subject in English schools, although the Relationships and Sex Education element of PSHE education will be statutory from September 2020, and the majority of schools choose to deliver some kind of PSHE education. So why would you 'choose' to deliver a subject if it is not a statutory requirement?

PSHE education specialists argue that PSHE education contributes to the development of healthy, happy and confident young people and that alone is reason enough. However, perhaps a significant factor is that schools have statutory responsibilities that would be difficult to meet without the contribution of PSHE education, for example, by:

- promoting children's and young people's well-being (Children Act, UK Parliament, 2004);
- helping children and young people to succeed, schools have a role to play in supporting them to be resilient and mentally healthy (*Mental Health and Behaviour in Schools*, DfE (2016b));
- supporting children and young people to keep safe (*Keeping Children Safe in Education*, DfE (2018c));
- promoting healthy lifestyles and healthy physical and mental development (*Healthy Child Programme 0-5 and 5-19 years old*, Department of Health (2009));
- achieve the whole-curriculum aims (Education Act, Section 78, UK Parliament, 2002 and Academies Act, UK Parliament, 2010);
- promote community cohesion (Education and Inspections Act, UK Parliament, 2006 and Education Act, UK Parliament, 2002).

Thus, PSHE education contributes to the wider aims of school education and school life, making the relationship between PSHE education provision and school ethos important. An effective school ethos requires a whole-school approach to health and well-being of which PSHE education is a part. Most schools recognise the benefits of providing quality PSHE education in terms of both health and well-being and academic success. PSHE education can potentially reduce or remove barriers to learning such as unhealthy risk-taking behaviours, bullying and low self-esteem. There is increasing evidence that PSHE education can support pupils to succeed academically as well as in other aspects of their lives (DfE, 2012a; Public Health England, 2014; DfE, 2015a; and Bonell et al., 2014). It can be argued that PSHE education contributes to the employability skills of young people; the Confederation of British Industry (CBI) and Pearson Education (2016) called for schools to be focusing on what has been given the misnomer of the 'soft skills' of communication, negotiation and self-management to equip school leavers for life after school.

In England (you may wish to look at how this links to your own curriculum if you are teaching outside of England), current government thinking is that the non-statutory status of PSHE education gives teachers and schools the flexibility to deliver 'tailor-made' PSHE education that best suits the needs of their pupils (DfE, 2013c). To this extent, schools are free to select which parts of the PSHE education curriculum they believe are most appropriate and relevant to their pupils. Potentially, the PSHE lead or head of year in your school has responsibility for providing and overseeing a PSHE education scheme of work (see the section below on 'Who is responsible for teaching PSHE education?'). Unfortunately, due to the status of PSHE in schools, you may find that there is no subject lead in your school and that any PSHE that is delivered is very ad hoc in nature. If there is a scheme of work then what it includes will vary from school to school. (The PSHE Association provides examples of PSHE Programme of Study, see the Further resources section at the end of this chapter.) There are elements of the PSHE education curriculum that are statutory and schools must refer to the statutory guidance on these areas: drug education, financial education, the new relationships and sex education and the importance of physical activity and diet for a healthy lifestyle. Parts of PSHE education may also be taught within the Science curriculum, such as life processes, the reproductive cycle and the effects of diet, drugs and disease. (See the section 'How is PSHE education organised in secondary schools?' below.)

Who is responsible for PSHE education?

Everyone within the school community has a responsibility for the personal, social and healthy development of the young people in its care. The care of the whole child including their academic achievement, well-being and personal development is the responsibility of many different people with different roles and can also involve working in partnership with parents, carers and external agencies.

PSHE education is not the only way in which schools support the personal development of young people, but it is the mechanism by which a planned programme supports pupils to access the knowledge, understanding, skills and confidence to enable them to live a life that they have chosen for themselves. The PSHE education curriculum supports the ethos and culture of the school by providing a taught programme, which includes a diverse topic area, including body image, diet, substance use and misuse, mental health, gender identity and personal relationships and other lifestyle issues. The PSHE lesson is not the place to give individualised personal advice. This is where the role of form tutor or a member of staff with pastoral responsibilities should step in. For example, a PSHE lesson might explore friendship issues generally, but a form tutor or pastoral lead would support an individual pupil with friendship issues. Here, the support would be individual and specific to the needs of that pupil. This might mean that as form tutor you would be liaising with a member of senior leadership or pastoral support, with family members or with external agencies such as a specialist service or a social worker. The role of the form tutor bridges the divide between PSHE education and therapeutic approaches of pastoral care, contributing to academic and personal development. The role of the form tutor varies from one school to another. In some schools the form tutor is little more than an administrative role, checking in pupils at registration, chasing up homework and day-to-day administrative tasks, whilst in other schools you may find yourself going through the school with the pupils and developing lasting connections with them as they go from Year 7 to Year 11. What is important is that you understand the difference between the individual support and advice that can be given as a form tutor to an individual pupil and what is appropriate in a planned PSHE lesson to a group of young people. (For more information and advice on this refer to McWhirter et al., 2017.) (The role of the form tutor is covered in Chapter 6.)

How is PSHE education organised and delivered in secondary schools?

There are many ways in which PSHE education can be organised in a secondary school. The organisation and leadership of PSHE education in a school reflects the value that the senior leadership places on PSHE education. Most schools have a named person with responsibility for leading, monitoring and managing PSHE education. Increasingly the title 'PSHE education lead' is being used. In some schools it is a member of the senior leadership team who takes on this role and if this is the case then PSHE education may be at the very heart of the vision for the school. In other schools the status of PSHE is much lower and the PSHE lead has very little influence on the direction of travel in a school. PSHE is a subject area that is vulnerable to high turnover of staff, particularly when there is not a champion for the subject at senior leadership level. One of the difficulties in writing a chapter on preparing beginning teachers for delivering PSHE education is that no other subject is organised in as many ways as PSHE education, however, here we explore the strengths and challenges of the most common models of delivery.

The 4 most common models are:

- teaching PSHE education through tutor time;
- 'drop down days' and outside agencies;
- cross-curricular provision of PSHE education;
- discrete PSHE education.

Teaching PSHE education through tutor time

The chances are that you are not a PSHE education subject specialist and that you have had very little, if any, PSHE training prior to arriving at your first school and yet you find that one of your responsibilities is to deliver the PSHE education curriculum via the form tutor period. Form tutors are usually managed by heads of year, heads of house or learning managers; if this is the case then they should be able to provide you with a programme of study and signpost you to resources. This depends on the structure of individual schools. Most schools provide a programme of study for PSHE education, however, be prepared for it to be called anything from 'personal development', 'life skills', 'health education' and many more. The organisation of tutor groups varies from school to school, some are made up of pupils from the same year group and in others you have an added challenge of a vertical tutor group with a mix of ages from 11 to 16 years old (see Chapter 6). It is unlikely that PSHE is taught in tutor time if the school is organised along a vertical system as pupils are at varying stages of personal development and some subject areas would not be appropriate for both Year 11 pupils and pupils from the younger year groups.

Form tutors can be expected to teach PSHE education as part of the tutorial programme and as a beginning teacher, this may be your first experience of delivering PSHE education. You are unlikely to have had any specialist PSHE subject teacher education and suddenly you are expected to teach the complex subject area of PSHE education. In some schools form tutors are well supported and trained to deliver well-thought-out and well-planned programmes of study. When this is the case, it can work very well as form tutors tend to know their pupils well. In the worst-case scenario, a form tutor is given a schedule of topic areas that need to be covered across the term during tutor time with little or no support or resources; in some cases the PSHE lead ensures that all tutors are given resources and a teaching pack.

You may find yourself in a school where there is a combination of PSHE education specialists working with form tutors. In some schools form tutors are supported with a programme of study and resources to cover the PSHE curriculum for Years 7-9 and the specialists teach Years 10 and 11.

The PSHE education specialists often provide twilight PSHE continuing professional development (CPD) training for form tutors.

All form tutors have some responsibility for personal development of the pupils in their care, irrespective of whether they are being asked to deliver the PSHE education curriculum and this usually comes under the umbrella of 'pastoral care' (see Chapter 6). Many schools also employ additional support workers to provide pastoral care and counselling services to individual pupils. The role of the form tutor is then to signpost individual pupils to appropriate support.

'Drop down days' and outside agencies

Schools organise whole days when the pupils come off the usual planned curriculum of weekly lessons and a whole day/days are blocked out for a focus on PSHE education. These days usually focus on one particular area of PSHE such as 'Relationships' or 'Financial and economic well-being'. These days can involve outside agencies, experts, specialist PSHE teachers, heads of year, heads of house and tutors.

In many schools the PSHE subject lead liaises with external agencies and experts to provide workshops and sessions with pupils. In some schools they operate a 'suspended timetable' or 'drop down days' to enable a focus on PSHE subject areas such as mental health, relationships and consent.

Cross-curricular provision of PSHE

A cross-curricular approach is more likely in the primary school than in the secondary school. There are examples of schools delivering parts of the Relationships and Sex curriculum through English, using key texts such as Shakespeare's *Romeo and Juliet* for example and of Biology teachers incorporating some of the PSHE curriculum into their lessons on reproduction or the effects of drugs. Theoretically, in a whole-school cross-curricular approach PSHE is embedded in all subjects and all teachers would then share the responsibility for meeting the learning objectives and outcomes for not only their main subject, but also for PSHE education as well. This model can seem appealing in the sense that every teacher would share responsibility for the delivery of PSHE education, but in practice this model is very difficult to get right. There is a danger that the PSHE element is lost when teachers are under pressure to cover the exam syllabus for their own subject. For example, a Biology teacher may teach the mechanics of reproduction and the nature of sexually transmitted infections but is less likely to find the time to fully explore the issues of consent or how to negotiate the use of contraception, or where to access sexual health services, when under pressure to cover the science curriculum. This approach to PSHE education can easily slip into being a tokenistic gesture towards PSHE education and a tick box approach to covering what the school identifies as the 'essential elements' of PSHE education. For the pupils, this approach can seem very disjointed and piecemeal, making it difficult for them to build on their learning in a way that makes it possible for them to make sense of it in relation to their own experiences and lives.

Discrete PSHE education lessons

In this model PSHE education is treated the same as any other curriculum subject with PSHE being part of the planned timetable. However, in some schools, PSHE education is merged with Citizenship or Religious Education. In schools where there are timetabled discrete PSHE lessons it is more likely that there is a PSHE subject lead who plans, co-ordinates, monitors and supports the delivery of PSHE curriculum in the school. It is likely that PSHE education enjoys a high status in the school and is valued by teachers and pupils alike. This model lends itself to developing a planned and comprehensive coverage of the PSHE curriculum, allowing the subject lead to ensure that there is continuity between year groups and key stages, progression and adequate differentiation to meet the needs of all pupils. This model allows the PSHE subject lead to organise, collect and collate data to assess progress and ultimately to be able to measure the impact of PSHE education. This model is the ideal; unfortunately, schools are under pressure to squeeze more and more into an already tight curriculum and the current non-statutory status of PSHE education makes it very vulnerable to being pushed off the timetable to allow space for other subjects.

The whole-school approach to PSHE education

The best-case scenario is when, as a beginning teacher, you find yourself in a school that values the contribution PSHE education can make to the education attainment, achievement and well-being of its pupils. In such a school, the very best elements of the models discussed above are present and these are supported by the ethos and culture of the school. There is a whole-school approach to health and well-being that supports the PSHE education curriculum. PSHE is taught in discrete PSHE lessons, by qualified teachers, supported by a planned tutorial programme and enriched by 'drop down days' where specialist agencies share their expertise through workshops and activities with the pupils and teachers. All of this is supported by the 'whole-school approach' to providing the best environment for the pupils and staff to flourish. School policies on anti-bullying support the PSHE curriculum coverage on specific issues such as healthy relationships and cyber-bullying. Staff model the behaviour of health relationships in the way they conduct themselves and the way they communicate and relate to other staff members, parents and pupils. The PSHE curriculum is the 'taught' element and the ethos and culture of the school provides the conditions for the 'caught' part of young people's personal and social learning. As part of a whole-school approach, PSHE education develops the qualities and attributes pupils need to thrive as individuals, family members and members of society (Long, 2017).

If you are fortunate enough to find yourself in such a school where PSHE education is valued and where there is a named PSHE lead, always seek their advice and support, particularly when delivering the more sensitive areas of the PSHE curriculum, such as Relationships and Sex Education (RSE). You should also be aware of relevant school policies and governmental guidance, which may include:

- Safeguarding (Child Protection)
- Anti-bullying – including cyber-bullying
- Equality
- Sex education
- Drug incident
- Healthy eating

Now complete Task 9.3, which asks you to consider how PSHE education is delivered in your school.

 Task 9.3   Reflect on how PSHE education is organised and delivered in your school

- Is PSHE education organised in your school using one or more of the models described above?
- What are the advantages and disadvantages of the model(s) used to deliver PSHE education in your school?
- Is there a named PSHE subject lead? Are they also a member of the senior leadership team?
- Do you feel supported in terms of resources, planning and advice on PSHE education?

Find out whether your school is a member of the PSHE Association. If so, make use of the online support materials. If not, investigate the possibility of joining either as an institution or as an individual.

Record your responses in your PDP and refer back to them as you read through the chapter.

What are the pedagogical principles that underpin effective practice in PSHE education?

To be an effective teacher of PSHE education you need to be both competent and confident in using participative or 'active' teaching to enable your pupils to learn about some of the most sensitive and challenging areas of the curriculum (Shaw in *LTT8*, 2019). PSHE education is perhaps unique in the sense that no other subject works as closely with the real-life, day-to-day experiences of young people. The PSHE Association has produced evidence-based principles of effective practice in PSHE education and these should inform your practice.

PSHE Association ten principles of effective PSHE

The PSHE Association has developed the following evidence-based principles of good practice in PSHE education that apply across Key Stages 1 to 4:

1. Start where children and young people are: find out what they already know, understand, are able to do and are able to say. For maximum impact involve them in the planning of your PSHE education programme.
2. Plan a 'spiral programme' that introduces new and more challenging learning, while building on what has gone before, which reflects and meets the personal developmental needs of the children and young people.
3. Take a positive approach that does not attempt to induce shock or guilt but focuses on what children and young people can do to keep themselves and others healthy and safe and to lead happy and fulfilling lives.
4. Offer a wide variety of teaching and learning styles within PSHE education, with an emphasis on interactive learning and the teacher as facilitator.
5. Provide information which is realistic and relevant, and which reinforces positive social norms.
6. Encourage young people to reflect on their learning and the progress they have made, and to transfer what they have learned to say and to do from one school subject to another, and from school to their lives in the wider community.
7. Recognise that the PSHE education programme is just one part of what a school can do to help a child to develop the knowledge, skills, attitudes and understanding they need to fulfil their potential. Link the PSHE education programme to other whole-school approaches, to pastoral support, and provide a setting where the responsible choice becomes the easy choice. Encourage staff, families and the wider community to get involved.
8. Embed PSHE education within other efforts to ensure children and young people have positive relationships with adults, feel valued and where those who are most vulnerable are identified and supported.
9. Provide opportunities for children and young people to make real decisions about their lives, to take part in activities that simulate adult choices and where they can demonstrate their ability to take responsibility for their decisions.
10. Provide a safe and supportive learning environment where children and young people can develop the confidence to ask questions, challenge the information they are offered, draw on their own experience, express their views and opinions and put what they have learned into practice in their own lives.

In PSHE education you address potentially controversial and sensitive subjects, therefore it is very important that you create and establish a safe and supportive learning environment.

Establishing a safe learning environment

One of the key tools that a teacher can have to support effective PSHE education teaching and learning is the establishment of a safe learning environment. You should not underestimate the importance of establishing a working agreement or ground rules with your pupils. However in the context of PSHE education, perhaps of greater importance is the concept of confidentiality.

Explaining the importance of confidentiality

It is important to be clear with your pupils about the issue of confidentiality and the disclosure of sensitive information. One of the most common ground rules suggested by young people is that 'whatever is said/shared in this room should stay in this room'; whilst there is nothing wrong in the sentiment of this statement, it is important that you are clear that there could be occasions when you would be obliged to share that information (in particular in relation to safeguarding). Therefore you should always follow the school's policies on safeguarding and confidentiality and ensure that pupils understand the policies on disclosure of confidential information and following up concerns in a more appropriate setting outside of lessons if necessary. The PSHE Association provides useful guidance on managing sensitive and controversial issue (PSHE Association, 2012).

Distancing strategies

Establishing clear ground rules alone is not enough. PSHE education by its very nature is 'personal' and you discuss sensitive issues. It is important to remember that PSHE education is a curriculum subject and not a therapeutic intervention. Teachers can signpost to specialist agencies and support within the lesson and make it clear where pupils can seek individual support and resources, e.g. details of an on-site school counsellor; local support groups and national phoneline support and websites from organisations such as Childline, the NSPCC and the Samaritans.

Distancing strategies are useful when teaching some of the more sensitive areas of the PSHE curriculum. To avoid individual pupils feeling uncomfortable it can be useful to 'distance the learning from the learner'. There are various techniques and strategies that you can use to help you to do this:

- using short video clips
- scenarios/case studies
- dialogues

It is also important to provide your pupils with the opportunity to ask anonymous questions, for example, by providing an Anonymous Question Box or an 'Ask it Basket', which should be available before, during and after lessons. Using the box before a lesson on sex and relationships can help you to prepare yourself for the types of questions your pupils may want to explore as well as avoiding the scenario where pupils feel too self-conscious or embarrassed to ask 'that' question. Further, using the box in the lesson before can help you to make the next lesson relevant to your pupils' needs (McWhirter et al., 2017).

PSHE education and internet safety

Growing up in the 21st century poses many challenges and opportunities to children and young people. Issues such as body image, harassment, pornography, exploitation and bullying are intensified by the internet (DCFS, 2008, 2010) (Chapter 17 looks at this in more detail). Schools can play a fundamental role in keeping young people safe online. The government's Green Paper on Internet Safety (HM Government, 2017) and subsequent response (HM Government, 2018), highlighted the opportunities presented by compulsory relationship and sex education from 2020 and PSHE education generally. The paper called for collaboration between the Department for Digital, Culture, Media and Sport (DCMS) and DfE in designing online safety aspects of the new RSE curriculum, working with a range of stakeholders, including young people and parents, to determine subject content, school practice and the quality of delivery. In the meantime there are a wealth of resources already available to support teachers in this area (please refer to Chapter 17 for more information). The PSHE education curriculum has the potential to address online safety and a range of related issues such as safe online relationships, media literacy and online gambling, in a planned and holistic way. New resources are constantly being developed to support teachers in dealing with online safety, some of which are listed here.

PSHE education – flexible approach within a planned framework

PSHE education, just like any other curriculum subject, should be planned and have clear aims, learning objectives and learning outcomes. The PSHE subject lead should oversee this programme. However, as a teacher responsible for delivering parts of the PSHE curriculum you must be prepared for the times when your pupils take you down a different direction than perhaps intended. At times you need to decide whether to let your pupils lead their own learning because where they are taking the class is more valuable or relevant to their needs than the original objective, or whether you need to bring them back on track. Thus, in PSHE education there are times when you are 'leading the learning' but also times when you must be prepared to 'facilitate their learning'. This is why it is so important to start from where your learners are and to try to involve them in all levels of curriculum planning in PSHE education. For a more in-depth study of how to plan the PSHE education curriculum to ensure that it meets the needs of your pupils, refer to *Understanding Personal, Social, Health and Economic Education in Secondary Schools* (McWhirter et al., 2017) and the PSHE Association's website.

Active learning in PSHE education

Teaching and learning in PSHE education is best achieved within a model of Active Learning. McLaughlin and Byers' (2001) 'Active Learning Model' is a good example of how this can be used to support personal/social learning in young people and focuses on four phases (see also Shaw in *LTT8*, 2019). Phase 1 (Do) requires the learner to undertake

Table 9.1 Key considerations around the phases in relation to planning for their inclusion

Phase	Possible strategies
1 - Do	Reading something Looking at something Doing a collaborative exercise Taking part in a debate/discussion
2 - Review	Discussion of activity Application to their own lives/personal reflection Assessment for learning strategies
3 - Learn	Identification of learning achieved Identification of next steps
4 - Apply	Introduction of new contexts (see transferable skills and concepts later in the chapter)

some form of activity. During Phase 2 (Review) they use the feedback to identify and reflect upon what was learned. Phase 3 (Learn) requires the learner to identify what they have learnt and what they may want or need to know in the future. Finally during Phase 4 (Apply) learners are provided opportunities to show how they are transferring this learning into a new context. Table 9.1 identifies some possible activities that can be used to support the planning of each phase, whilst Table 9.2 provides details of more specific strategies that can be used.

Task 9.4 encourages you to reflect upon Tables 9.1 and 9.2 to consider how you might plan for a unit of work. You are advised to seek out the support of your PSHE subject lead and to refer to the resources and planning tools available from the PSHE Association.

Table 9.2 Some examples of specific active learning strategies for the teaching of PSHE

Continuum 1	An imaginary line is drawn down the room. Pupils are told that one end of the line represents one extreme viewpoint, and the other end represents the opposite view. Statements relating to a particular issue are read out, and pupils stand along the continuum according to what they think. Pupils may discuss their view with someone else nearby, and/or with someone who has a different view. If the possibility of polarised views is undesirable or if pupils are less confident, 'islands' rather than a line can be used.
Continuum 2	Put up the signs: 'Agree', 'Not Sure', 'Disagree' on the walls of the classroom. One side is 'Agree', the opposite side is 'Disagree' and the middle of the room is 'Not Sure'. Read out the statements and ask the pupils to stand where they feel most represents their opinion/feeling on the statement. The teacher asks pupils to volunteer to discuss their view with the person next to them, and then asks for volunteers from the different stances to share their views. Pupils can then move positions if the discussion has led them to change their views. This helps pupils to explore different points of view.
Diamond 9	Small groups are given prepared cards (nine or more), each with a statement relating to an issue for discussion, e.g. 'The qualities of a good friend'. Each group arranges the cards in the shape of a diamond to represent their views on the relative importance of each statement.

Table 9.2 continued

Conscience Alley	A technique for exploring any kind of dilemma faced by a character, which provides opportunity to analyse a decisive moment in greater detail. The class or group forms two lines facing each other. One person (the teacher or a participant) walks between the lines as each member of the group speaks their advice. It can be organised so that those on one side give opposing advice to those on the other. When the person reaches the end of the alley, s/he makes her/his decision. Sometimes known as 'Decision Alley' or 'Thought Tunnel'.
Carousel	Half the group forms a circle facing outwards. The other half forms another circle around them, facing inwards. Each person in the inner circle should face someone in the outer circle. Each pair can be asked to talk about an issue or dilemma. Partners can be changed with ease by one or another circle moving round one place.
Snowballing	Pupils work alone for a few minutes, listing ideas related to a task. They then form pairs and share views. The pairs then double up and share their ideas.
Wordstorm	Pupils offer spontaneous suggestions regarding any issue. This is a short, quick activity where suggestions are recorded, but not discussed or challenged. Recorded material can be used later.
Rounds and Turns	All pupils are given the opportunity to express a view or opinion about a particular situation. This works well at the beginning or end of sessions.

✏ Task 9.4   Planning for PSHE education

In one of your units of work plan to use some of the active learning strategies above. Teach the lessons and then evaluate the effectiveness of the approach used and how you might improve it in the future. To what extent did the approach support you and your pupils in meeting the learning outcomes for this lesson/unit of work?

Transferable skills and concepts

The PSHE Association emphasise the importance of focusing on *transferable skills and concepts*, rather than just the knowledge and the 'facts'. Acquiring knowledge and understanding is essential to rational decision-making, however, the way we use this knowledge and understanding is dependent on our own and others' values and beliefs. When we are faced with choices that require us to make decisions, we need strategies, vocabulary and the resilience to help us to act on our decisions.

PSHE education should allow young people the opportunity to think about these 'crunch moments' in life before they experience them in their 'real lives' in a safe and supported environment, and to consider:

■   what they need to know;
■   what they feel;
■   what others may feel;

- what decisions they may choose to make;
- the consequences of those decisions.

These statements are useful as classroom prompts displayed around the teaching area for PSHE lessons.

PSHE education should allow pupils to develop and rehearse the skills and vocabulary they need to 'manage the crunch moments in life'. As a beginning teacher of PSHE education it is useful to recall what it was like to be a young person moving through adolescence. Think about some of the 'crunch moments' in life that can happen in your teenage years. Those times when you could decide on one path or another. To try a cigarette or not; to go on a date without telling anyone who you are meeting or where or to agree to meet this person, but to do so with precautionary measures in place; to have sex; to have 'safe sex' and so on. There are many 'crunch moments' or dilemmas to navigate as an adolescent and young adult, PSHE education can offer young people space to reflect upon these in a safe environment. Task 9.5 provides you with the opportunity to look at how you might embed this in your own teaching.

 Task 9.5   Crunch moment (adapted from the PSHE Association's CPD online programme)

Consider the two scenarios below and reflect on the implications for PSHE education.

Scenario 1

Imagine this scenario:

Fifteen-year-old Ben is at a party. He is with his friends, enjoying himself, when a bag containing some kind of tablets is passed around. Everyone seems to be taking one. The bag comes around to Ben. To Ben it feels as if everyone is waiting to see what he will do.

Think about what Ben would need to manage this situation safely. What would he need to:

- know and understand?
- feel about himself, his values and beliefs and attitudes?
- feel about the values, beliefs and attitudes of his friends and other people important to him?
- be able to say and do?
- understand about his responsibilities?

Reflection

Was it easier to focus on some of these questions more than others? As teachers we often find it easier to focus on factual knowledge; whereas in real-life situations, knowing the facts alone rarely helps us out of tight situations. Ben needs to know certain facts about the 'drugs' being handed round but, perhaps more importantly, he needs to feel confident in managing the situation. How is he going to say 'no', if that is what he wants to do? What strategies could he use? What skills may he need if his friends who have taken the tablets start to feel ill, lose consciousness etc.?

Scenario 2

Ben is now 16 years old. He is at a party with all his friends, including Katy, who he has known since Reception year. They are good friends and Ben really likes Katy. Everything is fine until she makes unwanted sexual advances to him, which make him feel uncomfortable ...

Reflection

Ask yourself the same questions as you did for Scenario 1.

Although the knowledge and understanding might be different, many of the values, beliefs and skills Ben would need would be similar in both scenarios. In both scenarios Ben would need to have personal attributes such as self-confidence to help him navigate through these 'crunch moments'. These are the transferable skills and concepts we need to help us manage life. The PSHE provision in your school should aim to offer pupils a range of opportunities to rehearse the skills and strategies that they would use when dealing with those 'crunch moments' in life.

Possible 'crunch moments' that could be part of the planned PSHE curriculum:

■ Whether to use contraception or not?
■ What information to share online?
■ Whether to drink alcohol/take a substance or not?
■ Whether to meet the person you have met online or not?
■ Whether to borrow money or not?

You could use the different scenarios to encourage pupils to think about the knowledge, skills and attitudes that they would need to manage each situation.

Store this information in your PDP for future use.

PSHE education can be approached with trepidation by beginning teachers and it should not be. If you spend time learning more about PSHE education and the pedagogy behind it, you will reap the benefits not only in your PSHE lessons but in everything you teach. The active learning strategies are usefully adapted to suit many other curriculum subjects and the higher communication skills that PSHE education helps to develop in your pupils equip them to be better all-round students and communicators for life. Likewise the active learning strategies you are using to teach your own curriculum subjects could be adapted for use in teaching PSHE education.

SUMMARY AND KEY POINTS

This chapter has introduced you to PSHE education and signposted you to further information and support.

- PSHE education contributes to the health and well-being of pupils but also improves academic attainment.
- PSHE education should be a *planned programme* of learning that starts from where your pupils are. PSHE education lessons should be planned, with clear learning objectives and learning outcomes, just as for your own curriculum subject.
- Your PSHE education programme should be a *spiral programme* that builds on prior knowledge, understanding and skills whilst introducing new and more challenging learning in an age-appropriate way.
- PSHE education deals with sensitive and controversial issues so establishing a safe learning environment is essential. A *safe learning climate* is of paramount importance and your pupils need to be involved in making clear ground rules for learning in PSHE education.
- Avoid 'worksheet' PSHE education and use a wide range of teaching and learning styles with an emphasis on *interactive learning*.
- Focus on *transferable skills and concepts* rather than knowledge. Encourage pupils to reflect on their learning and to transfer what they have learned in one scenario to another. Encourage your pupils to use the skills and strategies they have learned in PSHE education in other subject areas.
- PSHE education is not just taught in PSHE education lessons. PSHE education should be part of a *whole-school approach* and linked to whole-school policies such as Safeguarding and Anti-bullying.
- Find out who the PSHE subject lead is in your school. If unsure about any topic area within the PSHE education scheme of work seek advice and support.
- Take responsibility for your own PSHE CPD; join professional bodies such as the *PSHE Association*.

Record in your PDP, how the information in this chapter enables you to meet the requirements for your first year of teaching.

 Further resources

Coleman, J.C. (2011) *The Nature of Adolescence*, 4th edn, Abingdon: Routledge.
   This book provides an up-to-date introduction to the key features of adolescent development. It draws mainly on the North American literature on adolescence, however it does highlight European and British perspectives. Coleman places a particular emphasis on a positive view of adolescence.

McWhirter, J., Boddington, N. and Barksfield, J. (2017) *Understanding Personal, Social, Health and Economic Education in Secondary Schools*, London: Sage.
   This is essential reading for anyone teaching PSHE in a secondary setting. It is particularly useful to a beginning teacher. This book is invaluable for any teacher who wants to improve their practice and deepen their understanding of the theory underpinning best practice in

PSHE teaching and learning. Written by experts in the field of PSHE education, this is a 'must read' for any teacher who is serious about teaching effective PSHE education.

Scriven, A. (2010) *Promoting Health – A Practical Guide*, **6th edn, London: Baillière Tindall (also available as an e-book).**

A useful book for beginning teachers who are interested in improving their understanding of health and well-being and the role of health promotion generally. This is a seminal text that has been used in the training and education of health promoters over the last 25 years and has shaped health promotion practice in the UK. It provides an accessible practical guide for all those involved in health promotion. Part 1, chapter 1 is particularly useful in exploring the ideas of what is health and what is health promotion. Schools are identified as key settings for health education and health promotion.

Other resources and websites

www.pshe-association.org.uk – PSHE Association

www.pshe-association.org.uk/curriculum-and-resources/resources/programme-study-pshe-education-key-stages-1%E2%80%935 – Programme of Study for PSHE Key Stages 1–5 (accessed 25 October 2018).

www.sexeducationforum.org.uk – Sex education forum.

Useful resources for internet safety and related subject areas (body image, pornography)

■   **www.childnet.com/resources/pshe-toolkit/crossing-the-line** – 'Crossing the line' online safety PSHE tool kit. This supports young people to reflect on their online behaviour whilst also equipping them with the knowledge of how to respond to online safety issues, report any concerns and make positive decisions (PSHE Association, 2016 Quality Assured resource). This toolkit covers issues such as cyberbullying, sexting, peer pressure and self-esteem. This is toolkit is free to download from the Childnet website.

■   **https://assets.publishing.service.gov.uk/government/uploads/system/uploads/attachment_data/file/683895/Education_for_a_connected_world_PDF.PDF** – UK Council for Child Internet Safety (UKCCIS), CEOP, the NSPCC and Barnado's *Education for a Connected World framework (and online)* supports PSHE education teachers to review their curriculum to ensure that young people are prepared to understand and handle online risks. This framework is free to download.

■   **www.dove.com/uk/dove-self-esteem-project/school-workshops-on-body-image-confident-me/self-esteem-school-resources-confident-me-five-sessions.html** – Dove Self-esteem Project Teaching Pack. This free-to-download Key Stage 3 teaching pack explores body image and how personal identity and self-esteem are influenced by the media.

■   **www.pshe-association.org.uk/curriculum-and-resources/resources/frequently-asked-questions-pornography-and-sharing** – PSHE Association's Frequently Asked Questions on Pornography and Sharing Sexual Images in PSHE education.

■   **www.pshe-association.org.uk** – the PSHE Association offers CPD training days on Online Safety for all key stages.

Appendices 2 and 3 list subject associations, teaching councils and relevant websites.

Books in the *Learning to Teach* series that you may find helpful are as follows:

Capel, S., Leask, M. and Younie, S. (eds.) (2019) *Learning to Teach in the Secondary School: A Companion to School Experience*, **8th edn, Abingdon: Routledge.**

This book is designed as a core textbook to support student teachers through their initial teacher education programme.

Capel, S., Leask, M. and Turner, T. (eds.) (2010) *Readings for Learning to Teach in the Secondary School: A Companion to M Level Study*, **Abingdon: Routledge.**

This book brings together essential readings to support you in your critical engagement with key issues raised in this textbook.

The subject-specific books in the *Learning to Teach* series, the *Practical (subject) Guides*, *Debates in (subject)* and *Mentoring (subject) Teachers* are also very useful.

10 Becoming an inclusive educator

Developing your practice as a mainstream teacher of pupils with special educational needs and disabilities (SEND)

Mark Pulsford and Sana Rizvi

Introduction

There is increasing diversification in the ways schools are governed and in how teachers are educated in England, and these developments can be seen to have an effect on the provision available for pupils with 'special' and additional needs in mainstream schools. Where once it was the case that Local Authorities had an overview of services for these pupils, offering local schools access to centralised services, now the terrain is much more varied and market-orientated with schools having increased autonomy and responsibility for buying in services from both public and private bodies. There is an onus on head teachers, school managers and special educational needs coordinators (SENCos) to be savvy consumers and stretch their budgets at a time of rising costs – this can be an agonising matter, deciding to adequately support those relatively few pupils who have the most need, or choosing to suitably resource the wider 'mainstream' or 'typical' pupil body. This tension extends to the pressures on schools to perform well in 'high-stakes' tests; schools may feel acute challenges in ensuring meaningful and authentic inclusion for pupils who require more time and resources to achieve the best exam grades (Liasidou, 2012; Glazzard, 2013; Ainscow et al., 2016a; 2016b).

OBJECTIVES

At the end of this chapter you should be able to:

- Describe the historical and contemporary political developments that shape special educational needs and disability (SEND) provision;
- Discuss ideas for classroom practice, organised around the four recognised areas of SEND;

■ Reflect on how you might develop inclusive practice though a focus on pedagogy: your personal-professional values and your teaching materials and activities.

Check how the information in this chapter enables you to meet the requirements for your first year of teaching.

Building your knowledge base

There has been a diversification of the Initial Teacher Education (ITE) field in recent years (Jackson and Burch, 2016), resulting in more small-scale providers and an increase of shorter ITE courses, ranging from weeks or months rather than the three- or four-year undergraduate programmes that were once most common. It is therefore important to consider the inevitably varied experiences and knowledge of SEND that newly qualified teachers bring with them to their first jobs. How and where you undertook your ITE could be quite different to your colleagues; maybe you feel quite confident in some facets of your new role, but unsure about others. Research and government reviews agree that special educational needs and inclusion have not been prominent in ITE programmes in Britain (Mintz and Wyse, 2015; Wedell, 2008; Carter, 2015; Department for Children, Schools and Families (DCSF), 2010) – perhaps this describes your experience? This gap in preparation is important because, unsurprisingly, there tends to be a relationship between the amount of input teachers have had in this area and how successful they feel they can be as inclusive practitioners (Avramidis and Norwich, 2002; de Boer et al., 2010; Lechtenberger et al., 2012; Lindsay et al., 2013; Zagona, Kurth and MacFarland, 2017).

In Task 10.1 you are asked to review your current knowledge and to identify in-school support so that you can plan your personal professional development in SEND.

 Task 10.1   Review your current knowledge and identify in-school support

With one or two beginning teacher colleagues, discuss your experiences of SEND during your ITE programme. What did you learn from your teaching placements? What input did you receive during classroom-based ITE sessions? What are the similarities and differences between your experiences? What knowledge do you have and what knowledge do you need to support your SEND pupils? What seems to be relevant to the school that you are now teaching in and to the pupils you are teaching?

Meet with those responsible for SEND in your school and find out what systems operate to support you and your pupils.

Record the outcomes in your professional development portfolio (PDP) (or similar) for use when planning lessons and when you are asked about your professional development needs.

Against a backdrop of interlocking challenges – diversifying school governance structures, squeezed school budgets, marketisation of SEND provision, accountability regimes based on exam results, varied ITE routes and providers, and relatively unsubstantial training in SEND – this chapter seeks to offer some affirmative avenues via which you might develop as an inclusive educator. There is a need to be critically aware of the historical and contemporary political developments that impact on schooling and SEND provision, but we also want to encourage a sense that despite limited school budgets and even with limited experience or knowledge, you can work decisively towards inclusion through focusing on what you have most control over, and that is pedagogy: your personal-professional values, your teaching materials and activities, and your classroom ethos. As Thomas and Loxley (2007, p. 27) assert:

> Children who are slower to learn – for whatever reason – need the same in order to learn as any other child. They need the kinds of things which our humanity tells us they need: interest, confidence, freedom from worry, a warm and patient teacher.

The development of 'SEND' in the UK

Comprehensively exploring how 'special educational needs' (SEN) as a concept, a policy term and as a set of practices has developed within the UK education context is challenging in a short chapter. You are therefore encouraged to review Peacey's description (in *LTT8*, 2019) of the key legislation as this outlines how SEND has been framed within official government policies over time, and the evolution of SEND support for pupils in the UK. Below is a brief summary of the landmark developments in the last 25 years, with a focus on the most recent changes in England and Wales. As such, this section provides a general overview of developments and you are advised to consult the relevant legislation in your own area.

The 1993 Education Act in England and Wales (gov.uk, 1993) placed full responsibility on Local Authorities to coordinate SEN provision regardless of the type of school pupils attended. This Act led to the introduction of the first SEN Code of Practice (CoP) (Department for Education (DfE), 1994), a key document that has been revised and updated several times in the subsequent years. The first CoP outlined five stages in identifying and assessing pupils with SEN as well as introducing the role of the SENCo in facilitating this. Around this time, United Nations Education, Scientific and Cultural Organisation (UNESCO) released its Salamanca Statement (1994). This influential agreement, supported by 92 countries, stated that pupils with SEN must have access to mainstream schools, and that mainstream and special schools need to have a broader role in working collaboratively to support pupils with SEN.

The latest CoP (DfE and Department of Health (DOH), 2015) replaced previous codes in England and is viewed as a vital new framework for all educational providers (those under the control of Local Authorities as well as those in private, independent and voluntary sectors). The 2015 CoP replaced the graduated levels of support known as 'School Action' and 'School Action Plus' with a general 'SEN Support' category for pupils, and introduced an 'Assess, Plan, Do, Review' cycle for practitioners to follow in implementing this, a process that teachers should work on with their school's SENCo.

Tutt and Williams (2015) suggest this latest CoP represents a cultural shift because for the first time children, young people and parents are more able to see themselves as at the centre of the SEND system. The increased age range for support, from birth to 25 years old, aims to help families feel more confident of a smooth transition at various stages of their child's educational life, and by replacing 'Statements of Special Need' with 'Education, Health and Care' (EHC) Plans it is intended that professionals from relevant sectors work together to provide holistic assessment and provision for pupils with SEND. The CoP also enables families to have more control over the type of support they want by offering them a 'personal budget', and necessitating that providers (including schools) make clear their 'local offer' so families can pick from these SEN shop windows.

As of July 2017, there are approximately 1.2 million pupils in the UK with an identified SEND (DfE, 2017a). In state-funded secondary schools in England alone there are almost 54,000 pupils with Education, Health and Care (EHC) Plans, and a further 345,000 pupils receiving SEN Support (DfE, 2017a). Reflecting the stringencies of recent education funding, the percentage of state-funded secondary school pupils in England identified as having a SEN *and who have a Statement of Special Need/EHC Plan* fell from 28.28% to 22.2% between 2010 and 2017 (DfE, 2017a). Notwithstanding other factors influencing this decline, the figures suggest that there are now more likely to be pupils in secondary schools with a need for specific additional support beyond that which the school can customarily offer, yet without access to dedicated additional funds to provide this.

Definitions and areas of SEND

As a beginning teacher you need to make sure that you have a good understanding of the wide range of areas of SEND. The latest CoP in England retains the definition of SEN from its former versions. It is considered that:

> A child of compulsory school age or a young person has a learning difficulty or disability if he or she has a significantly greater difficulty in learning than the majority of others of the same age, or has a disability which prevents or hinders him or her from making use of facilities of a kind generally provided for others of the same age in mainstream schools or mainstream post-16 institutions ...
> *(DfE and DoH, 2015, pp.14-15)*

The framework in Scotland, 'Supporting Children's Learning Code of Practice' (Scottish Government 2010), uses the term 'Additional Support' rather than SEN.

The SEND CoP for England also provides guidelines for pupils with disability, defining it as:

> a physical or mental impairment which has a long-term and substantial adverse effect on their ability to carry out normal day-to-day activities. ... This definition includes sensory impairments such as those affecting sight or hearing, and long-term health conditions such as asthma, diabetes, epilepsy, and cancer ... Where a

disabled child or young person requires special educational provision they will also be covered by the SEN definition.

(DfE and DoH, 2015, pp. 14-15)

All educational providers have a legal duty to prevent the discrimination of pupils with disabilities, not only in terms of their admissions to mainstream schools but also in the provisions set out for them, with the aim being to ensure they are not treated less favourably than their peers.

It is important to note here that the guidelines outlined in all the CoPs across the UK are not in place to compensate for the absence of good teaching (Wearmouth, 2017) - all pupils, regardless of need, have a right to be taught in ways that support, stretch and inspire them. To emphasise this point, in Table 10.1 there are some descriptors used in different parts of Britain as minimum standards for entry into, and successful progression within, the teaching profession - some of this text is likely to be very familiar

Table 10.1 Examples of standards of practice in SEND for teachers in England and Scotland

All teachers need to adapt teaching to respond to the strengths and needs of all pupils:
■ Know when and how to differentiate appropriately, using approaches that enable pupils to be taught effectively.
■ Have a secure understanding of how a range of factors can inhibit pupils' ability to learn, and how best to overcome these.
■ Demonstrate an awareness of the physical, social and intellectual development of children, and know how to adapt teaching to support pupils' education at different stages of development.
■ Have a clear understanding of the needs of all pupils, including those with special educational needs; those of high ability; those with English as an additional language; those with disabilities; and be able to use and evaluate distinctive teaching approaches to engage and support them.
This excerpt is from the Teacher's Standards (DfE, 2011).
Teaching and learning:
■ Plan coherent, progressive and stimulating teaching programmes that match learners' needs and abilities.
■ Communicate effectively and interact productively with learners, individually and collectively.
■ Employ a range of teaching strategies and resources to meet the needs and abilities of learners.
■ Have high expectations of all learners.
■ Work effectively in partnership in order to promote learning and well-being.
This excerpt is from the Standards for Registration, General Teaching Council for Scotland (GTCS, n.d.).

to you by now as a qualified teacher recently graduated from an ITE programme! These particular excerpts refer to the expectations of teachers in relation to the range of needs that pupils may have. You'll note that there is no opt out here – all class teachers have a responsibility to know and understand about learning differences and be able to adapt their teaching appropriately.

The four areas of SEND

It is important that you, as a teacher, have an understanding of the four areas of SEND outlined in the current CoP (DfE and DoH, 2015). These are:

■   Communication and interaction
■   Cognition and learning
■   Social, emotional and mental health
■   Sensory and/or physical needs

Developing your understanding of these areas, however, should be accompanied by an awareness that identifying SENDs is far from straightforward and that the associated 'labelling' of pupils – although a crucial mechanism by which specialist support is secured – may have a detrimental impact on their educational experience (Caslin, 2014).

Once discussion turns to defining particular SENDs and how to support these categories of learners in appropriate ways, the terrain can become challenging. The four areas of need are not fixed and can, of course, overlap. Importantly, no two pupils either with SEND or without have the same set of abilities, learning preferences and developmental trajectory. We must therefore recognise, celebrate and support their individuality even though we may begin by understanding their needs in relatively general terms. Furthermore, it is important to consider these pupils as capable of significant progress and achievement, and that this is not limited because they are identified as having 'special educational needs'.

Below we outline the four areas of SEND and provide some techniques and practical advice for teaching pupils with some of the most prevalent SENDs (such as language impairment, dyslexia, Autism and ADHD). Such advice represents 'quality first' teaching – the basics of effective, inclusive classroom practice that does not require any particular specialist intervention, and as such it could be described as 'inclusive pedagogy' (Liasidou, 2012; see also Baglieri and Shapiro, 2017). As you read the following sections, imagine your actual pupils, lessons and topics, and think about how you could adopt and adapt the advice provided here (this will then lead you in to Task 10.2).

Communication and interaction

Communication is not just essential to facilitate learning but also to ensure pupils have positive relationships with their peers and teachers at school. Pupils who require support with communication and interaction may have language impairments, dyslexia, dyspraxia or speech and language delay. Communication also includes body language, gestures, facial expressions and eye contact (Wearmouth, 2017). These pupils could have a hearing impairment or be on the autistic spectrum. Pupils who have difficulties arising solely from English as an Additional Language (EAL) do not have SEND, however they may benefit from extra support often associated with communication-based SEND provision. Pupils with language impairment (See Table 10.2) have difficulties in either the receptive aspect (which includes understanding what is spoken and/or written), or expressive aspect (expressing their thoughts in either oral or written form); identifying receptive language impairment is more difficult. Pupils can have varying levels of difficulty in this area from mild to moderate to severe.

Some of these pupils may have dyslexia, which is a difficulty affecting the development of appropriate literacy and language-related skills. Traditional didactic and fast-paced teaching methods are less suitable for pupils with dyslexia because these pupils tend to have relatively more difficulties with phonological processing, processing speed, rapid naming, organisation and working memory (the part of our memory that allows us to transfer information correctly). See Table 10.3.

Table 10.2 Pedagogies for pupils with language impairments

Peacey (2019, p. 283) provides some useful pedagogical advice for teachers when working with pupils with language impairments:

- Regularly check understanding.
- Use visual aids and cues to the topics being discussed.
- Ensure the pupil is appropriately placed to hear and see.
- Explain something several different ways [to ensure you are understood].
- Repeat what pupils say in discussion or question and answer sessions.
- Allow time for pupils to respond in question and answer sessions and, if necessary, ensure they are pre-prepared for responding, perhaps by a TA.

You will notice that this advice essentially describes good teaching for all pupils; this is an important point for you to take away from this chapter.
For more educational resources, visit www.communication4all.co.uk and www.ican.org.uk

---

Table 10.3 Pedagogies for pupils with Dyslexia

Wearmouth (2017) suggests that any techniques that enhance a pupil's phonological awareness and memory, such as rhyming games and mnemonics, may prove useful. You may consider encouraging pupils with dyslexia:

- to listen to audiobooks or lesson recordings whilst they read and review text or notes;
- to record their own thoughts onto a digital recorder or use mind maps, so that the organisational and technical aspects of writing can be distinguished from the conceptual aspect;
- to use coloured filters on top of white paper (apps are available for computer screens), which help the words appear more clearly. You can also print handouts onto coloured paper and avoid asking pupils to read closely spaced chunks of text;
- to use lesson outlines, frames or key point prompts to help them take notes – these will also, of course, help all learners in your classes.

For further information and resources on dyslexia, you can refer to the British Dyslexia Association's website (www.bdadyslexia.org.uk/educator) and the Dyslexia MESHGuide (http://meshagain.meshguides.org).

Cognition and learning

Pupils in your classes may:

> learn at a slower pace than their peers, even with appropriate differentiation. Learning difficulties cover a wide range of needs, including moderate learning difficulties (MLD), severe learning difficulties (SLD), where children are likely to need support in all areas of the curriculum and associated difficulties with mobility and communication, through to profound and multiple learning difficulties (PMLD), where children are likely to have severe and complex learning difficulties as well as a physical disability or sensory impairment.
>
> *(DfE and DoH, 2015, pp. 97–98)*

Pupils with learning difficulties do not require a different *style* of teaching, however you need to ensure that their objectives and tasks are set at appropriate levels. Some education professionals recommend ideas such as using Makaton (a form of sign-language) and Numicon (shapes for numeracy activities), and incorporating structured images, symbols and multi-sensory approaches in teaching, learning and assessment activities that work to pupils' strengths; the Huddersfield Down's Syndrome Support Group (www.hdssg.org/education-2/resources/) has some excellent resources for teachers.

Pupils with learning difficulties may also be on the autistic spectrum (see Table 10.4). In England, around a quarter of Statements/EHC Plans are currently associated with pupils that have such needs (DfE, 2017a), making autism the most prevalent SEN in these terms. Pupils with autistic spectrum disorder (ASD) require support primarily in three areas: social interaction and social relationships, verbal and nonverbal social communication, and social imagination. These pupils may have difficulty in recognising social cues, the concept of danger, how their peers and others around them are feeling, or the meaning of gestures or implicit rules. They may also find changing routines difficult and experience sensory overload.

Table 10.4 Pedagogies for pupils on the Autistic Spectrum

As a teacher you can work to remove some of the barriers that classrooms can present to pupils with Autistic Spectrum Disorder (ASD) by:

■ providing the pupils with clear instructions, and consider using visual timetables;

■ having fixed lesson routines and procedures;

■ reducing any visual and sensory clutter;

■ using social stories (Gray, 2000);

■ providing a buddy system that allows the pupils to engage with their peers one-at-a-time, and developing social interactions skills.

The National Autistic Society (www.autism.org.uk/), and the Secondary Teacher's Toolkit from Wiltshire County Council (www.wiltshire.gov.uk/secondary-scd-toolkit-photocopy-version.pdf) among others, offer additional resources for teachers.

Social, emotional and mental health

There remains considerable stigma attached to mental health issues, despite mounting calls and campaigns to draw public attention to this area, such as the 'Where's Your Head At?', (www.wheresyourheadat.org) and 'Heads Together' (www.headstogether.org. uk) campaigns. Such stigma can often result in pupils with Social, Emotional and Mental Health difficulties (SEMH) being initially viewed as troublesome rather than understood as struggling with an identifiable condition. Therefore how their behaviour is interpreted and the interventions/support put in place is often deeply contested (Poulou and Norwich, 2000). Pupils with SEMH may be

> withdrawn or isolated, as well as displaying challenging, disruptive or disturbing behaviour. These behaviours may reflect underlying mental health difficulties such as anxiety or depression, self-harming, substance misuse, eating disorders or physical symptoms that are medically unexplained. Other children and young people may have disorders such as attention deficit disorder, attention deficit hyperactive disorder or attachment disorder.
>
> *(DfE and DoH, 2015, p. 98)*

The contemporary period seems to be one in which mental ill-health is on the rise (Thorley, 2016; LKMCo, 2018). Pupils with SEND are particularly at risk here, as they are more likely to experience physical or non-physical bullying (Chatzitheochari et al., 2014), and according to the DfE one in five pupils with SEND report being unhappy at their secondary school (DfE, 2017a). It is vital that your classrooms offer a safe and nurturing space for your pupils to raise and discuss their concerns. In some cases it may become necessary to warrant a referral to a local Child and Mental Health Service (CAMHS), especially if there is risk of self-harm or harm to others, and this is something your SENCo can support you with.

You may already have some awareness of Attention Deficit Hyperactivity Disorder (ADHD). Pupils with ADHD can be restless or fidgety during classes, may seem easily distracted and can struggle to concentrate during lessons (see Table 10.5). Pupils with

Table 10.5 Pedagogies for pupils with Attention Deficit Hyperactivity Disorder (ADHD)

As a teacher, you can support pupils with ADHD in your class by:

- ensuring the pace of tasks in lessons is appropriate for them;
- checking they understand what you have taught/the learning task you have set;
- aiding pupils' note-taking/task orientation with lesson outlines, frames or key point prompts;
- encouraging pupils to maintain personal mood diaries;
- offering a designated space in school as a retreat, if the pupil needs to temporarily leave a lesson;
- rewarding their completion of tasks.

For more resources for ADHD you can refer to www.additudemag.com/adhd-school-checklists-forms-letters/, and for a more comprehensive toolkit for supporting pupils' SEMH needs see the Anna Freud National Centre for Children and Families' resources for schools and colleges (www.annafreud.org/what-we-do/schools-in-mind/resources-for-schools/).

ADHD are often prescribed medication in accordance with the National Institute for Health and Care Excellence (NICE) guidelines, though this is a contested area (Moore et al., 2016; Ohan et al., 2011). There remains a view in some quarters that ADHD stems from poor parenting (Hinshaw, 1994), and that interventions are required to address both the parents' and child's deficiencies (Eiraldi et al., 2006). This is a prime example, though not an uncommon one in the field of SEN, where knowing the 'causes' and identifying the appropriate support for pupils are far from straightforward – as you navigate this terrain you should be aware that differing views circulate around your teaching and pastoral support of these pupils, and such contestation requires you to have reflected upon and examined your own attitudes, educational values and practices (see Task 10.3). Remember, you can always talk to your SENCo about any of your learners to gain support and further insight about SEND issues.

Sensory and/or physical needs

The 2015 CoP suggests that pupils with sensory and/or physical needs:

> have a disability which prevents or hinders them from making use of the educational facilities generally provided. These difficulties can be age related and may fluctuate over time. Many children and young people with vision impairment (VI), hearing impairment or a multi-sensory impairment (MSI) will require specialist support and/or equipment to access their learning, or habilitation support.
>
> *(DfE and DoH, 2015, p. 98)*

Pupils with hearing impairment can experience levels of difficulty ranging from mild, moderate, severe or profound, and may be late in starting to talk. They may also have poor language processing skills, difficulty in reading, spelling, comprehension and mathematics (Wearmouth, 2017). Many pupils with such an impairment wear hearing aids or have cochlear implants. However, as teachers you can also use radio aids (microphone and receiver) that help pupils hear your voice more clearly in class, and/or seek the support of specialist TAs who are trained in using British Sign Language and auditory-oral approaches; these can ensure pupils are learning and accessing the curriculum in the most effective way. See the four MESHGuides on Deaf Education pedagogies (http://meshagain.meshguides.org).

There are also varying degrees of visual impairment, and your school's SENCo is able to help you assess what level of support pupils need in class. Pupils with visual impairment often learn by relying on observation and copying their peers' actions, but they could require specialist codes such as Braille to help them access the curriculum. Again, you need to check they understand the lessons properly and provide them with flexible ways of accessing learning material, and ensure that where they are seated in the classroom maximises their opportunities to engage in class.

Now undertake Task 10.2 to consider some of these pedagogic strategies in relation to your learners.

Task 10.2   Plan support for one or more of your pupils

Having read the above sections, choose one of the four areas of SEND. Using the pedagogic strategies suggested, develop a subject-related plan of action for one pupil or a group of pupils you teach who have that particular set of needs. Plan what you could do in lessons next week to further support their learning.

Here you may find it useful to refer to the subject-specific chapters in Carpenter et al.'s (2017) edited collection *Enabling Access: Effective Teaching and Learning for Pupils with Learning Difficulties* and Bates' (2017) *A Quick Guide to Special Educational Needs and Disabilities.*

As you do this, it may be useful to incorporate the **Assess, Plan, Do, Review** cycle:

■ To begin with, what relevant **assessment** information (about pupil need or prior attainment) do you have?
■ Ensure that your **plan** addresses the conclusions drawn from those assessments.
■ Know what you are going to **do** precisely and then put this into practice.
■ Consider what information you will **review** afterwards to know if your plans and actions have been successful.
■ Then begin the cycle afresh.

Record the outcomes in your PDP for use when planning lessons.

The models of disability

Whilst it is heartening to note the progress made in terms of understanding and addressing pupils' varied educational needs, and ensuring that they have greater choice and control over their educational outcomes, many researchers maintain that the definition of SEND continues to be deficit-based (e.g. Trussler and Robinson, 2015; Slee, 2010; Thomas and Loxley, 2007). As early career education professionals, it is essential you understand how your own and others' belief systems affect how you work with pupils. Although there are many ways of thinking about this, we outline the most common 'models' for understanding SEND, which have shaped much of the discourse in this area in Table 10.6.

A third, more recent, view is the 'interactionist model of disability'. This suggests that disabling experiences for pupils are a result of the *interaction between* impairments (actual cognitive, behavioural, sensory or physical difficulties) and external structural and attitudinal barriers as emphasised by the 'social model'. The 'interactionist model of disability' helps us to understand that disabling experiences are different for each pupil and that they are contextual (Shakespeare, 2008). Therefore teachers require an understanding of a pupil's impairment *as well as* a firm sense that the 'norms' of social and school life are understood and organised in ways that produce what appears to be a deficiency – a '*special* need' or '*dis*-ability' – on the part of these pupils.

Table 10.6 The 'medical model' and the 'social model' for understanding SEND

Medical model	Social model
The 'medical/deficit model of disability' views any difficulty/disability that a pupil with SEND experiences as stemming from the pupil themselves. The focus of interventions is the pupils' impairment and their medical condition, as opposed to the environment in which they are situated. This view largely prevailed at the time of the UK Education Act of 1944, which categorised children and determined whether they were 'fit' to be educated.	The 'social model of disability' sees disabling barriers in the environment as preventing people from fully participating in various aspects of social life (Barnes, 2012; Oliver, 1996). The 'social model of disability' challenges what are now commonly termed 'able-ist' structures and attitudes within society, which privilege those classified as 'typical' and disadvantage those who are different. It is the social view that is currently prevalent and encouraged as the viewpoint for all education professionals, in order to address the goals of inclusion and social justice. However, it is clear that the 'medical model' retains significant influence on both public and professional attitudes.

Understanding self and others

Dominant discourses about SEND underpin our perspectives and practices as educators. It is therefore essential that we examine how our commonplace understandings of SEND and some school practices can be oppressive. As Sameshima argues:

> The teaching profession is dramatically strengthened when teachers understand who they are, know how their experiences have shaped their ideologies, and find and acknowledge their place of contribution in the broader context of the educational setting.
>
> *(2008, p. 34)*

However, there is a limited amount of research on the personal-professional dimension of teachers' work in SEND and inclusion within mainstream schools, where policy and procedure tend to dominate the agenda (Pulsford, 2019; Sakellariadis, 2007). Yet teachers' contextual and dialogic (shaped in relation to others') self-understandings are undoubtedly relevant to the ways policies are enacted in practice.

To address this, we want to introduce you to the 'triad of understanding' (see Task 10.3), which was developed as part of a research collaboration involving people with Asperger's syndrome discussing how service providers (e.g. social workers) could best understand and develop services for them (Robinson, 2017, 2015). However, this triad also has potential as a reflective tool for use *by practitioners themselves*, as it invites a set of critical questions that promotes a form of self-understanding directly tied with the perceptions and needs of others. For teachers, we suggest that this tool could be a particularly effective way of positioning oneself within the ongoing, intra- and inter-personal process of including pupils with SEND in mainstream schools.

M

 Task 10.3   Using the 'triad of understanding'

Using the 'triad of understanding' below, privately and honestly reflect on the following questions:

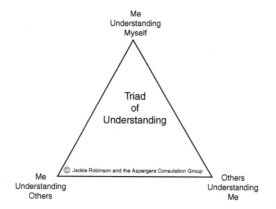

- *'Me understanding myself'*: How do I feel about people with learning difficulties and disabilities? Where does that feeling come from? What experiences or people have shaped this view? Do my own abilities and disabilities play a part here? Do my religious or political beliefs have an influence? Do I feel apprehensive, stressed, indifferent, enthusiastic, passionate (or something else) about teaching such pupils? What are my assumptions about their barriers to learning? How might this all effect how I teach?

- *'Others understanding me'*: What information do I want pupils and colleagues to know about me? How do I appear to pupils, in particular those with SEND? What would pupils say were my main priorities as a teacher? How do my actions and interactions influence how I am perceived in my classroom and around my department/school? Does this image reflect who I believe to be the 'authentic' or 'real' me, as a teacher and as a person? Is this OK?

- *'Me understanding others'*: What tends to be the view of inclusion of pupils with SEND in my school or department? Is there agreement amongst staff on this? Is there an inclusive 'ethos'? How do senior leaders engage with these debates and these pupils? How do my colleagues seem to see my role in relation to inclusion? Are there clear procedures and support structures for teachers in this area? Do I feel confident of receiving appropriate support if I ask for it? What sorts of things do I already know about my pupils' needs, and what insights do I feel I lack?

- Consider the consequences of these reflections. What conclusions can you draw and what actions present themselves? Consider what you could work on in your own teaching and start to think about what sorts of change might be needed in your school overall. Record the outcomes for use when planning lessons.

Discuss this information with your mentor (or another colleague) and store the information in your PDP to refer to later.

This leads us towards a sense that by thinking about pupils with SEND in our classes and schools, we are addressing something more than the minimum requirement that our instructional practices should meet all learners' needs. Inclusion means reflecting on who we are in relation to others; it means examining how and why we perceive 'the average pupil', 'normal progress' and 'mainstream schools' in the ways we do (Goodley and Runswick-Cole, 2016).

Developing a community of inclusive practice

The term 'inclusion' remains elusive, with multiple meanings, and it can be made to work in different ways depending on those who wield it. Norwich (2013) suggests that inclusion has typically been used to imply the physical placement of pupils with SEND into mainstream schools, however this is only the locational aspect of inclusion. We strongly view inclusion as an ongoing process, a language, and a set of beliefs and practices, which enables participation and learning for all pupils; a way of thinking and acting that 'subverts exclusionary social conditions and disabling educational practices' (Liasidou, 2012, p. 9). The Centre for Studies on Inclusive Education provides a useful definition:

> Inclusion is about making schools supportive and stimulating places for staff as well as students. It is about building communities which encourage and celebrate their achievements. But inclusion is also about building community more widely. Schools can work with other agencies and with communities to improve educational opportunities and social conditions within their localities.
>
> *(Booth et al., 2002, p. 4)*

This definition helps us conceptualise inclusion beyond classrooms and to see it as a means of challenging inequality, and celebrating diversity and difference. To an extent, it enables teachers to engage with their pupils in more enriching ways than through the reductive categorisations of the four areas of SEND discussed above. It also helps to situate you as part of a community of support and inspiration, rather than as an isolated figure anchored to your classroom striving to differentiate your lesson plans. Much recent research supports the argument that the potential of 'inclusion' to generate real change in educational practice is often only realised when stakeholders (e.g. teachers, SENCos, headteachers, TAs, parents, pupils) work closely together towards a shared goal (Roberts and Simpson, 2016; Mulholland and O'Connor, 2016; Rizvi and Limbrick, 2015; Montgomery and Mirenda, 2014; Laluvein, 2010).

SUMMARY AND KEY POINTS

- In this chapter we have outlined how historical and contemporary political developments have shaped SEND provision. These policy developments can be related to the 'models of disability' that were discussed as key discourses circulating in this area.
- We invited you to think about each of the four areas of SEND, and to reflect on teaching practices appropriate for pupils within these - the idea of 'inclusive pedagogy' was mentioned here.

- A main focus of the chapter was to encourage you to see yourself as an *agent of inclusion*; that you have capacity to make a difference, through honest and perhaps challenging reflections on your own pedagogy – your personal-professional values, and your teaching materials and activities.
- The chapter then noted how it is often through the actions – initially at least – of individual teachers seeking cooperative, equal and mutually beneficial relationships with key stakeholders that inclusive school cultures can evolve.

Record in your PDP how the information in this chapter enables you to meet the requirements for your first year of teaching.

Further resources

Resources referred to in the chapter

www.annafreud.org/what-we-do/schools-in-mind/resources-for-schools/

www.autism.org.uk

www.bdadyslexia.org.uk/educator

www.communication4all.co.uk

www.hdssg.org/education-2/resources/

www.ican.org.uk

www.additudemag.com/adhd-school-checklists-forms-letters/

http://meshagain.meshguides.org

www.wiltshire.gov.uk/secondary-scd-toolkit-photocopy-version.pdf

Other sources of information and resources

http://blog.optimus-education.com/categories/sencology

www.csie.org.uk/

https://educationendowmentfoundation.org.uk/

www.gdmorewood.com/

www.sendgateway.org.uk/

www.udlcenter.org/

Appendices 2 and 3 list subject associations, teaching councils and relevant websites.

Books in the *Learning to Teach* series that you may find helpful are as follows:

Capel, S., Leask, M. and Younie, S. (eds.) (2019) *Learning to Teach in the Secondary School: A Companion to School Experience*, 8th edn, Abingdon: Routledge.
This book is designed as a core textbook to support student teachers through their initial teacher education programme.

Capel, S., Leask, M. and Turner, T. (eds.) (2010) *Readings for Learning to Teach in the Secondary School: A Companion to M Level Study*, Abingdon: Routledge.
This book brings together essential readings to support you in your critical engagement with key issues raised in this textbook.

The subject-specific books in the *Learning to Teach* series, the *Practical (subject) Guides*, *Debates in (subject)* and *Mentoring (subject) Teachers* are also very useful.

Working to improve classroom climate and pupil behaviour

Terry Haydn

Introduction

Classroom management, and the ability to 'run a room' (Bennett, 2017), are major elements of the teaching and learning process, impacting on pupil attainment, pupil motivation and engagement, and the quality of teachers' working lives. Variations in classroom climate are also one of the most important causes of inequality of educational opportunity in England (Haydn, 2015).

This chapter draws on recent research and testimony from interviews with experienced and effective teachers to consider issues related to the working atmosphere in the classroom (sometimes referred to as 'classroom climate') and pupil behaviour. How do teachers get better at managing pupil behaviour, and why do some teachers develop to higher levels than others? How might you usefully consider and reflect on the extent to which there is an ideal classroom climate for learning in your classroom in order to further hone and refine your abilities in this facet of your teaching?

Classroom climate might be thought of as a continuum. At one end are classrooms where all the pupils are under the relaxed and assured control of the teacher, with the teacher able to undertake any form of lesson activity without concern; teacher and pupils working together, enjoying the experiences involved, and with all pupils doing their best to learn and do well (what I have termed, in my research, 'Level 10'). At the other end are classrooms where the amount of learning that takes place is severely constrained because many pupils are being disruptive, spoiling the learning of others, and preventing the teacher from teaching effectively ('Level 1'). (The full version of the scale is provided at the end of the chapter in Appendix 1. The scale and supporting materials can also be accessed from https://terryhaydn.co.uk/managing-pupil-behaviour/.)

What is the relationship between learner behaviour and classroom climate?

There is obviously a close relationship between learner behaviour and classroom climate. The interplay between the two has an important effect on how much learning takes place in a classroom, and the extent to which learners are able to enjoy the lesson and feel that the experience of being in the classroom is worthwhile. Even if there are just one or two pupils misbehaving, it is difficult for the teacher to relax and concentrate solely on getting pupils to learn. Other pupils will be aware of the fact that the teacher is not in full control of the lesson, may lose confidence in the teacher and start to feel frustrated by the negative impact on their right to learn. Often, other pupils become distracted from learning and the problem escalates. Deficits in classroom climate can influence not just the learning outcomes of the lesson, but the ways in which the teacher plans the lesson, sometimes resorting to defensive 'teaching for control' strategies (for example, building in lots of written work for pupils to do, to 'keep them busy, keep their heads down'). Levels 5-7 in the scale (see Appendix 1) give some descriptors of the effect of these deficits in classroom climate.

It is also difficult to overstate the effect that classroom climate has on the extent to which teachers are able to enjoy their job. It is difficult to enjoy working with a teaching group that is not fully under your control, but when you are teaching at 'Level 10', teaching can be a very fulfilling and enjoyable job. Below are some comments from teachers I interviewed about what it is like when you are teaching at Levels 9 and 10 on the scale:

> You come out feeling great. You know that you have their respect, they rate you, they think you are a good teacher (Newly qualified teacher (NQT))
>
> As you are walking round the classroom, or looking out of the window, you think to yourself, there aren't many people who have a job as fulfilling and enjoyable as this (Experienced teacher)
>
> In terms of how much you enjoy your teaching, there's a massive difference between operating at Levels 7 and 8 ... which are OK ... no big hassle ... and Level 10, when it's just a fantastic job, pure pleasure ... you can get a real buzz out of the interaction with pupils. It's like the adverts for teaching on the TV but in real life (NQT)
>
> (Haydn, 2012, pp. 11-12)

OBJECTIVES

At the end of the chapter, you should be able to:

- have a clear grasp of the range and complexity of factors that influence classroom climate;
- have an awareness of recent ideas and research evidence relating to classroom climate and pupil behaviour;
- have an awareness of the views of experienced professionals about which factors enable teachers to develop high levels of competence in managing pupil behaviour.

Check how the information in this chapter enables you to meet the requirements for your first year of teaching.

Context

Until as recently as 2012, the Office for Standards in Education, Children's Services and Skills (Ofsted) and the Department for Education (DfE) suggested that behaviour in English schools was relatively unproblematic, reporting that behaviour was 'satisfactory or better' in 99.7% of English schools (DfE, 2012; Ofsted, 2012b). However, more recently, this view has been questioned, and it is now generally acknowledged that deficits in classroom climate that affect behaviour in English schools are more prevalent than this (Haydn, 2014; Jenkins and Ueno, 2017). Deficits in classroom climate and concerns about pupil behaviour are a problem worldwide (Jenkins and Ueno, 2017; Organisation for Economic Cooperation and Development (OECD), 2009; Trends in International Mathematics and Science Study (TIMSS) (International Association for the Evaluation of Educational Achievement (IAEEA), n.d.). There are few, if any, education systems that can claim that there are no schools where some pupils at times impede the learning of others. As the English government's current behaviour advisor notes, having problems of behaviour is not abnormal (Bennett, 2017). You will be unusual if you go through your first few years of teaching operating at 'Level 10' with all your teaching groups. It is important for you to keep in mind that most teachers at some time face quite challenging decisions over issues relating to pupil behaviour as the following testimony from a year head demonstrates:

> This is not a school in desperate circumstances ... we are heavily oversubscribed, parents are desperate to get their kids into the school. But within a few days of becoming a year head, I had been obliged to make several quite difficult decisions about what to do with pupils who were spoiling the lesson for other pupils by behaving badly ... deliberately trying to undermine the teacher ... quite blatantly breaking the basic rules of behaviour.
>
> *(Haydn, 2012, p. 183)*

It is therefore unhelpful to suggest that any deficit in classroom climate is necessarily the result of poor teaching. Teachers sometimes have to work with large numbers of difficult and disengaged pupils, and such pupils are not spread evenly across schools (see, for example, Turner, 2017). It is also naïve to suggest that securing and maintaining a classroom climate that is ideal for learning is a simple and straightforward matter (for further examples see Department for Education and Skills (DfES), 2004; Wilshaw, 2014; Haydn, 2012, pp. 7-8). Deficits in classroom climate can be caused by a particularly difficult group of pupils, an inappropriate curriculum, poor pre-school experience, inadequate resources, lack of effective support and sanctions or lack of parental support, or any number of factors beyond the control of the classroom teacher. 'Level 10' is not a natural state of affairs; with some teaching groups it takes considerable skill to get all pupils to be perfectly behaved and keen to learn and do well, and in some challenging schools, even very experienced and accomplished teachers struggle to maintain a classroom climate that is ideal for learning (Haydn, 2012).

However, Ofsted's recent focus on school leaders, school systems and school ethos as the key determinants of levels of classroom control and classroom climate (Ofsted, 2014; Wilshaw, 2014) does not explain the phenomenon of 'in-school variation' in classroom climate. In England, as in many other countries, differences *within* schools have been found to be more significant than differences between schools in terms of the levels of behaviour that prevail in classrooms (see, for example, Elliott, 2009; Reynolds, 1999; Wubbels, 2011).

My experience as someone who taught at a challenging inner-city school for many years, and my interviews with over 140 teachers (Haydn, 2012) lean me towards Elliott's view that in spite of the existence of other variables, the classroom management skills of individual teachers are one of the most influential determinants of classroom climate and good pupil behaviour. The testimony of one student teacher is not untypical of many responses to the question of why classroom climate varied within schools:

> You couldn't do a placement at X school without realising what a fantastic difference the individual teacher makes. Groups that I had regarded as unteachable would behave like little angels [for teacher X], not just under control but relaxed, pleasant, helpful. They would just go quiet when he gave some small signal that he wanted to talk. At one level it was depressing because it made me realise how crap I was, but in another way it was inspiring ... it made you realise what a fantastic difference teachers can make.
>
> *(Haydn, 2015, p. 2356)*

It is for this reason that the chapter focuses predominantly on the question of the development of individual teachers' skills in managing pupil behaviour and 'running a room'. It is however important to remember that there are other factors, which have a significant influence on classroom climate. It is misleading to suggest that 'it is all down to the teacher'.

Complexity

There are so many variables involved in the complex process of teaching a lesson in very differing school cultures and with different pupils that it is artificial and misleading to suggest that the handling of any incident or experience can be, in all cases, reduced to a simple formula for prescribing the correct or appropriate action (along the lines of 'If A happens, you should respond by doing B'). Although there might be sensible *parameters* for action (that is to say, a range of possible responses, which would be appropriate given the policies and norms of a particular school culture), sometimes the answer is 'it depends ...'. Not every situation can be resolved by the application of a particular sanction 'tariff'. Of course, teachers should try to be consistent with their actions, but sometimes it is difficult to be consistent because of the complexity and subtle differences involved in an incident. In the words of Elliott:

> The dynamics (of the classroom) are such that skilled classroom management cannot simply be reduced to a set of behavioural guidelines or classroom routines independent of situational cues. Recognising, understanding and interpreting the complex social phenomena that underpin particular classroom dynamics in any given situation can prove problematic for less skilled teachers.
>
> *(Elliott, 2009, p. 200)*

Although behaviour 'checklists' (see, for example, Taylor, 2011) and guidance from behaviour experts can be useful, they are not guaranteed to work in all situations and circumstances. Lemov's research and guidance (see Lemov, 2015 and associated YouTube clips) is highly respected, but the suggestion that 'managing pupil behaviour is all in the eyebrow' (Lemov, 2017, p.24) might not work in all contexts.

In terms of the implications for your practice, it can be helpful to be aware of such guidance, but also to be open-minded, to be prepared to try things out and to reflect and adapt your practice in the light of these experiences. Stenhouse (1975) argued that the purpose of educational research was for teachers to test ideas out against their own practice and learn from them.

The limitations of such guidance can be gleaned from the contradictions and differences that sometimes exist between suggestions given by even the most talented and experienced experts.

I have always believed that a key level to aspire to in terms of classroom climate is that you can get the pupils to be quiet when you are talking. To me, it is one of the 'litmus tests' of whether you are in control of the class or not. Sue Cowley eloquently recommends the strategy of 'waiting for silence' before talking to a class (Cowley, 2002, p.22). Paul Dix, another highly respected expert in the management of pupil behaviour, radically disagrees with this approach, arguing that 'waiting for silence is not a behaviour technique, but an invitation for pupils to take control of the lesson' (Dix, 2010, p. 24). Now complete Task 11.1.

 Task 11.1   Getting the class quiet

A common criticism of less experienced teachers is that they sometimes 'talk over' the noise of the class, rather than waiting for the class to be quiet and listen (Haydn, 2012). Read the teacher testimony on the use of the 'waiting for quiet' strategy at https://terryhaydn.co.uk/how-to-get-the-class-quiet/. What influence (if any) does this testimony have on your ideas about the use of the 'waiting for quiet' strategy? Talk to colleagues about their views and experiences of using this approach to get the class quiet.

Store this information in your professional development portfolio (PDP) (or similar) to refer to later.

Another area where there are very differing views about good practice in managing pupil behaviour and establishing a calm and purposeful working atmosphere in the classroom is the question of rules. Rogers (2011) has suggested that teachers should try to negotiate and discuss classroom rules with pupils, with the idea that if pupils feel they have some ownership or say in the rules, they are more likely to respect them. Another view is that you just try to get pupils to comply with the rules for the school as a whole – most schools have a set of basic rules/expectations, and these are often on the walls of the classroom (which is not to say that they are always rigorously and unfailingly complied with). Dix (2012, pp.8–9) advised against starting out with a 'rules and expectations lesson':

> The children will think you are a prig and ignore you. It will not do anything to improve their behaviour or their respect for you. It will not inspire them, engage them or interest them. You can agree routines as you go along. Please, I beg you, don't tell them 'how it is going to be' before you have shown them something of who you are.

Bennett (2017) is at the opposite end of the spectrum, stating that in his own practice, he spends most of the first lesson spelling out routines, rules and expectations.

It isn't that these approaches are either right or wrong. It depends on the class, the school, but above all, how skilfully and resolutely you go about *establishing* the ground rules and expectations you have chosen to implement. Task 11.2 asks you to consider skills you need to establish rules and expectations in your lessons.

 Task 11.2   Establishing 'ground rules'

Read the list of teacher skills involved in establishing rules and expectations at https://terryhaydn.co.uk/classroom-rules-what-do-teachers-say/. Reflect on which of these skills and approaches you use and are already proficient in, and which you feel you have not explored, or you might hone and refine further.

Work with your mentor to develop your skills in establishing rules and expectations and record your progress in your PDP.

Similar tensions and ambiguities exist in other aspects of establishing a good classroom climate and managing pupil behaviour. 'Withitness' (Elliott, 2009) – the art of having very acute antennae for what is going on in the classroom, can easily shade into what Rogers (2011) terms 'manic vigilance', where the teacher betrays anxiety and lack of confidence by being over-zealous in looking round the room, almost giving the expectation that they expect the pupils to misbehave. There are those who argue that developing warm and friendly relationships with pupils is the key to developing a good classroom climate for learning, and others who advocate a 'Don't smile before Christmas' approach. As Elliott (2009) points out, it isn't that one of these strategies is 'correct' and one misguided, it depends on the adeptness and skill with which the approach is carried out. Some teachers are very effective with a stern and austere teaching approach, others are very successful with the 'cultivating good relationships' approach. 'What works' depends on both school context and the skill with which strategies are implemented (and of course, your own personality, and developing strengths and weaknesses in this aspect of your teaching). This extends to the widely advocated strategy of welcoming pupils into the room as they come into the lesson (see for example, Taylor, 2011). This is now sometimes official school policy, but done maladroitly, by a teacher who does not have high-level skills of interaction with pupils, it may do more harm than good. It does not *in itself* improve working relations between teacher and pupils, and there is the danger that if every teacher does this, in every lesson, there may be diminishing returns, and it may lose some of its value. It becomes the equivalent of 'Have a nice day', or 'Are you enjoying your meal?'. Now complete Task 11.3.

 Task 11.3   Welcoming pupils into the room at the door of the classroom

If it is possible to do this without upsetting pupils and colleagues, ask pupils (perhaps the pupils in your form, or 'A' level pupils), and colleagues that you get along with, what they think about the practice of being talked to and welcomed individually as they come into a classroom. Reflect on what comments and greetings might be most effective in using this strategy, and whether it might be a good idea to vary this approach (if it is not official school policy).

Record these in your PDP to enable you to build up a range of greetings to use in future.

The 'golden nugget' (Battersby, 2006) to keep in mind is that just about anything in teaching can be done well or badly, and that includes most of the ideas, techniques and strategies relating to managing pupil behaviour.

One further dimension of complexity in this area might be noted. Garner (2017) makes the important point that it is not just about you, the teacher. Behaviour for learning also encompasses understanding pupils and how they think about themselves (self-esteem, confidence, identity and so on), pupils' relations with others (both adults and other pupils), and how pupils view themselves as learners (their attitudes to the curriculum, to school and to the whole project of 'education'). (This is developed in more detail in Garner, 2016.)

In terms of the implications for your practice, this means that it needs time, patience and intelligent reflection in order to develop a good understanding of the pupils you teach and insight into how they feel about learning your subject, and being in your classroom. Some teachers are more accomplished than others in terms of getting to know their pupils as individuals, and knowing how to 'get the best out of them' in terms of their willingness to commit to working to the best of their ability and to wanting to do well in your subject.

Complex and sophisticated skills

Elliott (2007) argued that although schools have 'bureaucratic' systems for guiding pupils towards good behaviour, the most important source of teacher authority is the deployment of the teacher's own high-level expertise. He suggests that the teacher's authority comes from the respect that pupils have for the teacher's expertise in interacting with them and managing the classroom. He argues that the more authority the teacher has, in terms of commanding the respect of the pupils for their professional abilities, the more relaxed, friendly and approachable they can afford to be (Elliott, 2007). He argues that there are many complex and sophisticated skills that teachers need to develop – not all of them relating specifically to behaviour and control – which have an influence on the response of pupils to that teacher:

> Clearly, subject knowledge is crucially important, as is the capacity to provide high-quality teaching and learning. However, the third element of teacher expertise, interpersonal skill, is an element absolutely essential for ensuring teacher authority ... highly skilled teacher practice involves engaging in a range of behaviours that, in themselves, appear relatively unimportant but, taken cumulatively, are key to prevention and, where necessary, defusion of problem behaviour. Where these behaviours are exhibited, pupils are likely to perceive that their teacher has high-level expertise and adjust their behaviour accordingly.
>
> *(Elliott, 2009, p. 200)*

In other words, if your teaching skills are very well developed across a broad range of teaching competence – but perhaps especially in your skills of interaction with pupils, classes are more likely to respond well to your teaching. Bennett (2017) puts it slightly differently: while making the point that you should not seek popularity as a teacher, 'if you are a good teacher they will probably like you'.

So, what are these complex and sophisticated skills? Elliott (2007) identifies 'withitness' (the teacher's awareness of everything that is taking place around them), the ability to handle 'overlapping' ('overlapping' in the sense of the ability to show good judgement and calm efficiency in responding to lots of things happening at the same time), composure, non-verbal signals, voice and skills of 'teacher-talk' as being of particular importance, but stresses that there are many others. A more 'unpacked' and extensive explanation of the nature of these 'complex and sophisticated skills' can be accessed from https://terryhaydn.co.uk/complex-and-sophisticated-skills/. It includes an expanded version of Elliott's points together with advice from other expert practitioners, and some extracts from the 140 teachers interviewed about their views on managing pupil behaviour.

Talking to pupils, either as a group or as individuals, is a skill that is used in nearly every lesson taught. Some teachers develop to higher levels than others in their skills of interaction with pupils and in their use of teacher exposition and questioning. I worked for some years with a teacher where the pupils would sometimes sigh with disappointment when he stopped talking (I never reached that level of expertise). It is not just about tone, pitch, intonation – part of it is about the quality of what you say – have you got anything interesting to say, do you explain things well, can you hold their attention, is your questioning stimulating, lively and effective?

I taught for over 30 years before reading Philip Beadle's piece about the use of the pause (see below). I then experimented with the use of the pause in lectures and seminars and found that it did seem to work well (when not overdone):

> How effectively do you use the pause? 'Once you have pens down and everybody looking at you, wait ... then stretch the pause slightly ... wait a little ... then (long pause) ... speak. In doing this, you've assured that the attention is entirely on you, and that you haven't rushed it, losing the attention that was so hard won ... If you blast in, at a million miles an hour, you'll transmit nervousness or agitation.
>
> *(Beadle, 2010, p. 24)*

Now complete Task 11.4.

 Task 11.4   Developing skills in 'teacher-talk' and the use of the pause

- In at least one of your lessons, experiment with the use of the pause and see if it makes any difference to the quality of your delivery and the attentiveness of pupils.
- See if, in at least one of your lessons, you can hold the attention of the whole class for around 3–5 minutes simply by the quality of your teacher exposition. Reflect on why this was, or was not, successful and try to develop your skills of exposition from what you learn in this (and other) lessons.

Record your reflections in your PDP to help you with further development in using 'teacher talk' and pause.

Of course, it is not just about skill in using pauses; there are a number of strands in the use of voice and quality of oral 'delivery' to pupils which impact on pupil behaviour (see also Zwozdiak-Myers and Capel in *LTT8*, 2019). It should be an interesting part of the teacher's work honing and refining these skills, taking pleasure at getting better at them, and noting the improved response of pupils.

What are the characteristics of teachers who develop to excellence in the management of pupils' behaviour?

When I posed this question to head teachers and senior managers (Haydn, 2012) they were keen to stress that expert performance was *not* related to years of experience, innate charisma, or any genetic predisposition to manage pupil behaviour adeptly. Two responses that were fairly characteristic of the overall tenor of responses:

> Like most heads, I have some teachers who are exceptionally accomplished at working with difficult and troubled pupils, they are incredibly resourceful,

persevering ... and clever. Some students and NQTs learn from them, others don't pick things up.

I've got teachers here who have worked in this school for years who are still at Level 3 with some of their classes, and I've got NQTs who are already very assured in dealing with pupil behaviour, who have virtually no problems with their classes after the first term. Some teachers are much better than others at this ... it's not just a question of serving your time.

Good self-awareness, determination and perseverance, and the ability to learn and adapt from experience, advice and reading were also qualities that were frequently mentioned. Now complete Task 11.5.

 Task 11.5   'Keeping going'

Read Lisa McInerney's blog post on how she survived her NQT year (https://lauramcinerney.com/2013/03/23/surviving-the-first-year-of-teaching-nqt-teachfirst-trainee-pgce-survived/). It is an eloquent account of her NQT year and encapsulates what most commentators (and respondents in my study) say is important to keep in mind – that it usually takes time to develop high-level skills of interacting with pupils and running a classroom, even if you are intelligent, conscientious and keen to learn and improve. You wouldn't expect to be brilliant at playing the piano or speaking a foreign language after just a few weeks. Learning to get every child you teach to be keen to learn and behave perfectly is not simple and straightforward, it is very complex and difficult.

Next time you have a challenging class, make a conscious effort to keep in mind McInerney's points about the importance of resilience, keeping things in proportion, trying to keep your composure under pressure, and just carrying on doing your best for the pupils in your care even when it's difficult.

Record your progress in your PDP. You might also like to write this up to support other NQTs.

Expert teachers have a good understanding of the full breadth of benefits which pupils might derive from being in their classroom. Although it is important that you are an excellent subject teacher, there is more to being a good teacher than that. Many pupils arrive at secondary schools not perfectly socialised and have a lot to learn, on top of school subjects. Table 11.1 shows two lists that outline some of the other things that accomplished teachers try to develop in their pupils *as well as* getting better at the subject. If you want to cultivate a classroom climate that is ideal for learning, these things matter.

Garner also makes the important point that teachers need to have a clear grasp of the full breadth of desirable and undesirable behaviours that pupils may exhibit, and need to make expectations with regard to these behaviours explicit to pupils so as to develop the former, and minimise or eliminate the latter. (A helpful taxonomy of such strands of behaviour can be found in Garner, 2016, pp.184-185.)

Table 11.1 Non-subject-specific teaching objectives

Garner (2016)	Bennett (2017)
Pupils need to be taught to: ■ be effective and successful learners; ■ make and sustain friendships; ■ deal with and resolve conflict efficiently and fairly; ■ solve problems with others by themselves; ■ manage strong feelings such as frustration, anger and anxiety; ■ recover from setbacks and persist in the face of difficulties; ■ work and play cooperatively; ■ compete fairly and win and lose with dignity and respect for competitors.	Good habits you want pupils to develop to help them to succeed: ■ waiting their turn; ■ trying hard; ■ focusing; ■ being kind; ■ sharing; ■ interacting constructively with others; ■ learning how to debate. Pupils need these things (as well as knowledge) to help them to flourish as pupils and as people.

SUMMARY AND KEY POINTS

- There are different approaches to becoming accomplished at managing pupil behaviour: there is not one, single 'correct' approach.
- Becoming expert at 'running a room' is multi-faceted in terms of the number and range of skills you need to develop. It is not 'simple and straightforward'.
- It is important to be aware of the full range of ways in which pupils might benefit from being in your classroom. You are not *just* a subject operative.
- It takes time, patience, determination, open-mindedness and a willingness to learn, in order to get to expert levels of competence in this area.
- It is worth putting in the time, thought and effort to get to 'Level 10' on the Haydn Scale. Don't rest content if the working atmosphere in your classroom is quite good but not perfect. A classroom climate that is ideal for learning makes a big difference to how well learners do, and to how much you will enjoy your work as a teacher.

Record in your PDP, how the information in this chapter enables you to meet the requirements for your first year of teaching.

Appendix 1: The working atmosphere in the classroom: a ten-level scale (Haydn, 2014)

The scale was devised to encourage student teachers (and teachers, departments and schools) to think about the degree to which teachers are in relaxed and assured control of their classrooms and can enjoy their teaching, and also the extent to which there is a 'right to learn' for pupils, free from the noise and disruption of others. It is not designed as an instrument to pass judgement on the class-management skills of teachers (not least because there are so many other variables that influence the levels – most obviously, which school you are working in). Its purpose is to get teachers to think about the factors influencing the working atmosphere in the classroom, the influence of the working atmosphere in classrooms on teaching and learning, and the equal opportunities issues surrounding the tension between inclusion, and situations where some pupils may be spoiling the learning of others.

Level 10	You feel completely relaxed and comfortable; able to undertake any form of lesson activity without concern. 'Class control' not really an issue – teacher and pupils working together, enjoying the experiences involved.
Level 9	You feel completely in control of the class and can undertake any sort of classroom activity, but you need to exercise some control/authority at times to maintain a calm and purposeful working atmosphere. This can be done in a friendly and relaxed manner and is no more than a gentle reminder.
Level 8	You can establish and maintain a relaxed and co-operative working atmosphere and undertake any form of classroom activity, but this requires a considerable amount of thought and effort on your part at times. Some forms of lesson activity may be less calm and under control than others.
Level 7	You can undertake any form of lesson activity, but the class may well be rather 'bubbly' and rowdy; there may be minor instances of a few pupils messing around on the fringes of the lesson, but they desist when required to do so. No one goes out of their way to annoy you or challenges your authority.
Level 6	You don't really look forward to teaching the class, it is often a major effort to establish and maintain a relaxed and calm atmosphere. Several pupils will not remain on task without persistent surveillance/exhortation/threats. At times you feel harassed, and at the end of the lesson you feel rather drained. There are times when you feel it is wisest not to attempt certain types of pupil activity, in order to try to keep things under control. It is sometimes difficult to get pupils to be quiet while you are talking, or stop them calling out, or talking to each other at will across the room *but* in spite of this, no one directly challenges your authority, and there is no refusal or major disruption.
Level 5	There are times in the lesson when you would feel awkward or embarrassed if the head/a governor/an inspector came into the room, because your control of the class is limited. The atmosphere is at times rather chaotic, with several pupils manifestly not listening to your instructions. Some of the pupils are in effect challenging your authority by their dilatory or desultory compliance with your instructions and requests. Lesson format is constrained by these factors; there are some sorts of lesson you would not attempt because you know they would be rowdy and chaotic, *but* in the last resort, there is no open refusal, no major atrocities, just a lack of purposefulness and calm. Pupils who wanted to work could get on with it, albeit in a rather noisy atmosphere.
Level 4	You have to accept that your control is limited. It takes time and effort to get the class to listen to your instructions. You try to get onto the worksheet/written part of the lesson fairly quickly in order to 'get their heads down'. Lesson preparation is influenced more by control and 'passing the time' factors than by educational ones. Pupils talk while you are talking, minor transgressions (no pen, no exercise book, distracting others by talking) go unpunished because too much is going on to pick everything up. You become reluctant to sort out the ringleaders as you feel this may well escalate problems. You try to 'keep the lid on things' and concentrate on those pupils who are trying to get on with their work.

Level 3	You dread the thought of the lesson. There will be major disruption; many pupils will pay little or no heed to your presence in the room. Even pupils who want to work will have difficulty doing so. Swearwords may go unchecked, pupils will walk round the room at will. You find yourself reluctant to deal with transgressions because you have lost confidence. When you write on the board, objects will be thrown around the room. You can't wait for the lesson to end and be out of the room.
Level 2	The pupils largely determine what will go on in the lesson. You take materials into the lesson as a manner of form, but once distributed that will be ignored, drawn on or made into paper aeroplanes. When you write on the board, objects will be thrown at you rather than round the room. You go into the room hoping that they will be in a good mood and will leave you alone and just chat to each other.
Level 1	Your entry into the classroom is greeted by jeers and abuse. There are so many transgressions of the rules and what constitutes reasonable behaviour that it is difficult to know where to start. You turn a blind eye to some atrocities because you feel that your intervention may well lead to confrontation, refusal or escalation of the problem. This is difficult because some pupils are deliberately committing atrocities under your nose, for amusement. You wish you had not gone into teaching.

 ## Further resources

Bennett, T. (2017) *Creating a Culture: How School Leaders Can Optimise Behaviour*, London: DfE. Available from: www.gov.uk/government/publications/behaviour-in-schools (accessed 25 November 2018).

>   An up-to-date study that complements the emphasis on teacher skills in this chapter.

Dix, P. (2017) *When the Adults Change, Everything Changes*, Carmarthen, UK: Independent Thinking Press.

>   This text presents ideas and opinions rather than research and evidence (no references, no index), but is interesting and potentially useful nonetheless.

Elliott, J. (1991) *Action Research for Educational Change*, London: McGraw-Hill.

>   The section 'Professional competence and the development of situational understanding' (pp. 128-132) provides a summary of Klemp's model of professional competence. I find this one of the most plausible explanations of why some professionals develop to excellence, and others don't.

Garner, P. (2019) 'Managing classroom behaviour: adopting a positive approach', in S. Capel, M. Leask and S. Younie (eds.) *Learning to Teach in the Secondary School: A Companion to School Experience*, 8th edn, Abingdon: Routledge, pp. 164-183.

>   This chapter should be read in conjunction with Philip Gardner's chapter, which provides a more developed explanation of some of the ideas mentioned briefly in this chapter.

Haydn, T. (2019) *Managing Pupil Behaviour*. Available from: https://terryhaydn.co.uk/managing-pupil-behaviour/ (accessed 18 August 2019).

>   This site provides further teacher testimony on common behaviour dilemmas (such as how best to cope if the class is not fully under your control, and decision making over sending pupils out of the classroom).

Lemov, D. (2015) *Teach like a Champion 2.0*, San Francisco, CA: Jossey-Bass.

>   Based on video analysis of expert teachers, these suggested techniques can be tried out to explore whether they might work for you.

Appendices 2 and 3 list subject associations, teaching councils and relevant websites.

Books in the *Learning to Teach* series that you may find helpful are as follows:

Capel, S., Leask, M. and Younie, S. (eds.) (2019) *Learning to Teach in the Secondary School: A Companion to School Experience,* **8th edn, Abingdon: Routledge.**
This book is designed as a core textbook to support student teachers through their initial teacher education programme.

Capel, S., Leask, M. and Turner, T. (eds.) (2010) *Readings for Learning to Teach in the Secondary School: A Companion to M Level Study,* **Abingdon: Routledge.**
This book brings together essential readings to support you in your critical engagement with key issues raised in this textbook.

The subject-specific books in the *Learning to Teach* series, the *Practical (subject) Guides, Debates in (subject)* and *Mentoring (subject) Teachers* are also very useful.

12 Understanding learners' primary experiences and transition

Brian Matthews and Lyn Matthews

Introduction

The transition between primary and secondary school is an important life change that affects learners' attainment and well-being in the long term. Assisting in the transition process is a key responsibility of all primary, middle and secondary teachers who work with learners at this time. This chapter focuses on transition at age 11, i.e. Year 7, but transition ages may be different in the region (and country) in which you are teaching.

A primary school would have had a vision statement. Both primary and secondary schools can have similar vision statements with typical aims, which include: to provide a 'welcoming community where children are supported, through a wide range of opportunities, to develop the skills and character needed to prepare them for a successful future'.

Do you recall your primary school? We suspect you do, very clearly. Spare a thought for the petite, Year 7 child obscured by their oversized uniform arriving late for your first lesson, overwhelmed. Their last educational experience may have been a small rural primary school with four classes. The average size of a primary school is around 200 learners, but secondary schools are at least four times bigger. An analogy that we find helpful is that the primary school provides a family orientated environment, whereas the secondary school is a more business/work environment. The aim of this chapter is for you to understand the difference between primary and secondary school and how to support learners during the transition between the two. (See also Jindal-Snape in *LTT8*, 2019.)

OBJECTIVES

At the end of this chapter you should be able to:

- understand the experiences and concerns of primary pupils as they enter secondary school;
- have knowledge of the primary experiences of your learners;
- have ideas on how to build on the learning from primary schools and gradually integrate pupils into the secondary school culture.

Check how the information in this chapter enables you to meet the requirements for your first year of teaching.

The fundamentals of primary education

Knowing about the curriculum shaping your pupils' experiences in the primary school helps you to understand the transition they are experiencing. In England, the Primary National Curriculum provides the statutory part of the school curriculum where all of the experience should be met through a broad and balanced curriculum that:

- promotes the spiritual, moral, cultural, mental and physical development of pupils at the school and in society, and
- prepares pupils at the school for the opportunities, responsibilities and experiences of later life (Department for Education (DfE), 2014a, para 2.1).

The English National Curriculum documents for primary and secondary schools state that there should be time and space to develop each child in order that they become 'educated citizens'. However, in today's climate in England, too often the relentless drive with the data-driven performance-evidenced culture means that many schools are pushed towards a restricted English and Maths focus that many teachers consider uncreative and demotivating. As former conservative Secretary of State for Education, Justin Greening stated:

> When children leave primary school, they should have acquired a firm grasp of the basics of literacy and numeracy.
>
> *(Greening, 2016, para 1)*

In England, testing at primary school begins with baseline assessment at Early Years Foundation Stage; for Mathematics & English at Key Stage 1 (KS1); Mathematics Tables tests for Y4 and finally KS2 Standard Assessment Tasks (SATs) tests. As the Office for Standards in Education, Children's Services and Skills (Ofsted) themselves suggest, the primary school culture is in danger of becoming just a matter of teaching to the test (Brooker, 2017). These are problematic areas for us all to consider because they impact on children's creativity and well-being (a point that we will return to later).

Now complete Task 12.1. If you are working in a country other than England, adapt the tasks to your context.

 Task 12.1   What was included in your pupils' primary curriculum?

In creating a learning continuum, it is essential that you familiarise yourself with what your pupils have been taught before. Pupils will have come from a range of schools and countries that have different curricula.

What can you remember and what do you know about the primary curriculum? Secondary teachers can go over the same materials as in primary schools so pupils wonder, 'Why are we doing this again?'. If you do repeat, explain why.

Make notes of your subject requirements in the primary curriculum used in your country.

Store the information in your professional development portfolio (PDP) (or similar) to refer to when planning lessons so that your lessons reinforce and build on the primary curriculum foundation.

Generally though, a primary-school day is literally more *enclosed* than the secondary-school day. The one teacher/one class is pivotal in this. In this situation, children are more likely to develop secure and stable relationships that support their development through each year. We, as teachers, have witnessed some dramatic changes in cognitive and social development, especially with children who have had challenging backgrounds, who can thrive and develop in one year. Each primary school context, driven by its pedagogy, provides learners with a perception about what valuable learning is, a belief in their own capabilities and, alongside close parental connections, that develops the child through to the end of Year 6 for 'secondary school readiness'.

The primary school years are fundamental in providing the foundations for later educational experiences. Most subjects are taught by the class teacher in the same room: specialist subjects, like music, can be taught separately. Some schools spread the curriculum load by having Science or Arts weeks. Lessons tend to be interactive, have many short active learning tasks, using talk in paired or group situations. Children are known by most adults working in the school. Often learning is enriched with whole-school foci: book week, poetry day, outdoor learning week etc. Primary schools give parents more opportunity than secondary schools to meet and speak regularly with class teachers (most schools welcome this as informal practice at the end of the day). Schools may also provide a wider service to the whole local community, and provide a focus for all families, through events, to share their child's educational life.

Many teachers report that, at the end of primary school, children can feel they are at the top of the educational tree. They are the learners that are given the most homework (commonly about 2.5 hours each week) and they have tasks with responsibilities such as getting the benches out for assembly and controlling the football leagues in the playground. A good primary school will have taken pupils to the required academic standard and provided them with some excellent learning opportunities. This may include, for example, sport; visual arts; leadership skills; acting and performing; and behavioural, social and emotional skills. On completing Year 6, many children have had some increased responsibility to do with school and their own learning. Now complete Task 12.2.

 Task 12.2   Learning about your pupils' individual needs and experiences

Primary school pupil transfer documents can be very useful as the primary teachers know the pupils well and have built up a detailed knowledge of them. Check the primary school transfer documents for your pupils and gather as much information about the 'real' child, such as their interests, clubs they have joined and their physical activities, through meeting them on induction days and meeting with their parents/ carers. Become involved in this process as soon as you can. Particularly find out more about the special educational needs and disabilities (SEND) children and set a meeting up early on with your SENCo to check the needs and support for individual children. Also see Chapter 10 for more information on becoming an inclusive educator and developing your practice as a mainstream teacher of pupils with SEND.

Record your findings in your PDP. Discuss these with other staff who are teaching your pupils and use the information to plan your lessons.

Primary schools and transition

Unfortunately, we know that the process of primary–secondary transfer is not plain sailing. Transition is characterised by a decrease in academic achievement and motivation. This 'hiatus' in children's academic achievement has been reported widely (Measor and Woods, 1984; Galton et al., 2003). Indeed, Galton, Morrison and Pell (2003) suggest that up to 40% of pupils are affected negatively by the transfer. Government and local educational intervention have consequently been directed at pre-empting this shortfall through academic support.

The English National Curriculum is set out to provide curriculum from early years through to age 16. The transition period should be a part of this continuum. In its report, 'The Wasted Years', Ofsted (2015) is clearly concerned about the lack of general progress found at Key Stage 3 and found that during transition:

> too many secondary schools did not work effectively with partner primary schools to understand pupils' prior learning and ensure that they built on this during Key Stage 3.
> *(Ofsted, 2015, p. 5)*

Programmes that contain on-site lessons, day visits, open events with parents and Transition Units, where tasks are begun in the primary school and then completed in the secondary school (Department for Education and Skills (DfES), 2002), are some of the many ways schools can support transition. These initiatives prioritise the management of learning and in doing so adhere to a preconceived set of regulatory and behavioural expectations. However, what happens more often is that children feel in a state of limbo during the summer holidays with apprehension about joining the youth culture of the secondary school (Haigh, 2005).

So, what is good practice in the transition process? What makes a successful transition to secondary school? Evangelou et al. (2008) argue that there are eight key strands that need to be considered:

1. academic attainment
2. social adjustment
3. linkages between schools
4. organisational issues
5. pupil perceptions
6. cultural factors
7. socio-economic factors
8. gender differences

Children settle better when primary schools have, prior to transition, allowed pupils to be more responsible for their learning, to be taught about strategies for learning on their own, and provided with a challenging curriculum, with clear goals of academic achievement (Evangelou et al., 2008). Most schools have a variety of ways in which positive learning strategies are fostered both in the classroom and in school at large. In Year 6, or before, this could range from, for example, enquiry-based learning opportunities, individual project-based homework, group work sessions in class or final end-of-year class performances that support that particular school's culture.

However, there is another significant side to the transition process, which is of the children's own self-identity. Goleman (1996) suggests that during transition many children experience a decrease in self-esteem and a rise in self-consciousness. It is a time when the success of navigating this period can affect not only their academic performance but also that general sense of well-being. Zeedyk et al. (2003) report this is a time of considerable stress and worry, which may affect later development and attainment, and that pupils appear to have predominantly emotional issues. In the *School Transition and Adjustment Research Study* (STARS) project, Rice et al. (2008) found that the key concerns of Year 7 were, in order: getting lost, being bullied, discipline and detentions, and homework and losing old friends. As you can see, there is little concern about academic attainment but more to do with their own identity.

Learners going through the transition processes are individuals who can be seen to be developing through learning about and engaging with their self-identity (Lucey and Reay, 2000) but the learner's self-identity is changing to adapt to their new situation. Learners therefore, are not changing their learning; they are changing friendships, teachers and a secure environment they have known for up to 7 years. We do know that SEND pupils, and other vulnerable groups, do not transfer as well compared to others (Evangelou et al., 2008). In essence, aspects of all teaching should be directed towards supporting a changing self-identity. However, even learners whom one might think would make the transition smoothly may be struggling. Here are some facts about the mental health of young children. Public Health England (2017) reported that (verified by the organisation *Young Minds*):

- 8% of 5- to 10-year-olds have a diagnosed mental problem;
- 1 in 10 children have a diagnosable mental health disorder – that's roughly 3 children in every classroom;
- almost 1 in 4 children and young people show some evidence of mental ill health.

At this time of stress of the movement to the secondary stage of their educational life, for some children their well-being needs will be heightened. This can however be addressed within your teaching and the way you deliver the curriculum.

In a particular research project, Matthews (2007) found that a six-week creative arts approach to support this transition process proved to be successful. In this project children were enabled to explore their feelings about transition through the arts. At the end of the project they reported feeling more able to approach their new school positively. As the National Curriculum dictates there 'should be time and space to develop each child in order that they become "educated citizens"' (DfE, 2014a, para 3.1). Now complete Task 12.3.

 Task 12.3   Planning lessons to provide continuity of experience for learners

Begin thinking about your first lessons with a primary school approach in mind. Make them interactive, fun, talk focused and structured with up to six parts over a single lesson (for example, in Maths, see www.ncetm.org.uk/resources/47230

Record your plans in your PDP and evaluate your success perhaps by a simple survey asking the learners how they felt about the lesson pace and structure (e.g. if you can create a list of questions with tick boxes under a smiley face, a neutral face and a sad face, this can provide quick feedback).

Most parents actively support their child during the transition to secondary school. Parental, sibling and family influence are important and often determine the choice of school from the outset. Research (Evangelou et al., 2008) has found that most parents' concerns are similar to those of the children: bullying, finding and keeping friends, dealing with the discipline and being organised. In conclusion, where there is good and effective communication between primary schools, secondary schools, learners and parents, most concerns were allayed (Evangelou et al., 2008).

Teaching Year 7s (11–12-year-olds) in secondary school

Teachers should build on the learning from primary schools and gradually integrate pupils into the secondary school culture.

When you have a class of Year 7 learners, usually your main concerns are about classroom management (see Chapter 10) and how well learners are likely to do in your subject. It is common for teachers to give tests in their subject to find out how well learners are achieving. Many schools put learners into ability groups based on the results. Other schools believe that learners need to settle in and get to know the teachers before trying to assess them. Some teach in mixed-ability groups. These factors affect how learners feel about the transition if they are anxious about tests, especially if they are then categorised as a 'failure' in comparison to others (Putwain, 2008). Now complete Task 8.4.

M

Task 12.4   Ability is not static! Establishing 'growth mindsets'

Year 7 pupils already have perceptions about their abilities. Some learners, and teachers, believe in a fixed mindset where learners think that ability is static: you are either 'bright' or not (Dweck, 2000). The alternative to this is a growth mindset, where learners believe that ability is linked to effort and application and can be changed over time. These learners are more likely to use failure to learn more, as it is part of the effort of learning.

Look up more about Dweck (www.youtube.com/watch?v=_XOmgOOSpLU or www.youtube.com/watch?v=-71zdXCMU6A).
Think how you can promote a growth mindset.
Can you see why giving tests and putting learners into ability grouping encourages a fixed mindset?

Neuroscientists describe the brain as being 'plastic', i.e. capable of development through life. We suggest you take the quiz to check your assumptions about how to promote learning. See the MESHGuide on Neuromyths (www.meshguides.org/neuromyths/). See also Booth (in *LTT8*, 2019) on the impact of mindset on achievement.

Record your findings in your PDP. Discuss these ideas with other staff teaching the children at your school and use the information to plan your lessons.

Learners may believe that tests give accurate results, and so think that they have a fixed ability, which leads them to a fixed mindset. However, one of the difficulties with tests is that they can give inaccurate results, for example, a learner may have done better with a different set of test items, or they may not have felt well. SATs results are not reliable (Weale, 2017). Test results can give you a snapshot of attainment about areas of the curriculum or particular skills that could benefit the majority of the class if you spent a bit of time working on these. Be careful of looking at one test result and thinking that a particular learner is 'good' or not because of the 'Pygmalion' effect (Rosenthal and Jacobson, 1968). This is where a learner who is seen by a teacher, say as weak, is then more likely to do poorly through the way the teacher interacts with them. This is part of the reason why when learners are put into ability groups they rarely move because they are likely to conform to their label. In order to avoid this labelling of 'good' and 'poor' learners, it is important to get to know the learners and to try to delay, for as long as possible, from forming a view of how able a learner is. You have an advantage in not knowing the pupils so you can start with an open mind. This enables the pupils to make a fresh start. Check what they have done by talking to them individually, ideally in a non-formal setting such as in the corridor when they are lining up or in class so that they know you have an interest in them and want them to improve. You can ask a few learners about what they have done in their primary schools and even ask to see their primary books and ask what their primary teachers were like. The more relaxed you make them the more you will understand individual learners. This sort of interaction and communication is also important in building up a good relationship with the learners and class as a whole. In turn, these both impact on their development and can aid their transition.

While secondary schools focus on academic achievement during transition, as mentioned earlier, learners' anxieties are mainly about the personal and social aspects of transition, along with homework (Jindal-Snape and Miller, 2008; Jindal-Snape in *LTT8*, 2019). Indeed, Jindal-Snape and Miller (2008) argue that the transition can be considered a 'challenge of living' because of the social and emotional challenges and changes at this period. They argue that to help learners cope with transition, personal experiences should be focused on. In particular, lower-attaining learners were more anxious, more likely to experience bullying and likely to be more upset at the beginning of secondary schooling. These effects continued beyond Year 7 and these learners were more likely to be depressed, have lower well-being and be disengaged from school (West, Sweeting and Young, 2010). Hence, unless social and emotional development is focused on, learners, often from families with low incomes, are even more likely to fail. Similarly, research has shown that most learners stated that they had experienced difficulties because of peer relationships (West et al., 2010). One crucial aspect is how you can support learners to develop friendships. However, do not assume that learners from the same school are friends, it can be the opposite. Talking to the learners to find out how they feel about their classmates can help. Girls, more than boys, may not form friendships and are more likely to have volatile relationships (Kucharski et al., 2018). Since learners come from different primary schools, some will feel very isolated as they may not know anyone and see others from the same school talking to each other. Some will have had SEND provision and with the altered support arrangements can feel rejected or lost so we suggest you take account of this in the induction programme. Now complete Task 12.5.

 Task 12.5   Learners' induction programme

Think about your school's system for induction of learners and how it is approached. What is it focused on, learners' cognitive abilities or their personal development? Based on your experience and the information from the tasks above, what else might you do to help them settle in to the ways of working in secondary school?

Record your findings in your PDP. Discuss these ideas with other staff teaching the children at your school and use the information to plan further induction.

Implications for teaching

So, the evidence clearly points to some key factors that support a successful transition.

- Learners are able to **develop** new friendships, and **improve** their self-esteem and confidence.
- They **settle in** to school life in a way that causes no concerns to their parents and teachers.
- They show an **increased interest** in school and school work.
- They get used to their **new routines** and school organisation with great ease.
- They experience curriculum **continuity**. (Rice et al., 2008; West et al., 2010)

A Year 7 teacher should be active in employing positive teaching strategies to enable many of the above to be met within their class. Your incoming Year 7 will see the secondary school primarily as a place, a social institution where friendships are formed as well as a site of academic learning. The emphasis for the Year 7 teacher is to ensure that there is time and space within the security of the classroom to allow the building of firm and secure relationships. This may contribute to the development of learner's self-confidence and future engagement with the learning that your school has to offer. When you teach and plan lessons you obviously focus on the subject matter and how to enable learners to learn. However, it is crucial that you plan in a way that integrates the social and emotional development of the learners, enables you to get to know them, helps them get to know each other and allays their fears about homework. The overall theme here is that relationships help humanise learners both to you as well as to each other. You should see them as learners who can grow and change and not as a label (especially never see them as numerical data). Getting to know learners personally also helps with behaviour and classroom management. Now complete Task 12.6.

 Task 12.6   Monitoring and supporting transition

Keep short written notes about the social development of the class and how supportive they are of each other. Include a set of items that are relevant to your class, the following are examples: help others, listen and respond, show empathy, get on with pupils of different backgrounds, respond well to helpful criticism and keep calm.

Discuss these findings with the pupils as you find appropriate.

Record your findings in your PDP. Discuss these ideas with other staff teaching the children at your school and use the information to plan your lessons.

Group work and the use of language is central to learners learning, not only the subject, but about each other and developing socially and emotionally. However, just putting them in groups is not sufficient as they need to be taught to learn together. For example, in my own research (Matthews, 2006) with Year 7 (11-12-year-old) learners, the learners had to discuss how well they functioned as a group. There were a range of sheets learners had to fill in individually after group work so they could compare how each of the others felt and compare it to what they felt. The sheets helped learners focus on such things as how much they talked and listened, if they felt they could speak, if it was any different for boys or girls, how they felt about each other and if they helped each other learn (Matthews, 2004). The stages included were:

1. Verbalise (through writing and talking) what the interactions meant to them.
2. Compare this with what other pupils thought had gone on (understand that there are different perceptions of the same discourse). Hence they have some evidence about different feelings.
3. Have time to think, reflect and analyse. Discuss their perceptions so that they come to understand their own and each other's viewpoints – emotional and cognitive.
4. Learn about each other and empathise with each other. This is both individually and across groups such as gender, ethnicity and social class. Become aware of power differences across and within groups. [This stage can help learners develop a sense of equity and to experience that emotional literacy is connected to equity issues.]
5. Learn to understand the subject and become aware that it involves social interactions. (Matthews, 2006, p. 96)

The teachers involved in this research reported that they learnt a lot more about the learners and their capabilities (Morrison and Matthews, 2006). The learners reported that they learnt to get on together (and behavioural difficulties reduced), to help each other learn and to support each other. This all helps learners to form friendships as they communicate with each other. The learners in the research reported how this aspect had helped them settle in to their secondary school and so helped them with the transition.

There are many materials that give ways of enabling learners to learn cognitively and emotionally at the same time, although they usually focus on the emotional (DfES, 2003b; Faupel, 2003; Casel, 2016). The point is to get to know your learners and to make them feel valued for what they can achieve, not bad for what they cannot yet do. This links to the earlier points about talking to learners to find out what they learnt in primary schools, and how they are feeling about the transition. The emphasis on learning cognitively and socially at the same time can help learners gain a growth mindset as they experience learning as an emotional event where learners help each other to learn.

Other small things can help learners feel supported and help the transfer processes. For example, never put up test results, or read out a list as this makes it seem you are only interested in how each learner compares with the others. Except for the learners who gain the top marks most learners will feel demotivated. This can lead to feelings of alienation from the school and a more anxious transfer process. You can help them by saying that what matters to them and to you is if they are improving. They can share their results with friends if they want to. See Booth (in *LTT8*, 2019) for more detail.

You can also think of ways of reducing anxiety over homework: make it simple; model how to do it; get them to pair up or do the homework as a group. These are simple examples to show you how you can think about reducing the anxiety learners feel. Now complete Task 12.7.

Task 12.7   Learner anxiety and building resilience

What can you think of to help reduce learner anxiety and build learner resilience? Is there a mechanism in the department (or school) for sharing such ideas?

Record your findings in your PDP. Discuss these ideas with other staff teaching the pupils at your school and use the information to plan your lessons.

SUMMARY AND KEY POINTS

■ Pupils come from primary schools both excited and anxious. The more you can find out about them as people, the better.

■ While all learners can experience problems during the change from primary to secondary schools, remember that lower achieving learners and vulnerable learners are more likely to have difficulties with transition. So be aware of all at-risk learners.

■ While cognitive learning is often seen by teachers as being important, learners are more concerned about social and emotional factors.

■ Tests can make learners anxious and likely to underperform. So be aware of testing regimes, especially in the early weeks for Year 7.

■ It is vital that learners are helped to settle in, develop good friendships, and learn cognitively and emotionally at the same time. Be proactive, use classroom strategies to develop your and their relationships.

■ Put yourself in your learners' shoes.

Record in your PDP, how the information in this chapter enables you to meet the requirements for your first year of teaching.

 Further resources

Resources to give help on transfer:

Jindyl-Snape's work on transitions provides further information, including Jindal-Snape, D. (2019) 'Primary-Secondary transitions', in S. Capel, M. Leask and S. Younie (eds.) *Learning to Teach in the Secondary School: A Companion to School Experience*, Abingdon: Routledge, pp.184–197.

Also see:

www.asdan.org.uk/courses/programmes/lift-off

www.ero.govt.nz/publications/evaluation-at-a-glance-transitions-from-primary-to-secondary-school/6-transition-from-primary-to-secondary-school/

www.mentalhealth.org.uk/sites/default/files/moving-on-15042013-d2125.pdf

www.nasen.org.uk/.../download.E57C5F2E-CFE0-4B75-BA50C7BF00085DBE.html

www.tes.com/news/transition-isnt-just-matter-first-term-impact-can-last-years

Reports that include advice for SENCOs:

www.nasen.org.uk/.../download.E57C5F2E-CFE0-4B75-BA50C7BF00085DBE.html

www.mentalhealth.org.uk/sites/default/files/moving-on-15042013-d2125.pdf

A book that shows how to integrate cognitive and social learning:

Matthews, B. (2006) *Engaging Education: Developing Emotional Literacy, Equity and Co-education,* Buckingham, UK: McGraw-Hill/Open University Press.

Appendices 2 and 3 list subject associations, teaching councils and relevant websites.

Books in the *Learning to Teach* series that you may find helpful are as follows:

Capel, S., Leask, M. and Younie, S. (eds.) (2019) *Learning to Teach in the Secondary School: A Companion to School Experience,* 8th edn, Abingdon: Routledge.
This book is designed as a core textbook to support student teachers through their initial teacher education programme.

Capel, S., Leask, M. and Turner, T. (eds.) (2010) *Readings for Learning to Teach in the Secondary School: A Companion to M Level Study,* Abingdon: Routledge.
This book brings together essential readings to support you in your critical engagement with key issues raised in this textbook.

The subject-specific books in the *Learning to Teach* series, the *Practical (subject) Guides, Debates in (subject)* and *Mentoring (subject) Teachers* are also very useful.

13 Learning beyond the classroom

Mark Chidler and Elizabeth Plummer

Introduction

> Learning outside the classroom is about raising achievement through an organised, powerful approach to learning in which direct experience is of prime importance.
> *(Department for Education and Skills (DfES), 2006, p.3)*

As a teacher you always seek opportunities to make learning exciting and interactive. Learning outside and beyond the classroom is a vehicle for you to develop and extend both learning opportunities for pupils by creating quality learning experiences in 'real' situations and your own teaching.

This chapter focuses on how activities supporting learning outside and beyond the classroom can be used as effective tools to facilitate and enhance pupils' learning and your teaching. A wide range of supporting evidence, as cited by Sedgewick (2012) and Learning Outside the Classroom (LOtC) (DfES, 2006), demonstrates how learning beyond the classroom can actively improve engagement of pupils with learning, whilst promoting skills and attributes such as:

- improving academic achievement;
- providing a bridge for higher order learning;
- developing skills and independence in a widening range of environments;
- making learning more engaging and relevant to young people;
- developing active citizens and stewards of the environment;
- nurturing creativity;
- providing opportunities for informal learning;
- reducing behaviour problems and improving attendance;
- stimulating inspiration and improving motivation;
- developing the ability to deal with uncertainty;
- providing challenge and the opportunity to take acceptable levels of risk;
- improving young people's attitudes to learning.

DfES (2006, p.3)

This chapter aims to help you, as a teacher new to the profession, gain an understanding of how innovative approaches to learning *beyond* the classroom (LBtC) can facilitate a transformative learning experience for pupils. The tasks in this chapter, taken together, comprise a toolkit of activities and suggestions you can work through to develop your practice, 'open up' your classroom teaching and promote the skills and attributes that can be enhanced through teaching beyond a traditional classroom setting. Some of the tasks require you to physically move outside your classroom, whereas others ask you to think about expanding your teaching into other areas of the school and indeed varied locations (locally, nationally and internationally).

OBJECTIVES

At the end of this chapter you should be able to:

■ explain the term learning beyond the classroom;
■ be aware of ways to embed learning beyond the classroom within your own practice;
■ consider a range of resources to support learning beyond the classroom (for example, locations for outdoor learning opportunities, field guides, information sheets, websites, new technologies, virtual reality head sets and personal reflections of learning beyond the classroom);
■ reflect and consider how learning beyond the classroom can be used as an effective tool to meet the requirements of your first year of teaching and beyond.

Check how the information in this chapter enables you to meet the requirements for your first year of teaching.

What is learning beyond the classroom (LBtC)?

LOtC is all learning that takes place *outside* the classroom. On the other hand, Learning Beyond the Classroom (LBtC) is broader. It encompasses learning opportunities for pupils beyond the classroom, as explained below.

However, it does not necessarily require pupils and teachers to physically leave the classroom. In its simplest sense, LBtC is the creation of learning opportunities in a variety of environments (physical or virtual).

Examples of physical environments outside the classroom include the school grounds, natural and built environments, cultural and historical sites of interest, residential and overseas experiences and indeed theme parks! Whilst by no means an exhaustive list, common locations for LBtC include state buildings such as Parliament Buildings, libraries, parks, beaches, rivers, farms, museums, art galleries, businesses and factories, business parks, shopping centres, airports and train stations. LBtC can be local, national or overseas. LBtC comes in many guises and should not be confused simply with fieldwork. Whilst fieldwork is a tool for encouraging and embedding learning experiences, LBtC is a term that encompasses a myriad of out-of-classroom learning designed to enhance, extend and stimulate a love of learning across the curriculum.

However, LBtC is not just about a physical space or location. It also encompasses the use of technology as a way of extending the learning experience. Consider the popular use of the internet as a way of researching and finding answers to questions posed. Further, consider the use of YouTube, for example, as a repository for film that, when used thoughtfully, creates extended learning experiences. Low cost virtual reality (VR) headsets now provide opportunities for immersive experiences. For example, exploring historical sites, such as Pompeii and the Grand Canyon from anywhere in the world. Development and accessibility of online forums as a means to continue discussions all add to LBtC.

Thus, LBtC includes a broad range of learning activities away from the school - locally, nationally and internationally, on the school site but beyond the classroom, and class-based through the use of new technologies. We use the term LBtC throughout this chapter, except where the term LOtC is used explicitly by others.

No doubt, you have experienced LBtC yourself. Now complete Task 13.1.

 Task 13.1   Your experiences of LBtC

1.   Reflect upon your own experiences as a pupil and list all LBtC experiences that you encountered at school (both primary and secondary).
2.   How did they extend your learning?
3.   In what ways did they encourage active learning?
4.   How were these experiences linked with the subject curriculum and the wider school curriculum, e.g. educating the whole person or preparing you as a pupil for your adult role in society or for the world of work?

Make notes in your professional development portfolio (PDP) (or similar) about what made these successful LBtC experiences and what detracted from them being a successful experience for you. Refer to these notes when planning such experiences for your pupils.

LBtC provides opportunities for teachers to be innovative in creating active learning experiences (see Shaw in *LTT8*, 2019). Active learning is simply learning by doing, which is exactly what LBtC is all about. This was reinforced by DfES (2006, p.2) who were clear that LOtC is about raising achievement through an organised, powerful approach to learning, in which direct experience is of prime importance. Whether you lead your class on a visit to investigate how river meanders are formed or chair an online debate following a class discussion or task, LBtC has the power to facilitate unique and powerful personal learning experiences. Some pupils, may also experience a sense of awe and wonder.

It is important to remember that, as discussed by Shaw (in *LTT8*, 2019), learning by doing is not enough by itself to ensure learning. LBtC experiences are linked typically with developing pupils' understanding of core concepts in the curriculum, project work and homework. As with all learning, linking experiences with tasks and actions deepens learning as does embedding a period of reflection through discussion with others, especially with you, the teacher. This facilitates not only pupils' recall but also develops 'thinking skills'. In addition, the Office for Standards in Education, Children's Services and Skill (Ofsted, 2008, p.5) consider that LOtC contributes significantly to raising standards and improving pupils' personal, social and emotional development.

LBtC and the curriculum

When considering many curricula, you will not see specific reference to the term LBtC, although some subject areas make reference to fieldwork. However, as you develop your repertoire of pedagogical skills and innovative approaches to teaching, you should consider how LBtC can be used within your particular subject area to enhance pupils' learning. Consider, for example, how you can facilitate activities and learning opportunities to consolidate and extend learning through a whole-class off-site experience or through the use of a range of multi-media, film, audio and online discussions. Task 13.2 asks you to audit LBtC opportunities in your specialist subject and to consider the range of opportunities in your subject area. Task 13.3 asks you to reflect on the LOtC manifesto (DfES, 2006) in relation to your subject.

 Task 13.2   Audit current LBtC in your specialist subject in your school and identify other opportunities

Undertake an audit of your specialist subject area to identify how LBtC is facilitated in your school. Importantly, this audit requires you to consider extended learning opportunities that are available either locally, nationally or internationally, as well as virtually. An example for physical education is shown in Table 13.1. Complete the table for your own subject area.

Table 13.1 Audit of learning opportunities for your subject

Subject area	Physical Education
Local	School grounds/local stadiums
National	Visit top national sports arena
International	Sports tour
Virtual	YouTube, Vimeo, Vevo, Google Video

Now speak to your departmental colleagues about what they do and what they recommend. It may be that teachers bring together several classes for certain LBtC activities.

Now consider:

What other LBtC activities could you use in your subject area?

What other innovative ideas for LBtC could you create yourself for your pupils? For example:

■   whole-class visits to museums/art galleries/sites of specific interest;
■   online virtual learning environment (debates);

- YouTube;
- virtual reality animations/films;
- others.

Create a section in your PDP to keep records of the LBtC activities. Store this audit in it to refer to when considering planning LBtC opportunities for your classes.

 Task 13.3 Reflecting on your subject within the context of LBtC

Critically evaluate the DfES, LOtC Manifesto (DfES, 2006) in relation to your specialist subject area. Write a critical analysis of how your subject could be enhanced when taken beyond the classroom.

Store this analysis in your PDP.

When starting to consider opportunities for LBtC, we advise you to start with those in the school grounds and the local area as well as virtual opportunities – particularly those which can be undertaken within lesson time; rather than those which require a half or full day or longer. Although there are still considerations regarding (for example, safeguarding, pupils' safety, risk assessment, adult/pupil ratios, insurance, transport, protocols covering parental consent and costs), they do not involve, for example, changes to the school timetable, permission for pupils to miss other lessons etc. (see the section 'Planning for LBtC' below). Some schools have periods within the school year that are 'off timetable' and these provide opportunities for extended LBtC activities but these need to be planned well in advance and often involve other colleagues and liaison with others over months. This may allow for LBtC activities further afield that require more time.

LBtC and developing everyday classroom practice

As you incorporate LBtC into your planning and teaching, you become accomplished at using a range of activities to enhance pupils' learning. Long-term planning enables you to be strategic in ensuring that a variety of activities and experiences can be created and used to extend learning and provide additional depth of understanding. Task 13.4 asks you to identify LBtC in a scheme of work and Task 13.5 asks you to consider apps you might use.

 Task 13.4 Identifying LBtC in a scheme of work

In school, you are likely to be given schemes of work from which you plan. Take one scheme of work and as you read through, begin to annotate opportunities for LBtC.

Use Table 13.2 to identify opportunities locally, nationally, internationally and virtually. Store this in your PDP when complete.

Table 13.2 Opportunities for LBtC in a scheme of work

Classroom	School grounds	Local	National	International

 Task 13.5 Apps you could use to support LBtC in your subject

Identify which of the apps in Table 13.3 could be used in your subject area to support learning and clearly outline how they could be used within your subject area. Consider any other apps and digital technologies you might use to support LBtC in your teaching. Store this in your PDP and add to it as you identify other apps and digital technologies that you could use.

It is important to consider the notion that many educationalists advocate, that the main focus of education is to build upon an individual's capacity to learn for example, making meaningful connections and developing knowledge and understanding. As Claxton (2002) states, for individuals to develop the capacity to learn they need to firstly develop four specific characteristics.

■ *Resilience*: being ready and willing to enjoy learning, whilst staying focused even in the face of many distractions. Developing the ability to face difficulties and fears.
■ *Resourcefulness*: being able to learn in different ways. Developing a wide range of different learning strategies.
■ *Reflectiveness*: being ready and willing to look at different approaches to solve problems. Considering one's own strengths and areas of development.
■ *Reciprocity*: being able to learn alone and with others. Developing the ability to contribute whilst learning from other approaches.

It is important to consider the development of learning capacity when planning activities and learning opportunities that arise outside of the perceived normal classroom environment in LBtC. You may well have experienced how some pupils react positively and some negatively to learning in different environments. For example, learning in an unconventional environment may well challenge pupils in terms of their behaviour, responsibilities and roles. Furthermore, a day visit to an art gallery or a residential field trip may well be the first time that pupils have had this opportunity, and it is not uncommon for them to find this challenging, both physically and mentally. This may manifest itself in poor behaviour or indeed, result in improved engagement from pupils.

Table 13.3 Examples of apps for use in your subject area

Examples of apps	Yes – could be used or No – could not be used	If could be used, how it could be used in the subject area?
Google Maps		
Google Earth		
Pacer		
Dictionary		
BBC News		
Kahoot!		
Dropbox		
FaceTime		
Skype		
YouTube		
Other apps and digital technologies		

Now complete Tasks 13.6 and 13.7.

Task 13.6   Claxton's four R's

Consider the identified educational benefits for LOtC as listed at the start of the chapter and assign each to one or more of Claxton's four R's. An example is given:

Resilience	
Resourcefulness	
Reflectiveness	Improving academic achievement
Reciprocity	

Record this analysis in your PDP and use it when setting objectives for lessons that fall into the LBtC category.

Table 13.4 Commonly used resources and places for LBtC in your subject

	Subject area	Activity
School grounds	*Geography*	*Environmental audit*
Local area		
Museums		
Art galleries		
New technologies	*History*	*VR headsets – virtual tour of Pompeii*
Other		
Other		

  Task 13.7   Extended learning opportunities

To begin to use LBtC with your pupils, consider the commonly used places and resources in Table 13.4, and reflect how you could use these to provide LBtC opportunities to extend teaching and enhance pupils' learning in your subject. Table 13.4 shows two examples of how this can be undertaken (note, school grounds, local opportunities and virtual are listed as these are likely to be possible within your normal timetable time). Complete Table 13.4 in relation to your own subject area.

File this in the LBtC section of your PDP for reference when planning your long-term schemes of work. Overtime, these records make it much quicker and easier for you to provide LBtC experiences for your pupils.

The links in the Further resources at the end of this chapter might help with some ideas.

Museums as an example of an LBtC resource for teaching and learning

The value and importance of using museums as a tool to encourage and extend LBtC should not be overlooked or underestimated. As Talboys (2010) reflects, museums encourage active learning in a variety of ways. They can provide access to genuine artefacts that enable learners to conceptualise cultural material and cultural heritage. They also provide opportunities to engage with new technologies through the use of quick response (QR) codes linked to exhibits that can be scanned and other innovative interactive display material. In order to further extend learning, many museum services provide access to artefacts through dedicated loan services.

Museums come in all shapes and sizes and, as identified by Talboys (2010), often fall into five particular categories:

1. national
2. provincial

3.   university
4.   independent
5.   private

Now complete Task 13.8.

 Task 13.8   Identifying museums for your subject area

Consider your local area, identifying the museums that are easily accessible and what resources are available that would be beneficial in your subject area. Visit as many as you can and whilst there identify any educational services that may be available, such as guides, taught sessions, interactive lectures and teaching resource packs, all of which provide a strong foundation for the planning and leading of a visit. Keep your record in your PDP for future reference.

Of course, visiting a museum is only one key aspect of using such a valuable resource. It is important to be mindful that in order to get the best out of such a visit you plan and prepare thoroughly for the visit, including identifying and reviewing available online and digital resources that may be available. Furthermore, consider carefully all follow-up activities to ensure they facilitate the extension of the learning experience.

Earlier in the chapter you considered Claxton's (2002) four R's of resilience, resourcefulness, reflectiveness and reciprocity. Museum visits, whether organised by you or used as a directed task to be undertaken out of school hours, have the power to build upon each of the four R's. As Claxton advocates, it is important to create a culture that cultivates habits and attitudes that enable young people to become confident and competent learners who are able to face the many challenges of learning in a calm and diligent manner. Task 13.9 asks you to consider how this can be achieved.

  Task 13.9   Claxton's four R's and museums

Choose one of the museum websites listed below, or another museum relevant to your subject, and review the content. Identify how, by visiting the location (physically or virtually), resilience, resourcefulness, reflectiveness and reciprocity could be developed in pupils. Consider and identify the challenges your pupils may face when learning in an unfamiliar environment. Discuss these with your mentor or another teacher in your subject area.

   British Museum - www.britishmuseum.org
   Birmingham Museum and Art Centre - www.birminghammuseums.org.uk/bmag
   National Museum Wales - https://museum.wales/cardiff
   National Museums Northern Ireland - www.nmni.com/Home.aspx
   National Museums Scotland - www.nms.ac.uk

File your notes in the LBtC section of your PDP for use when planning your long-term schemes of work.

Resilience	
Resourcefulness	
Reflectiveness	
Reciprocity	

Museums were included here as an example, other locations can have an equal impact (see examples listed on p.173).

Planning for LBtC

When you consider using museums and other off-site venues as teaching and learning tools, there are a number of very important considerations and procedures you must follow. Also you require a range of skills, some of which may be new. For example, you need clear and effective organisational capabilities and the ability to communicate your intended outcomes to a variety of audiences. Planning early LBtC opportunities with another member(s) of your subject department is a good way of identifying the skills you need. Discuss with other members of your subject department or your mentor how you might go about developing such skills and plan activities to help your development.

You need to consult your school fieldwork policy documentation and undertake a risk assessment. You need to find out about the school's requirements for such activities, which include, for example adult/pupil ratios, safeguarding, insurance, transport as well as the protocols covering parental consent and costs for any such activities. You need to consider timetable constraints, additional staffing and costs, depending upon where the off-site venue you wish to visit is located. These are necessary and should not be seen or considered as barriers; rather good practice and a way of ensuring you meet and maintain pupils' safety. Always liaise with your line manager and school Senior Leadership Team to ensure that all requirements are met before embarking upon any LBtC activities. It is advisable to support the planning of an activity by an experienced member of staff before trying to do this on your own.

Professional development

As you think about developing this aspect of your teaching also consider opportunities for your own development, e.g. through undertaking national and international experiences yourself. Below are some links that may give ideas for developing your own practice through extended opportunities overseas. Talk to other staff about other possible links/opportunities, locally, nationally, internationally and virtually.

British Council –www.britishcouncil.org
Camp America – www.campamerica.co.uk

Erasmus Exchange Programme – www.erasmusprogramme.com and www.erasmusplus.org.uk
www.buildingfuturesinthegambia.com

These may give you the chance to develop not only your own interests but also your understanding of pedagogy within national and international settings. From this you might go on to devise lesson plans, schemes, projects or pursue further academic study – studying at Masters level and/or taking recognised accredited courses.

You might also work across subjects in such activities. Task 13.10 looks at using LBtC across the school.

M

 Task 13.10   Analysis of LBtC across the school

Conduct a whole-school audit to identify opportunities that currently take place for LBtC for all subject areas. Analyse and identify the benefits to pupils learning and reflect upon how this could enhance specialist subject knowledge. This aids knowledge and understanding of whole-school issues.

Store this information in your PDP for later reference.

SUMMARY AND KEY POINTS

After reading this chapter you should understand that LBtC is not necessarily an expedition to a far-flung corner of the earth. It is about providing enhanced learning opportunities that extend and develop individual capacity to learn, including:

■ improving pupil engagement with learning;
■ promoting resilience, resourcefulness, reflectiveness and reciprocity;
■ providing learners with a transformative learning experience.

These opportunities include, but are not limited to:

■ the use of new technologies such as VR headsets;
■ YouTube videos to explore distant places;
■ museums and art galleries as a rich resource for teaching and learning;
■ field work experiences in the local area or further afield.

However, to incorporate LBtC effectively into your teaching and embed it into your own practice to enhance pupils' learning needs careful thought and in all instances careful planning and preparation of the visit itself and follow up activities.

In conclusion, it is important as a teacher to remember, as stated by the DfES (2006, p. 1) 'that every young person should experience the world beyond the classroom as an essential part of learning and personal development, whatever their age, ability or circumstances'. As advocated throughout this chapter, this can be undertaken through a variety of creative and imaginative activities.

Record in your PDP, how the information in this chapter enables you to meet the requirements for your first year of teaching.

Further resources

www.lotc.org.uk – Council for Learning Outside the Classroom
This website is designed to support anyone working with children and young people to provide high-quality educational experiences by providing a large range of resources developed with the support of many experts in learning outside the classroom.

www.outdoor-learning.org – Institute for Outdoor Learning
Examples of websites follow that might be useful for extending learning opportunities (there are many others of course that are relevant to your own subject; Appendix 2 lists subject associations and teaching councils).

https://bletchleypark.org.uk – Bletchley Park

www.cwgc.org – Commonwealth Graves Commission

www.forestschools.com – Forest Schools

www.gov.uk/find-your-local-park – Local Parks

www.iwm.org.uk – Imperial War Museums

www.nationaltrust.org.uk – National Trust

www.rsc.org.uk – Royal Shakespeare Company

www.sciencemuseum.org.uk – Science Museum

https://spacecentre.co.uk – National Space Centre

www.youthsporttrust.org – Youth Sport Trust

Appendices 2 and 3 list subject associations, teaching councils and relevant websites.

Books in the *Learning to Teach* series that you may find helpful are as follows:

Capel, S., Leask, M. and Younie, S. (eds.) (2019) *Learning to Teach in the Secondary School: A Companion to School Experience,* **8th edn, Abingdon: Routledge.**
This book is designed as a core textbook to support student teachers through their initial teacher education programme.

Capel, S., Leask, M. and Turner, T. (eds.) (2010) *Readings for Learning to Teach in the Secondary School: A Companion to M Level Study,* **Abingdon: Routledge.**
This book brings together essential readings to support you in your critical engagement with key issues raised in this textbook.

The subject-specific books in the *Learning to Teach* series, the *Practical (subject) Guides, Debates in (subject)* and *Mentoring (subject) Teachers* are also very useful.

14 Improving pupil progress through quality questioning and talk

Nikki Booth

Introduction

Talk is a key tool that we as teachers have for guiding learning in the development of constructing knowledge. Indeed, research has shown that the interaction and collaboration learners have between adults and peers can provide important opportunities for both learning and cognitive development (Mercer and Littleton, 2007). The notion of constructivism, as a theory of learning, describes a way in which we are able to work side-by-side with thinking learners whose ideas are central to the teaching and learning process (Shively, 2015). Constructivism, therefore, supports you in adopting a more learner-centred approach based on active, rather than passive, learning. This is an important concept because understanding cannot simply be passed from you, the teacher, to the learner; it must be built up by each learner on the basis of their experience (Garnett, 2013). A key element within constructivist learning theory is *scaffolding*. This is a powerful pedagogical tool and, as the name suggests, is when the teacher supports learners just like scaffolding can support a building. Over time, the scaffolds can be gradually withdrawn by the teacher as the learner grows towards mastery. The use of scaffolding through classroom-based talk is an effective element of constructivism and allows for cognitive development where learners can become more accomplished problem-solvers. Teachers who use scaffolding through talk effectively are able to guide learners in the process of learning, push them to think more deeply and model the sorts of questions and responses that learners need to be developing for themselves without simply giving them the final answers (Hmelo-Silver, 2006).

Because of the importance of talk, this chapter focuses on how you can use it more effectively within the day-to-day classroom. The main emphasis of the first part of this chapter unpicks teacher-learner discourse and, with the use of effective formative assessment, explores how you can improve this to develop the quality of your learners' responses during lessons. From this, the second part deals with notions of learner-learner discussions and, through the modelling of teacher-learner talk, how these can become more effective overtime.

OBJECTIVES

At the end of this chapter you should be able to:

■ understand how to use formative assessment effectively to enhance the quality of teacher-learner talk;

■ pre-plan effective questions;

■ use questions as feedback to move learning forward;

■ model and scaffold effective questioning to develop quality learner-learner talk.

Check how the information in this chapter enables you to meet the requirements for your first year of teaching.

Using formative assessment to enhance the quality of teacher-learner talk

What is formative assessment?

Formative assessment (also commonly referred to as assessment *for* learning) can be described as an ongoing *process* that involves working *with* learners so that they know where they are in their learning, where they need to be and how they are going to get there. In relation to classroom talk, formative assessment normally involves a conversation that enables teaching and learning to move forward. What makes formative assessment truly *formative*, though, is not only the collecting and giving of information, but that the information is *used*, by all involved, to improve learning. A comprehensive discussion of formative (and summative) assessment is presented by Booth (in *LTT8*, 2019).

What does research say about teachers' questioning?

Teachers ask hundreds of questions every day (Marzano, 1991). It has been shown, however, that a large proportion of these questions actually require simple, factual or recall responses from learners (Wiliam, 2000). Research on teacher questioning (for example, Barnette, Orletsky and Sattes, 1994) has found that the number of surface-level questions (also known as 'closed' as opposed to 'open' questions) was in the region of 80% plus. This can be a problem in the classroom as these 'closed' questions often require single-word or very short answers and can easily favour learners who 'have this information at their fingertips' (Fautley and Savage, 2008, p. 38). This is not to say that all surface-level questions are bad and that you should only ever ask higher-level questions because we know that higher-level thinking cannot occur without a surface-level foundation. What the research above is saying is that there is a clear imbalance between the two types. (Detailed advice on questioning is provided by Zwozdiak-Myers and Capel in *LTT8*, 2019.)

It is also possible, of course, that questioning may not elicit more productive talk because it can often be a way of the teacher leading and controlling the classroom.

Furthermore, since learners are already aware that you know the answers, they may see little or no need to think about the answers at all (Wade and Moje, 2000). What you need to be mindful of, as Moore and Stanley put it, is that 'if you teach them facts, what you're going to get back is facts' (2010, p. xvii). That said, there is good evidence, however (for example, Black et al., 2003), that when learners are engaged in deep, rich, higher-order conversations, based on an understanding of the surface knowledge, enhanced learning takes place.

For many years it has been believed that teacher-learner talk is the best source to enhance progress in the classroom (Flanders, 1970) within the secondary setting (van den Akker, 1998). Research into teacher-learner talk has found, however, that teachers would often dominate the talk (Hardman, Abd-Kadir and Smith, 2008) and control topics and learning (Cazden, 2001). Liu and Le (2011), for example, found that in lessons of 45 minutes in duration, an average of 31 minutes was taken up with teacher-talk time and an average of 9 minutes was for learner talk. What is clear from this research is that learner talking time was severely reduced and they were found to only speak for short periods in response to teacher prompts. Chapter 19 provides advice about undertaking research into your practice and your use of questioning may be a useful focus for you if you wish to undertake a small-scale research study. Task 14.1 provides a starting point in analysing your practice.

In their research, Sinclair and Coulthard (1975) found a regular structure in the oral interactions between teachers and learners. These exchanges consisted of a teacher *initiation* (I), which was usually in the form of a question, a learner *response* (R) and teacher feedback (F) based on the learner's response. For example:

Teacher: What is the capital of Spain? (I)
Learner: Madrid. (R)
Teacher: Good. (F)

This notion of 'IRF' has been found to still be a common feature in classrooms today not only in the United Kingdom (Mercer and Dawes, 2008), but also internationally (Friend, 2017; Tainio and Laine, 2015). This is because teachers frequently use oral questioning to assess learners' understanding, maintain their attention and to provide feedback on the responses they hear (Mercer and Dawes, 2008). This common structure, however, has been criticised as talk can be 'overwhelmingly monologic' (Alexander, 2004, p. 10). Furthermore, these types of questions only allow learners to reiterate information, which has probably already been provided by the teacher at an earlier phase of learning. Other research (for example, Wegerif and Dawes, 2004) found that teachers would sometimes allow an 'IDRF' structure where learners would be able to *discuss* (D) their answers before giving a response to the question. Although this means that learners are able to take a more active role in constructing their knowledge, they are still likely to be responding with a single or short answer. What we need, then, is a taxonomy in order to develop more 'open' and higher-level questions to help elicit better quality responses from our learners.

Now complete Task 14.1.

Task 14.1   Reflecting on classroom talk

Video record or ask a colleague to observe a lesson and respond to the following reflective questions about your classroom:

1. What was the proportion of teacher-talk and learner-talk in the lesson? How did you calculate this?
2. What was the proportion of 'closed' and 'open' questions in the lesson?
3. How did you respond to learner responses throughout the lesson?
4. If you teach in a mixed school, how much time did you spend with girls – boys?
5. How much time did you spend with learners at the front of the class compared to those at the back?
6. What was the balance between IRF and IDRF questions? Was that what you planned? If not, why was it different?
7. Reflect on how you could enhance the quality of your teacher-learner talk in your lessons.

Store your recordings and/or observation notes in your professional development portfolio (PDP) (or similar) and refer to these when planning lessons so your lessons reinforce your growing professional understanding.

Taxonomies for higher-level thinking and talking: Bloom's and SOLO

Bloom's Taxonomy

Possibly the most well-known and frequently used taxonomy is Bloom's Taxonomy. The original version (Bloom et al., 1956) shows a six-point hierarchical scale that differentiates types of thinking that are undergone when learners answer questions. From lower-order thinking to higher-order, these different types include: knowledge, comprehension, application, analysis, synthesis and evaluation. As teachers naturally you want your learners to be 'evaluators' of their own work. This notion, however, requires some thought. During a question, a learner may 'evaluate' something by responding with 'I think that's awful'. Whilst this is indeed an evaluation, consideration needs to be given to the fact that the learner may not be able to communicate suitable thoughts as to *why* they have come to such a negative evaluation. At the other end of the taxonomy the notion of 'knowledge' (knowing things) can also be seen as problematic because it has been separated from a learner's ability to *use* such knowledge. As Spruce asserts:

> 'knowledge' is no longer independent from them [the learners] but part of their being – of their consciousness … knowledge and the relationship of knowledge to the learners has been reconceptualised to one where it does not exist independently of them but is created by them.
>
> *(Spruce, 2010, p.189)*

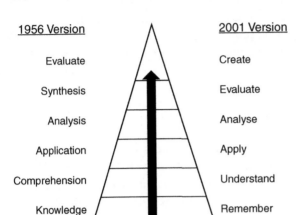

1956 Version		2001 Version
Evaluate		Create
Synthesis		Evaluate
Analysis		Analyse
Application		Apply
Comprehension		Understand
Knowledge		Remember

Figure 14.1 A comparison of Bloom's Taxonomies (Bloom et al., 1956; Anderson and Krathwohl, 2001) in Hook, Booth, Price and Fobister (2019)

Bloom's Taxonomy was revised (Anderson and Krathwohl, 2001) and changes to the cognitive hierarchy were made. The new hierarchy includes: remember, understand, apply, analyse, evaluate and create. A comparison between the two Bloom's versions has been provided by Hook, Booth, Price and Fobister (2019) and is shown in Figure 14.1.

One obvious change worth mentioning between the 1956 and 2001 versions is the alteration from nouns to verbs. This is an important consideration as it shows a clear change in the approach to understanding about learner thinking (Fautley and Kinsella, 2015). In other words, this means that learning is being seen as a frequent ongoing *process* rather than a set of isolated products.

To have 'create' at the top of the new hierarchy, though, also needs further analysing. Regardless of the subject, you want your learners to be creative from the earliest possible experiences of learning. The term 'create', according to Padget is when: '[l]earners ... are engaged in making meaning together through stimulating learning tasks of which they feel ownership' (2013, p.2). If you want your learners to be creative from the earliest possible opportunities then does this mean that they can 'jump to the top of the Bloom pyramid' (Fautley and Kinsella, 2015, p.115) and that they have nothing more to learn? Absolutely not! A further problem with both versions is that there is an assumed relationship between the question asked and the resulting response (Schrag, 1989). This is not necessarily the case, as shown in the 'evaluation' example above, because a supposedly higher-order question could actually receive a lower-order response (Fairbrother, 1975).

The SOLO Taxonomy

The lesser-known taxonomy, in comparison to Bloom's 1956 and 2001 versions, is SOLO (Structure of Observed Learning Outcomes). The SOLO Taxonomy is a model of learning that appears to provide a simple, reliable and robust framework of understanding: surface, deep and conceptual (also referred to as transfer) (Biggs and Collis, 1982). It should be pointed out that although Biggs and Collis (1982) originally designed the SOLO Taxonomy with learner outcomes in mind (for example, the assessing of written work), it is now also frequently used in classrooms throughout the world as a teaching and learning strategy during the process of learning (Hook, Booth, Price and Fobister, 2019).

What makes the SOLO Taxonomy particularly interesting is that it can make the outcome of a question 'visible' to teachers (and learners). SOLO has proved to be a reliable and valid tool across a variety of curriculum areas (Biggs and Collis, 1982) where learner responses are 'assigned' one of five hierarchical levels. In its simplest language, each 'level' can be described as: no idea, one idea, multiple ideas, relating the ideas and extending the ideas (Hook, Booth, Price and Fobister, 2019). In addition, SOLO consists of three principle categories, surface (*unistructural* and *multistructural*), deep (*relational*) and (deeper) conceptual (*extended abstract*). Figure 14.2 shows key symbols and terminology associated with the SOLO Taxonomy.

Within the classroom, the two surface-level categories involve understanding ideas, for example, a *unistructural* response to a question would require the knowledge of only one piece of information. With an increase in quantity, a *multistructural* response would require two or more pieces of information. The two deeper categories show a change from quantity to quality, which is more cognitively challenging. A *relational* response, then, would require learners to integrate or relate the separate pieces of information from the multistructural level. At the top of the SOLO Taxonomy, an *extended abstract response* would require learners to go beyond the information given by making predictions or hypotheses in a new context – without or with very little teacher scaffolding (Hook, Booth, Price and Fobister, 2019). During the process of questioning, SOLO makes it possible to identify, in broad terms, which 'level' a learner is currently working at and, for effective formative assessment to take place, how a learner's understanding of a concept can become deeper.

Using SOLO offers potential remedies to the problems with both Bloom's versions (1956 and 2001). First, the clear hierarchical structure enables the evaluation of a learner's response through the progression of quantitative knowledge to qualitative knowledge, establishing connections and relationships and extending current knowledge into new, untaught, concepts. In other words, there is a progression from *how much* the learner knows about a topic to *how well* they know it. Second, with SOLO, unlike Bloom's, there is no assumed relationship between the question asked and the resulting correct response. Supported by effective formative assessment, the SOLO Taxonomy then is able to offer you as teachers a clear method for asking questions so that learning can progress.

	Surface learning		Deep(er) learning	Conceptual learning
Prestructural	Unistructural	Multistructural	Relational	Extended Abstract

Figure 14.2 SOLO-based symbols and terminology

Developing effective questions for deeper responses using the SOLO Taxonomy

Questioning is an excellent strategy that both teachers and learners engage with during every lesson and is an ideal opportunity for formative assessment to take place. The purpose of questioning is not to just find out what learners know and do not know, but for you to engage in a conversation with your learners with a view of challenging their thinking at a variety of levels. Asking questions using SOLO means that you are able to develop progressive questions, which help move learning (and teaching) within the lesson forward. A particular advantage of oral questions (as opposed to written questions) is that they allow immediate feedback where both teachers and learners can be reactive, and further questions to probe a deeper level of understanding can be asked rather than just simply recalling information. The progressive nature of the SOLO Taxonomy means that some questions can be pre-planned (Fautley, 2009) and that, with effective formative assessment, learners are able to move up the levels of the SOLO Taxonomy during the lesson. It should be noted that the *extended abstract* questions are designed for information to be transferred into new contexts based on current information (Hook, Booth, Price and Fobister (2019)). From a planning perspective, this does not mean that some learners are doing a different unit of work at the same time as the others, but aims to provide suitable challenge for them to transfer their knowledge. Table 14.1, for example, shows some possible pre-planned starting points for a music lesson provided by Hook, Booth, Price and Fobister (2019) in relation to key SOLO Taxonomy verbs.

Now complete Task 14.2.

 Task 14.2   SOLO-based questioning

Using the SOLO Taxonomy and the music examples in Table 14.1 as a guide, pre-plan a set of starting questions for a lesson you are going to teach. Try and include at least one question for each level that:

- might result with a single piece of information (*unistructural*);
- might result with several pieces of information (*multistructural*);
- might result in several pieces of information being linked together (*relational*); and
- might result in learners thinking beyond by predicting or hypothesising where the concept in question is transferred into another context (*extended abstract*).

Record your notes in your PDP to refer to when planning lessons so your lessons reinforce your deepening professional understanding.

With formative assessment you need to think carefully about how learning, through questioning, can be moved forward. The following examples in Tables 14.2, 14.3 and 14.4 are taken from a series of Year 10 music lessons, which illustrate how a learner's response can progress using the SOLO Taxonomy as a formative assessment strategy. The names used, of course, are pseudonyms. Read these tables now.

Table 14.1 Examples of SOLO-based, pre-planned question stems in music (from Hook, Booth, Price and Fobister, 2019)

SOLO level	Example questions	SOLO verb
Unistructural	■ What does the word 'tempo' mean?	Define
	■ Can you name one composer of the Classical period?	Name
	■ Can you point to the treble clef?	Label
	■ What is this instrument you are listening to?	Identify
	■ Can you find middle C on the keyboard?	Find
	■ Which orchestral family does this instrument belong to?	Match
Multistructural	■ Can you describe the mood of this music?	Describe
	■ Can you name three instruments that are playing?	List
	■ Can you outline the features of the Baroque period?	Outline
	■ Can you tell me more about that?	Elaborate
	■ Can you give two musical reasons why this piece is joyful?	Combine
Relational	■ Can you place these composers in historical order?	Sequence
	■ Which period of music is this piece from and why?	Classify
	■ What are the similarities and differences between these two pieces?	Compare and contrast
	■ Can you explain the effect World War Two had on music?	Explain
	■ Can you analyse the development of instrumentation during the romantic period?	Analyse
	■ Can you organise these composers into their correct period giving reasons for your answers?	Organise
	■ What is the difference between these two pieces of music?	Distinguish
Extended abstract	■ In general, from what you know about Blues music, what can you tell me about Jazz music?	Generalise
	■ From what you know about Stravinsky, what do you expect to hear from this piece?	Predict
	■ Can you evaluate the use of elements in this new piece?	Evaluate
	■ Can you now create a piece of music inspired by minimalism?	Create
	■ How could you improve your composition and how do you think this will improve your piece of music?	Reflect
	■ Can you explain your practice plan to your partner and how you think it will improve your playing?	Plan
	■ Can you justify the choice of instrumentation in your composition?	Justify
	■ Why do you think Classical music is less popular now than in its day?	Argue
	■ Can you compose a piece of gamelan music?	Compose

Table 14.2 Example of a learner's response progressing from unistructural to multistructural

Teacher:	What are the main instruments playing in this piece, Victoria?	multistructural
Learner:	A flute, Sir.	unistructural
Teacher:	Okay, listen again, what else do we hear after the flute?	prompt - multistructural
Learner:	Erm … a trumpet and then a violin.	multistructural

Table 14.3 Example of a learner's response progressing from multistructural to relational

Teacher:	Describe how tempi are used in this piece, Martin.	multistructural
Learner:	It starts off fast then gradually gets faster and faster. After a while it suddenly slows down.	multistructural
Learner:	Do you think the choice of tempi is suitable for the title of this piece?	relational
Learner:	I do, 'cause since it's called *Rollercoaster* the getting faster and faster is like when you have just started the ride and the end slows down just like it, too.	relational

Table 14.4 Example of a learner's response progressing from relational to extended abstract

Teacher:	Why do you think this piece is distinctly Baroque, Helen?	relational
Learner:	Because it has a harpsichord.	unistructural
Teacher:	Okay, anything else? Did you notice anything fancy about the melodies?	prompt - multistructural
Learner:	Oh yer … it had lots of trills and mordents in it and the tune kept on coming back … erm … ritornello form.	multistructural
Teacher:	Ok, good. And why do you think these are important in the Baroque period?	prompt - relational
Learner:	Well … the harpsichord was one of the most popular keyboard instruments of the period, the trills and mordents help keep the listener interested because the long notes would be boring without them.	relational
Teacher	And what about the ritornello form? Why is that important?	relational
Learner:	It's important because there are so many ideas and the little returns of the tune help keep the listener interested in the music.	relational
Teacher:	Right. So, is there anything that you think would be different in the Classical period, then?	extended abstract
Learner:	Erm … I think the biggest difference would be that there wouldn't be a harpsichord because the piano became more popular then.	extended abstract

In the example shown in Table 14.2, the teacher is looking for more than one correct answer to the question (multistructural). Victoria, however, has only given one correct answer, which has fallen short of the demands of the question. The teacher then prompts her with a follow-up question as more information is still required. Her second response becomes multistructural with the inclusion of two additional instruments she has heard.

Again, in the example shown in Table 14.3, the teacher asks a question and is clearly looking for more than one piece of information. The learner, Martin, is able to respond by giving several pieces of accurate information (multistructural). Rather than simply moving on to another learner, the teacher then challenges Martin with a relational question, which requires him to think about (relate) the music he heard and the title of the piece. In response to this question, Martin is able to explain what being on a rollercoaster is like and successfully apply this to the music.

In the example shown in Table 14.4, the teacher starts by asking the learner, Helen, a relational question. As her response is only based on a single piece of information (unistructural), the teacher follows up with a multistructural question to help scaffold a better response. After this has successfully been done, the teacher re-attempts questions at a relational level to which Helen is able to give more developed answers compared to her previous ones. In an effort to challenge her, the teacher attempts an extended abstract question, which requires Helen to use the information she currently has and transfer it into a context that the teacher has not taught her – the Classical period. This allows Helen to use her current knowledge about the Baroque period and any previous knowledge she might have about the Classical period and bring the two together.

Whilst some of these examples might be classed as 'in an ideal world', there is often a limit to what a learner in your class can actually answer. In SOLO terms, there might be times when, at a questioning point, a unistructural response, for example, is as best as the learner can do at that time, and prompting them for more information will not work. In addition, there are times when a learner simply does not know the answer (prestructural). An effective strategy in these cases would be for you to say 'that's ok, I'll come back to you'. What happens next is that you would continue to collect responses from other learners in the class and circle back to this learner who, having listened to their peers, would contribute with an answer. This can be seen as a very positive formative assessment strategy as the learner needs to listen to their peers in order to contribute to the activity (Hodgen and Webb, 2008).

Enhancing the quality of learner-learner talk

Although good teacher-learner talk is important, more recent research (for example, Pay, 2016) shows that learner-learner talk is able to offer greater benefits including engagement, behaviour and decision making. On analysing the Office for Standards in Education, Children's Services and Skills (Ofsted) report of the quality of teaching Paton (2014) found that the inspectorate had criticised a number of schools for hindering learners' autonomy by reducing opportunities to discover their own learning through 'chalk and talk' teaching. Indeed, Vygotsky (1978) argued that language is a key psychological and cultural tool where social involvement through group-based problem-solving is a key factor for an individual's development. Furthermore, Mercer (2015) states that there are wider benefits of using learner-learner talk than just for attainment and progress and goes on to say that such talk, when done effectively, can have additional benefits for formative assessment and higher-order thinking.

According to Sinclair and Coulthard (1975), the 'IRF' structure is not fit for purpose for learner-learner interactions as there is no agreement as to who has control over the discourse. Peer discussions allow learners the opportunity to disagree, reflect and develop roles and relationships with one another in developing learning within the classroom (Zack and Graves, 2001) through social interaction (Mercer and Littleton, 2007). As Pierce and Gilles state: 'having students build on one another's ideas and create meaning together is the essence of critical conversations' (2008, p. 40). Barnes and Todd (1977) posit that learners are more likely to involve themselves in open and extended group discussions when the teacher is not visible to them. They go on to say:

> Our point is that to place the responsibility in the learners' hands changes the nature of that learning by requiring them to negotiate their own criteria of relevance and truth. If schooling is to prepare young people for responsible adult life, such learning has an important place in the repertoire of social relationships which teachers have at their disposal.
>
> (Barnes and Todd, 1977, p. 127)

Whist this may be the case, it is important to differentiate between learners working *in* a group to those working *as* a group. Research has shown (for example, Alexander, 2004) that although learners may well be sitting in close proximity to one another they may actually be working alone.

Mercer (2004) developed a three-part typology on the different types of learner-learner talk; *disputational talk, cumulative talk* and *exploratory talk. Disputational talk* might involve all the learners in a group, but can be characterised by disagreement and individualised decision making with few attempts of constructive criticism being made. A typical discourse here is likely to involve commands and assertions between learners. *Cumulative talk* is when learners build on what others have said through co-operative working but without any criticality of ideas. *Exploratory talk* is when learners are engaged in talk that is critical but constructive of others' ideas. In other words, they challenge one another's ideas. A key feature here is when all learners are actively participating and all opinions and points of view are carefully considered before a joint decision is made. Observational research (for example, Mercer and Littleton, 2007) has revealed that although exploratory talk is a powerful means of learners thinking and reasoning together (for example, 'Why do you think that?'), this type of talk seldom happens within group settings.

The use of exploratory talk does not just happen overnight or even within a short period of time. What needs to happen, in order to develop this, is the careful modelling and scaffolding of effective and deep teacher-learner dialogue in order for learners, as Sadler puts it, 'to hold a concept of quality [talk] similar to that of the teacher' (Sadler, 1989, p. 121). Using the SOLO Taxonomy as a tool for progressive questioning means that you are able to judge the quality of a learner's response and provide further questioning, as a means of formative feedback, to either scaffold or challenge them further to develop their answers. With a move from the less frequent use of the common 'IRF' structure to a more developed and progressive dialogue within the classroom, learner-learner talk can become an effective question-and-answer learning activity of its own. Reading the MESHGuide on 'Classroom Dialogue and Learning' (Cook et al., 2018) from the Cambridge University research centre, which specialises in research on classroom talk, should further extend your understanding of the pedagogical issues raised in this chapter.

Now complete Task 14.3

Task 14.3   Analysing the quality of learner-learner talk

As you walk around your classroom during paired or group work complete the following action research-based exercises:

1. *Quantitative data collection*: Is the group-based talk mainly *disputational*, *cumulative* or *exploratory*?
2. *Qualitative data collection*: What is being said within this type of talk?
3. How does the quality of the group-based talk develop over time as you model and scaffold more developed and challenging questions as a means of feedback to your learners?
4. Reflect on how you can develop this further in your practice and plan accordingly.

Record your observation notes and findings in your PDP to refer to when planning lessons so your lessons reinforce and build on your growing professional understanding.

SUMMARY AND KEY POINTS

- Formative assessment, in relation to classroom talk, normally involves a conversation that enables teaching and learning to move forward.
- Pre-planned questions, using the SOLO Taxonomy enables you to develop learners' responses to progress in quantity and quality, while providing opportunities for the transfer of information into other contexts. This in turn helps develop higher-order thinking skills.
- Using SOLO-based questions as a means of providing formative feedback can help scaffold and challenge the quality of learners' responses.
- The embedded use of effective questioning (as well as questioning as feedback) can act as a model for learner-learner discussion to develop in quality overtime.

Record in your PDP how the information in this chapter enables you to meet the requirements for your first year of teaching.

📚 Further resources

Cook, V., Major, L., Hennessy, S., with Ahmed, Calcagni and others (2018) MESHGUIDE: Classroom Dialogue and Learning Cambridge Educational Dialogue Research Group (CEDiR). Available from: www.meshagain.meshguides.org (accessed 18 August 2019).

Hodgen, M. and Webb, M. (2008) 'Questioning and dialogue', in S. Swaffield (ed.) *Unlocking Assessment: Understanding for Reflection and Application*, Abingdon: Routledge.
A useful chapter on developing questioning and oral feedback.

Hook, P. and Mills, J. (2011) *SOLO Taxonomy: A Guide for Schools. Book 1. A Common Language of Learning*, New Zealand: Essential Resources Educational Publishers.
An introductory guide to using SOLO in the classroom.

Mercer, N. and Hodgkinson, S. (eds.) (2008) *Exploring Talk in School*, London: Sage.
A useful book for developing dialogic teaching in the classroom.

Mercer, N. and Littleton, K. (2007) *Dialogue and the Development of Children's Thinking: A Sociocultural Approach*, Abingdon: Routledge.
A useful book for developing dialogic teaching in the classroom.

www.robinalexander.org.uk/dialogic-teaching
Other books and downloadable resources on dialogic teaching.

Appendices 2 and 3 list subject associations, teaching councils and relevant websites.

Books in the *Learning to Teach* series that you may find helpful are as follows:

Capel, S., Leask, M. and Younie, S. (eds.) (2019) *Learning to Teach in the Secondary School: A Companion to School Experience*, 8th edn, Abingdon: Routledge.
This book is designed as a core textbook to support student teachers through their initial teacher education programme.

Capel, S., Leask, M. and Turner, T. (eds.) (2010) *Readings for Learning to Teach in the Secondary School: A Companion to M Level Study*, Abingdon: Routledge.
This book brings together essential readings to support you in your critical engagement with key issues raised in this textbook.

The subject-specific books in the *Learning to Teach* series, the *Practical (subject) Guides*, *Debates in (subject)* and *Mentoring (subject) Teachers* are also very useful.

15 Assessment, marking and homework

Helen Cassady and Barry Harwood

Introduction

In this chapter, we explore data collection at a teacher, departmental and school level and how you have a role in the process. For examples we use the agenda in England at the time of writing, which has a specific focus on accountability and progress measures. Reference will also be made to practices that could be described as dubious in an attempt to shield poor performance. The role of marking and homework will also be discussed with a view to identifying how these two processes can support pupil learning.

OBJECTIVES

At the end of the chapter you should:

- know what data is collected in a secondary school and how it can support assessment as a teacher;
- know how and why data is collected, how it is analysed and how it improves teaching and learning;
- have become aware of the issues of accountability as a beginning teacher;
- have explored the role and purpose of homework;
- have developed a greater awareness of how you can mark to support pupil progress and teacher effectiveness.

Check how the information in this chapter enables you to meet the requirements for your first year of teaching.

Accountability measures, curriculum design and their impact on assessment

As is mentioned in Chapters 1, 2 and 16, you will find that politicians frequently introduce changes into the education system in England and schools and teachers find themselves adapting practices to meet the new requirements. Knowing the political nature of educational decisions may help you to understand some of the requirements that are placed on you by your school.

For example, on 14 October 2013, the Rt. Hon. David Laws, Minister of Schools, made an announcement about school accountability in England, in particular the future of secondary school accountability measures following a consultation during February–May 2013. In his statement, he outlined that schools have been judged by the proportion of pupils awarded five GCSEs at grade C and above, including English and Maths, pointing out that:

> schools currently improve their league table position if pupils move over the C/D borderline. This gives schools a huge incentive to focus excessively on the small number of pupils around the 5Cs borderline.
>
> *(Department for Education (DfE), 2013d, p. 2)*

Further, that:

> This is unfair to pupils with the potential to move from E grades to D grades, or from B grades to A grades. [But also] ... unfair to those on the C/D borderline because it leads schools to teach to the test.
>
> *(DfE, 2013d, p. 2)*

Laws argues that 'The 5 A*–C measure also encourages schools to offer a narrow curriculum. Mastery of just 5 subjects is not enough for most pupils at age 16' (DfE, 2013d, p. 2). He also states that the measure of 5 A*–C grades including English and mathematics 'permits many schools, particularly in affluent areas "to coast". These schools find it easy to hit targets based on 5 C grades' (DfE, 2013d, p. 2). Furthermore, he argues that the school may look successful but Cs are not a success when pupils are capable of more. Laws (DfE, 2013d) reinforces that: 'the accountability system must set challenging but fair expectations for every school, whatever its intake' (DfE, 2013d, p. 2).

As a result, the Coalition Government announced on 7 February 2013 proposals to reform school accountability, which were designed to hold schools to account for all their pupils' progress across a broader range of subjects. As a part of such reforms, the government ensured there was a close link between qualifications and accountability. Consequently, as a result of these reforms, new GCSEs were introduced that saw the removal of coursework in subjects such as English Language and Literature and a significant increase in the content of the courses and lengthy final examinations (for example, 2 hours 30 minutes for the Eduqas (examination board) component 2 GCSE English Literature paper). These newly reformed qualifications for both academic and vocational subjects are published via the DfE's approved qualifications list along with their discount codes. Each qualification is given a discount code, which means schools must look carefully to make sure one course does not cancel out the other in the accountability measures. Therefore, when designing the best curriculum for secondary school pupils it has become inevitable that 'what counts' and what schools are 'held to account' for are reliant on one another. Headteachers therefore need to both safeguard their schools in the accountability measures, whilst also ensure that they are providing the best possible education and qualifications for their young people. It is a balancing act and there is a great need for teachers to ensure pupils acquire and develop effective knowledge, skills and understanding in their subject, that content is stored to memory and that it can be effectively recalled. Task 15.1 will allow you to consider this in a little more detail.

 Task 15.1   Getting to know assessment in your subject

Identify the requirements for your subject for knowledge, skills and understanding, and planning progression of learning. Review the content of your subject in the National Curriculum and also the examination boards.

- Identify the knowledge, skills and understanding learners must master.
- What will the five-year curriculum plan be made up of so that there is suitable challenge for learners?
- What will the curriculum plan be for Key Stage 3 so that learners have a secure foundation from which to build?
- How will you plan the content delivery of the examination across two academic years?

Record the information in your professional development portfolio (PDP) (or similar) to refer to as you plan your lessons.

Accountability measures

After Laws' (DfE, 2013d) initial announcement of the new accountability and qualifications reforms the government outlined new accountability measures for schools in England. September 2016 saw the introduction of Progress 8 (P8) and Attainment 8 (A8). These new measures impact on the curriculum design secondary schools can offer. The government (DfE, 2015b) argues that:

> The new performance measures are designed to encourage schools to offer a broad and balanced curriculum at Key Stage 4 and reward schools for the teaching of all their pupils, measuring performance across 8 qualifications.
>
> *(DfE, 2015b, p. 5).*

So long as the qualification is on the 'approved' list.

So, what are Progress 8 and Attainment 8?

Progress 8 (P8) measures a pupil's achievement across eight subjects. It:

> aims to capture the progress a pupil makes from the end of primary school to the end of secondary school. It is a type of value-added measure, which means that

pupils' results are compared to the actual achievement of other pupils with the same prior attainment.

(DfE 2015b, p. 5)

Within P8 every grade is worth a number of points and it is these points across the eight subjects that are calculated to determine the P8 score of a school. A score of 0 means pupils made the expected progress or the school has performed as it should have done; a score of 0+ means they exceeded and a score of -0 indicates that there is a lack of achievement and also underperformance. It is a school's P8 score that is the main accountability measure and the floor measure from which a school is judged.

Attainment 8 (A8) shows the average grade across the same eight subjects that make up P8. The government (DfE, 2013e) states that this will 'show achievement across a broad curriculum in a clear way' (DfE, 2013e, p. 7). In short, A8 and P8 are based on pupils' performance across eight subjects. Task 15.2 asks you to consider your current level of understanding in relation to Progress and Attainment 8.

 Task 15.2   Questions to ask yourself in relation to Progress 8 and Attainment 8

- ■   What is the Progress 8 score and Attainment 8 score for your current school?
- ■   What does it tell you about the school's performance?
- ■   How does it compare with local schools and nationally?
- ■   Do the scores give a real picture of the school's achievement?
- ■   Is there reference in the School Improvement Plans as to how scores will be improved or maintained?

Record the information in your PDP to refer to as you plan your lessons.

However, there are restrictions on which eight subjects schools can count. The eight subjects are subdivided into three sections or, as they are referred to in the profession, as 'The Buckets'! In bucket one is mathematics and English, known as the Mathematics and English element. Within this element English Language or English Literature can count, but it is the one with the highest grade that counts for reporting purposes. English and Mathematics are double weighted and by this we mean they are worth double the points. For example, a grade 3 is equivalent to 3 points but in bucket 1 it is double its value so is equal to 6.

The second bucket is known as the EBacc element and is made up of the following subjects: discrete sciences, double science, history, geography, computer sciences and languages. In this bucket, there are three slots. The government points out that the EBacc element '... will continue to show the percentage of pupils who achieve good grades in a range of academic qualifications' (DfE, 2013e, p. 7).

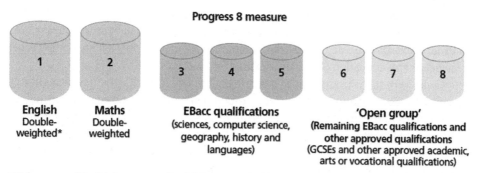

*Higher score of English language or English literature double-weighted if student has taken both subjects|

Figure 15.1 Progress 8 measures (NCFE, 2015a, p. 2)

The third bucket is known as the Open element. This element is made up of any three recognised qualifications from the range of EBacc subjects, or any other high value arts, academic or vocational qualifications. English Literature can also count in this group of subjects (DfE, 2013e). Figure 15.1 shows a visual representation of the qualifications that are allocated to buckets and make up P8.

In total eight subjects make up P8 and A8 but academic subjects in English, Mathematics and the EBacc elements constitute 70% of the measures. The points for each grade are calculated to produce the overall P8 and A8 point scores. Although the government (DfE, 2016c) published how to calculate a school's P8 and A8 scores, in 2017 the DfE announced that they are not going to share the formulae, as schools should focus on the performance of pupils rather than the performance of the school in league tables and accountability measures. This is a somewhat ironic statement when you realise that a school's quality of education is judged on the outcomes that pupils achieve. From a leadership perspective, it could be suggested that not to work in partnership with headteachers shows distrust, as well as applying unnecessary pressure on teachers and school leaders.

In short, the headteacher has a responsibility to ensure *all pupils receive a broad and balanced curriculum and are provided with a high-quality education*. They must ensure a school is not only well placed in the accountability measures of P8 and A8 but also offer a curriculum that suits the individual pupil. Designing the curriculum therefore is a challenge and it must ultimately start with the development of the pupil, how they are prepared for society so that they will make a positive contribution as an adult citizen. The DfE (2014d) states:

> The national curriculum provides pupils with an introduction to the essential knowledge that they need to be educated citizens. It introduces pupils to the best that has been thought and said; helps engender an appreciation of human creativity and achievement.
>
> (DfE, 2014d, p. 5)

The National Curriculum (2014) outlines that every state-funded school must offer a curriculum that is balanced and broadly based. The curriculum should also be one that promotes spiritual, moral, cultural, mental and physical development of pupils when at the school and as a part of society and prepares them for the opportunities, responsibilities and experiences of later life (DfE, 2014d). An outline of your responsibilities for personal social and health education (PSHE) is provided in Chapter 9.

However, with the introduction of academies and free schools, the government has given academies and free schools greater freedom in curriculum design, as they do not have to adhere to the National Curriculum guidelines. However, in 2010 the government announced that 90% of pupils should be studying the English Baccalaureate (EBacc). As a result of its 18-month consultation, this has been revised and on 19 July 2017, Justine Greening, Secretary of State for Education (Busby, 2017), announced that only 75% of Year 10 pupils in state-funded mainstream schools will start to study GCSEs in the EBacc combination of subjects by 2022 and 90% of year 10 pupils studying GCSEs in the EBacc subjects by September 2025 (Long and Bolton, 2017). As a result of this, the expectation limits what choice pupils have to study at each key stage (as set out in Figure 15.1, which shows P8 and how the EBacc subjects apply) and also places constraints on curriculum models. The challenge that schools face is ensuring that there is sufficient time in the curriculum for the breadth and depth of the subject content to be learnt whilst not marginalising subjects in the areas of the arts and technology for example.

What does P8 and A8 mean for you as a classroom teacher?

- You must plan for the knowledge, skills and understanding that need to be delivered, reviewed and tested across Key Stage 4 so that pupils are well prepared for the demands of the final examinations.
- The pupils will need to be taught not only subject content but also the skills they need to have mastered by the end of the course. It is therefore essential that teachers plan the curriculum well across the secondary school so that the Key Stage 3 curriculum teaches the knowledge, skills and understanding needed for Key Stage 4. The pupils must have the firm foundations from which to build.
- Curriculum mapping must be in place to ensure effective coverage of the subject content and the understanding and skills to be mastered. Assessments must also prepare pupils for the demands they will face in the final examinations.

With the removal of Key Stage 3 levels in 2014, schools and teachers are now able to set their own assessment criteria, this has many advantages but can also bring risk. The teacher must ensure there is progression in content and sufficient demand year on year.

Some schools have adopted GCSE criteria that progress from Years 7–11 and others have written their own depending on the needs of their pupils. Whichever approach is taken you must safeguard pupils' learning and success so that they are well prepared for the final examinations and achieve their potential.

Teachers must also be clear about what they want their pupils to learn in every lesson and that pupils are making sufficient progress. Assessment criteria must be integral to learning and pupils must have ownership of it (see also Chapter 14; Booth in *LTT8*, 2019; and McLaughlin in *LTT8*, 2019).

Pupils must know:

- what they are to achieve by the end of the lesson;
- what they have learnt;
- what they need to do next to improve further.

Overtime, pupils must know the criteria they need to attain and what they need to do to achieve the next criteria. It is therefore vital that teachers:

- plan tasks that enable pupils to understand how their learning relates to the assessment criteria;
- give feedback (marking and verbal) that must encompass the identified criteria;
- ensure each pupil acts on their area of development to ensure progress is made in key areas.

Task 15.3 encourages you to consider your current level of understanding in relation to examinations in your subject.

 Task 15.3   Understanding the mark scheme for the GCSE in your subject

Review the mark scheme for the GCSE examination you are currently using. Read the examiner report to identify the national picture of the strengths of learners' responses and also areas for development.

- Are you securing learners' knowledge and understanding in these areas?
- Liaise with your school examinations officer and find out how many points are allocated to each grade awarded.
- Identify what areas you have identified as requiring some development.

Record the information in your PDP to refer to as needed.

Marking

'... Classroom life can sometimes feel like "Do, Do, Do" – and when you've finished that, do some more!' (Watkins, Carnell and Lodge, 2007, p.71). Trying to juggle the demands of teaching and learning and all of the other aspects of being a teacher can, for a recently qualified teacher, feel daunting, especially in the area of marking. The never-ending pile of books and folders seem to be forever increasing in size rather than diminishing (see Chapter 20, which looks at teacher well-being and resilience).

So, what can you do to stop the 'Do, Do, Do' approach?

- Identify:
  - What is it that worries you/causes the greatest challenge about marking?

- Explore:
    - So, what does this mean for day-to-day practice in class?
    - What does the available literature suggest?
    - Find out how other teachers in your department and other beginning teachers manage. See Task 15.4.
- Act – Identify:
    - Now, what are you going to do next to support your practice?
    - Who will be able to support you?

Further advice regarding the management of time and workload can be found in Findon and Johnston-Wilder (in *LTT8*, 2019).

A recommendation from the Independent Teacher Workload Review Group (*Eliminating Unnecessary Workload around Marking*, 2016) was that marking should be:

- *Meaningful*
- *Manageable*
- *Motivating*

Reflecting on these three key points may help you move from the '*Do, Do, Do*' approach. See Table 15.1 for further details and undertake Task 15.4.

 Task 15.4   Managing your workload

Having asked others, observed different practices and considered what the current literature suggests, what could you do differently to use your time efficiently, as a teacher, prior to a lesson when planning the tasks, during a lesson and after a lesson?

Record your intentions in your PDP and review your success in time and workload management periodically.

Table 15.1 Recommendations of the Independent Teacher Workload Review Group

Meaningful: Marking varies by age group, subject and what works best for the pupil and teacher in relation to any particular piece of work. Teachers are encouraged to adjust their approach as necessary and trusted to incorporate the outcomes into subsequent planning and teaching.
Manageable: Marking practice is proportionate and considers the frequency and complexity of written feedback, as well as the cost and time-effectiveness of marking in relation to the overall workload of teachers. This is written into any assessment policy.
Motivating: Marking should help to motivate pupils to progress. This does not mean always writing in-depth comments or being universally positive: sometimes short, challenging comments or oral feedback are more effective. If the teacher is doing more work than their pupils, this can become a disincentive for pupils to accept challenges and take responsibility for improving their work. Independent Teacher Workload Review Group (2016, pp. 8–10)

Figures 15.2 and 15.3 – devised from *The Final Report of the Commission on Assessment without Levels* (DfE, 2015c) have been used with initial teacher education (ITE) student teachers that we work with to help them to engage with and reflect on the purpose of formative and summative assessment. They help you to decide the value of any assessment you intend to do. Likewise, they can be used with a 'marking' perspective.

Can you plan for marking?

From experience, the model for teaching tends to be: plan a lesson, deliver a lesson and mark the output – with assessment often seen as a separate activity rather than an integral part of the teaching and learning process. We would suggest that marking and also homework needs to be planned for; to be an integral part of the process. The following question may help you to plan for marking: How can you make your marking *meaningful*, *manageable* and *motivating* (see Table 15.2)? The key question is who is your AUDIENCE? Parent, senior leadership team (SLT) or pupil? For whom are you marking? For impact on learning it **must** be the pupil.

Now complete Task 15.5, which encourages you to reflect on your current approach to marking.

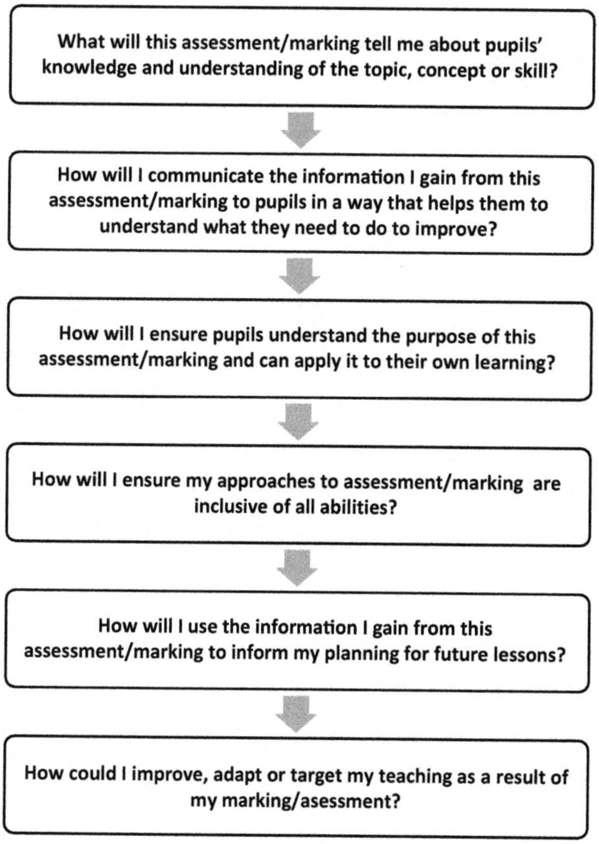

What will this assessment/marking tell me about pupils' knowledge and understanding of the topic, concept or skill?

How will I communicate the information I gain from this assessment/marking to pupils in a way that helps them to understand what they need to do to improve?

How will I ensure pupils understand the purpose of this assessment/marking and can apply it to their own learning?

How will I ensure my approaches to assessment/marking are inclusive of all abilities?

How will I use the information I gain from this assessment/marking to inform my planning for future lessons?

How could I improve, adapt or target my teaching as a result of my marking/asessment?

Figure 15.2 Principles of in-school formative assessment (devised from DfE, 2015c)

Who will use the information provided by this assessment/marking?

How will it be used to support broader progress, attainment and outcomes for the pupils?

Will it give them the information they need for their purposes?

How should the assessment/marking outcomes be communicated to pupils to ensure they have the right impact and contribute to pupils' understanding of how they can make further progress in the future?

How should the assessment/marking outcomes be communicated to parents to ensure they understand what the outcomes tell them about their child's attainment, progress and improvement needs?

How should the assessment/marking outcomes be recorded to allow the school to monitor and demonstrate progress, attainment and wider outcomes?

Figure 15.3 Principles of in-school summative assessment (devised from DfE, 2015c)

 Task 15.5   Reflecting on marking

Critically reflect on Table 15.2 and consider how your practice can be adapted to ensure that your marking supports both your learners and also supports your teaching.

▪ Will your approach only support the performative culture of schools or will it also enhance the learning experience of your learners?

Record your reflections in your PDP and develop a personal action plan. You may want to use a SWOT (Strength, Weaknesses, Opportunities and Threat) analysis to support the development of your plan. Review your practice from time to time in the light of your developing experience.

Table 15.2 Questions to ask yourself when marking

How can you make your marking *Meaningful*	■ Does it help the learner to understand what they KNOW, UNDERSTAND and DO? ■ How does it? ■ Does it identify their NEXT STEPS?
How can you make your marking *Manageable*	■ Can you give feedback in a session? ■ Does it have to be written? ■ Do you have a coding system used by: School? Faculty? Department? ■ Do you plan when you will take in work and balance that against all of your timetable? ■ Do you identify specific areas to comment on: SUCCESS CRITERIA? ■ Are you writing more than the pupil?
How can you make your marking *Motivating*	■ Is it personal to their work? ■ Does it mention their name? ■ Does it recognise progress and what they can do? ■ Does it set challenges for the pupil? ■ Can it be an ongoing dialogue; a comment not just seen in isolation? ■ How do you involve your pupils in the assessment process? ■ Do you model good practice to your pupils? ■ Do you use feedback to support your teaching based on marking, rather than seeing it as that was yesterday, now it is today?

Homework

In the previous section we identified the need to see assessment and marking as: meaningful, manageable and motivating to be effective in the teaching and learning process. The same is true for homework if it is to support the pupils' learning and not just be a bolt-on task with little relevance to the pupil. However, before we look at homework in further detail, Task 15.6 encourages you to think about how you use homework in your own practice.

 Task 15.6   Reflecting on your homework practice

Check the practice in your school and department for the setting of homework and answer the following questions:

■ Why do you set homework?
■ What sort of homework do you set?
■ Have you considered if your pupils have the facilities to do the homework at home?
■ How do you use homework: a task to do or a task to enhance and develop future learning?
■ What do your department's and the school's policies say?

> ■ Are you aware of the homework pattern of your pupils? Does a pupil have some days where there is no official homework and others where they have 3 or 4 subjects?
> ■ Do you need to take the above into account?
>
> Record your reflections in your PDP and personal action plan. Review your practice from time to time in the light of your developing experience.

From experience, we would suggest that the effective approach is to see homework as an integral part of the learning process as shown in Figure 15.4.

At times, the home learning provides the stimulus for in-class learning and at others, in-class learning provides the stimulus for home learning.

As a means of developing a more interactive and diverse approach to home learning, Bloom's Taxonomy (Bloom et al., 1956) may offer a way of supporting in-class and home learning (see Table 15.3). Such an approach, we believe, allows you to provide homework that is not just recall and understanding but allows for deeper thinking and challenge.

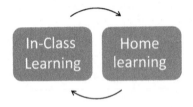

Figure 15.4 Relationship between in-class learning and home learning

Table 15.3 Homework planner using Bloom's Taxonomy (Bloom et al., 1956)

Homework planner		
Skill	*How the learners can use the skill as part of the learning journey* *Questions I can ask learners to show use and ownership of the skill* *Tasks I could set learners as part of home learning*	*How it will be built upon in class as a result of the homework task* *This is how I will use it ...*
Remembering		
Understanding		
Applying		
Analysing		
Evaluating		
Creating		
Skills I need to teach in-class:		

The planning sheet in Table 15.3 may help with the planning of a deeper, richer, more meaningful homework experience.

The key to setting meaningful homework we believe, is that:

- You see homework, not as an add on, but as integral to the pupils' learning journey.
- You consider how you will value the homework.
- How and when will you assess the homework?

SUMMARY AND KEY POINTS

This chapter aimed to develop your knowledge of:

- what data is collected in a secondary school and how it can support assessment as a teacher;
- how and why data is collected, how it is analysed and how it improves teaching and learning;
- the issues of accountability as a beginning teacher;
- the role and purpose of homework;
- how you can mark to support pupil progress and teacher effectiveness.

In summary these are the key facts to know about performance measures:

- Progress 8 (P8) measures a pupil's achievement across eight subjects.

Within P8, every grade is worth a number of points and it is these points across eight subjects that are calculated to determine the P8 score of a school.

- A score of 0 means pupils made the expected progress or the school has performed as it should have done; 0+ means they exceeded and –0 means there is a lack of achievement and underperformance.
- It is a school's P8 score that is the main accountability measure and the floor measure from which a school is judged.
- Attainment 8 shows the average grade across the same eight subjects that make up P8.
- The eight subjects are subdivided into three sections or what are referred to in the profession as 'The Buckets'
    - *Bucket 1* is Maths and English.
    - *Bucket 2* is known as the EBacc element.
    - *Bucket 3* is known as the Open element.
- In total, eight subjects make up P8 and A8 but academic subjects in English, Mathematics and the EBacc elements constitutes 70% of the measures.
- The points for each grade are calculated to produce the overall P8 and A8 point scores.

Below are the key questions you need to ask yourself about marking and homework:

- How can you make your marking *Meaningful*?
- How can you make your marking *Manageable*?
- How can you make your marking *Motivating*?
- Who is your AUDIENCE? Parent, SLT or pupil? For whom are you marking? For impact on pupil learning it **must** be the pupil.

Record in your PDP how the information in this chapter enables you to meet the requirements for your first year of teaching.

 Further resources

www.aaia.org.uk - Association for Achievement and Improvement through Assessment
The website has a number of useful blog posts covering many aspects of assessment. For example:

- Assessment for Learning: www.aaia.org.uk/blog/category/afl
- Assessment of Learning: www.aaia.org.uk/blog/category/aol

Black, P., Harrison, C., Lee, C., Marshall, B. and William, D. (2003) *Assessment for Learning: Putting it into Practice*, **Maidenhead, UK: Open University Press.**
This resource provides insight into assessment for learning based on teachers sharing how they changed their assessment practice.

Black, P., Harrison, C., Lee, C., Marshall, B. and William, D. (2004) 'Working inside the black box: Assessment for learning in the classroom, *Phi Delta Kappan*, 86(1), 9–21.
This is an important text on assessment and how it can be used to ensure attainment and progress is enhanced in your classroom.

Wiliam, D. (2011) *Embedded Formative Assessment*, **Bloomington, IN: Solution-Tree.**

Wiliam, D. (2014) *Redesigning Schooling: Principled Assessment Design*, **SSAT (The Schools Network). Available from: www.ssatuk.co.uk (accessed 19 August 2019).**
William outlines five key strategies of formative assessment and supports the impact of these strategies with research evidence. Practical activities for teachers are also presented.

Framing the workload and assessment agenda

Independent Teacher Workload Review Group (2016) *Eliminating Unnecessary Workload Around Marking.* **Available from: www.gov.uk/government/publications/reducing-teacher-workload-marking-policy-review-group-report a (accessed 18 August 2019).**
The working party explored the workload associated with marking and offered suggestions on how it could be reduced. This is an easy read and places assessment in the workload agenda.

Higgins, S., Katsipataki, M., Coleman, R., Henderson, P., Major, L.E., Coe, R. and Mason, D. (July 2015) *The Sutton Trust - Education Endowment Foundation Teaching and Learning Toolkit*, **London: Education Endowment Foundation.**
The Sutton Trust provides accessible resources to support the evidence-informed teaching agenda.

Lange, J. and Burroughs-Lange, S. (2017) *Learning to be a Teacher*, **London: Sage Publications.**
This book explores professional learning approaches that might make your work less stressful and more rewarding. It is very readable and offers you powerful reflection points to reflect on your own developing practice.

Appendices 2 and 3 list subject associations, teaching councils and relevant websites.

Books in the *Learning to Teach* series that you may find helpful are as follows:

Capel, S., Leask, M. and Younie, S. (eds.) (2019) *Learning to Teach in the Secondary School: A Companion to School Experience*, **8th edn, Abingdon: Routledge.**
This book is designed as a core textbook to support student teachers through their initial teacher education programme.

Capel, S., Leask, M. and Turner, T. (eds.) (2010) *Readings for Learning to Teach in the Secondary School: A Companion to M Level Study*, **Abingdon: Routledge.**
This book brings together essential readings to support you in your critical engagement with key issues raised in this textbook.

The subject-specific books in the *Learning to Teach* series, the *Practical (subject) Guides*, *Debates in (subject)* and *Mentoring (subject) Teachers* are also very useful.

16 Making the curriculum your own

Chris Shelton and Julia O'Kelly

Introduction

This chapter is about the curriculum that you teach. As a beginning teacher you are likely to be given an outline curriculum for each year group or perhaps an examination syllabus, thus, topics are set. However, you are able to decide how that curriculum is implemented, for example, through how long you spend on each aspect of the curriculum, how deeply you explore each topic, your use of examples or through setting project and homework tasks that extend the core curriculum.

Whatever subject you specialise in teaching, in the UK and many other countries, you need to negotiate the demands of national curriculum guidance, the expectations from your exam syllabus and also your own interests when choosing what to teach and how to teach it. These decisions are important because they affect whether your pupils meet the expectations that you have for them, how motivated your pupils are in your lessons and, as we argue, how satisfied you are with your work. This chapter is intended to help you consider the different influences on the school curriculum and support you in developing professional autonomy as a curriculum designer.

The chapter begins with a brief reminder of some of the different definitions and elements of the school curriculum and how these relate to your values and the aims of education. Then, the chapter explores where a curriculum comes from and the process and influences that shape it. Finally, we discuss your role as a teacher and professional in moulding the curriculum in your own classroom.

OBJECTIVES

By the end of this chapter you should be able to:

- recognise and critique the influences on the curriculum for your school and your subject;
- understand how the curriculum relates to your aims when teaching;

■ begin to identify ways of using your professional judgement to design your teaching curriculum

Check how the information in this chapter enables you to meet the requirements for your first year of teaching.

Understanding the school curriculum

Recent research from the Office for Standards in Education, Children's Services and Skills (Ofsted) in England has suggested that there is a "dearth of understanding about the curriculum in some schools" (Spielman, 2018) resulting in many children having their secondary education narrowed due to a focus on shallow test content rather than more in-depth learning. As Spielman (2018) states: 'The curriculum is not the timetable. Nor is it what we think might be on the exam' (Spielman, 2018). In their research, Ofsted have focused on teachers' intentions for their curriculum, how these are implemented and what impact this has. So, before you can implement a successful curriculum, you need to be clear about your curriculum intent.

Haydon and Heilbronn (2016a, 2016b) and Heilbronn, Orchard and Haydon (in *LTT8*, 2019) discuss the purpose and place of the curriculum, highlighting the connections between the curriculum and our society's aims for education. Haydon and Heilbronn discuss the diversity of views about what the aims for education might be, including individual aims 'aims characterised by individual achievements or qualities that contribute towards making the lives of individuals better' (2016a, p. 495) and societal aims 'aims characterised by some possible state of society that is seen as desirable (such as an affluent society, or a free society, or a society with a strong sense of community)' (2016a, p. 495). As teachers, you work within a context of local and national aims for education set by governments and school leaders that reflect their values about what is best for individuals and society as a whole. Because there is room for debate about what these aims and values should be and tensions over their relative importance, there is also debate about the aims of education. As a teacher, you have your own views about what is best for your pupils and for society more generally and these may or may not match the views of others in your school. Your personal aims for education are important but need to be considered carefully and critiqued. Task 16.1 asks you to review your aims and values taking into account the country and school context in which you work.

 Task 16.1 Your aims

At the heart of this chapter is the idea that you will find teaching more satisfying, fulfilling and enjoyable if the curriculum that you teach aligns with the values in which you believe. Hence, it is important that you can analyse the curriculum for your classes in terms of your beliefs about the aims, purposes and values of education. So, the best place to start is by reminding yourself of what you believe is truly important in teaching. Spend ten minutes listing what you think are the key aims for your subject in the age range you teach:

- What knowledge do you want pupils to acquire?
- What concepts or processes do you want pupils to be able to understand?
- What skills and techniques do you want pupils to develop?
- What attitudes towards your subject or the world do you wish to promote and why?

Finally, can you justify the importance of your subject within the school curriculum in terms of these aims. Record this brief justification in your professional development portfolio (PDP) (or similar).

According to Haydon and Heilbronn (2016b), the curriculum is 'one of the most important "tools" through which educational aims can be realised' (p.501). However, they also argue that it is not obvious what the 'curriculum' actually is and this is reflected in a wide range of different definitions and explanations of the term 'curriculum' (see, for example, Ross, 2000). The term 'curriculum' is often used to refer to the prescribed content of teaching, although Barrow (1984) noted that this content is 'both less and more than what individual students get out of it' (p.5). It is *more* in the sense that the curriculum may contain more content than pupils will actually learn and remember, and *less* in the sense that pupils will always learn other things in school that are not part of the official curriculum. Haydon and Heilbronn (2016b) distinguish between the planned or formal curriculum, the informal curriculum and the hidden curriculum (see Table 16.1).

According to Giroux the hidden curriculum is 'those unstated norms, values, and beliefs embedded in and transmitted to students through the underlying rules that structure the routines and social relationships in school and classroom life' (2001, p. 47). As a class teacher, you are concerned with what values and beliefs you are transmitting to your pupils through the ways that you speak to pupils, how you organise your classroom and in what you value in your teaching. See Heilbronn, Orchard and Haydon (in *LTT8*, 2019) for a discussion about values, beliefs and teaching.

Table 16.1 Types of curriculum (based on Haydon and Heilbronn, 2016b)

Types of curriculum	Meaning
Planned or formal curriculum	The intended content of an educational programme set out in advance – it may contain 'core' and 'optional' components
Informal curriculum	Things that the school wishes pupils to learn but that are not taught as part of the formal curriculum (e.g. cooperation, consideration of others)
Hidden curriculum	Things that pupils learn that the school does not intend them to learn. These may be positive (e.g. developing respect for others) or negative (e.g. sexist or racist attitudes, seeing themselves as failures, etc.)

It is also helpful to distinguish between the curriculum of a school (i.e. the breadth of subjects and other learning that pupils experience throughout the school) and the curriculum within a subject (the specific learning intentions and topics within each subject). The secondary school curriculum is influenced by many factors, including ensuring that pupils experience the breadth of subjects mandated by the national curriculum but also by the expectations of parents, school inspectors and politicians. For example, in England, judgements of schools are made by Ofsted against a number of performance indicators. Currently, Ofsted assesses attainment in the English Baccalaureate (EBacc) subjects (Department for Education (DfE), 2017b) and against 'progress 8' (DfE, 2016d) (see also Chapter 15). Ofsted judgements are crucial for a school's status, for public perception and for recruitment, so schools are under pressure to ensure that these measures are as high as possible. A consequence has been that there was a 28% drop in the number of pupils in England taking arts General Certificate of Secondary Education (GCSE) courses between 2010 and 2017 (Cultural Learning Alliance, 2017) and a survey for the BBC in 2018 suggested that nine out of ten secondary schools had cut back on time, facilities or staff in at least one creative arts subject. Given the pressures on schools, it is important that you, as a representative of your subject, are clear about the purpose and place of your subject in the school curriculum and able to justify its importance. You can keep up to date in your subject through being an active member of your subject association (see Appendix 2).

How a subject curriculum is made

For beginning teachers, the curriculum can appear to be a fixed and permanent statement of what is most important in a subject – an expert view of what they should be teaching. And such a view can be encouraged by those who write the curriculum, for example, the aims of the National Curriculum for England state that it provides pupils with 'an introduction to the essential knowledge that they need to be educated citizens. It introduces pupils to the **best** that has been thought and said' (DfE, 2014d, p.5).

This intention to select what is 'best' deliberately references the work of Matthew Arnold (1822-88) and demonstrates that underpinning this curriculum is a specific view of what knowledge is 'essential' for pupils. However, it is important to remember that any curriculum is a construction and that its finished form may not hint at the arguments and debates that occurred during its creation. In fact, a curriculum is a political document and is very much an artefact of the time and place in which it is created. It is a selection from the culture of a society (Lawton, 1975) and reflects the views of those who did the selecting. Haydon and Heilbronn (2016b, p. 506) suggest that there can be three approaches to this selection – an attempt to define what is 'best', an attempt to define what is 'distinctive' or an attempt to define what is 'foundational': the knowledge that pupils require in order to support further learning.

The political and controversial nature of decisions about the curriculum lead to regular curriculum changes and adapting to these challenges is part of the professional life of a teacher. This is why this book includes advice about building your resilience to cope with change (Chapter 1) and advice about the management of change (Chapter 2).

By considering how curricula have changed over time or how they differ between countries or even the different parts of a single country, you can see the range of influences that have shaped our current curricula. For example, Ross (2000) gives a detailed account of the ways in which curriculum changes in twentieth-century England were marked by conflict and controversy. For Ross, the attempts to define the curriculum reflect conflicting ideas about what education is for and what it can achieve. He notes how political agendas and memories of school have been held in conflict with 'progressive' views about education and describes how power over the curriculum has oscillated between local and central control. Throughout much of the twentieth century, schools in Britain have had a great deal of autonomy (Haydon and Heilbronn, 2016a) and schools were able to determine their own curriculum. But having the curriculum outside government influence led to the announcement in 1960 from the Minister of Education in England, Sir David Eccles, that he would open the 'secret garden of the curriculum' (Ross, 2000) eventually leading to a National Curriculum for England in 1988.

The principles that underpin the development of each subject curriculum have varied widely between the four nations of the UK (and, indeed, in other countries). For example, in contrast to the subject-based curriculum in England, at the time of writing, the curriculum in Wales was being redeveloped around four key purposes: that pupils would be ambitious and capable learners, enterprising and creative contributors, ethical and informed citizens, and healthy and confident individuals. These principles are applied across six 'Areas of Learning and Experience': expressive arts; health and well-being; humanities; languages, literacy and communication; mathematics and numeracy; and science and technology.

Now undertake Task 16.2.

 Task 16.2   Comparing curricula

Look at the curriculum for your subject at Key Stage 3 in another of the nations of the UK:

England:
https://www.gov.uk/government/publications/national-curriculum-in-england-secondary-curriculum

Northern Ireland:
http://ccea.org.uk/curriculum/key_stage_3/overview

Scotland:
https://education.gov.scot/scottish-education-system/policy-for-scottish-education/policy-drivers/cfe-(building-from-the-statement-appendix-incl-btc1-5)/Experiences%20and%20outcomes

Wales:
http://gov.wales/topics/educationandskills/schoolshome/curriculuminwales/curriculum-for-wales-curriculum-for-life/?lang=en

These curriculum documents reflect different assumptions and starting points – so how do they differ for your subject?

Discuss the differences that you have found with a colleague who teaches the same subject as you. Record notes of the discussion in your PDP.

Designing the curriculum

When comparing the curriculum specifications for different subjects, you begin to see how different influences have shaped the documents but, also, how the most powerful influences vary for different subjects. For some subjects in some countries, the curriculum reflects a desire to ensure inclusivity and to consider the needs of individual pupils and families, whilst in other places and for other subjects, the focus may be on developing skills for future employment. However, within all subjects there is a need to find a balance between competing aspects of the subject, and this always means that there are tough decisions to make. For example, your subject curriculum may need to balance engendering an appreciation of the beauty or scale of a subject with ensuring pupils gain skills for employability. It may also be challenging to promote intellectual development, learning and achievement whilst also ensuring pupils' social, emotional and moral development. For some subjects, notably English and mathematics, international comparisons in the form of the results of international tests are very influential. The results of the Programme for International Student Assessment (PISA), a set of international tests for 15-year-olds managed by the Organisation for Economic Co-operation and Development (OECD), and those of Trends in International Mathematics and Science Study (TIMSS) from the International Association for the Evaluation of Educational Achievement (IAEEA) are publicised widely. As a result, governments may design policies to respond to the results of these and to raise their nation's position in the international PISA and TIMSS rankings.

A possible consequence of this for you as a class teacher may be that certain departments are prioritised (in terms of resources or curriculum time) in order to address perceived priorities and to raise certain international test results, notably in English and mathematics. A mathematics teacher may find that the content of a curriculum or exam syllabus is altered in ways that are perceived to make the curriculum more challenging in those areas that are assessed in international comparisons.

Case Study: From information and communications technology (ICT) to computing

An illustration of how diverse interests can affect the design of a school curriculum can be found in the introduction of 'Computing' to English schools. In 2014, the subject of ICT was replaced in the English curriculum with the subject 'Computing'. In September, teachers who had worked as ICT teachers in the previous year found themselves expected to become 'Computing' teachers and teach a new curriculum having had very little involvement in the changes or design of this curriculum. This was presented by the government at the time as a response to dissatisfaction with the existing curriculum but as Williamson (2017) has shown, the changes resulted from an 'anarchic' mess of influences including businesses, professional societies, charities, media groups, think-tanks, venture capitalists and others. Although initial drafts were written by a fairly large consultative group, Williamson describes insider accounts that the final version of the curriculum was created by two people over a weekend in response to a deadline set by a government adviser. As a result, Williamson argues that the final version of the curriculum lost the sense of differentiation between the different aspects of computing and also missed opportunities for pupils to develop a critical understanding of the subject.

The curriculum and your professional autonomy

Wiliam (2013) draws a distinction between the 'intended' curriculum - the content specified by documents such as the national curriculum, the 'implemented' curriculum formed by the textbooks and lesson plans based on those intentions, and the 'enacted' curriculum that is actually experienced by the pupils. Those experiences of the 'enacted' curriculum are the outcome of teachers taking the specified outcomes of the intended curriculum and developing these into exciting and engaging classroom activities. This is a creative process that is much more than just 'delivering' a curriculum. As Wiliam says, 'Curriculum development is therefore not some special process done in committee meetings after school. Teachers create and develop curriculum every day, whenever they plan and deliver lessons' (2013, p.10).

The process of making the curriculum (whether devised nationally or inside your school) your own is part of your role as an autonomous professional, capable of exercising 'discretionary judgement' (Freidson, 2001, p.35). It is also a crucial element of effective teaching, as, according to Pollard, 'pedagogy is impoverished if it is disconnected from the capacity and responsibility to engage in curriculum development' (2010, p.5).

This requires you not only to use technical or craft skills, but also to draw on your academic knowledge and your values (Furlong and Whitty, 2017). It provides scope for you to develop further, to adapt to different teaching contexts and revised curriculum statements, not to stand still professionally, repeating technical skills (Freidson, 2001; Winch, 2010). This involves you making use of all the different forms of professional knowledge that underpin your expertise as a teacher. Now complete Task 16.3.

 Task 16.3   Teacher expertise and knowledge

Observe a lesson taught by an experienced teacher.

Create your own observation schedule for this activity. This should consist of a few headings listing some of the different forms of professional knowledge for you to reflect on during on the observation. For example, you may use headings such as academic knowledge, craft knowledge, values or personal knowledge and contextual knowledge.

As you observe the lesson use your observation schedule to note where the teacher is drawing on these forms of knowledge.

For example, where in the lesson have they drawn on their academic knowledge? Have they applied their knowledge of school context in order to design their lesson, e.g. in terms of following school policy or tailoring the activities for the pupils? How does the lesson content or pedagogic approach reflect the teacher's personal values, e.g. empathy, tolerance or respect?

Reflect on which forms of your professional knowledge are your strengths and which you would like to develop. Consider how you draw on your professional knowledge in your own lessons and make notes about your plans to refer and reflect on periodically. Store the information in your PDP and use to support the development of your professional knowledge.

A way of thinking about the relationship between the different types of knowledge you might draw on to exercise professional, discretionary judgement is Bernstein's characterisation of knowledge as vertical and horizontal. His model suggests that vertical knowledge includes specialised, academic knowledge (of your subject, or of education) while horizontal knowledge comes from practical experience. To explore this further, you might like to read the chapter by Hordern (particularly pp. 197-199) in Whitty and Furlong's book *Knowledge and the Study of Education* (Hordern, 2017). In your initial and continuing teacher education you will have spent a great deal of time in school acquiring and practising skills of teaching but also reflecting on that practice (Schön, 1983) as a process of continuous improvement. If that reflection relies on horizontal, craft knowledge, it may be reduced to identifying practical issues of, for example, classroom management. It is vertical knowledge that provides a meaningful framework in which to investigate your practice.

Indeed, Freidson goes so far as to suggest that identifiable academic knowledge is a key feature of a profession, a foundation of its status and value (Freidson, 2001). Without it, teaching may be de-professionalised because 'deliberation and judgment are no longer of value' (Ball, 2008a, p. 67). Belief in the value of what you do as a teacher may well have been a reason you saw teaching as worthwhile when you chose to join the profession. It may even provide the foundation for your professional resilience. For example, for the teacher quoted below, a belief in the value of their subject to those they teach is a continuing motivating factor:

> the subject alone is what drew you to teaching that subject, otherwise arguably you would have chosen a different subject, so I think the, for me, for PE, the want to educate children about how they can be the fittest, healthiest, more … version of themselves is something that can always keep me in, keep me going as a PE teacher.

Gu and Day (2013) suggest that teacher resilience is far more than the ability to 'bounce back' after negative events but that it is 'the capacity to maintain equilibrium and a sense of commitment and agency in the everyday worlds in which teachers teach' (p. 26). They describe resilient teachers whose 'intrinsic motivation and emotional commitment to provide the best service for their students was associated with an ethic of care for the wellbeing of their students which was at the heart of what they did and how they lived their lives in the profession' (p. 35). For these teachers, their sense of moral purpose and values provided the strength that enabled them to cope under pressure. As Gu and Day show, such resilience can become eroded over time, and the context in which a teacher works and the relationships they build are important in order for them to remain resilient in the face of external pressures. See Findon and Johnston-Wilder (in *LTT8*, 2019) for advice on building your resilience.

Therefore, as personal values and ethics are so important to longevity as a teacher, it is crucial that our teaching and, in particular, our curriculum aligns with and supports those values. Now undertake Tasks 16.4 and 16.5 and consider while you are doing this how your values and ethics fit with what you are required to do.

 Task 16.4   Analysing the subject curriculum

What are the influences on the curriculum for the subject(s) that you teach? Look closely at the curriculum documents for your school.

■   How do they relate to the National Curriculum?
■   What is the relationship to the relevant exam syllabus?
■   What is not included in your curriculum that you would like to see there?
■   What external influences can you identify in the content that was chosen (or not chosen) for inclusion in the curriculum? Can you identify economic, ideological and political influences?

Look back at the justification for your subject that you wrote for Task 16.1. How do the influences that you have identified here relate to your own aims for your subject? Record your ideas in your PDP.

M

 Task 16.5   Professionalism, curriculum and pedagogy

Read the introduction and first chapter of Pollard's *Professionalism and Pedagogy*. Which of the 'curricular concepts' (see p. 11) needs to be your focus for curriculum development? Make notes in your PDP.

Pollard, A. (ed.) (2010) *Professionalism and Pedagogy: A Contemporary Opportunity. A Commentary by TLRP and GTCE*. London: TLRP. Available from: http://reflectiveteaching.co.uk/media/profandped.pdf (accessed 18 August 2019).

Set yourself a calendar reminder to look again at your curriculum in six months' time and see how you have developed the curricular concepts that you identified in Task 16.5.

Moving forward

While the process through which a school curriculum is created and adopted can feel remote from the classroom, this does not mean that all of the responsibility and power is taken away from the teacher. In fact, as a class teacher you make the ultimate decisions about how curriculum statements are implemented in your classroom. This provides an opportunity for you to become a curriculum designer rather than merely a curriculum user. Twistelton (2004) describes three types of beginning teacher: 'task managers', who are concerned with organisation and ensuring work is completed; 'curriculum deliverers', who are concerned with ensuring everything is covered; and 'concept/skill builders', who are focused on pupils' development and use the curriculum as a catalyst and tool to develop the deeper skills and understanding they want pupils to learn. In order for you to be a 'concept builder' you need to take control of your curriculum. In fact, part of the professional role of the teacher is to 'take an overview of the curriculum, have a sense of "where it comes from" and be able to engage in discussion on whether it could be improved and, if so, in what ways' (Haydon and Heilbronn, 2016b, p. 504).

There are many ways of doing this but it can be helpful to work with colleagues (in your school or others) to reflect on and to adapt your curriculum. For example, can you explore opportunities for teacher enquiry? Work with two or three colleagues in your subject to design, trial and evaluate how you can improve the curriculum you teach. Thinking critically about your practice and how you might improve this helps you to develop your confidence and professional autonomy. See the tasks in Chapter 19.

You might also engage with your subject association to discover new approaches to curriculum design, to learn from the expertise of other association members and to take part in curriculum debates about your subject.

Another approach is to find out what your pupils think about the curriculum. Ask them to evaluate parts of your curriculum and find out if your pupils' perspectives on the curriculum match your own.

Finally, spend time reflecting on how well your curriculum reflects the interests and contexts of your pupils. Roegman et al. (2017) discuss how a meaningful curriculum should reflect a deep knowledge of your students and they associate this with teacher retention. They suggest that for the teachers they worked with, responding to pupil interest went 'beyond what students like or what they think is fun but rather underscores developing curricula that support them in making meaningful connections to their lives' (p. 440). Making meaningful connections is not about livening up lessons with fun quizzes or tenuous references to popular media characters but is about helping pupils to understand why you think what you are teaching is worth learning and making deep connections between pupils' lives and your subject. A clear understanding of your curriculum's aims and intent and how pupils will develop and make progression in your subject enables you to achieve this.

SUMMARY AND KEY POINTS

- Although you work from a published curriculum or syllabus, there are many opportunities to make this curriculum your own.
- The curriculum you teach should reflect your values and beliefs about what is most important for pupils to learn. In order to do this, you need to be a 'curriculum maker', not just a 'curriculum user', and develop a clear sense of your curriculum intent.
- There are many competing influences on the curriculum and these reflect different political and social contexts.
- You need to keep sight of your values and sense of professional autonomy - the curriculum will change, governments will change - how will you respond? What will you base your professional decisions on? What will keep you going and keep your teaching fresh?

Record in your PDP how the information in this chapter enables you to meet the requirements for your first year of teaching.

Further resources

The following resources will support you in understanding curriculum principles, however, for specific guidance, you need to refer to subject-specific advice, for example, the *Learning to Teach* textbooks for specific subjects.

Hordern, J. (2017) 'Bernstein's sociology of knowledge and education(al) studies', in J. Furlong and G. Whitty (eds.) *Knowledge and the Study of Education*, Oxford: Symposium Books.

Pollard, A. (ed.) (2010) *Professionalism and Pedagogy: A Contemporary Opportunity. A Commentary by TLRP and GTCE*, London: TLRP. Available from: http://reflectiveteaching. co.uk/media/profandped.pdf (accessed 12 January 2018).

Wiliam, D. (2013) *Principled Curriculum Design*, London: SSAT (The Schools Network).

Wyse, D., Baumfield, V.M., Egan, D., Hayward, L., Hulme, M. and Gallagher, C. (2013) *Creating the Curriculum*, Abingdon: Routledge.
While focused on the primary curriculum, many of the issues raised by this book are relevant to secondary education.

Appendices 2 and 3 list subject associations, teaching councils and relevant websites.

Books in the *Learning to Teach* series that you may find helpful are as follows:

Capel, S., Leask, M. and Younie, S. (eds.) (2019) *Learning to Teach in the Secondary School: A Companion to School Experience*, 8th edn, Abingdon: Routledge.
This book is designed as a core textbook to support student teachers through their initial teacher education programme.

Capel, S., Leask, M. and Turner, T. (eds.) (2010) *Readings for Learning to Teach in the Secondary School: A Companion to M Level Study*, Abingdon: Routledge.
This book brings together essential readings to support you in your critical engagement with key issues raised in this textbook.

The subject-specific books in the *Learning to Teach* series, the *Practical (subject) Guides*, *Debates in (subject)* and *Mentoring (subject) Teachers* are also very useful.

17 Digital technologies

Pedagogies and classroom practice

Andrew Csizmadia and Jon Audain

Introduction

Teachers are expected to integrate digital technologies into their teaching and promote online safety. For example, in England, *Essential Digital Skills Framework* (Department for Education (DfE), 2018d) and in Wales, *Digital Competence Framework* (Welsh Government, 2017) have been developed to enable learners to thrive in an increasingly digital world. The Welsh government regards digital competence as one of the three cross-curricular responsibilities for schools, alongside literacy and numeracy. Internationally, European Schoolnet, on behalf of the European Union, advocates digital citizenship as a right for all, and that digital skills enable people to exercise this right. Furthermore, the United Nations Education, Scientific and Cultural Organization (UNESCO) has developed an information and communication technology competency framework for teachers (ICT-CFT) (UNESCO, 2011).

This chapter's focus is on the use of digital technologies to facilitate and enhance teaching and the learning experience in your classroom. Digital technologies used innovatively within your subject teaching enhance learning for your learners. Good subject teachers already make good use of digital technologies and are always looking out for new ways of using them to stimulate learners and extend their learning. These teachers understand that digital technologies are a tool to be applied selectively but are not the complete solution to meeting an individual pupil's needs. They are also able to learn from learners who may have a better grasp of certain aspects of digital technologies than they themselves have.

The purpose of this chapter is to encourage you to become a teacher who uses digital technologies creatively in your teaching to enhance learning. One key objective is to erase some of your fears and present some clear signposts for you to using digital technologies to support your subject teaching. After all, in reality 'The only thing we have to fear is fear itself' (Roosevelt, 1933, p. 1).

> **OBJECTIVES**
>
> At the end of this chapter you should be able to:
>
> ■   understand the relevance of digital technologies for you and your learners;
> ■   use an appropriate framework for auditing your knowledge and understanding of digital technologies;
> ■   plan to teach using digital technology resources to enhance the earning experience;
> ■   understand your role and responsibilities in promoting digital wisdom for both yourself and the learners you teach.
>
> Check how the information in this chapter enables you to meet the requirements for your first year of teaching.

Digital technologies

What is digital technology?

The Education Endowment Foundation (EEF) defines digital technology as 'the use of computer and technology assisted strategies to support learning in schools' (EEF, 2018). Whilst Laurillard (2012) defines digital pedagogical competence as 'the proficiency in using ICT in teaching, applying pedagogic and didactic judgment, and being aware of its implications for learning'.

According to the report 'The Use of ICT in Education: A Survey of Schools in Europe' (Wastiau et al., 2013), two-thirds of teachers in the European Union learnt about information and communications technology (ICT) in their own time and almost all were positive about the impact of ICT on their pupils. However, despite this readiness, many teachers in Europe still have a lack of competence in using ICT in their teaching and admit they use it to only a small extent in their classrooms.

Bennett-Worth (n.d.) has compiled an A to Z of digital technologies for performing arts, which is partly shown in Table 17.1.

Selecting digital technologies

Guzdial (2016a) identified five principles for selecting a digital technology for learners. These principles are:

1. connect to what learner's know (Bruner, 1960);
2. keep cognitive load low (Weintrop and Wilensky, 2015; Morrison, Margulieux and Guzdial, 2015);
3. be honest about what the digital technology can do (Shaffer and Resnick, 1999);
4. be generative and productive (Kafai, Bruke and Resnick, 2014);
5. test, don't trust (Guzdial, 2016).

Table 17.1 A to Z of digital techniques for performing arts (adapted from Bennett-Worth, n.d.)

Animation	Blogging	Coding	Digital storytelling	Extratemporality	Forms
Gender	Haptic theatre	Improvisation techniques	Javascript	Keyboard – Makey Makey	Live feed
Motion sensors	Networks	Open source	Processing	Query string	Raspberry Pi
Social media	Telepresence	Upload	Via Positiva	Webcams	X
Y	Z-space parallax design				

These five principles can be aligned to Papert's concept of 'Low Threshold, High Ceiling' (Papert, 1980) that was used to describe the goals of Logo, an educational programming language. 'Low threshold' means that it should be easy for a novice to get started with a specific digital tool or technology and that the interface should not be intimidating (Principles 1 and 2). 'High (or no) ceiling' means that it's possible for an expert to work on increasingly sophisticated projects using powerful tools (Myers, Hudson and Pausch, 2000) (Principles 3 and 4). Guzdial (2016a) asserts that "we just don't know where the threshold and ceilings are until we try" (Principle 5). Resnick et al. (2005) added a third goal: 'Wide Walls' to indicate that the tools within digital technology should support and suggest a wide range of explorations.

Adoption of and attitude towards digital technology

Based on the adapted Rogers' technology adoption model (1962) (see Figure 17.1) consider your own adoption of and attitude towards new digital technologies.

Where do you see yourself? Are you someone who is a trailblazer/innovator who has to explore the newest technology? Do you prefer to wait for the majority of people to be using the technology before you begin your own exploration? Or are you someone who is the last to try out the technology? How does this impact upon your use of digital technology in your classroom?

The EU-funded Mentoring Technology Enhanced Pedagogy project (MENTAP) (Abbiati et al. 2018) sought to address this need in Europe for teachers to be able to innovate using ICT in the classroom and improve data on teachers' digital competence. MENTAP developed an online, open educational resource, technology-enhanced teaching self-assessment tool (TET-SAT) to support teachers to reflect and act upon their digital pedagogical competence. This online tool assesses four dimensions of digital pedagogical competence, which are divided into 15 sub-areas and 30 competences, as illustrated in Figure 17.2.

After answering 30 questions, teachers receive an individual, personalised confidential feedback, an overall average score, including a brief explanation of their level, and the percentage for each sub-area. The feedback provided is linked to both national and European ecosystems of training mapped against the competence areas of the tool.

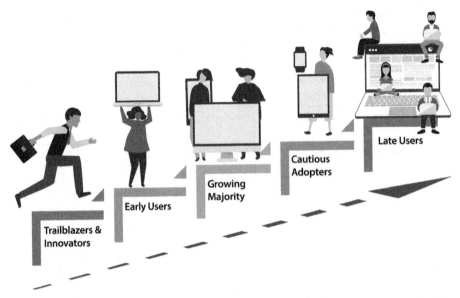

Figure 17.1 Adapted technology adoption model (Rogers, 1962) (image created by Jon Audain)

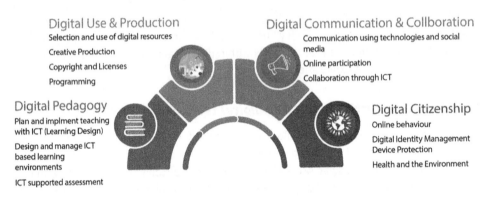

Figure 17.2 Overview of TET-SAT (image created by Jon Audain)

Thus, allowing a teacher access to resources for their professional learning to develop their digital maturity in using digital technologies appropriately. A teacher does not teach in isolation but as part of a community of practice and therefore there is a need to take into consideration the school's adoption of digital technologies.

Maturity models for schools

Several maturity models exist for schools to assess their usage and integration of ICT not only into the curriculum but also in order to manage the school (Solar, Sabattin and Parada, 2013; Rodriguez, Nussbaum and Dombrovskaia, 2012; Underwood and Dillion, 2011). One of the schemes that secondary schools have adopted is Naace's ICT Mark as it recognises schools for their good use of technology to support teaching, learning and school administration. To assist schools in working towards the ICT Mark, Naace provides schools access to their online Self-Review Framework tool, which provides schools with a structured route for reviewing and improving the school's use of digital technology. Now complete Task 17.1.

 Task 17.1   Assessing your own digital competences

Use MENTAP's online TET-SAT tool (http://mentep.eun.org/tet-sat) to discover your own digital competences and as a stepping-stone to further develop your own digital pedagogical competence.

Carefully reflect on the personalised feedback that you receive from using TET-SAT.

What are your identified strengths regarding digital technologies and what are your areas for development?

What course of action do you need to take to further develop your digital competences?

Record your findings in your professional development portfolio (PDP) (or similar) for later reference.

Digital pedagogies

In this section we explore several pedagogies that support the use of digital technologies in the classroom as well as several international and national digital competence frameworks.

Pedagogies for digital technologies

In 2001 Church published *Bloom's Digital Taxonomy* (Church, 2001), which applied 'Bloom's Revised Taxonomy of educational objectives' (see Anderson and Krathwohl, 2001) to the use of digital technologies. For example, processes and actions associated with Web 2.0 technologies, infowhelm (the exponential growth in information) and increasing ubiquitous personal technologies or cloud computing.

Church's *Bloom's Digital Taxonomy* is less about digital tools or technologies, rather it is about using them to facilitate the achievement of learning objectives. Outcomes are measured by competence of use and more importantly the quality of the process or the product. Church's *Bloom's Digital Taxonomy* lends itself to problem- and project-based learning where learners work through the entire process of development and evaluation.

Substitution Augmentation Modification Redefinition (SAMR) model

The Substitution Augmentation Modification Redefinition (SAMR) model, developed by Puentedura (2006, 2014a, 2014b) provides a method of seeing how digital technology might impact teaching and learning as indicated in Table 17.2. It also indicates a progression that

Table 17.2 SAMR Model (Pueutedura, 2006, 2014a, 2014b)

Enhancement	Substitution	Technology acts as a direct tool substitute with no functional change
	Augmentation	Technology acts as a direct tool substitute with functional improvements
Transformation	Modification	Technology allows for significant task redesign
	Redefinition	Technology allows creation of new task, previously inconceivable

adopters of digital technology often follow as they progress through teaching and learning with technology. The important concept to grasp here is the level of a learner's engagement. Progression can be measured by examining who is asking the important questions as the activity unfolds. As one moves along this continuum, digital technology becomes more important in the classroom, but at the same time becomes invisibly interwoven into the demands of effective teaching and learning.

UNESCO ICT Competence Framework

UNESCO and its partners are currently revising the ICT Competency Framework for Teachers (UNESCO, 2011) to ensure that all teachers can harness technology for education. The UNESCO ICT-CFT highlights the role that technology can play in supporting six education focus areas across three phases of knowledge acquisition, as shown in Figure 17.3.

This framework is being updated to maintain its currency and covers emerging technologies and digital services now available to teachers and the competences that teachers need to use these technologies and services effectively and effortlessly within the classroom for teaching and learning. In addition to providing the ICT-CFT framework, UNESCO have curated an ICT-CFT Toolkit to assist teachers to transform from being technology literate to being knowledge creators, not just for themselves but for their learners too.

DigCompEdu, the European Framework for the Digital Competence of Educators

In 2017, the European Union published DigCompEdu, the European Framework for the Digital Competence of Educators (Redecker, 2017). This framework has been developed with the aim of enabling and empowering teachers to harness the potential of digital technologies to encourage enhancement of and innovation in education and training practices, improve access to lifelong learning and professional learning. The DigCompEdu framework consists of six interrelated strands: professional engagement, digital resources, teaching and learning, assessment, empowering learners and facilitating learners' digital competence. It is summarised in Table 17.3.

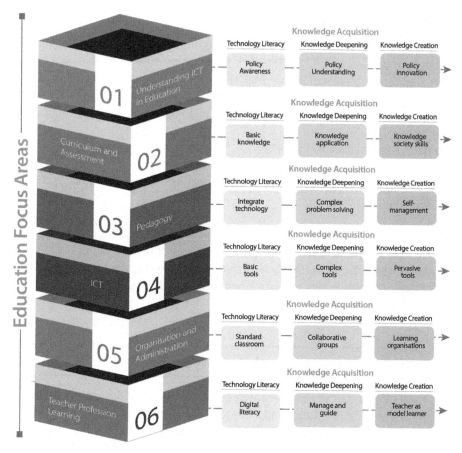

Figure 17.3 Overview and summary of UNESCO's ICT competency framework for teachers (image created by Jon Audain)

Table 17.3 Educators' pedagogic competences (adapted from the DigCompEdu project)

Teacher competence	Specific skills required of the teacher	Pedagogic strategies	Benefits for the learner's digital competence
Using digital resources for teaching	■ selecting ■ creating and modifying ■ managing protecting and sharing	■ active and collaborative learning ■ self-regulated learning ■ inclusion, differentiation and personalisation	■ information and media literacy ■ communication ■ content creation ■ responsible use ■ problem-solving
Using digital resources for assessment	■ Assessment strategies ■ analysing evidence ■ feedback and planning		

Jisc digital capability framework

In the United Kingdom, Jisc (formerly the Joint Information Systems Committee) has developed a digital capability framework for teaching staff in further and higher education that is applicable to those who teach in secondary schools. This digital capability framework is built around six interrelated elements. ICT proficiency is seen to come from competency in four areas:

- information data and media literacies;
- digital creation, problem solving and innovation;
- digital communication, collaboration and participation;
- digital learning and development.

Competence in these areas leads to ICT proficiency and, JISC suggests, to giving individuals a clear digital identity and well-being with respect to ICT usage.

Jisc has developed resources for teaching staff to assist their learners to develop their digital capability and for teachers to develop and embed digital literacy in the curriculum.

Now complete Task 17.2.

 Task 17.2   Investigating digital pedagogies

Taking a unit of work that you teach, consider how *Bloom's Digital Taxonomy* and the ideas from the projects listed above might be applied to it in order to supplement and complement your teaching of that unit and support your learners' learning.

You may wish to draw a concept map either by hand or by using an online tool, such as MindMap (www.mindmup.com).

Record your findings in your PDP for later reference.

Digital tools and techniques to support teaching and learning

Learning management systems

Schools have either invested in a commercial learning management system (LMS) or chosen to implement an offering from a multinational IT organisation, such as Microsoft Teams or Google Classroom. An LMS is intended to provide access to both a virtual classroom, that is, a digital repository of teaching and learning resources and formative digital assessment tools, and tasks that learners can access either in class or outside class. Common features of an LMS include an electronic mark book for learners for the activities they have undertaken and the ability to track how long and what specific activities an individual learner has actively engaged with or not. The functionality of an LMS can be customised to meet the needs of different users so they can perform specific tasks as indicated in the Table 17.4.

Table 17.4 Functionality of an LMS allocated to different user types

Users	*Tasks they carried out with the virtual classroom*
Teachers	■ create and manage classes, assignments and grades. ■ give direct, real-time feedback and grades.
Pupils	■ keep track of classwork and materials. ■ share resources and interact in class stream or by email. ■ submit assignments. ■ receive feedback and grades.
Parents/guardians	■ receive an email summary of their learner's work; the summary can include information about missing work, upcoming assignments and class activity. Note that parents/guardians can't sign in directly to the LMS but receive summaries emailed through another account or via a portal on the school's website
Administrators	■ can create, view or delate a class. ■ add or remove learners or teachers from a specific class. ■ view all work in created classes.

Normally, an LMS is integrated with the school's management information system (MIS) so that a learner's data can be transferred between each system seamlessly. This is so that you, your head of department and senior managers at the school can monitor and track an individual's progress as well as the progress of an individual class or an entire year group, not just in your subject but in all the subjects that the learner studies. The data that is generated by the LMS can be interrogated and analysed to determine how an individual learner is performing against their baseline assessment for any specific subject and their target grade for that subject. This is achieved by using learning analytics and can automatically determine if an intervention is required.

ePortfolio

An ePortfolio is a digital version of a portfolio (you have used a portfolio during your initial teacher education programme to collate and present evidence against the grading criteria for the *Teachers' Standards* in England (DfE, 2011)). This is a repository in which a learner can store digital content they have created or curated from other sources. This digital content can include digital artefacts such as text, static images, photographs, scanned documents, animations, embedded or imported videos, voice recordings and hyperlinks to websites the learner wants to refer to. An ePortfolio can be customised and personalised by a learner so that they take ownership of it. In addition, the learner can determine with whom they share the whole ePortfolio or alternatively to whom they provide access to specific pages. Individuals who have access to an ePortfolio cannot only view it but also post constructive comments to its owner. There is a tension for the teacher in either providing the learner with the artistic freedom to determine the presentation of the content or provide a template for the presentation of the content that the learner populates with content.

Flipped learning

This pedagogical strategy is an inversion of the usual approach of the teacher teaching in the classroom and assigning homework and group work for outside of class. Instead, in a flipped classroom, pupils engage in passive learning (e.g. viewing teaching material, assigned reading) at home and class time is devoted to collaborative projects, answering questions and engaging with the subject material at a deeper level. The dynamics involved in flipped classrooms are outlined in Figure 17.4.

Digital technology and activity learning are two key components of the flipped classroom environment model as they both influence pupils' learning environments in fundamental ways. The advantages and disadvantages of the use of flipped learning are summarised in Table 17.5.

Despite the various disadvantages, the flipped classroom model continues to grow in popularity. Many teachers have seen at first hand the power of this pedagogical model to transform their classroom into spaces of creativity, collaboration and thoughtful enquiry.

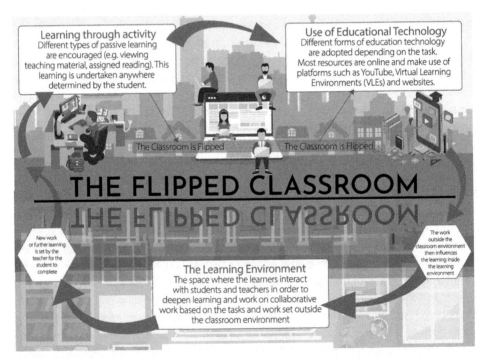

Figure 17.4 Dynamics of the flipped classroom (image created by Jon Audain)

Table 17.5 Advantages and disadvantages of flipped learning

Advantages	Disadvantages
■ When pupils are expending the most energy, in attempts to solve problems, answer questions or work in a group, then the teacher is there in the classroom to assist pupils. ■ Instead of being sent home with questions to grapple with on their own, pupils come to classes with questions they have devised themselves after watching the pre-recorded video. ■ Assists teachers in understanding where individual pupil's comprehension is actually faltering; thus, the teacher discovers individual pupil's misconceptions or misalignments. ■ Pupils can learn at their own pace, pause and rewind the recording when they need to. ■ Class time is used to work on group activities, enhancing peer-to-peer teaching and learning.	■ Time is required for a teacher to pre-record the videos to use in flipped learning. ■ Pupils must have the necessary equipment at home and an internet connection to watch the recording outside school.

Gamification

An example of gamification is that of Kahoot! (http://kahoot.com) with its philosophy of *Create – Play – Learn*. Kahoot! is a pupil response system that engages pupils through game-like pre-made quizzes, discussion or surveys (Byrne, 2013; Cross, 2014). With Kahoot!, a teacher can create a learning game, called a Kahoot!, which can be a multiple-choice single-answer quiz, and learners using online devices can answer the questions within a given response time. The learning system supporting Kahoot! provides instant feedback to the learners and also provides an integrated learning management system for creating quizzes for and tracking the progress of individual learners. Kahoot! has a professional development certification programme for teachers so that they can utilise its full potential. Several studies have been conducted investigating the use of Kahoot! in the classroom either by individual teachers (Dellos, 2015; Johns, 2015) or researchers (Plump and LaRosa, 2017) with a clear focus on investigating pupil engagement and motivation.

Simulation

Simulations are instructional scenarios where the learner is placed in a scenario in a 'virtual world' defined by the teacher or the organisation that has created the scenario. These scenarios represent a view of reality in which learners can interact with characters (actors) in the virtual world presented to them and manage the virtual world by altering environmental parameters and viewing the resultant effects. Learners can use the simulation as a vehicle to develop and enhance self-efficacy and resilience, and develop problem-solving, communication and teamworking skills by solving problems presented in the scenario. A simulation is a form of experiential learning and as a teaching and learning strategy aligns with that of pupil-centred and constructivist learning and teaching (Bellou, Papachristos and Mikropoulos, 2018; Erlam, Smythe and Wright-St Clair, 2017). Simulations can take a number of forms and may contain elements of a game, role play or an activity that acts as a metaphor. Simulations are characterised by their non-linear nature and by their controlled ambiguity within which learners must respond by making decisions. The inventiveness and commitment of the learner determine their successful engagement with the simulation.

Simulations provide an opportunity to promote the use of critical and evaluative thinking, due to their ambiguous and open-ended nature. They encourage learners to contemplate the implications of a scenario and engage their higher-order thinking skills by answering "What if …" questions. Learners often find themselves more deeply engaged with simulations than other activities, as they are actively experiencing the activity at first hand rather than as passive knowledge consumers. In addition, simulations promote concept attainment through experiential practice as the learners actively explore the nuances associated with a concept. Moreover, simulations allow learners to appreciate more deeply the management of the environment, politics, community and culture.

When using simulations, you need to be aware that resources and time are required to develop a quality learning experience and that assessment of pupil learning using simulations is often more complex that other methods. You may wish to apply the following principles when using simulations: prepare in advance as much as possible, brief the learners beforehand, note what you want the learners to accomplish when using a simulation, monitor the process closely so that learners both understand it and can benefit from it, and consider carefully what you want to assess. You might find it best to use simulations as part of the learning process, rather than as a formative or summative measure of it, in which case follow-up activities can be used to measure comprehension and as a debriefing mechanism in which learners reflect on the process undertaken rather than the simulation itself.

In summary, a simulation utilises an immersive experience to engage learners. It is framed by a set of parameters in which learners solve problems in the scenarios that they are presented with by responding to changes, and they gain an awareness of the factors that govern and influence the scenario presented in the simulation.

QR codes

Quick Response (QR) code is the trademark for a type of matrix (two-dimensional) barcode. The barcode is a machine-readable optical label that contains information about the item it is associated with. It was initially designed in 1994 for the automotive industry in Japan to track vehicles through the manufacturing process.

Miller (2014) outlines twelve ideas for teaching with QR codes, presented in Table 17.6.

Table 17.6 Twelve ideas for teaching with QR codes

Create 21st-century biographies	Show exemplars	Provide a service	Make a classroom greener
Rewards and praise	Make learning stations	Check answers and reflect	Provide extension activities
Compile research	Create interactive labs or dissection	Differentiate instructions	Vote

QR codes can be used in a Library Quest, for example, in which learners are engaged by scanning QR codes using a mobile device (e.g. smartphone, tablet) with a camera and a QR reader app, which are distributed through the library to inform them what that section of the library is and to guide them to where the next clue in their quest is (Ojino and Mich, 2018). Marcus, Stiddard and Woodward (2017) outlined strategies for teaching history using museums. One strategy involved learners scanning a QR code, which is positioned closely to a museum artefact that the learners are investigating, which then provides them with further information or a link to a multimodal website to engage them further with animation, augmented reality or a video.

QR code generators are freely available on the internet. They convert the URL of a website into a QR code, which can be printed or copied and pasted into another application.

The benefits of using QR codes as a digital technology include a slight learning curve to master the technology, interactivity, easy connections, accessibility and portability. The disadvantages include perception of the learning curve, whether learners are permitted to have access to and use smartphones on a school's premises.

As mobile learning becomes prevalent within schools, teachers must find effective ways of leveraging mobile tools in the classroom.

Virtual reality/augmented reality

Google fund Virtual Reality Research Grants that could fund a collaboration between your school and your local university in evaluating the effectiveness and impact of virtual reality field trips. For example, the Open University, funded by Google, is working with the Field Study Council, Geographical Association and the Association for Science Education investigating the role of virtual reality-based field trips in encouraging and supporting outdoor fieldwork.

Twitter

Twitter is one of greatest resources available to teachers if used correctly. This all begins when you start following people. Twitter provides you access both to resources and ideas that you can either adopt or amend and to digestible conversations and discussions that you can either follow or contribute to. A whole new world will open up for you. The companion website contains a list of educators who you might want to follow.

Wordle

Wordle (www.wordle.net) is a digital tool for generating 'word clouds' from text that you provide. The cloud gives greater prominence to words that appear more frequently in the source text, as shown in the following Wordle of Dr Martin Luther King's 1963 speech, 'I have a dream' (see Figure 17.5).

You can customise your word cloud with different fonts, layouts and colour schemes. It can be used as a supplementary research tool (McNaught and Lam, 2010) and formative assessment of pupils' short written responses (Brooks et al., 2014). Pearcy (2016) reports on a research study of using Wordles to visualise text in history lessons. Now complete Task 17.3.

Figure 17.5 Wordle from Dr Martin Luther King's 1963 speech 'I have a dream' (image created by Jon Audain)

M | **Task 17.3   Tools, techniques and tactics**

Investigate one of the digital tools that we have introduced in this section to see how you can use it for either your professional development or to assist you with learning and teaching in the classroom. When evaluating the digital tool that you have chosen, ask yourself the following questions:

a)   What do I need to do to use this digital tool in my classroom?

b)   How do I need to prepare my learners so this digital tool can be used to both supplement and complement teaching and learning in the classroom?

c)   How am I going to progress from being a novice user of this digital tool to mastering it?

Record your findings in your PDP for later reference.

Professional learning

Digital technologies within the classroom emerge, evolve, embed and may even become extinct. This section highlights initiatives offered by organisations and universities that may support teachers in developing and enhancing their digital skills and evidence-based research for the adoption and usage of digital technologies within the classroom.

Several international IT corporations provide free continuous professional development and free professional certification so that you can explore and master digital technologies for teaching your subject and be accredited for the training you have received. These corporations include:

- Apple offers Apple Education as a portal for teachers to learn how to embed core creative skills in their subjects and develop their confidence, capability and competence in using Apple products via the Apple Teacher programme. In addition, they recognise pioneers in education through their Apple Distinguished Educators programme.
- Google operates the Google for Education Teacher Center, which provides guidance on how to embed and incorporate technologies in the classroom and offers Google Educator certification for those teachers who want their expertise to be externally recognised.
- Microsoft maintains the Microsoft Education Community and provides access to online courses that teachers can use to develop their digital skills as well as integrating digital technology in the classroom. As an incentive to completing these online courses, Microsoft awards a digital badge for each course that a teacher completes. Eventually, a teacher can be recognised as a Microsoft Innovative Educator (MIE) when they have gained the required number of digital badges.

In addition, several educational charities or not-for-profit organisations provide access to resources for professional learning with regard to the use of digital technologies in the classroom. These include the following:

- Edutopia is the George Luca Educational Foundation and provides free access to ideas, projects and research for incorporating digital technologies in the classroom.
- MESH seeks to connect educators with summaries and sources of educational research. These summaries are published as open access MESHGuides in order to distribute evidence-informed practices in the classroom as widely as possible.
- TED is devoted to spreading ideas, usually in the form of short, powerful talks; TED Student Talks is part of the TED-Ed initiative, whose mission is to celebrate the ideas of pupils and teachers around the world. This is achieved through the production of a library of original animated videos and the provision of an international platform for teachers to create their own interactive lessons.

In addition, to support professional learning from IT multinational organisations, a number of universities have invested in and continue to invest in designing and developing massive open online courses (MOOCs) for individuals worldwide to gain access to subject matter experts delivering open access online courses on different aspects of digital technologies. For example, the University of York has a MOOC entitled 'Digital Wellbeing', which explores how digital technologies affect our well-being.

Within school you might want to speak to your head of department, lead practitioners or your mentor for advice and guidance regarding how to develop your digital skills further and embed digital technologies within your teaching. Now complete Task 17.4.

Task 17.4 Professional learning

Subject-based Communities of Practices (CoPs) exist to support your development as a teacher and provide guidance and support to develop not only your subject knowledge but also the use of digital technologies to support your teaching. Research, identify and bookmark websites that can support you as a teacher and help your learners develop their digital skills.

Research the Ideas website (https://idea.org.uk/) and the Microsoft Education website (https://education.microsoft.com/badges-points-certificates/badges-and-points) to identify digital badges that you can work towards to develop your digital skills and promote with the learners you teach.

Record your findings in your PDP for later reference.

Digital wisdom

As a teacher you have a moral responsibility to model to your learners not only how to behave in the real world but also in the virtual world. In addition, you have a responsibility to model to your learners how to use digital tools appropriately and wisely. Netiquette refers to guidance not only for how to communicate in an appropriate manner online but also for how to behave in the virtual world.

Addressing fake news

The Guardian Foundation, in collaboration with the National Literacy Trust and the PHSE Association funded by Google, produce a free, cross-curricular news literacy project, entitled *NewsWise*. The aim of NewsWise is to empower learners with the skills and knowledge to recognise and navigate fake news. These organisations want to assist learners to engage with and enjoy news, feel confident to ask questions and to challenge misinformation, to develop their own values and opinions and endow them with a clear and authentic voice to articulate their thoughts.

Guidelines for designing digital resources

On International Literacy Day in 2018, the UNESCO-Pearson Initiative for Literacy launched its Guidelines for Designing Inclusive Digital Solutions and Developing Digital Skills (UNESCO, 2018a). These guidelines have been developed following a two-year landscape review of digital inclusion strategies for low-skilled and low-literate people (UNESCO, 2018b), in recognition that, in an increasingly digitised world, learners need digital and literacy skills to live, learn and communicate and for their future employment and productivity. Without these skills, learners face marginalisation not only in the physical world but in digital realms as well. Fortunately, digital exclusion is avoidable, and you can play your part in eradicating it in your classroom.

Assistive and accessible technology in teaching and learning

Accessibility involves designing systems to optimise access. Being inclusive as a school and a teacher is about providing equal access and opportunities to every learner in your classroom wherever possible. This involves reducing and overcoming the barriers that might occur in digital content, teaching, learning and assessments. The social model of disability suggests that society (i.e. the school) or the environment (i.e. the classroom) are disabling the learner, rather than their impairment or difficulties. For example, it is not clear that not providing subtitles on videos disadvantages anyone watching in a noisy classroom, but a lack of subtitles disadvantages deaf learners all the time.

Accessibility is about designing learning and teaching activities and resources that utilise digital technologies to minimise and, if possible, remove unnecessary barriers that make it harder for learners to engage and participate in learning and teaching episodes in the classroom. As with video subtitles, digital technologies are very useful tools in providing a level playing field for all learners within the classroom.

Assistive technology is the term used for technology that assists a learner to do something they would otherwise be unable to do or have difficulty with. Some assistive technology can be more accurately described as productive tools because they make learning or teaching easier or more efficient.

Jisc provides digital solutions for United Kingdom education and research and has produced guidance on the use of assistive technologies that can support learners with special educational needs (www.jisc.ac.uk/full-guide/using-assistive-and-accessible-technology-in-teaching-and-learning). Although these guides are intended for learners in further and higher education, the principles are applicable to learners with special educational needs in secondary schools. Jisc provides the following six tips for inclusive practice:

1. maximise resources online;
2. make presentations meaningful;
3. make documents easy to navigate and understand;
4. provide alternative media but make them accessible;
5. use hyperlinks for multiple support options;
6. provide opportunities for self-assessment.

In addition, technical guidance is available from the Benetech Diagram Center (http://diagramcenter.org/) on how to produce accessible diagrams in mathematics.

Ranaldi (2010) produced a case study on using digital resources across the curriculum in schools and the impact that this had had on teaching and learning.

Professional use of social media

The General Teaching Council for Scotland (GTCS) has produced professional guidelines on the use of electronic communication and social media (GTCS, n.d.), which is applicable to all teachers throughout the United Kingdom. This practical guidance is presented in Table 17.7, so that you have a yardstick with which you can measure your professional use of social media.

Table 17.7 GTCS professional guidance on use of electronic communications and social media (from GTCS, n.d.)

As a teacher you should:

■ always maintain a formal and courteous and professional tone in communicating with pupils and ensure that professional boundaries are maintained;

■ only use official channels of communication e.g. GLOW and work email addresses, and be aware of and comply with employer's policies and guidance;

■ not exchange private text, phone numbers, personal e-mail addresses or photos of a personal nature with pupils;

■ firmly decline pupil-initiated 'friend' requests from pupils and do not instigate any yourself. Use your own discretion when dealing with friend requests from parents. It is acceptable to decline these invitations and remind parents of more formal channels which they can discuss their child's education;

■ operate online in a way in which would not call into question your position as a professional;

■ realise that pupils are naturally curious about your personal life outside school and may try to find out more about you;

■ Manage your privacy setting and keep them under review. These are particularly important in regard to photos. Remember that no privacy mechanism is 100% guaranteed;

■ ensure your settings prohibit others from tagging you in any photos or updates without your permission and you can ask others to remove any undesirable content related to you;

■ audit and re-evaluate the information about you and who has access to it if you are entering a programme of teacher education, or your Teacher Induction Period;

■ be aware that potential employers may try and view your online social media profiles;

■ consider that conversations held online may not be private. Be aware of who may have access to what you post;

■ assume that information you post can be accessed and altered;

■ not discuss pupils, colleagues, parents or carers online or criticise your employer or others within the school community;

■ respect pupil privacy and confidentiality at all times;

■ use strong passwords and change them regularly. Protect your mobile phone/smartphone/ tablet computer with a PIN, especially when in school to protect access to its content and potential misuse;

■ bring the matter to the attention of your employer using the proper procedures, if you are the victim of cyber-bullying or uncomfortable with comments, photos or posts made by pupils of or about you.

Online safety

The UK Safer Internet Centre advocates that the most effective approach to online safety in a school is to treat it as a whole school community issue, with educational messages not just embedded across computing, personal, social, health and economic (PSHE) education, sex and relationship education (SRE) and citizenship, but articulated in all subjects across the curriculum whenever and wherever learners are using digital technologies.

The importance of this is recognised by the Office for Standards in Education, Children's Services and Skills (Ofsted) in their report *Not Yet Good Enough: Personal, Social, Health* and Economic Education in Schools (Ofsted, 2013b), which makes it clear that digital issues must be addressed in order for a school to achieve an 'Outstanding' grade.

In 2015, the South West Grid for Learning (SWGfL) produced a cross-curricular digital curriculum (SWGfL, 2015), which allows teachers to access resources to empower learners to think critically, behave safely and participate responsibly not only in the classroom but in the digital world too. This cross-curricular digital curriculum focuses on the following eight topics:

- privacy and security
- digital footprint and reputation
- self-image identity
- creative credit copyright
- relationship and communication
- information literacy
- cyberbullying
- internet safety

Although these themes ideally may have been introduced to learners in primary schools, they are introduced, within a secondary school, to learners in Key Stage 3, and developed throughout both Key Stages 4 and 5. Further guidance (Education for a Connected World) was also released in 2018 by the UK government, who produced a framework describing the skills and understanding learners should be equipped with in terms of current technology (www.gov.uk/government/publications/education-for-a-connected-world).

Hopefully, this section has highlighted the importance of developing not only the individual learner's digital wisdom but also your own as you work, learn and rest in both the physical world and the digital world. Now complete Task 17.5.

 Task 17.5   What is your digital footprint?

We live in an age where we exist simultaneously in two worlds, the physical world and the virtual world. Within the virtual world we exist as a collection of data (e.g. audio, numerical, text, images, videos) and within interdependent, interwoven and interlinked networks that connect us to others. In order to discover and review your online presence, take the following steps:

a)   Google your name and see how many search results relate to you.
b)   Which search results would you want the pupils you teach to see?
c)   Review your privacy settings on any social media platform that you belong to and any social media apps.

Discuss this information with your mentor (or someone else) and store the information in your PDP to refer to later.

SUMMARY AND KEY POINTS

This chapter has aimed to:

■   enable you reflect on how to use digital technologies to enhance teaching and learning in your subject area;

■   help you consider how digital technology refers to many of the things you may see and use every day without thinking about them and to reflect on ideas about how you may use them in your teaching;

■   enable you to undertake a digital literacy competency audit – this should be encouraging, as it probably shows you know more than you thought;

■   encourage you to use digital technologies in your lessons, including ways in which you are able to control the direction, pace and learning to keep pupils engaged;

■   Highlight the importance of online safety for yourself and the pupils that you teach.

Record in your PDP how the information in this chapter enables you to meet the requirements for your first year of teaching.

 ## Further resources

The suggested further resources have been selected to encourage you to think about opportunities for using all types of digital technologies in both an innovative and effective manner to enhance teaching and learning in your subject. They also seek to demonstrate that inspiration can come from an unexpected range of sources, and so pose the question 'That looks interesting: could I adopt that to enhance my subject teaching?'

Bradshaw, P. and Younie, S. (2018) 'Understanding online ethics and digital identity', in S. Younie and P. Bradshaw (eds.) *Debates in Computing and ICT Education*, Abingdon: Routledge.
  This provides an understanding for both pupils and teachers of key ethical issues concerning digital technologies and an awareness of our online identities.

Cych, L., Williams, L. and Younie, S. (2018) 'Using Web 2.0 technologies to enhance learning and teaching', in S. Younie and P. Bradshaw (eds.), *Debates in Computing and ICT Education*, Abingdon: Routledge.
  This chapter outlines the use of digital technologies for enhancing teaching and learning across subjects, specifically how Web 2.0 tools can be used to create a social constructivist learning environment. The authors discuss how digital technologies can be used to stimulate learner engagement and how to deploy Web 2.0 technologies effectively in the classroom.

Appendices 2 and 3 list subject associations, teaching councils and relevant websites.

Books in the *Learning to Teach* series that you may find helpful are as follows:

Capel, S., Leask, M. and Younie, S. (eds.) (2019) *Learning to Teach in the Secondary School: A Companion to School Experience*, 8th edn, Abingdon: Routledge.
  This book is designed as a core textbook to support student teachers through their initial teacher education programme.

Capel, S., Leask, M. and Turner, T. (eds.) (2010) *Readings for Learning to Teach in the Secondary School: A Companion to M Level Study*, Abingdon: Routledge.
  This book brings together essential readings to support you in your critical engagement with key issues raised in this textbook.

The subject-specific books in the *Learning to Teach* series, the *Practical (subject) Guides*, *Debates in (subject)* and *Mentoring (subject) Teachers* are also very useful.

18 Leadership and management

Rachel Peckover

Introduction

> Effective heads build the capacity for school improvement by empowering others to lead and to develop the school.
>
> *(Harris and Lambert, 2003, p. 3)*

At a time of widely reported retention and recruitment issues within the teaching profession in many countries, including pronounced recruitment difficulties for the main middle leadership roles in schools (National Association of Head Teachers (NAHT), 2016), there is an increasing trend in 'grow your own' policies towards internal promotion (Bush et al., 2012). Schools often recognise and nurture their own leadership talent, providing opportunities and training for staff to develop their skills from the beginning of their career, in the hope that they will stay with the school and apply for any future leadership roles.

This means that opportunities for progression are greater than ever for you as a beginning teacher if you wish to take on a leadership role at an early stage in your career. When you have successfully completed your induction, you have the opportunity to consider your own teaching career path. Although this will be unique to you, if middle or senior leadership is something that you aspire to, it is important to start planning for progression as soon as possible. For the truly ambitious, it is wise to begin your career with a five-year plan. Although achieving your goals requires a certain amount of luck - being in the right place at the right time - it is also about making the right choices, getting noticed and taking on smaller roles and responsibilities as and when they arise.

OBJECTIVES

At the end of this chapter you should be able to:

- understand leadership structures within schools;
- identify your strengths and interests;

- ▪ understand different types of leadership and associated skills;
- ▪ recognise the type of leader you would like to become;
- ▪ begin to identify ways to develop your leadership skills.

Check how the information in this chapter enables you to meet the requirements for your first year of teaching.

School structures

Although secondary and primary school structures differ, typically both have a senior leadership team made up of the head, deputy and assistant heads. These may be joined by an extended leadership team of phase leaders, a special educational needs and disability coordinator (SENDCo) and core subject coordinators. Figure 18.1 provides examples of two different types of school leadership structure. Table 18.1 then summarises the roles and responsibilities usually found in schools.

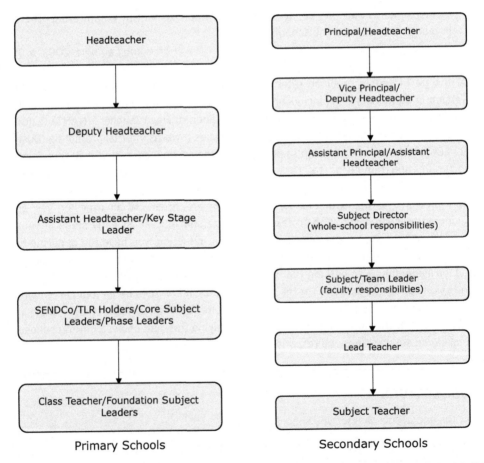

Primary Schools   Secondary Schools

Figure 18.1 Primary and secondary leadership structures (see Table 18.1 for further details)

Table 18.1 A brief description of roles within schools

Role	Responsibilities
Headteacher/Principal	Overall responsibility for the school, its staff, its pupils and the education they receive
Deputy headteacher/Vice principal	Plays a major role in managing the school, particularly in the absence of the headteacher
Assistant headteacher	Supports the head and deputy with the management of the school. May have a teaching commitment
Key Stage manager	Employed to lead and manage a Key Stage. Usually includes a class teaching commitment
Early years/Phase leader	Responsible for children at a specific stage of their education, leading a team of teachers, nursery nurses or teaching assistants
Special educational needs and disabilities coordinator	Responsible for day-to-day provision for pupils with special educational needs.
Subject director	Usually a member of the extended leadership team. Responsible for whole-school development in key subjects: English, Maths, Science or ICT.
Subject leader/Team leader/Curriculum coordinator e.g. Maths lead More able Lead Student voice Principal teacher (Scotland)	Responsible for a particular area in the curriculum: taking part in the review and development of teaching materials and programmes. In primary schools, class teachers may be expected to accept responsibility for an area of the curriculum as part of their normal professional duties. **Teaching and Learning Responsibility (TLR) positions have an additional responsibility in that the post holder is accountable for the quality of the work of pupils and other staff in this area. They may also have line manager duties.**
Lead teacher/Specialist leader of education (SLE)	Employed as a specialist teacher with outstanding teaching skills. May be required to provide line management duties and mentoring for newer members of staff. May support the development of teaching and learning in other schools.
Classroom teachers	Plan, prepare and deliver lessons to meet the needs of all pupils, setting and marking work and recording pupil development as necessary. Often work in partnership with teaching assistants.

In order to develop your career path, it is important to understand these structures and the roles and responsibilities that go with them. See, for example, the now closed Training and Development Agency (TDA) guidance (2011). However, it should be noted that, in England, with the increase in the number of academies and the autonomy that goes with this, these structures may become more varied over time. Now undertake Task 18.1.

Task 18.1   Identifying your strengths and areas of interest

Consider the structures in Figure 18.1 and the roles and responsibilities outlined in Table 18.1.

Begin to consider which roles appeal to you.

Review your PDP and induction action plans. Identify your current strengths and any areas identified for further development linked to your leadership ambitions.

Record your reflections in your professional development portfolio (PDP) (or similar), perhaps in a personal development section.

Types of leadership

If you read books on educational leadership you come across a confusing number of different terms: positional, managerial, transactional, instructional, transformational, distributed, democratic, the list goes on. Until relatively recently, there was little research into the impact that these different styles of leadership had. Research by Hay/McBer (Goleman, 2000), provides a framework, which has since been developed and adopted by the (now closed) National College for Teaching and Leadership (NCTL) in England, detailing six distinct types of leadership outlined in Table 18.2: coercive, authoritative, affiliative, democratic, pacesetting and coaching.

Outstanding leaders should be able to demonstrate all of these styles, depending on school circumstances. However, they are likely to have a preference for, or be more dominant in, some rather than others. Now undertake Task 18.2.

M   **Task 18.2   Identifying leadership styles**

Look at Table 18.2.

Consider which styles of leadership you have seen enacted within your school.

When were they used?
Which were successful?
Were there any that were less successful?
Which style do you favour?

Record your notes in your PDP to use as a benchmark for developing yourself.

Preparing for leadership – first steps

'The door into leadership has "confidence" written upon it' (Adair, 1997, p. 33). Not only should you be identifying what you are good at, but it's also important that other people begin to notice this as well. Have conversations with headteachers and heads of department, explaining where you feel your strengths and passions lie. Ask for advice

Table 18.2 A summary of Goleman's (2000) six types of leadership

Leadership style	Summary
Coercive	This can be successful in an immediate short-term crisis, for example when a new headteacher inherits a failing school and needs to make changes quickly. However, in the long term, coercive leadership is incredibly damaging to morale as it is based on micro-management and inflexibility, with staff potentially frightened into doing as they are told. Its overall impact is most often negative.
Authoritative	Authoritative leaders are visionaries whose enthusiasm and dedication inspire others to work hard and improve performance, helping everyone to understand their role in moving a school forward and giving them a sense of pride in their work. Authoritative leadership welcomes flexibility and innovation.
Affiliative	This type of leadership is people-centred, valuing individuals rather than the end result. Leaders create bonds between the community of practice, allowing for good communication, innovation and risk-taking. Positive feedback motivates staff. This style of leadership is effective when dealing with low morale. It works best when used alongside authoritative leadership.
Democratic	This has a positive effect on communities of practice and, in schools, works well when fresh approaches and everyone's ideas are required. It creates 'buy in' for new initiatives and encourages trust, respect and commitment among staff, allowing for flexibility and a collective responsibility. Leaders who enact this type of leadership need to be very good listeners. However, care needs to be taken to ensure that crucial decisions are not delayed.
Pacesetting	Pacesetting leadership can be successful in motivating highly skilled and knowledgeable teachers who require little direction. In these circumstances, the leader is able to exemplify the high performance expected. However, when used in other circumstances, pacesetting leadership can see the decline of morale and trust within a group. It can leave staff feeling overwhelmed and vulnerable.
Coaching	Coaching (see Chapter 3) would appear to be the most suited to an educational environment. Unfortunately, the pressures of time can mean that this style of leadership is often overlooked. When executed well (as a result of excellent communication and delegation skills), coaching ensures that staff are accurately able to reflect on their own practice and provides constructive feedback and advice on how to develop, allowing creativity. Staff who experience this type of leadership feel valued.

and support and be proactive in finding yourself an informal mentor, someone whose leadership style appeals to you. Discuss your ambitions and ask to shadow them as they go about some of their leadership responsibilities.

Once you have identified your strengths, leadership styles and interests, you need to begin to develop your skills. This will often be without any extra pay, formal position or additional time but it is imperative that you gain experience in order to progress. As Irvine and Brundrett (2017) argue, this should be seen as an investment, even when classroom teaching feels all consuming. You need to demonstrate your enthusiasm and skill set. Case Study 18.1 shows how one beginning teacher did just that.

Case study 18.1   A beginning teacher's first steps towards leadership in a secondary school

Tom is a beginning teacher in the PE department of an outstanding secondary school. Nearing the end of his first year, he has spoken to his faculty head about his ambition to one day lead PE, identifying that his strengths and interests lie in the curriculum side of teaching.

In response, his faculty head has given him responsibility for running the school's sport specialism programme, which involves developing Year 9 pupils as coaches for neighbouring primary schoolchildren.

This is very much a first step towards Tom achieving his overall ambition. As part of his new role, he will be managing a small budget; planning the structure of the sessions (at times having to decide whether to follow his head of department's plans or implement a new approach); learning about curriculum design; developing critical thinking skills; and leading and managing his department colleagues in this specific area, using his emotional intelligence and communication skills.

Tom is aware that there is no extra pay attached to this role, although he has been told that there may be the opportunity for some non-contact time. Crucially, he is willing to take on this extra responsibility anyway to help him to develop the skills he will need for future leadership opportunities.

Competencies required of a successful leader

The SecEd Guide (2015b) suggests that competencies required of any successful leader are emotional intelligence, strategic thinking and effective communication. Delegation skills should also be added to this list.

Danielson (2007) points out that there is a growing recognition that leadership is a very different role from that of classroom teaching and, as such, requires additional preparation. Not all of the skills required may have been adequately addressed as part of initial teacher education (Pont, Nusche and Moorman, 2008). However, research by Conger (quoted in Burke and Cooper, 2006) found that for the right individuals, those with talent and motivation, these competencies can be learnt.

Emotional intelligence

A good leader demonstrates expertise, knowledge and reasoning. However, an outstanding leader demonstrates emotional intelligence (Goleman, 2011; Goleman, Boyatzis and McKee, 2013).

The link between emotional intelligence and leadership has not always been obvious (Cherniss, 2006). Understanding emotion helps leaders to make decisions. In fact, research by Goleman (1998) found that 85 per cent of the competencies required for effective leadership were related to emotional intelligence. Leadership is essentially about the ability to influence others. You therefore need to begin to understand your emotions and how they can be a motivating or limiting factor.

As a teacher, you are probably already highly skilled in using emotional intelligence within your own classroom, responding to pupils' and parents' characters and moods, whilst holding your own in check. These same skills are required when leading other adults.

One of the hardest aspects of emotional intelligence is the ability to handle your own feelings in a demanding and often exhausting job (Department for Education (DfE), 2015d). High levels of anxiety make it more difficult to process information and cope effectively when making decisions. However, the use of mindfulness techniques is becoming increasingly popular. A quick internet search provides many useful websites and resources, such as the National Health Service (NHS) Choices page, which discusses mental well-being and provides tips on being more mindful. It is worth investigating some of the daily activities that this page recommends. There are also useful summaries of Carol Dweck's (2017) work on growth mindset.

Communication skills

Once again, you are continually refining your communication skills within your own classroom. However, you need to ensure that they are effective not only with your class, but with other adults too. Just as you explain a task to your pupils, you need to check that information has been interpreted correctly. It is not enough to assume that silence means understanding (Rees and Porter, 2015). As a result of embarrassment, politeness or impatience, even adults can say that they have understood when they have not. This needs to be addressed through a positive check, which goes beyond rhetorical questions such as, 'do you understand?', as well as by using your own active listening skills.

Body language is as much a part of communication as the words that we use. People's attitudes and feelings are not always easily expressed through language. It is important to look for other cues (Rees and Porter, 2015). Looking around at your colleagues' body language in staff meetings can tell you how they are really feeling about the information being imparted. Are they mirroring the person who is speaking: showing signs of agreement; fidgeting: have other things on their mind; or is their head bent down: disagreeing with what is being said?

In addition, the role of technical language should also be considered. Education is awash with acronyms and jargon that may not be clear to everyone a teacher engages with, for example, hampering communication when talking to parents. Now undertake Task 18.3.

 Task 18.3   Developing communication skills

After a parent-teacher meeting reflect critically on the experience.

Think about the words used, listening skills deployed and body language cues.

Discuss this with your mentor or a colleague and record your reflections in your PDP for reference before the next parent and teacher meeting.

Resilience and assertiveness

In order to become a successful leader, you need to negotiate your school's community of practice and, from a position of legitimate peripheral participation (Lave and Wenger, 1991), attract enough attention and create purposeful relationships with established colleagues to have your voice heard.

Understandably, the early years of a teacher's career can be a particularly difficult time. Ruohotie-Lyhty (2013, p.120) argues that it can severely challenge beginning teachers' former beliefs about teaching and themselves. You may have faced differences between expectation and reality, resulting in 'transition shock' (Patrick et al., 2010, p.278). Good experiences at the beginning of your career can allow you to develop resilience and sustain you through these difficulties and any that you may encounter in the future (Ulvik and Langørgen, 2012).

While you are trying to shape your identity, you may be unlikely to want to disrupt the status quo within your school. Wenger (1998) discusses this in some detail, providing evidence in his research that beginning teachers often adopt a 'strategic compliance' (Flores and Day, 2006), adhering to established routines and ways of teaching at the expense of their own values and ideals. As a beginning teacher, you need to develop the confidence to influence your own community and a resilience to persevere with your own beliefs (Keay, 2009).

This is where an informal mentor, chosen by you, can help (as suggested in Chapter 3). They can encourage you to adopt an assertive attitude, described by Rees and Porter as 'recognising the right of all parties to speak in a direct, honest and open way' (2015, p.100) and ensure that your valid ideas and opinions are listened to by the rest of your colleagues.

Strategic thinking

One of the most common mistakes made by inexperienced leaders is to try to take on too many new initiatives at once. As a teacher, it can often feel that you are being pulled in different directions as the demands of the Maths coordinator vie with those of your English coordinator, or your head of faculty wants you to devote time to one new initiative, while your SENDCo has something else that they would like you to implement. As a leader, you should never forget how it feels to have extra demands made upon your time. New initiatives should never be implemented just for the sake of it. Developing a reputation for making carefully considered, necessary changes helps to ensure that staff trust your decisions and will strive to implement your vision.

Once you secure the opportunity to lead a subject or project, start by setting clear goals. Know what you want to achieve and create a realistic timeline for progress. Set up a monitoring schedule to assess the current situation and identify next steps. Ensure that success is measurable. You need to ask your colleagues, wherever possible, to work smarter rather than harder. Gill (2011) explains the need for a 'helicopter view' - switching being able to get a broad feel of the issue in context and the ability to focus on specific details at the same time.

Delegation skills

Delegation is a vital day-to-day tool in the classroom if you are to carry out all the activities required of you. However, it can be daunting. As a beginning teacher, you are most likely to be delegating tasks to teaching assistants who may well be older than you and well established within the school. It becomes ever more important should you take on further leadership roles as how you delegate to colleagues sets the limit of your leadership impact (Sostrin, 2017).

There are a number of reasons that people in middle and senior leadership positions find delegation challenging (Creative Education, 2015). These include the feeling that it is disrespectful to colleagues; fears that they may appear lazy or incompetent; and the belief that it's often quicker to carry out a task themselves – the old adage 'if you want a job done properly ...'.

Leaders who are able to successfully delegate know their own strengths and weaknesses and those of their team. Colleagues feel trusted and valued and this encourages commitment to the school. Key to successful delegation is to show respect towards every member of the workplace community, from the lunchtime supervisor, office staff and caretaker through to the headteacher. This ensures that everyone knows the importance of their contribution, particularly when asked to carry out what may be considered to be menial tasks. Now undertake Task 18.4.

M

 Task 18.4   Delegating

Talk with colleagues about how they work with teaching assistants and any other support available within the school.

1.   Look at your current workload and identify a task that could be delegated.
2.   Approach a teaching assistant, teaching partner or classroom volunteer to help you, explaining why you're giving them a particular task.
3.   Give clear information on what needs to be achieved, the timescale and the desired outcome.
4.   Allow them to approach the task in their own way and give them responsibility for decision making linked to its completion – don't micro-manage!
5.   Show appreciation for a job well done.

Write reflective notes on how this delegation made you feel; how effective this was and what you have learnt from this task to store in your PDP.

Leadership development

> Leadership development is broader than specific programmes of activity or intervention and can be done through a combination of formal and informal processes throughout the stages and contexts of leadership practice.
>
> *(Pont, Nusche and Moorman, 2008, p. 107)*

The manner in which teachers engage with continuing professional development (CPD) has changed over the last few years. External professional development opportunities, once provided by local authority (LA) employees, are now accessed through private consultants, often at a greater economic cost (Pedder and Opfer, 2011).

Therefore, you need to be more inventive in the ways that you engage with leadership development. It is worth discussing the opportunity to take part in more formal CPD, such as the National Professional Qualifications (DfE, 2017c), which require you to undertake and reflect upon leadership projects within your own school. However, these can be prohibitively expensive at a time of concern over school budgets.

As stated earlier, seeking out informal opportunities, with the support of a mentor, is an excellent way to develop leadership skills. However, having the time to take on extra responsibilities, whilst still keeping up with your planning, marking and every other pressure that teachers face, requires serious consideration. If you are determined to set yourself on the path to leadership, the Chartered College of Teaching and teaching unions offer a wide range of advice, resources and courses, often at no extra cost. There are also opportunities to take part in leadership coaching activities through programmes such as Women Leading in Education (Teaching Schools Council).

Additionally, your subject association, the Education Development Trust, MESHGuides, MirandaNet, Teach Meets and researchED offer opportunities for teachers to engage with research online and at national conferences in order to develop practice. TES Institute offers a range of online courses and it is well worth engaging with online teacher forums and TED Talks. Knowledge Hub offers the opportunity to join a variety of networks linked to education.

However, vitally important in developing successfully as a leader, is the support that you get from your school. Is the ethos supportive of your leadership ambitions? Ultimately, if your current school is not the right place to develop your career, don't be afraid to look for jobs that offer more of the opportunities that you are interested in. Now undertake Task 18.5.

 Task 18.5   Developing your career plan

Thinking back to Task 18.1, begin to develop your own five-year career development plan.

Consider the skills that you need to develop, the support required and the opportunities available to gain experience in your chosen area.

Store this in your PDP.

SUMMARY AND KEY POINTS

This chapter has:

- provided you with information on school leadership structures;
- identified six distinct types of leadership (Goleman, 2000) to help you understand the situation in which you're working;
- encouraged you to consider your areas of strength and interest and think about ways in which you can develop identified leadership capabilities.

Record in your PDP how the information in this chapter enables you to meet the requirements for your first year of teaching.

Further resources

Burke, R.J. and Cooper, C.L. (2006) *Inspiring Leaders*, **London: Routledge.**

Although not directly linked to educational leadership, this book is helpful in further exploring the competencies required to be a successful leader.

Goleman, D. (2000) 'Leadership that gets results', *Harvard Business Review,* **78(2), 78-90.**
This article provides further details on leadership styles and is a handy primer on the emotional intelligences that accompany them.

Other resources and websites

Dweck: **https://mindsetonline.com/whatisit/about/index.html**

This website provides an overview of Dweck's work.

NHS Choices: **https://www.nhs.uk/conditions/stress-anxiety-depression/improve-mental-wellbeing**

The NHS Choices website provides a useful starting point for developing mindfulness practices.

Wenger-Trayner: **http://wenger-trayner.com/resources/what-is-a-community-of-practice**

This website provides a useful overview on communities of practice.

The following websites provide a range of educational research useful for your own professional development.

Education Development Trust: **https://www.educationdevelopmenttrust.com/en-GB/our-research/our-research-library**

Knowledgehub: **https://khub.net**

MESHGuides: **http://www.meshguides.org/**

MirandaNet: **http://mirandanet.ac.uk**

researchED: **https://researched.org.uk/**

The following websites provide opportunities for CPD and coaching.

DFE list of national professional qualification (NPQ) providers: **https://www.gov.uk/government/publications/national-professional-qualifications-npqs-list-of-providers/list-of-national-professional-qualification-npq-providers**

Teaching Schools Council - Women Leading in Education: **https://tscouncil.org.uk/women-leading-in-education-coaching-pledge/**

The Chartered College of Teaching: **https://chartered.college/**

Appendices 2 and 3 list subject associations, teaching councils and relevant websites.

Books in the *Learning to Teach* series that you may find helpful are as follows:

Capel, S., Leask, M. and Younie, S. (eds.) (2019) *Learning to Teach in the Secondary School: A Companion to School Experience*, **8th edn, Abingdon: Routledge.**
This book is designed as a core textbook to support student teachers through their initial teacher education programme.

Capel, S., Leask, M. and Turner, T. (eds.) (2010) *Readings for Learning to Teach in the Secondary School: A Companion to M Level Study*, **Abingdon: Routledge.**
This book brings together essential readings to support you in your critical engagement with key issues raised in this textbook.

The subject-specific books in the *Learning to Teach* series, the *Practical (subject) Guides*, *Debates in (subject)* and *Mentoring (subject) Teachers* are also very useful.

19 Researching your teaching

Eira Wyn Patterson

Introduction: a case for research informed practice

A recent review of the role of research in education concluded that research carried out by teachers has the potential to make a major impact on their practice and the resulting quality of learning taking place (British Educational Research Association and the Royal Society of Arts (BERA-RSA), 2014a). However, progress towards establishing evidence-based practice within education has proved to be a slow process, with many barriers to overcome (BERA-RSA, 2014b). The development of your practice and identity as a teacher can be enhanced by engagement in research and this chapter is designed to support you in that process.

> ### OBJECTIVES
>
> At the end of this chapter you should be able to:
>
> - understand key principles of research in education;
> - develop research designs to investigate research questions that are important to you in your own educational context;
> - ensure that your research attains high ethical standards.
>
> Check how the information in this chapter enables you to meet the requirements for your first year of teaching.

As you work through this chapter it would be useful to explore how the ideas it presents could support you in meeting the Teachers' Standards (Department for Education (DfE), 2011). There are many books and resources available to support the development of your research skills, including the Research Methods MESHGuides (see Patterson, 2016a, 2016b and 2016c in the Further resources section).

Developing your research design

A model of the research process

The following model of the research process illustrates possible stages in the development and implementation of your research design (adapted from Punch and Oancea, 2014):

- identify a research focus that aims to explore an aspect of practice;
- develop research questions to plan in more detail what you intend to research;
- identify the types of data that you need to collect to answer those questions;
- identify the methods you will use and design research tools to collect your data;
- analyse the data you have collected to provide insights into your research questions.

Identifying factors to focus on in your research

In education contexts different elements exist that have the potential to impact on the area of focus that you aim to research. Your research will enable you to explore how these elements interact within that context and how they influence the question or problem you want to explore. In quantitative research these elements are termed *variables*. In this chapter the focus is on qualitative research where these elements are often referred to as *factors*. An important part of developing your research design is to identify the factors that could potentially be important to focus on and to develop your research questions based on these. Table 19.1 illustrates a range of different factors that could be researched when investigating opportunities for enhancing cooperative learning within Key Stage 3 or 4.

Table 19.1 Factors that may impact on learning during cooperative group activities within Key Stages 3 or 4

Factors that may impact on learning within cooperative group activities	Examples of how factors could be researched: operationalised
Features of the physical environment	Resources available, e.g. how resources can be used to scaffold cooperative interactions
Behaviours or actions	Learners' engagement and interest in activities, e.g. use of a framework to assess the degree of engagement in an activity
Attainment of learners (this might focus on knowledge, understanding, skills or creative traits)	Analysis of the learning taking place during talk episodes, e.g. using a framework of indicators of effective learning
Types of talk	Analysis of the talk taking place between learners using a framework of indicators, e.g. to enable identification of exploratory talk
Social and emotional aspects	Categorisation of the types of interaction taking place, e.g. using a framework to analyse roles within the group

Task 19.1   Developing a research focus within a structured context

To give you practice in identifying a research focus Table 19.1 provides a list of factors that may impact on learning taking place during cooperative group activities. Using the information in Table 19.1, identify a possible research focus that could provide insight into how to improve the learning taking place during cooperative group activities. The research focus could be represented in the form of a statement or a question that could be explored (see examples in Table 19.2).

Record your ideas in your professional development portfolio (PDP) or reflective journal etc.

Choose a topic of interest to you that will be the focus of Task 19.2.

Task 19.2   Identifying a focus for your own research

Reflect on the context in which you work and identify a research focus that you would find interesting to explore further, that may provide insights to help develop an aspect of your practice. You may find it useful to record (using a journal or research notebook) your observations and developing ideas as you begin to reflect on your own teaching context. Once you have some ideas, reading related research is helpful in developing your thinking.

Record your ideas building on these as you engage with the tasks below.

Developing researchable questions: operationalisation

Once you have established a research focus, the next step is to develop your research questions. As a first step it is useful to list the possible factors that could potentially be important in relation to your research focus (see Table 19.1 for an example of possible factors that could influence learning in cooperative group activities). Reading published research that has been carried out in your area of interest can help you to identify these factors. Once you have developed your list, select the factors that you want to explore and draft research questions that will enable you to collect relevant evidence to provide insights into these factors within the context you are researching.

The term *operationalisation* can be used to describe the process of translating your initial research focus into specific research questions, followed by the development of tools to investigate these (Cohen, Manion and Morrison, 2017). This process of *operationalisation* can be subdivided into five stages:

Stage 1: starting from your central research focus, identify the *factors* that could have an impact on the focus you want to study within your education context.

Stage 2: begin to frame research questions to explore these factors.

Stage 3: develop an *operational definition* or *indicator* for each of the factors you want to study to enable you to identify this practically (Newby, 2014). This is particularly useful for factors that represent abstract concepts, such as resilience.

Stage 4: identify the kind of evidence you need to answer your research questions and select the most appropriate research methods that will enable you to collect this evidence.

Stage 5: design the research tools that you will use to collect this evidence.

It is useful to create a *research design* that maps each of these stages and this can be organised in different ways, for example a table, mind map or flow chart.

Research questions should be *researchable*, that is, the wording of the questions should facilitate the development of your research design (Cresswell, 2018). Word your research questions as simply as possible and check that there are no terms that are ambiguous. In addition, it is important that your research questions are concise, as too many words can result in the focus of the research being unclear. The way a question is worded can also reflect assumptions held by the researcher, so it is important to analyse your wording carefully to identify assumptions you may have made. Task 19.3 will enable you to practice operationalising your research focus.

 Task 19.3   Creating your research design: operationalising your research focus

Begin creating a first draft for your research design by following the five stages of the *operationalisation process*. Explore different ways to record your research design (e.g. table, mind map or flow chart) to find out which works best for you.

When recording your research design in your PDP or reflective journal consider how you could make links to other tasks in this chapter. The notes from the other tasks in this chapter.

Starting with the literature: doing your literature review

When designing a research project, it is important for you to find out what other work has been done in your area of focus. To search the literature, first establish a clear idea of what you are looking for by having a well-thought-out research focus to direct your literature search. Developing an organised and systematic approach to searching the literature will make the process of searching more efficient and effective.

When carrying out electronic searches you will need to identify *key terms* to use in your searches. Here are some suggested steps to follow in searching for literature:

1. Identify some initial key terms that relate to your focus area.
2. Enter these terms into a search engine such as Google Scholar and select relevant journal articles, reports, etc.

3. Use the sources you have found to help you to identify further search terms. It can also be useful to follow up the sources in the reference lists in the journals and reports that you find.

Strategies for carrying out electronic searches

Some strategies that can be used to improve your electronic searches include:

- using Boolean operators: AND, NOT and OR can be used to combine words in a search string to allow you to, for example, narrow the search by using NOT, which will reduce the number of sources retrieved, or broaden the search by using AND or OR;
- broadening the search by putting ~ in front of a word, which will facilitate related words being found;
- using truncation symbols such as * (most common) or ? or $ can be attached to the suffix of a word to allow you to search for possible variants;
- including wildcards such as ? or # to represent letters that may vary in words;
- using inverted commas around phrases such as 'high attaining' to facilitate phrase searching.

Strategies for efficient information searching within texts

To evaluate how useful the sources that you find are for your enquiry, here are some skills that can help you:

- read quickly by *skimming*, to focus on signposts within the article, such as the contents, headings, introductions and conclusions;
- look for keywords or other specific information by *scanning* the text.

When you have found a relevant source, the reference list can be useful to help you to identify other literature.

M   **Task 19.4   Finding literature to inform your research**

Identify search terms related to your research focus and use these to carry out electronic searches to find literature such as journal articles and reports that will help you develop your research design. Aim to be systematic in your search and limit the scope of your search, for example searching over a set timescale, otherwise you will find yourself faced with choosing from thousands of possible articles. As you read, make notes about interesting themes that emerge, ideas for developing your research design and directions that you could take your research.

Recording notes in your PDP or reflective journal on the themes you find in the literature from your searches can be useful in informing your research design e.g. by giving you ideas of questions to ask participants.

Understanding research methodology

Research approaches

The two basic research approaches that you will come across are qualitative and quantitative approaches:

Qualitative research is based on a research question that is often open in nature, at least at the start of the research. Data is collected using methods that aim to develop an in-depth understanding of the interrelationship between factors in a research context.

Quantitative research is based on a specific and narrow research question that is closed-ended and focuses on exploring the relationships between variables in a context.

Mixed methods designs that integrate both qualitative and quantitative approaches are also possible.

The way the main research focus and the research questions are worded determines the approach you will choose. In small-scale research carried out in educational contexts, qualitative research is usually the preferred approach. A range of different methodologies have been developed, including case studies, action research, ethnography, phenomenology, grounded theory, narrative research and experimental design. In this chapter we briefly explore two methodologies commonly used in small-scale education research, namely case studies and action research.

Case studies

Case studies normally focus on a small number of contexts, often just one. This narrow focus makes it possible to generate in-depth data that facilitate exploration of a range of interrelated factors within natural settings. Case studies lend themselves to the use of a range of data collection methods such as observation, interview and document analysis.

Action research

This type of research aims to enable the researcher to develop a greater understanding of the factors impacting on issues or problems that exist in a research context, with a focus on developing new strategies for implementing change to bring about improvement in practice. Action research is a cyclical process, with ongoing analysis of the impact of new strategies that then become the focus of the next phase of the research.

Establishing validity and reliability

One of the main functions of a research design is to ensure the highest possible quality of the evidence collected and this involves considering validity and reliability. There has been extensive debate over the extent to which the terms validity and reliability can be applied within a qualitative context. Consequently, alternative terms have been suggested by some researchers, such as credibility in place of validity and dependability in place of reliability.

However, Newby (2014) advocates the use of the terms validity and reliability within qualitative research, where a process of triangulation enhances the validity and reliability of the evidence collected. Therefore, in this chapter the terms validity and reliability are used when exploring ways to enhance the quality of data collection within a qualitative design.

How can validity be improved?

The validity of your research findings relates to the extent to which your data provides insight into the questions you are aiming to research. Validity is influenced by a range of factors including choice of sample, researcher bias and design of the research tools. The design of your research tools is critical in ensuring a high level of validity and you need to consider how effective they are in collecting data that answer your research questions.

How can reliability be improved?

In qualitative research, reliability can be thought of in terms of the extent to which the data collected represent what is really happening within in the context being studied. In qualitative research, reliability can be evaluated through:

- taking your interpretation of the data back to participants and asking them to evaluate the extent to which the data represent their views;
- getting different researchers to interpret the same data.

Triangulation to improve validity and reliability

Triangulation involves the use of two or more different approaches within your research design with the aim of improving the validity and reliability of the data being collected. Four types of triangulation commonly used in education research are:

- methodological triangulation, in which different methods are used to investigate the research questions;
- data triangulation, which involves collecting different sources of information, for example, interviewing different groups within a school such as teachers, pupils, governors;
- environmental triangulation, which is achieved by carrying out the study at two or more different times or in different settings;
- investigator triangulation, which requires different researchers to either collect or analyse the data, for example, two researchers analysing the same video evidence.

Research methods and research tools

A range of research methods can be used to gain insight into your research questions, including observation, interview, survey and document analysis. Once you have chosen appropriate methods you need to design research tools to collect your data. This chapter provides insights into how to develop research tools for two research methods that are commonly used in educational research: interview and observation.

Interview

Using interviews in your research enables you to explore participants' experiences and views in depth. This section focuses on semi-structured interviews, in which the researcher creates a series of open questions as a starting point for the discussion that can be used flexibly to follow up interesting avenues of discussion that arise during the interview. Semi-structured interviews are particularly useful for exploring what people find meaningful in their lives and create potential for the participant to direct the discussion, which reduces the impact of the researcher's own bias on what is said (Newby, 2014).

The following checklist will help you to identify the key features you need to consider when designing your interview questions:

- Will you carry out the interview face-to-face or by telephone or via a form of online communication?
- Will you interview participants individually, in pairs or as a group?
- What initial questions will you ask to put the participant at ease and engage them in the interview process? Useful opening questions can focus on lived experiences or explore what the participant knows about a particular topic.
- What types of follow-up questions will you need to explore your participants' responses to your main questions?

Prompt questions: designed to support interviewees who are struggling to interpret a question or to think of a relevant response;

Probing questions: designed to explore a response in more depth to clarify meaning or follow up an interesting theme.

Interview technique takes time to develop and it is worth investing time in practising by asking interview questions to colleagues or friends. This also enables you to evaluate how effective your questions are at getting the kind of data you need to provide insight into your research questions. It is very useful to record interviews as then you can focus on the dialogue and are not distracted by writing notes. Also, transcription of recorded data is more reliable. A useful programme for recording is Audacity, which is free to download. Following the interview, you need to transcribe the data and analyse it.

Observation

Observation is a particularly important research method as it gives researchers a direct window into the issue being researched without relying on the perceptions of the participants. This enables you to explore the impact of different factors within the events unfolding in the context within which you are observing. However, observation has its own challenges, as it is not easy to identify events and interactions that may be of significance to your research questions. Also, observation is particularly prone to the findings being influenced by observer bias and assumptions. An observation schedule can be useful for helping to focus your observations on events and interactions that are relevant to the questions you are researching. Without a schedule it is more likely that you focus on unusual events that may not be of relevance to your research focus.

The following checklist will help you to identify the key features you need to consider when planning your observations:

■ When carrying out observations consider the impact of your presence as an observer on the events taking place in the setting and whether you will be a participant (engaging in activities) or non-participant (interacting as little as possible with activities).

■ Consider creating a semi-structured observation schedule that provides a clear focus for your observations, whilst also allowing flexibility in what you will observe. This may take the form of a checklist with indicators of the factors you want to investigate.

■ A more structured approach could involve time sampling using a checklist to collect observations of particular events or behaviours at regular intervals.

■ The use of technology in recording observations can be useful, for example audio recording of dialogue or video recording to gain insight into nonverbal interactions. However, the potential impact of the use of technology on the behaviour of participants needs to be considered. Safeguarding needs to be a priority when storing and analysing video data.

Considering ethics in your research

It is important to consider the possible ethical issues that may arise at each stage of your research when you are developing your research design. The British Educational Research Association (BERA) (2018) *Ethical Guidelines for Educational Research* are useful to support you in identifying ethical considerations related to your research design. The following list shows some of the things that you need to consider to facilitate developing a research plan that meets the highest possible ethical standards:

■ ensuring that the rights and dignity of participants in the research are respected;
■ gaining informed consent from participants (and parents/carers where appropriate) prior to starting the research;
■ ensuring participant anonymity and confidentiality at each stage of the research;
■ analysing and interpreting the evidence you have collected with honesty and integrity.

(adapted from Cresswell, 2018)

The ethical considerations of research are diverse and complex, and this section aims to enable you to understand key principles underpinning ethics in research within education contexts. This section will help you to develop and present your research design in a way that informs participants' decision making by ensuring a clear understanding is gained of what participation in the research will involve and any implications that publication of the data may have for them.

Professional gatekeepers, such as those leading education institutions, *do not* have legal rights in relation to the decisions of individuals in their care to participate in the research, and *cannot* give consent for individuals to participate in a research project. However professional gatekeepers do have legal responsibility for their pupils' well-being and, as part of this remit, they need to make decisions about the access that researchers have to individuals within the context that they are responsible for. Also, professional gatekeepers can make decisions about the information that is given to potential participants and their parents or carers.

Participant consent must be sought, even where a parent/carer is involved in the process of gaining informed consent (in general for participants under the age of 16 or those who are vulnerable). It is *essential* that the potential participants are given the opportunity to gain an understanding of the research and that their wishes regarding whether to participate are fully considered and acted on. To make this possible, information about the project needs to be provided in an accessible form and the researcher needs to make explicit the essential role of participants themselves in the decision-making process.

Providing information to participants

The process of gaining informed consent from potential participants in your research is a complex process in which you need to consider:

- What information needs to be provided and what form should this take?
- Who should be involved in the process of giving consent?
- How will you go about the process of gaining informed consent?

Providing information about the research in a clear and accessible format enables potential participants (often supported by parents/carers and gatekeepers) to make informed decisions about whether to participate in a research project. This information can take the form of an information sheet that provides details about the research. In addition, researchers should always make themselves available to explain their research design and answer potential questions that prospective participants might have. Following this information-sharing process it is necessary to gain evidence of consent. This usually takes the form of a signed declaration, but other forms of evidence of consent are also possible, such as audio recording. Requiring formal agreement to participate in the research ensures that participants are protected and that their rights are respected, however data protection issues also need to be considered such as ensuring participant anonymity and confidentiality.

Aspects to consider when designing an information sheet

In the design of the information sheet that you give to the gatekeeper and participants, you need to think about how you will provide sufficient information so that they can make an informed decision about involvement in the research, without overwhelming them with unnecessary detail. Also, the wording and layout of the information sheet needs to be accessible and not off-putting. Consider using text boxes, bullets and other approaches to formatting that break up the text and make the information sheet look less daunting

The following checklist will help you in the design of your information sheet:

- Have you explained the key points about your research clearly? Check that you have not used jargon and complex language that will make it difficult for the intended audience to understand.
- Have you considered the accessibility of the layout of the information sheet?
- Who will have access to the data prior to the process of anonymisation and have you made this clear?
- What will the data be used for and have you explained this? For example, published as part of a dissertation, published to a wider audience, e.g. as part of a journal article
- How will confidentiality by ensured in data storage?
- How will anonymity be achieved in presentation of the data?
- Is the right of individuals to withdraw from the research clearly explained and are any time limits associated with this clear? For example, often it is not possible to withdraw data once the data analysis phase has started.

To gain a written record of consent you also need to design a letter of consent that will repeat some of the information from the information sheet, emphasising the main ethical considerations. If participation in the research involves different elements, such as individual interviews, focus groups, video recordings, etc., consider including a checklist detailing each data collection method to provide participants with the choice to opt in or out of each element of the research. The information sheet will be retained by the participant and the consent form returned to you once it has been signed by the participant or their parent/carer to agree to their participation in the research project.

Enabling participants to exercise the right to withdraw

In practice, exercising the right to withdraw from a research study may be difficult for certain groups of participants, for example pupils may be reluctant to tell the researcher that they do not want to be involved in the project any more, particularly if that person is their teacher, due to the power dynamics involved. Alternatively, a participant may not want to answer a certain question, however they may feel obliged to do so. Insights into whether a participant may be feeling uncomfortable or under pressure can be gained by observing their body language. This enables you to then explore reasons for this and take appropriate action. An approach that has been used in research with pupils is the use of a 'stop' card, where participants can hold up the card if they decide they do not want to answer a question or if they no longer want to participate in the project (Wiles, Heath, Crow, and Charles (2005).

Anonymity and confidentiality

The key difference between anonymity and confidentiality is that anonymity involves protecting the identity of a research participant, whereas confidentiality ensures the personal information of participants is protected. The General Data Protection

Regulation (ICO, 2018) has implications for how information is collected, stored and communicated and a legal requirement exists that requires that the identities and personal information of participants in research projects are protected. For further information about the General Data Protection Regulation (2018) access the Information Comissioner's Office Guide to the General Data Protection Regulation: https://ico.org.uk/for-organisations/guide-to-the-general-data-protection-regulation-gdpr/ and www.gov.uk/government/publications/guide-to-the-general-data-protection-regulation

Safeguarding

The BERA (2018) guidelines for ethics are underpinned by principles that state that all educational research must ensure that participants are respected and that researchers' responsibilities to participants are carefully considered. Although there is no legal mandate to report child protection and safeguarding concerns, researchers should be aware of the reporting procedures in the organisation they are researching and that they have a moral duty to contribute to whatever actions are needed to promote each individual participant's safety and welfare. An important aspect of safeguarding relates to ensuring secure storage of images of pupils, for example video data, and making provision for secure disposal of these images after the data analysis phase.

M

 Task 19.5   Developing your research design

Building on the research design you began in Task 19.3 and drawing on what you have learned from searching the literature (Task 19.4) develop your research design further so that it would be detailed enough for someone else to undertake the research by following your plan. Ask for feedback on your design from a colleague who has undertaken their own research and annotate your research design based on their input. If it is possible for you to carry out this research, remember to gain agreement of the headteacher as a first step. Seeking formal ethical approval from a responsible body such as the senior management team is usual practice before embarking on a research project. This should then be followed by a process of gaining informed consent from potential participants (and their parents/carers where appropriate).

You will find it helpful to record the notes in your PDP or reflective journal and to make links to your notes from the other tasks in this chapter.

An introduction to analysing qualitative data

When you have collected your data, you need to decide on how you will go about your data analysis in order to interpret what the evidence is telling you in relation to your research questions. A range of approaches exists for analysing quantitative data. This chapter focuses on a brief introduction to the thematic analysis of qualitative data using coding. Coding involves looking for themes in your data, which you can code for example through highlighting in different colours to help you to identify themes and organise your findings. There are various ways you can arrive at the codes you will use to analyse your data, for example:

1. use an existing coding framework that has been developed in another research project;
2. develop your own codes from theory or the findings of published research;
3. use your own data as a starting point for developing codes by searching for emergent themes from the data.

Coding of data is not a precise process and it can be challenging deciding on whether data best fit one code or a related code. Also, it is possible that during the analysis additional codes will need to be created as new themes emerge from the data. Conversely, you may want to merge some of your initial codes for related themes into a single overarching code. Once you have developed codes from the emergent themes you identify in your data, colour coding enables you to identify relevant examples from your data that provide evidence to inform your analysis. Data can be presented in figure boxes where evidence is organised by being grouped into themes. Different types of data can be included in a figure to provide enhanced insights into a theme. For example, a figure may contain a transcript from a talk episode, together with associated observation data, and perhaps a diagram that the pupil had drawn as part of their work that was being discussed in the talk episode. In your analysis you can identify and reflect on the insights that can be gained from the data within each figure and then make links between your reflections and related findings from published research.

Examples of small-scale research study designs

This section gives you some insights into the design of small-scale research projects that have been carried out in secondary schools in England. This will enable you to consider the scale of projects that you might realistically carry out in your own school or setting.

Table 19.2 Example research questions and research design overviews from small-scale research studies carried out in secondary schools in England

Research focus and researcher	Research questions	Research design summary
Stretch and Challenge: Improving classroom provision for potentially high-attaining students Dom Burrell	What actions can be taken to improve the challenge provided for potentially high-attaining students within Key Stage 3?	*Background*: This research is responding to the issue of insufficient challenge for students who have the potential for high attainment but are not being given opportunities to achieve what they are capable of (Office for Standards in Education, Children's Services and Skills (Ofsted), 2013 and Montacute, 2018). *Data collection methods*: Surveys pre- and post- intervention

Metacognitive strategies to support problem-solving in mathematics Jake Wilson Article: Wilson (2018)	Q1: What prompts are useful to support mathematical problem solving and why? Q2: Does the ordering of prompts impact on their effectiveness? Q3: How can student ownership of the problem-solving process be facilitated?	*Background*: This research involved the development of 'prompts' to structure the process of mathematical problem-solving based on a problem-solving framework devised by Polya (1971): Step 1: Understanding the problem Step 2: Devising a plan Step 3: Implementing the plan Step 4: Reflecting. *Data collection methods*: survey to gain students' perceptions of the usefulness of the prompts; analysis of students' written approaches to solving problems.
Reflecting on resilience and growth mindsets Tina Herringshaw	Q1: How can I build resilience in students so that they 'know' they are doing well? Q2: How can I use feedback to help students improve?	*Background*: This study builds on the work of Dweck (2007), which explores the potential impact of praise on students' mindsets (growth/fixed) and possible implications for motivation and achievement. *Data collection methods*: peer observations and discussions; videoing the researchers' own practice to facilitate self-evaluation.
Developing students' self-regulation Jan Avery-Harris and Kate Thirwall	Q1: How do we move our students from teacher-dependency to becoming agents in their own learning? Q2: What interventions and strategies can be developed that facilitate this shift without adding to teacher burden?	*Background*: Claxton's (2007) concept of 'split-screen thinking' was used to encourage meta-cognitive awareness in students. Existing activities were adapted to always include an element of self-reflection or strategies that encouraged self-regulated learning. *Data collection methods*: Video, reflective diaries, simple, short questionnaires, notes from interactions with students, analysis of student work, semi-structured interviews with students.

Table 19.2 Continued

In what ways can effective formative feedback inculcate the intrinsic motivation of lower prior attaining boys? Luke Brewer	*Q1: What constitutes effective formative feedback for lower-attaining boys?* *Q2: How is the intrinsic motivation of lower-attaining boys impacted upon by the process of receiving formative feedback?* *Q3: What are the implications arising from student responses upon future design of effective formative feedback practices?* *Q4: Are there additional factors that create strong impacts upon lower prior attaining boys?*	*Background*: This study draws on conceptions of self-efficacy (Bandura, 1982) and motivation (Lai, 2011) to explore the potential interrelationship between formative feedback and intrinsic motivation. *Data collection methods*: Phase I – Multi-stage questionnaires Phase II – Semi-structured paired interviews

The contribution of Dr Katherine Burn and her students at the University of Oxford, UK, is gratefully acknowledged.

Bandura, A. (1982) 'Self-efficacy mechanism in human agency', *American Psychologist*, 37, 122–47.

Claxton, G. (2007) 'Expanding young people's capacity to learn', *British Journal of Educational Studies*, 55 (2), 115-34.

Duijnhouwer, H., Prins, F.J. and Stokking, K.M. (2010) 'Progress feedback effects on students' writing mastery goal, self-efficacy beliefs and performance', *Educational Research and Evaluation*, 16 (1), 53–74.

Dweck, C. (2007) 'The perils and promises of praise', *Educational Leadership*, 65 (2), 34-9.

Lai, E.R. (2011) *Motivation: A Literature Review. Pearson Research Report.* Available from: https://images.pearsonassessments.com/images/tmrs/Motivation_Review_final.pdf (accessed 9 January 2018).

Montacute, R. (2018) *Potential for Success: Fulfilling the Promise of Highly Able Students in Secondary Schools*, London: Sutton Trust. Available from: www.suttontrust.com/wp-content/uploads/2018/07/PotentialForSuccess.pdf (accessed 12 November 2018).

Ofsted (2013) *The Most Able Students: Are They Doing as well as They Should in our Non-Selective Secondary Schools.* Available from: https://assets.publishing.service.gov.uk/government/uploads/system/uploads/attachment_data/file/405518/The_most_able_students.pdf (accessed 9 November 2018).

Polya, G. (1971) *How to Solve It: A New Aspect of Mathematical Method*, 2nd edn, Princeton, NJ: Princeton University Press.

Wilson, J. (2018) 'Metacognition through prompts in mathematical problem solving', *Impact: Journal of the Chartered College of Teaching*, 3, online. Available from: https://impact.chartered.college/article/wilson-metacognition-mathematical-problem-solving (accessed 12 November 2018).

How to find out more:

Further details of these projects together with a range of other projects across different subject areas are available from: www.educationdeanery.ox.ac.uk/research-activities

SUMMARY AND KEY POINTS

Some key actions to consider when planning your research design:

■ develop clear and specific research questions based on careful consideration of the possible factors that it may be important for you to explore within the context you aim to research;

■ find authoritative and reliable published literature related to your research focus and use this to inform the development of your research design;

- identify the ethical issues that need to be considered in your research and the actions you need to take to ensure your research design is of the highest possible ethical standards;
- make informed decisions about your choice of research methodology and methods and the design of your research tools, keeping your research questions at the forefront of your decision-making process;
- consider joining a network where you can become part of a research community that can support your research, for example, a subject association or a research hub.

You may find it helpful to explore how the ideas and information in this chapter could support you in meeting the Teachers' Standards (DfE, 2011) by facilitating engagement with a research-informed approach to developing your practice.

You may find it helpful to record in your PDP or reflective journal, how the information in this chapter enables you to meet the requirements for your first year of teaching.

 Further resources

Sources to support the development of your research design

Higher Education Academy, *Action Research: Practice Guide*: https://www.heacademy.ac.uk/knowledge-hub/action-research-practice-guide

National Centre for Research Methods (NCRM) resources: http://eprints.ncrm.ac.uk/view/subjects/

Open University Guides to Research (select Course Content, then Resources): http://www.open.edu/openlearncreate/course/view.php?id=1592#

Patterson, E.W. (2016a) *Research Methods 1: Doing a Literature Review: How to Find and Make Sense of Published Research, MESHGuide*, University of Winchester, UK. Available from: http://www.meshguides.org/ (accessed 18 August 2019).

Patterson, E.W. (2016b) *Research Methods 2: Developing Your Research Design, MESHGuide*, University of Winchester, UK. Available from: http://www.meshguides.org/guides/ (accessed 18 August 2019).

Patterson, E.W. (2016c) *Research Methods 3: Considering Ethics in Your Research, MESHGuide*, University of Winchester. Available from: http://www.meshguides.org/guides/ (accessed 18 August 2019).

Sources to support good practice in ethics and safeguarding

British Education Research Association (BERA) (2018) *Ethical Guidelines for Educational Research*. Available from: https://www.bera.ac.uk/wp-content/uploads/2018/06/BERA-Ethical-Guidelines-for-Educational-Research_4thEdn_2018.pdf?noredirect=1

ESRC (Economic and Social Research Council), *Research Ethics*: https://esrc.ukri.org/funding/guidance-for-applicants/research-ethics/

Information Commissioner's Office, *General Data Protection Regulation Guide* (ICO, 2018): https://ico.org.uk/for-organisations/guide-to-the-general-data-protection-regulation-gdpr and https://www.gov.uk/government/publications/guide-to-the-general-data-protection-regulation

Sheffield Hallam University, *Safeguarding Children in Research Contexts*: http://www.shu.ac.uk/_assets/pdf/Safeguarding-Children-in-Research-Contexts.pdf

University of Leicester, *Ethical Appraisal Framework*: https://www2.le.ac.uk/colleges/ssah/research/ethics

Books in the *Learning to Teach* series that you may find helpful are as follows:

Capel, S., Leask, M. and Younie, S. (eds.) (2019) *Learning to Teach in the Secondary School: A Companion to School Experience*, 8th edn, Abingdon: Routledge.
This book is designed as a core textbook to support student teachers through their initial teacher education programme.

Capel, S., Leask, M. and Turner, T. (eds.) (2010) *Readings for Learning to Teach in the Secondary School: A Companion to M Level Study*, Abingdon: Routledge.
This book brings together essential readings to support you in your critical engagement with key issues raised in this textbook.

The subject-specific books in the *Learning to Teach* series, the *Practical (subject) Guides*, *Debates in (subject)* and *Mentoring (subject) Teachers* are also very useful.

20 Looking after yourself and your professional development

Derek Boyle

Introduction

Developing and embedding good emotional well-being into your daily routines enables you to become an empathic teacher that pupils can connect with, thereby building good relationships with your learners. Being aware of the signs and symptoms of decreasing mental health in yourself is key to managing your own well-being and becoming emotionally literate. The end result of this is a greater understanding of how your own emotional state influences those of your pupils and the outcomes for them both individually and collectively.

The transition from being a student teacher to an early career professional is as important as reaching Qualified Teacher Status (QTS). The personal development and growth you undertake during your early years of teaching equip you with the emotional resilience and empathy you need to thrive during your first few years of teaching.

Developing and refining your professional network as you enter the profession enables you to gain deeper insight into teaching and your place within it. Although teaching can be a solitary process when you are teaching the pupils in your classes, the wider community of professionals you work within helps you not only to survive the first few years of teaching, but also to thrive through building good relations with staff and pupils.

Through developing your professional persona, you are able to consider your future career prospects in a more favourable light and start to map out where you see yourself in the longer term.

OBJECTIVES

By the end of this chapter you should be able to:

- have an understanding of how to manage your own mental health during your early years of teaching to set a firm foundation across your career;
- recognise the signs of decreasing mental health and well-being in yourself;
- identify and work with your support network to help them recognise when your emotional well-being and mental health are suffering;

■ embed good habits to build your resilience and develop into the teacher you want to be;

■ have the foundations of early career planning.

Check how the information in this chapter enables you to meet the requirements for your first year of teaching.

Surviving

According to the work of Westerhof and Keyes (2010), well-being can be defined under the following three facets: can be defined under the following three facets:

■ 'emotional well-being – this includes being happy and confident and not anxious or depressed;

■ psychological well-being – this includes the ability to be autonomous, problem-solve, manage emotions, experience empathy, be resilient and attentive;

■ social well-being – this includes the ability to have good relationships with others and being able to be without behavioural problems, that is, to have the ability not to be disruptive, violent or a bully.

Using these three definitions as a starting point, the interplay between your own well-being and that of the staff, pupils and wider stakeholders within the school community determine the success of the relationships you develop in your role as a teacher.

If the pupils in your care need their emotional, psychological and social well-being to be considered and met through the learning environment you establish and the relationships you engender, then this model can also be extended to all your interactions within the school environment.

Your own emotional, social and psychological state is a key driver for the emotional, psychological and social well-being of the pupils in your care. If you are lacking confidence or anxious about the lessons you are teaching, then that is perfectly understandable, but the moment those internalised emotions surface during the lesson then that is when you are at your most vulnerable professionally.

Experienced teachers have the ability to sail 'swan-like' through lessons, but the observer or pupils in the room may not appreciate that under the surface they are paddling hard to keep the lesson on track and to manage the demands placed upon them. One of the hardest habits to master in the early part of your career, is the ability to simultaneously manage all the competing demands in the classroom and to manage your own emotions. Being able to demonstrate empathy while being resilient and attentive to the individual needs of all pupils is a key attribute for successful teachers. Through separating the impact of the exhibited behaviours being demonstrated by your pupils from your professional demeanour is key to remaining 'swan-like'.

Groups of pupils very quickly ascertain the emotional well-being or state of the teacher in front of them and as such mirror that state themselves. If the teacher is in an agitated or disorganised state themselves, then the pupils take longer to settle and engage with the learning environment. It is important that, through good preparation, planning and poise, the teacher is externally exhibiting the behaviours they would like the pupils to exhibit as well.

Outside of the classroom environment, the health and the social well-being of the teacher has a marked effect on the wider relationships within the school environment. The 'rippling out' effect of having good social well-being is a benefit to the whole workforce, as relationships can be built and cemented much more quickly to the benefit of everyone within the school. If a pupil has trust in a teacher, that they are fair and even-handed, then the impact of the pupils' perception of their teacher pays dividends in pastoral and extracurricular settings.

Well-being and the mentoring relationship

Your relationship with your mentor is pivotal in the success in your early career. If you approach the mentoring relationship in a proactive and open manner, being receptive to the advice and guidance that you are given, then this helps with development of your professional expertise and competence, in England against the Teaching Standards (Department for Education (DfE), 2011).

It is worth bearing in mind that your mentor is undertaking this role in addition to their wider professional responsibilities and they have a number of competing demands placed upon them during your time in placement with them. Their own emotional well-being needs to be considered in your interactions with them and, at times, mentoring meetings may become strained. You should approach every mentoring experience with a fresh slate as the mixture of daily experiences and professional responsibilities vary on a daily basis.

If the emotional well-being of the mentor is poor and it is affecting your ability to have a productive mentoring relationship, then you need to seek further advice from a colleague.

Chapter 3 focuses on your relationship with your mentor.

Self-realisation to actualisation

In order to survive and thrive during your early years of teaching, you need to gain a deeper understanding of how you respond to change, internal pressures you place upon yourself, external pressures that are placed upon you by your school and external influencing factors such as family commitments and caring responsibilities.

When you have a good understanding of your own responses to these different pressures you are able to plan for mitigating the effects of these competing demands and establish the natural rhythm that you need to discover as a qualified teacher.

Most importantly when it looks like your response to the pressures and demands of being a teacher go 'wrong' and your normal coping mechanisms are not working, talk to someone straight away.

Now complete Task 20.1.

    Task 20.1   Your weekly commitments

List your weekly professional commitments as a teacher within your school. By the side of each commitment, identify who you could seek help from if you feel overwhelmed. In addition to your mentor, try to identify two or three key people within your school who would listen and understand and who you could talk to or ask for advice and guidance.

Store this information in your professional development portfolio (PDP) (or similar) to refer to when needed.

The first step to managing the emotional and physical demands of teaching is to 'normalise' the feeling that it is okay to seek help and advice from others in the workplace.

Support networks

The support network you sustain and develop during your early years of teaching is instrumental in your success as a teacher. From your initial teacher education you may have developed a support network of those going through the same events and experiences, who you can rely on to be a listening ear and sounding board. Joining your subject association and a union may provide access to supportive networks (see also Appendices 2 and 3). As you settle in to your teaching job your support network grows and you get to know who you can call upon for advice and guidance focused on the practicalities of teaching within the ethos and culture of that school.

Your personal support network, which comprises your family, friends and close colleagues are those who you feel that you are able to turn to without them making a value judgement on your need to open-up about the pressures that you face.

The professional support network that you can rely on within school would be your immediate line manager, colleagues and your mentor. This is supplemented by your subject associations or a union that you may have joined.

Further, your existing social and familial support network needs to be cherished and nurtured. Keep time each week to spend with friends and family to keep a sense of perspective and remain grounded in why you wanted to become a teacher in the first instance. Ensuring that you have ring-fenced time within the working week to nourish these support networks helps you to keep a sense of proportion with the workload challenges that you are facing. Outside term time you should give yourself days off to help reset your internal balance and to recover emotionally and psychologically from the demands placed on you. Using this time to have a break away from the marking pile and emails helps to recharge your batteries.

Remember the importance of sleep to help recharge your inner self and get yourself into a routine, specifically to take a mental break from working late into in the evenings. Setting a specific 'stop time' and giving yourself the task of closing your books, packing your bag for the next day and switching off the emails, gives you a chance to mentally 'switch-off' before going to bed, which aids quality sleep.

Recognising your own indicators

Understanding the extrinsic behaviours or habits that you exhibit when your own well-being is poor is a key factor in managing your own mental health. Talk to the people in your support network, both within and away from school and ask them when you would know that you were suffering from poor personal well-being. Through having a better understanding of when the intrinsic pressures of being a teacher are expressed extrinsically, you start to understand the key triggers for the build-up of internal anxiety. Once these have been identified then you should look at refining your coping mechanisms, addressing the root causes of the anxiety or evaluating the way in which you manage workload.

Ask those around you in your personal support network, how they *know* when you are under pressure and any changes in behaviour that they notice in you as your workload increases.

You need to remember that the only constant in teaching is that you are always going through change (see Chapter 2).

The way in which you respond individually to change determines your own happiness and the ability to thrive. Now undertake Task 20.2.

 Task 20.2   Identifying external pressures and your body's responses

Draw an outline of a body and around it draw arrows showing all of the external pressures that come at you pointing inwards towards the body.

From within the body name all of the ways in which other people know that you are under pressure, such as mood swings, loss or gain in appetite, poor sleeping patterns, etc.

Once you have completed the diagram, start considering how you can better manage the effect of the external pressures, as well as what you could do to better manage how this increase in pressure exhibits itself to others.

Record your analysis in your PDP and add your coping strategies as you develop these and come across strategies used by colleagues.

Who is in your support network?

You may find that different parts of your personal support networks overlap and some key people that you know fall into several different categories.

The people who are the most significant in your life, who have known you before you became a teacher, know the 'real' you without your professional persona. When you join the teaching staff at a new school, you quickly find out who you can call on for help at a professional level from those colleagues that you worked with at previous schools. Each year, new teachers starting at the same time form professional networks because they are all going through the same induction process and acquiring the culture and ethos of the school. These shared experiences help to form support networks that can help you to navigate your new role and the expectations placed on you.

Consider how the three different support networks intersect. Take a piece of paper and draw three intersecting circles (a Venn diagram) representing the overlap between the three different support networks that you have:

■   personal – long-term friends and family;
■   new school and previous schools – teachers, support staff and other beginning teachers;
■   fellow beginning teachers within your school or setting.

Put the names of different people who you can rely on to be ready to give you emotional or practical support during your early years of teaching into the different parts of the Venn diagram you have created.

If you find that, over the course of your early years in teaching, some people move into the overlap between these different aspects of your life then these usually become part of your long-term support network that sustains you in your early career. Now undertake Tasks 20.3 and 20.4.

 Task 20.3   Identifying support mechanisms

Reflect on the support mechanisms you found it during your initial teacher education. For example, within your placement school, what practical support did you give to and receive from those around you?

During your time with your fellow student teachers, did you spend your time celebrating successes, sharing anecdotes, helping to find answers to fellow student teachers' difficulties or worrying about your teaching? Was this type of support network a constructive or destructive influence? Why?

Now identify possible support mechanisms in the school where you have begun or are beginning your teaching. Once you have identified these support mechanisms, how do you access them? Are there key people that you need to approach?

Record your reflections in your PDP and add to your list of supporting mechanisms as you identify sources useful to you personally.

 Task 20.4   Your external signs that you are not managing workload or pressure

Talk to the people in your support networks and ask them how they know that you are under pressure? What are the external signs that you are not managing workload or pressure well?

When you have discussed them with the key people you trust within your support network, identify what sorts of pressures lead to you exhibiting those external signs. For each of these pressures, what can you and the people in your support network do to help mitigate those pressures?

Are there any lifestyle changes you can make to mitigate the effects of those pressures? Examples could include having a regular shopping delivery, leaving the hoovering and cleaning for a few days, going for a regular walk, meeting up with non-teacher friends for a chat, making time to read a book for pleasure or listening to music away from your marking, assignments and lesson preparations.

Make a list of changes that you could make to help mitigate the identified pressure points. Try these out when you are under pressure.

Record the changes in your PDP and review how effective they were when you were under pressure.

Making time for you and developing coping strategies

As a beginning teacher you need to learn to be gentle with yourself. Remember, every teacher has been through the same process in order to get where they are and there is no shame in asking for help or advice from anyone, whether it is your mentor, head of department, colleagues or those in other schools. Remember, do not take things personally; no teacher was amazing on their first day. Teaching is a constant learning journey and each new year and new class presents the opportunity for you to learn.

- The pupils you are teaching are young adults; they make mistakes and misjudgements of situations but that does not mean they hate you. Try and go into each lesson afresh and do not dwell on issues from previous lessons with the pupils. If you carry over the emotional baggage from previous incidents, so will the pupils.
- Remember to look after yourself, still go out and relax, ensure you are eating and sleeping enough, manage your workload (harder than it sounds), as an exhausted teacher is less inspiring.
- Reflect on your lessons, but don't dwell on the parts that did not go to plan. Learn from your mistakes and move on.
- Don't try to do everything as the book (or your initial teacher education) suggests. Pupils are different, as are schools, and what does not work with one class/school/ pupil may work with another. Read widely, but remember who *you* are ... a successful strategy for one teacher may not be as successful for another.
- Reflect on the effectiveness of your teaching, but put a lid on that box and divert to another task/go home/to the pub ... you can always reopen that box.
- Don't be afraid to ask or clarify something, even if it sounds silly. Don't think you need to know it all straight away.
- Make regular time with a trusted friend to meet for a coffee who can perhaps help you put your worries into perspective.
- Make after school on a Friday night a regular pub night with other staff – it can help you process your week with someone other than those closest to you.
- Don't take feedback as criticism, its job is to support and develop ... if it does not feel developmental after sleeping on it, organise a meeting with the coach, mentor etc.

to discuss. Don't dwell on mistakes ... if you find yourself doing this say 'stop' out loud and divert your thinking.

- Make packed lunches the night before – you'll eat better.
- Remember: you are not Mr Smith. You play Mr Smith between 8:30 and 4:30 every day. He's different from John, you. The pupils don't know John. They don't need to like Mr Smith, but they do need to trust him, value his knowledge and opinion and respect him. They do that if Mr Smith values their needs, their desires and cares for who they are. Play Mr Smith well and you'll be a great teacher. Don't worry if he's not John, and certainly don't take it personally if they don't like Mr Smith, because he isn't you.

The changing relationship with your mentor – mentoring moving to coaching

During the early part of your school placement, the relationship with your mentor was very much within a mentoring framework. You were learning your craft and getting to know the pupils and classes you were teaching as well as digesting the curriculum and assessment requirements for your different classes. During this phase you were drawing upon your own reading, observations and the expertise of your mentor and other teachers within the school to secure your confidence and competence in the classroom and around the school.

As a newly qualified teacher, with more confidence and competence, the relationship with your mentor may have moved more towards a coaching style where they are working alongside you to help develop your craft and resilience. The relationship with your mentor is one built on trust and a mutual understanding that you are learning and that you will make mistakes. It is how you respond to those mistakes that defines the sort of teacher you become and how you develop resilience.

Looking ahead – what sort of teacher do you want to be?

During your initial teacher education, you had the chance to work with a wide range of qualified and experienced teachers, who helped to guide you to develop your professional practice. You internalised aspects of their personal and professional behaviours and these have helped to formulate your own external professional habits as well as your personal educational philosophy. The way in which you develop these habits and behaviours is a product of your previous exposure within education and how you have amalgamated the variety of experiences from any previous career and your initial teacher education.

There is a tendency for new teachers to aspire to exhibit behaviours that belong to an influential teacher that they have either had as a pupil themselves, or to try to be a clone of a teacher they are working with during their school placements. This should be seen as admirable, but you should remember that the exhibited professional behaviours of that influential role model are the result of the specific blend of experiences and education that were peculiar to that individual. Now undertake Task 20.5.

 Task 20.5   What characteristics would you like people to see in you?

Think about some staff you would consider as key role models from your current school. What characteristics do you admire that they exhibit with the pupils and staff?

Why do you admire those characteristics?
Would you like other staff to see those characteristics in you? Why?
What other characteristics would you like others to see in you?

Record this in your PDP.

Building long-term networks

As you progress, you should be considering how you develop your wider professional network so that you can stay up to date with developments both within your subject, but also across the education sector.

The wider professional networks

During this stage in your career, you should consider joining your relevant subject association, as the benefits of joining enable you to get access to news and events that support your early career development. Local branch events and conferences are just some of the ways in which you can remain up to date with developments in the teaching of your subject as well as having a collective voice for future curriculum changes. Now undertake Task 20.6.

 Task 20.6   Identifying membership benefits of your subject association

Identify the membership benefits of becoming a member of your subject association. (See Appendix 2 for a list of subject associations and teaching councils.)

Are there any local branch meetings for your subject association? When are their annual conferences held? Plan to attend if you can. Many subject associations rely on members to undertake key roles.

Record this in your PDP as well as activities that might be useful for your development as a teacher.

There is a worldwide network of teaching councils. These have varying responsibilities and provide a wide range of services. Appendix 2 includes information on teaching councils in the UK. These are briefly described below.

Chartered College of Teaching (in England)

'The Chartered College of Teaching is an independent chartered organisation for the teaching profession that has three key aims:

■ Creating a knowledge-based community to share excellent practice
■ A collective voice for the teaching profession
■ Enabling teachers to connect with rigorous research and evidence'.

The college publishes regular articles on a range of key issues for teachers and provides local and regional networks of events for teachers at all points in their career. Members are able to get a deeper sense of the role and purpose of the profession they are joining and to engage with the latest evidence-based research.

The General Teaching Council for Northern Ireland

'The Education (Northern Ireland) Order 1998 allocates the following functions to the General Teaching Council for Northern Ireland (GTCNI/the Council)

■ The establishment and maintenance of a register of teachers.
■ The approval of qualifications for the purposes of registration.
■ Regulatory functions relating to unprofessional conduct and serious professional misconduct.
■ The provision of advice to the Department of Education and employing authorities on:
    ■ Registration;
    ■ Training, career development and performance management of teachers;
    ■ Standards of conduct for teachers'.

General Teaching Council for Scotland (GTCS)

'GTCS carries out a wide range of statutory functions to promote, support and develop the professional learning of teachers. The functions include:

■ Maintaining a register of teachers in Scotland
■ Setting the Professional Standards expected of all teachers
■ Accrediting programmes leading to the award of GTCS Standards, including Initial Teacher Education programmes at Scottish universities
■ Advising the Scottish Government on matters relating to Scotland's teachers and teacher professionalism
■ Providing public protection and assuring the high quality of the teaching profession by investigating and adjudicating on the Fitness to Teach of registrants through robust and fair regulation processes'.

Education Workforce Council (Wales)

The Education Workforce Council (EWC) was established by the Education (Wales) Act 2014 from a reconfiguration and renaming of the General Teaching Council for Wales (GTCW). The EWC came into being on 1 April 2015.

The EWC is 'the independent regulator in Wales for teachers in maintained schools, Further Education teachers and learning support staff in both school and FE settings, as well as youth workers and people involved in work-based learning.

The principal aims of Council are to:

■ contribute to improving the standards of teaching and the quality of learning in Wales;
■ maintain and improve standards of professional conduct amongst teachers and persons who support teaching and learning in Wales;
■ safeguard the interests of learners, parents and the public and maintain public trust and confidence in the education workforce'.

Onwards and upwards

Although the completion of your induction year is your immediate concern, you should be putting thought to where you see your career developing and professional aspirations.

Many teacher education programmes include Masters level credits and these can lay the foundations of further study at this level, leading eventually to a full Masters degree. The additional workload that this further study entails is something you need to consider as well as the time period that your Masters level credits can be transferred into a full Masters degree programme.

Future career - steps that you can take

As you embark on the start of your career you should start to consider which aspects of your role as a teacher you enjoy and find rewarding. If it is within your specialist subject, then, for example, is your first step on the promotion ladder coordinating your subject within a specific key stage, or taking responsibility for an aspect such as marking and assessment, or enhancing the profile of your subject across the school? For those wanting to work within a pastoral role, how can you work with those within your school in pastoral leadership roles to develop experience and confidence working across the school and with parents or carers?

As you progress through your induction period, you should look at being involved in working parties or in school groups that focus on an enhancement aspect of the curriculum such as science, technology, engineering and mathematics (STEM) activities or cross-curricular projects. Working on cross-school projects is a good way of developing confidence in working with wider teams and to identify areas that, in the future, you may want to seek promotion in.

If your aspiration is to move into middle then senior leadership, then arrange a meeting with a leader within your school and ask them about their career path to date and their aspirations as suggested in Task 20.7.

Task 20.7 Considering career pathways

Interview a teacher you know or someone within your school who has a post of responsibility who is three to five years into their career and ask them about how they reached the position that they hold.

What early experiences did they have in their induction year that put them on this career pathway?

How did they take on that first additional responsibility?

What was a key learning point that they wished they had known before they took on the post?

Make notes in your PDP to help you identify your own route to career development and promotion.

SUMMARY AND KEY POINTS

- You are at the start of the process of becoming a teacher and it is a great vocation to be in as you are always learning and growing as a professional. The impact you have on the life chances of young people is immense and you are in a privileged position within society.

- Your teacher education programme and the school placements that you undertook provided the formative experiences that helped you to develop your early appreciation of the craft of teaching. The habits that you established during your initial teacher education and early years in teaching have a huge influence on your personal resilience and how well you respond to change during your career.

- How well you look after your well-being and keep the role of the teacher in balance with the rest of your life determines how well you cope with the pressures that teaching puts on you, as the only constant in teaching is that it is always changing. Each new year brings new classes, new pupils to work with and a changing community of teachers within the school.

- Your well-being is intricately linked to your own mental and physical health, and remember to be gentle with yourself. Remember to learn when to say 'that is good enough'.

When you need a moment to put everything into perspective, I suggest you read 'Desiderata' by Max Ehrmann, as it reminds the reader that 'there will always be greater and lesser persons than yourself' and that, as far as possible, try to be gentle with yourself.

Record in your PDP how the information in this chapter enables you to meet the requirements for your first year of teaching.

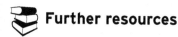

Further resources

Education Support Partnership. Available from: www.educationsupportpartnership.org.uk (accessed 17 August 2018).
The UK's only charity providing mental health and well-being support services to all education staff and organisations.

Findon, M. and Johnston-Wilder, S. (2019) 'Developing your resilience: Managing stress, workload and time', in S. Capel, M. Leask and S. Younie (eds.) *Learning to Teach in the Secondary School: A Companion to School Experience*, 8th edn, Abingdon: Routledge.
This chapter gives detailed research-based advice on building your resilience, managing your stress, workload and time.

MIND, *How to Improve Your Mental Wellbeing.* Available from: www.mind.org.uk/information-support/tips-for-everyday-living/wellbeing/#.WTRUHuvyuUk (accessed 17 August 2018).

NHS mental health services online resources pages. Available from: www.nhs.uk/conditions/online-mental-health-services/Pages/introduction.aspxReferences (accessed 17 August 2018).

Time to Change, *Managing Stress and Anxiety.* Available from: www.time-to-change.org.uk/sites/default/files/stress%20and%20anxiety.pdf (accessed 17 August 2018).
Specifically the section on ideas for dealing with stress and anxiety.

Appendices 2 and 3 list subject associations, teaching councils and relevant websites.

Books in the *Learning to Teach* series that you may find helpful are as follows:

Capel, S., Leask, M. and Younie, S. (eds.) (2019) *Learning to Teach in the Secondary School: A Companion to School Experience*, 8th edn, Abingdon: Routledge.
This book is designed as a core textbook to support student teachers through their initial teacher education programme.

Capel, S., Leask, M. and Turner, T. (eds.) (2010) *Readings for Learning to Teach in the Secondary School: A Companion to M Level Study*, Abingdon: Routledge.
This book brings together essential readings to support you in your critical engagement with key issues raised in this textbook.

The subject-specific books in the *Learning to Teach* series, the *Practical (subject) Guides*, *Debates in (subject)* and *Mentoring (subject) Teachers* are also very useful.

Appendix 1

Glossary of terms

Terms shown in bold within a definition have their own entry in the glossary. All URLs were checked July 2018.

A level. See **GCE**.

A2 level. See **GCE**.

Academies. - and related types of school such as Free schools - are schools in England funded by the central government but run as independent schools. An academy is not the same as community schools, voluntary schools or foundation schools as all these types of school are controlled - to a greater or lesser extent - by local authorities. Academies do not have to follow the national curriculum or keep to usual school holidays. They can be organised into multi-academy trusts (MATs).

- are schools in England funded by the central government but run as independent schools. An academy is not the same as community schools, voluntary schools or foundation schools as all these types of school are controlled - to a greater or lesser extent - by local authorities. Academies do not have to follow the national curriculum or keep to usual school holidays. They can be organised into multi-academy trusts (MATs).

They were formed as part of a central government political initiative in England to bring sponsors from business, faith or voluntary groups into school management removing local accountability and local authority oversight. See also **State maintained schools in England** and **Other state schools in England**.

ACCAC (Awdurdod Cymwysterau, Cwricwlwm ac Asesu Cymru) formerly the Qualifications, Curriculum and Assessment Authority for Wales. Merged with **DCELLS** in 2006.

AEB. See **AQA**.

Analyse School Performance. Replaced RAISEonline in 2018.

Annual review. The review of a statement of special educational needs **(SEN)** in England, which an **LA** must make within 12 months of making the statement or from a previous review.

AQA Assessment and Qualifications Alliance. An **Awarding Body** for **GCSE, GCE A** and **AS levels** and **Diplomas**. Online: http://www.aqa.org.uk. Formed in 2000 by a merger of City and Guilds GNVQ, Associated Examining Board (AEB), Southern Examining Group (SEG) and Northern Examination and Assessment Board (NEAB).

AS level. See **GCE**.

Assessment. Assessment covers all those activities that are undertaken by teachers and others to measure the effectiveness of their teaching and of pupils learning. See also **Assessment for learning, Assessment of learning, Criterion-referenced assessment, Formative assessment, Ipsative assessment, Norm-referenced assessment** and **Summative assessment**.

Assessment for learning. Assessment for which the first priority is promote pupils' learning. It allows teachers and pupils' to decide where the learners are in their learning and encourages pupils to take ownership of their learning. See also **Assessment, Assessment of learning, Formative assessment, Ipsative assessment, Norm-referenced assessment** and **Summative assessment**.

Assessment of learning. The summative assessment of pupils' attainments and progress periodically in a variety of ways and for a variety of purposes. See also **Assessment, Assessment for learning, Criterion-referenced assessment, Formative assessment, Ipsative assessment, Norm-referenced assessment** and **Summative assessment**.

Attainment targets (ATs) of **NC** for England. The knowledge, skills and understanding that pupils of different abilities and maturities are expected to have by the end of each **Key Stage**. Attainment targets previously consisted of eight **Level descriptions** of increasing difficulty, plus a description for exceptional performance above level 8. The latest National Curriculum (2014) has removed all level descriptions. See also **Programmes of Study**.

Awarding Body. There are three Awarding Bodies that set public examinations in England: the Assessment and Qualifications Alliance (**AQA**); **EdExcel** (Pearson); Oxford and Cambridge Regional (**OCR**).

BA/BSc (QTS) Bachelor of Arts/Bachelor of Science with **QTS (Qualified Teacher Status)**. A teaching qualification awarded in England – a combined course with a route to QTS. Note: a teaching qualification may not be recognised in other countries.

Banding. The structuring of a year group into divisions, each usually containing two or three classes, on grounds of general ability. Pupils are taught within the band for virtually all the curriculum. See also **Mixed ability grouping, Setting** and **Streaming**.

Baseline testing. Any process that sets out to find out what the learner can do now in relation to the next stage of learning. For example, the assessment of practical skills and familiarity of pupils with equipment and tools prior to a **D and T** course. Or the assessment of pupils in Year 1 and reception classes for speaking, listening, reading, writing, mathematics and social skills. See also **Benchmarking**.

BEd Bachelor of Education. A teacher training qualification in England leading to **QTS**.

Benchmarking. A term used to describe a standard against which comparisons can be made. Can be used by schools, for example, to measure the success of the school in public examinations relative to a national norm.

BESD – Behavioural, Emotional and Social Difficulties. A group of pupils with special educational needs. The term is often applied to pupils whose behaviour is consistently poor and not obviously related to the circumstances and environment in which pupils find themselves. Pupils who are withdrawn also fit into this category. See also **SEN, SEND**.

BTEC Business and Technician Education Council. Part of **EdExcel Foundation** that offers courses called BTEC Nationals.

C and G City and Guilds. See **AQA**.

Career Entry and Development Profile (CEDP). All **ITT** providers in England are required to provide newly qualified teachers with a **CEDP** to help them in their first teaching post and support **induction**.

Careers education. Designed to help pupils to choose and prepare for opportunities, responsibilities and experiences in education, training and employment. See National Careers Service: https://nationalcareersservice.direct.gov.uk

CPD.   Continuing professional development.

CEDP.   See **Career entry and development profile.**

CEHR   Commission for Equality and Human Rights; also referred to as Equality and Human Rights Commission. http://www.equalityhumanrights.com.

Certificate of Achievement (COA).   An examination designed to give a qualification to pupils who may not gain a GCSE grade, offered by the **Awarding Bodies.** Also called **Entry Level Certificate**; see Directgov website.

Church and faith Schools.   A faith school is a British school teaching a general curriculum but with a particular religious character or having formal links with a religious organisation. Regulations differ in detail among constituent countries of the United Kingdom. In England the curriculum, admissions criteria and staffing policies may reflect their religious foundation. See also **State maintained schools in England** and **Other state schools in England**.

Citizenship.   A statutory subject of the English **NC** at **Key Stages** 3 and 4. See also **Cross-curricular** elements. See researchbriefings.files.parliament.uk/documents/SN06798/SN06798.pdf.

Collaborative group.   A way of working in which groups of children are assigned to groups or engage spontaneously in working together to solve problems; sometimes called cooperative group work. See the now archived DCFS Standards website Grouping pupils for success: http://webarchive.nationalarchives.gov.uk/20110809101133/nsonline.org.uk/node/84974.

Combined course.   A course to which several subjects contribute while retaining their distinct identity (e.g. history, geography and RE within humanities). See also **Integrated course.**

Comprehensive school.   A type of state-maintained secondary school that admits pupils of age 11 to 16 or 19 from a given catchment area, regardless of their ability. See also **State maintained schools in England** and **Other state schools in England**.

Community and foundation special schools.   For children with specific special educational needs, such as physical or learning difficulties. See also **State maintained schools in England** and **Other state schools in England**.

Community of practice.   Groups of people who share a concern for something or have knowledge and skills to share. For example, a subject association network or a network of teachers working on solving a particular problem.

Community school.   A school run by the **LA,** which employs the staff, owns the land and buildings and decides admission criteria. It develops links with community. See also **State maintained schools in England** and **Other state schools in England**.

Continuity.   A feature of a curriculum and of lesson plans that ensures that learning builds on what has already been taught and experienced and prepares pupils for what is to come. See also **Progression.**

Core skills.   Skills required by all students following 14–19 courses. See **Functional skills** and **Personal learning and thinking skills.**

Core subjects.   These are **Foundation subjects** that are taught at both KS3 and KS4 comprising English, mathematics and science in the National Curriculum for England. See also **Entitlement subjects**; researchbriefings.files.parliament.uk/documents/SN06798/SN06798.pdf.

Coursework.   Work carried out by pupils during a course of study marked by teachers and contributing to the final examination mark. Usually externally moderated.

CPD   Continuing professional development.

CRE   Commission for Racial Equality; now part of **CEHR.**

Criterion-referenced assessment.   A process in which performance is measured by relating candidates' responses to predetermined criteria. See also **Assessment, Assessment for learning, Assessment of learning, Formative assessment, Ipsative assessment, Norm-referenced assessment** and **Summative assessment.**

Cross-curricular elements. Additional elements of a curriculum beyond statutory subjects that in England includes careers, **Citizenship**, economic education, **Key skills, Personal learning and thinking skills (PLTS)** and personal, social and health education (**PSHE**).

Curriculum. A course of study followed by a pupil.

Curriculum guidelines. Written guidance for organising and teaching a particular subject or area of the curriculum. See also **Programmes of Study**.

Church and faith schools. Similar to other **State maintained schools in England** but they follow a locally agreed religious education curriculum and have religion-centred admissions criteria and staffing policies. See **Other state schools in England**.

DCELLS Department for Children, Education, Lifelong Learning and Skills of the Welsh Government. http://www.accreditedqualifications.org.uk/department-for-children-education-lifelong-learning-and-skills-dcells.html.

DES, DfE, DfEE, DfES, DCSF; various names for the Ministry of Education in England, see **Government education departments and chronology**.

Differentiation. The matching of work to the differing capabilities and learning needs of individuals or groups of pupils in order to extend their learning.

Disapplication. Arrangement for lifting part or all of the **NC** in England requirements for individuals or for any other grouping specified by the Secretary of State.

EAL English as an Additional Language.

EBDD Emotional and behavioural difficulties and disorders. Used with reference to pupils with such difficulties or schools/units that cater for such pupils.

EdExcel Foundation. An **Awarding Body**. Online http://www.edexcel.org.uk.

Education welfare officer (EWO). An official of the **LA** concerned with pupils' attendance and with liaison between the school, the parents and the authority.

Entitlement subjects (in English NC). Non-statutory subjects in four curriculum areas, Arts, Design and Technology, Humanities and Modern Foreign Languages. (See 'About the School Curriculum: what is statutory?' on DfE website.)

Entry level. See **National Qualifications framework; Certificate of achievement;** https://www.gov.uk/what-different-qualification-levels-mean.

ESL English as a second language.

Exclusion. Headteachers of **State maintained schools in England** and **Other state schools in England** are empowered to exclude pupils temporarily or permanently when faced with a serious breach of their disciplinary code. The exclusions are either a fixed term or permanent. Schools may send pupils to a **Pupil referral unit (PRU)**.

EYFS Early Years Foundation Stage (of the **NC** for England).

Formative assessment. Or assessment for learning, linked to teaching when the evidence from an assessment is used to adapt teaching to meet pupils' learning needs. See also **Assessment, Assessment for learning, Assessment of learning, Criterion-referenced assessment, Ipsative assessment, Norm-referenced assessment** and **Summative assessment**.

Forms of entry (FE). The number of forms (e.g. of 30 pupils) that a school takes into its intake year. From this can be estimated the size of the intake year and the size of the school.

Foundation schools. The governing bodies of these schools employ the staff and set the admissions criteria. The school land and buildings are owned by the governing body or a charitable foundation. See **State maintained schools in England** and **Other state schools in England**.

Functional skills. Functional skills in the **NC** for England are those core elements of English, mathematics and **ICT** that provide individuals with the skills and abilities they need to operate confidently, effectively and independently in life, their communities and work. They can be examined individually. See Directgov website.

Foundation subjects.   Subjects that **State maintained schools in England** are required by law to teach. In England four **Foundation subjects** are designated **Core subjects**. Different subjects are compulsory at different **Key Stages** in England. See **Basic curriculum, Core subjects, Entitlement subjects**.

Free schools.   – and related types of school such as **academies** - are schools in England funded by the central government but run as independent schools. An academy is not the same as **community schools, voluntary schools or foundation schools** as all these types of school are controlled – to a greater or lesser extent – by **local authorities**. Academies do not have to follow the national curriculum or keep to usual school holidays. Established under to Academies Act in 2010 as a result of a political initiative to set up independent, state-funded schools, non-selective and outside **LA** control. Free schools are set up by parents, teachers, charities or businesses. Grants are available to support the initial setting-up process. They are subject to the Schools Admissions Code of Practice but priority is given to founders' children. In time, subject to **Ofsted** inspection. See also **State maintained schools in England** and **Other state schools in England**.

GCE   General Certificate of Education, also called Advanced Level of the GCE. An award after two years study, usually post-**GCSE**. Comprises two awards; an AS level taken after one year study and A2 level after two years study.

GCSE   General Certificate of Secondary Education.

GNVQ   General National Vocational Qualifications.

Government education departments and chronology.   For England and Wales to 2006, then England.

DES   (Department of Education and Science) pre-1992;

DfE   (Department for Education) 1992–1995; title reappeared 2010–present;

DfEE   (Department for Education and Employment) 1995–2001;

DfES   (Department for Education and Skills) 2001–2007;

DCSF   (Department for Children, Schools and Families) 2007–2010.

Grade-related criteria.   The identification of criteria, the achievement of which are related to different levels of performance by the candidate.

Grammar schools.   State maintained or independent schools that select all or almost all of their pupils based on academic ability, usually through the 11 plus examination. Parents often pay for extra tuition to give their children a higher chance of being admitted. See also **State maintained schools in England** and **Other state schools in England**.

Group work.   A way of organising pupils where the teacher assigns tasks to groups of pupils, to be undertaken collectively although the work is completed on an individual basis.

GTC   General Teaching Council for England. Was the professional body for teaching in England between 2000 and 2012. Duties taken over by **National College of Teaching and Leadership (NCTL)** which was repurposed to become the Teaching Regulation Agency. Northern Ireland, Scotland and Wales have their own teaching councils

HEI   Higher Education Institution.

HMCI   Her Majesty's Chief Inspector of Schools in England.

HMI   Her Majesty's Inspectors of Schools in England.

House system.   A structure for pastoral care/pupil welfare within a school in which pupils are grouped in vertical units, i.e. sections of the school that include pupils from all year groups. Alternative to the **Year system**.

IB   International Baccalaureate. A post-16 qualification designed for university entrance.

In-class support.   Support within a lesson provided by an additional teacher, often with expertise in teaching pupils with special educational, disability or language needs. See also **Learning support, Learning support assistant, Partnership teaching, Withdrawal**.

Inclusion.   Inclusion involves the processes of increasing the participation of pupils in, and reducing their exclusion from, schools. Inclusion is concerned with the learning participation of all pupils vulnerable to exclusionary pressures, not only those with impairments or categorised as having special educational needs.

Independent school.   A private school that receives no state assistance but is financed by fees. Often registered as a charity. See also **Public school**.

Induction.   For teachers, the first stage of **Continuing professional development (CPD)**. A statutory requirement for newly qualified teachers (**NQTs**) in England in the first year of teaching. Successful completion of induction requires NQTs to meet standards set by the regulatory body in the country in which they wish to practise.

Integrated course.   A course, usually in a secondary school, to which several subjects contribute without retaining their distinct identity (e.g. integrated humanities, which explores themes that include aspects of geography, history and RE). See also **Combined course**.

Integration.   Educating children with special educational needs together with children without special educational needs in mainstream schools. See **Inclusion**.

Ipsative assessment.   A process in which performance is measured against previous performance by the same person. See also **Assessment, Assessment for learning, Assessment of learning, Criterion-referenced assessment, Formative assessment, Norm-referenced assessment, Summative assessment**.

ITE   Initial Teacher Education.

ITT   Initial Teacher Training.

ITTE   Initial Teacher Training and Education.

Key skills.   See **Functional skills** and **Personal learning and thinking skills**.

Key Stages (KS) England.   The periods in each pupil's education to which the elements of the **NC** for England apply. There are four **Key Stages**, normally related to the age of the majority of the pupils in a teaching group. They are: Key Stage 1, beginning of compulsory education to age 7 (Years R (Reception), 1 and 2); Key Stage 2, ages 7-11 (Years 3-6); Key Stage 3, ages 11-14 (Years 7- 9); Key Stage 4, ages 14 to end of compulsory education (Years 10 and 11). Post-16 is a further Key Stage 5.

LA.   See **Local Authority**.

Language support teacher.   A teacher provided by the **LA** or school to enhance language work with particular groups of pupils.

Learning objectives.   What pupils are expected to have learned as a result of an activity, lesson or topic.

Learning outcomes.   Assessable learning objectives; the action or behaviour of pupils that provides evidence that they have met the learning objectives.

Learning support.   A means of providing extra help for pupils, usually those with learning difficulties, e.g. through a specialist teacher or specially designed materials. See also **Learning support assistants, In-class support, Partnership teaching, Withdrawal**.

Learning support assistants.   Teachers who give additional support for a variety of purposes, e.g. general learning support for pupils with **SEND** or **ESL**; most support is given in-class although sometimes pupils are withdrawn from class. See also **Learning support, In-class support, Partnership teaching, Withdrawal**.

Lesson plan.   The detailed planning of work to be undertaken in a lesson. This follows a particular structure, appropriate to the demands of a particular lesson. An individual lesson plan is usually part of a series of lessons in a **Unit of work**.

Level description (**NC** for England). A statement describing the types and range of performance that pupils working at a particular level should characteristically demonstrate. Level descriptions have been removed in the latest version of the NC (2014). Level descriptions provide the basis for making judgements about pupils' performances at the ends of each of **Key Stages** 1, 2, 3. At Key Stage 4, national qualifications are the main means of assessing attainment in National Curriculum subjects.

Levels of attainment in England. Eight levels of attainment, plus exceptional performance, are defined within the National Curriculum **Attainment targets** in England. These stop at **Key Stage** 3; see **Level description**.

Local Authority (LA). An LA has responsibility for local services, including education, libraries and social services. It has a statutory duty to provide education in their area. Many schools have opted out of LA control, see e.g. **Academies**, **Free schools**.

Maintained boarding schools. State-funded schools that offer free tuition but charge fees for board and lodging. See also **State maintained schools in England** and **Other state schools in England**.

Middle school. A school that caters for pupils aged from 8–12 or 9–13 years of age. They are classified legally as either primary or secondary schools depending on whether the preponderance of pupils in the school is under or over 11 years of age.

Minority ethnic groups. Pupils, many of whom have been born in the United Kingdom, from other ethnic heritages, e.g. those of Asian heritage from Bangladesh, China, Pakistan, India or East Africa, those of African or Caribbean heritage or from countries in the European Union.

Mixed ability grouping. Teaching group containing pupils representative of the range of ability within the school. See also **Banding**, **Setting**, **Streaming**.

Moderation. An exercise involving teachers representing an **Awarding body** external to the school whose purpose is to check that standards are comparable across schools and teachers. Usually carried out by sampling coursework or examination papers.

Moderator. An examiner who monitors marking and examining to ensure that standards are consistent in a number of schools and colleges.

Module. A definable section of work of fixed length with specific learning objectives and usually with some form of terminal assessment. Several such units may constitute a modular course.

Multi-academy Trusts. A group of academies in England in partnership with each other often, but not always, because they are geographically close to one another.

National Assessment Agency (NAA). Set up as a separate body by QCA in 2004 to deliver and administer **National Curriculum Tests**. Closed 2008 and functions subsumed into **QCA**. Later **QCDA** and **STA**.

NC (National Curriculum) for some schools only in England (https://www.gov.uk/national-curriculum). The **Core** and other **Foundation** subjects and their associated **Attainment targets**, **Programmes of Study** and assessment arrangements of the curriculum.

National College for Teaching and Leadership (NCTL) was an executive agency of the Department for Education from 2013 to 2018. Was replaced by Department for Education **(DfE)** and **Teaching Regulation Agency**.

National Curriculum Tests formerly **Standard Assessment Tasks (q.v.)**.

National Qualifications Framework (NQF). A framework that links academic and vocational qualifications and shows their equivalence at several levels of attainment. See also **Awarding Bodies**, **Vocational Courses**, **GNVQ**, **NVQ**. See Directgov website at https://www.gov.uk/what-different-qualification-levels-mean.

NEAB. See **AQA**.

NFER National Foundation for Educational Research. Carries out research and produces educational diagnostic tests.

Non-contact time. Time provided by a school for a teacher to prepare work or carry out assigned responsibilities other than direct teaching.

Norm-referenced assessment. A process in which performance is measured by comparing candidates' responses. Individual success is relative to the performance of all other candidates. See also **Assessment**, **Assessment for learning**, **Assessment**

of learning, **Criterion-referenced assessment, Formative assessment, Ipsative assessment, Summative assessment.**

NQT   Newly qualified teacher.

NSG   Non-statutory guidance (**NC** in England). Additional subject guidance but not mandatory; to be found attached to National Curriculum Subject Orders such as PSHE, Citizenship.

NVQ   National Vocational Qualifications.

OCR   Oxford and Cambridge Regional **Awarding Body.** Online http://www.ocr.org.uk.

OFQUAL.   The Office of Qualifications and Examinations Regulation is a non-ministerial government department set up in 2008. Regulator of examinations and tests in England, taking over that aspect of **QCA**. Independent (of **DfE** ministers) and responsible directly to parliament. https://www.gov.uk/government/organisations/ofqual.

Ofsted   Office for Standards in Education, Children's Services and Skills. Non-ministerial government department established under the Education (Schools) Act (1992) to take responsibility for the inspection of schools in England. Ofsted inspects pre-school provision, further education, teacher education institutions and **Local authorities. Her Majesty's Inspectors (HMI)** form the professional arm of Ofsted. See also OHMCI.

OHMCI   Office of Her Majesty's Chief Inspector (Wales). Non-ministerial government department established under the Education (Schools) Act (1992) to take responsibility for the inspection of schools in Wales. **Her Majesty's Inspectors (HMI)** form the professional arm of OHMCI. See also **Ofsted.**

Other state schools in England. These include **Academies, Community and foundation special** schools, **Church and faith** schools (see **Voluntary schools), Free schools, Grammar schools, Maintained boarding schools, Specialist schools** and **Pupil Referral Units**. See Directgov website. See also **State maintained schools in England.**

PANDA.   See **Raiseonline.**

Parent.   Under Section 576 of the Education Act 1996 a parent includes any person who is not a parent of the child but has parental responsibility (see **Parental responsibility**), or who cares for the child.

Parental responsibility.   Under Section 2 of the Children Act 1989, parental responsibility falls upon:

■   all mothers and fathers who were married to each other at the time of the child's birth (including those who have since separated or divorced);

■   mothers who were not married to the father at the time of the child's birth;

■   and fathers who were not married to the mother at the time of the child's birth, but who have obtained parental responsibility either by agreement with the child's mother or through a court order. Under Section 12 of the Children Act 1989, where a court makes a residence order in favour of any person who is not the parent or guardian of the child that person has parental responsibility for the child while the residence order remains in force.

Partnership teaching.   An increasingly common means of meeting the language needs of bilingual pupils in which support and class teachers plan and implement together a specially devised programme of in-class teaching and learning. See also **Learning support, Learning support assistants, In-class support, Withdrawal.**

Pastoral care.   Those aspects of a school's work and structures concerned to promote the general welfare of all pupils, particularly their academic, personal and social development, their attendance and behaviour.

PAT   Pupil Achievement Tracker. Now part of **Raiseonline**.

Pedagogic content knowledge.   The skills to transform subject content knowledge into suitable learning activities for a particular group of pupils.

PGCE   Post Graduate Certificate in Education. The main qualification for secondary school teachers in England and Wales recognised by the **DfE** for **QTS**.

Policy.   An agreed school statement relating to a particular area of its life and work.

PoS.   See **Programmes of Study**.

Pre-vocational courses.   Courses specifically designed and taught to help pupils to prepare for employment.

Profile.   Samples of work of pupils, used to illustrate progress, with or without added comments by teachers and/or pupils.

Programme of Study (PoS)   for **NC** in England. The subject matter, skills and processes that must be taught to pupils during each **Key Stage** in order that they may meet the objectives set out in the **Attainment targets**. They provide the basis for planning **Schemes of work**.

Progression.   The planned development of pupils' knowledge, skills, understanding and attitudes over time. See also **Continuity**.

Project.   An investigation with a particular focus undertaken by individuals or small groups of pupils leading to a written, oral or graphic presentation of the outcome.

PSE   Personal and Social Education.

PSHCE.   This is **PSHE** with a specific additional **citizenship** component.

PSHE   Personal, Social, Health and Education. A non-statutory subject in the English National Curriculum. See also **PSHCE**.

PSHEE.   This is **PSHE** with a specific additional economic component.

PTA   Parent-Teacher Association. Voluntary grouping of parents and school staff to support the school in a variety of ways.

PTR   Pupil:Teacher ratio. The ratio of pupils to teachers within a school or group of schools (e.g. 17.4:1).

Public school.   An **Independent school**, not state funded. So-called because at their inception they were funded by public charity.

Pupil referral units (PRUs).   For children of compulsory school age who may otherwise not receive suitable education, focusing on getting them back into a mainstream school.

Pupil Achievement Tracker (PAT).   See **RAISEonline**.

QCA   Qualifications and Curriculum Authority. Initiated in 1997 by the merger of **SCAA** and National Council for Vocational Qualifications (**NCVQ**), it was responsible for the overview of the curriculum, assessment and qualifications across the whole of education and training, from pre-school to higher vocational levels. The QCA advised the Secretary of State for Education on such matters. Aspects of assessment were delegated by QCA to the **NAA**. Dissolved in 2010 the responsibilities were shared between **QCDA** and **Ofqual**. The Welsh equivalent of the QCA was **ACCAC,** later **DCELLS**.

QCDA   Qualification, Curriculum and Development Agency. Formerly **QCA**. Set up in 2008. Responsible for the **National Curriculum** and associated assessments, tests and examinations. Dissolved in 2012, its functions were taken over by the **Standards and Testing Agency (STA)**.

QTS   Qualified teacher status. This is usually attained by completion of a Post Graduate Certificate in Education (**PGCE**) or a Bachelor of Education (**BEd**) degree or a Bachelor of Arts/Science degree with Qualified Teacher Status (**BA/BSc (QTS)**). There are other routes into teaching.

RAISEonline   Reporting and Analysis for Improvement through School Self-Evaluation. Closed in 2017. In England it provided interactive analysis of school and pupil performance data. It replaced the Ofsted Performance and Assessment (**PANDA**) reports and the Pupil Achievement Tracker (**PAT**). Replaced by Analyse School Performance.

Record of achievement (ROA).   Cumulative record of a pupil's academic, personal and social progress over a stage of education.

Reliability.   A measure of the consistency of the assessment or test item; i.e. the extent to which the test gives repeatable results. See also **Validity**.

RSA   Royal Society of Arts.

SACRE   Standing Advisory Council on Religious Education in each LA to advise the LA on matters connected with religious education and collective worship, particularly methods of teaching, the choice of teaching materials and the provision of teacher training.

SATs.   See **Standard Assessment Tasks**.

Scheme of work.   A planned course of study over a period of time (e.g. a **Key Stage** or a Year). In England it contains knowledge, skills and processes derived from the **Programmes of Study** and **Attainment targets** together with **Units of work** and **Lesson plans**.

School Improvement Plan (SIP).   A coherent plan required to be made by a school, identifying improvements needed in curriculum, organisation, staffing and resources and setting out action needed to make those improvements.

SEG.   See **AQA**.

SEN (Special Educational Needs).   Children have special educational needs if they have a *learning difficulty*. Children have a *learning difficulty* if they:

a) have a significantly greater difficulty in learning than the majority of children of the same age; or (b) have a disability that prevents or hinders them from making use of educational facilities of a kind generally provided for children of the same age in schools within the area of the local authority; (c) are under compulsory school age and fall within the definition at (a) or (b) above or would so do if special educational provision was not made for them. Very able or gifted pupils are not included in SEN. See also SEND, SENCO.

SEN Code of Practice.   Act of Parliament describing and prescribing the regulations for the support of pupils with SEN.

SENCO   Special Educational Needs Coordinator in schools. See also **SEN**, **SEND**.

SEND   Special Educational Needs and/or Disability. In England a widening of the scope of **SEN** (Ofsted 2010).

Setting.   The grouping of pupils according to their ability in a subject for lessons in that subject. See also **Banding, Mixed ability grouping, Streaming**.

Short course.   A course in a National Curriculum foundation subject in **Key Stage** 4 that, by itself, does not lead to a full **GCSE** or equivalent qualification. Two short courses in different subjects may be combined to form one full GCSE or equivalent course.

Sixth form college.   A post-16 institution for 16–19-year-olds. It offers **GCSE, GCE A level** and **Vocational courses**.

SLD   Specific learning difficulties.

SOA   Statements of attainment (of **NC** subjects).

Special school.   See **Community and foundation special schools**.

Specialist schools.   Teach the whole curriculum but with a focus on one subject area such as arts, business and enterprise, engineering, humanities, language, mathematics and computing, music, science, sports, technology. See **Other state schools in England**.

STA (Standards and Testing Agency).   An executive agency of the **DfE** set up in 2011. It is responsible for the development and delivery of all statutory assessments from early years to the end of Key Stage 3, which formerly were carried out by **QCDA** (dissolved in March 2012).

Standard Assessment Tasks (SATs).   Externally prescribed **National Curriculum for England** assessments that incorporate a variety of assessment methods depending on the subject and **Key Stage**. The term SAT is not now widely used, having been replaced by **'National Curriculum Tests',** overseen by **STA**.

State maintained schools in England. In England there are four main types of schools, **Community schools, Foundation and Trust schools, Voluntary-aided** and **Voluntary controlled schools**. All are funded by **LA** and/or central government. Many of these schools admit pupils from a wide range of ability; see **Comprehensive schools**. Within the four categories are schools with special characteristics; see **Other state schools in England**.

Statements of special educational needs. Provided under the 1981 Education Act and subsequent Acts to ensure appropriate provision for pupils formally assessed as having **SEN**. See **SEN Code of Practice** and **SEND**.

Statutory order. A statutory instrument that is regarded as an extension of an Act, enabling provisions of the Act to be augmented or updated.

Streaming. The organisation of pupils according to general ability into classes in which they are taught for all subjects and courses. See also **Banding, Mixed ability grouping, Setting**.

Summative assessment. Assessment linked to the end of a course of study. It sums up achievement in aggregate terms and is used to rank, grade or compare pupils, groups or schools. It uses a narrow range of methods that are efficient and reliable, normally formal, i.e. under examination conditions. See also **Assessment, Assessment for learning, Assessment of learning, Criterion-references assessment, Formative assessment, Ipsative assessment, Norm-referenced assessment**.

Supply teacher. Teachers appointed temporarily to fill vacancies.

Support teacher. See **In-class support** and **Learning support**.

TA Teaching Agency. Set up in 2012. Responsible for the initial and in-service training of teachers and other school staff in England. Comprised the former bodies **TDA, GTC** (General Teaching Council for England) and **QCDA**. Replaced by the **Teaching Regulation Agency**.

TDA Training and Development Agency for schools for England. Set up in 2005, closed 2010 replacing the **Teacher Training Agency**, now replaced by the **Teaching Regulation Agency**. The TDA had a remit for overseeing standards and qualifications across the school workforce and supporting the quality of teacher training.

Teacher Assessments. Assessments made by teachers alongside **National Curriculum Tests** at some **Key Stages** in England.

Teacher's record book. A book in which teachers plan and record teaching and learning for their classes on a regular basis.

Teaching Regulation Agency. An executive agency of the DfE which began to operate from 1st April 2018. It has responsibility for the regulation of the teaching profession, including misconduct hearings and the maintenance of the database of qualified teachers.

Team teaching. The teaching of a number of classes simultaneously by teachers acting as a team. They usually divide the work between them, allowing those with particular expertise to lead different parts of the work, the others supporting the follow-up work with groups or individuals. See also **In-class support, Learning support, Partnership teaching**.

Thinking skills. Additional skills to be promoted in lessons. See also **Cross-curricular elements**.

T Levels (Technical Levels) are for vocational courses, which will be on a par with A levels and will provide young people with a choice between technical and academic education post-16. They start in 2020. https://www.gov.uk/government/news/new-t-levels-mark-a-revolution-in-technical-education.

Travellers. A term used to cover those communities, some of which have minority ethnic status, and either are or have been traditionally associated with a nomadic lifestyle, and include gypsy travellers, fairground or show people, circus families, New Age travellers and bargees.

Traveller education. The development of policy and provision that provides traveller children with unhindered access to and full integration in mainstream education.

Trust schools. These are **Foundation schools** supported by a charitable foundation or trust, which appoints school governors. A trust school employs its own staff, manages its own land and assets, and sets its own admissions criteria.

Tutor group. Grouping of secondary pupils for registration and pastoral care purposes.

Unit of work. Medium-term planning of work for pupils over half a term or a number of weeks. The number of lessons in a unit of work may vary according to each school's organisation. A unit of work usually introduces a new aspect of learning. Units of work derive from **Schemes of work** and are the basis for **Lesson plans**.

Validity. A measure of whether the assessment measures what it is meant to measure – often determined by consensus. Certain kinds of skills and abilities are extremely difficult to assess with validity via simple pencil and paper tests. See also **Reliability**.

Vocational courses. Programmes of study leading to vocational qualifications that are work-related, preparing learners for employment. **Awarding Bodies** offer vocational courses. See also **NVQ, GNVQ, BTEC, National Qualifications**.

Voluntary-aided schools. Often religious schools. The governing body, often a religious organisation, employs the staff and sets admissions criteria. The school land and buildings are also owned by a charitable foundation. See also **State maintained schools in England** and **Other state schools in England**.

Voluntary-controlled schools. Mainly religious or 'faith' schools, but run by the LA. The land and buildings are often owned by a charitable foundation, but the LA employs the staff and has primary responsibility for admission arrangements. See also **State maintained schools in England** and **Other state schools in England**.

Voluntary schools. Schools that receive financial assistance from the **LA**, but are owned by a voluntary body, usually religious. See **State maintained schools in England** and **Other state schools in England**.

Withdrawal. Removal of pupils with particular needs from class teaching in primary schools and from specified subjects in secondary schools for extra help individually or in small groups. In-class support is increasingly provided in preference to withdrawal. See also **Learning support, Learning support assistants, In-class support, Partnership teaching**.

WJEC (Welsh Joint Education Committee). Provides examinations, assessment, professional development, educational resources, support for adults who wish to learn Welsh and access to youth arts activities. It also provides examinations throughout England.

Work experience. The opportunity for secondary pupils to have experience of a work environment for one or two weeks, usually within school time, during which a pupil carries out a particular job or range of jobs more or less as would regular employees, although with emphasis on the educational aspects of the experience.

Year system. A structure for pastoral care/pupil welfare within a school in which pupils are grouped according to years, i.e. in groups spanning an age range of only one year. An alternative grouping is the **House system**.

Years 1-11. Years of schooling in England. Five-year-olds start at Year 1 (Y1) and progress through to Year 11 (Y11) at 16 years old. See **Key Stages** for details.

Appendix 2

Subject associations and teaching councils

Teaching councils

England - Chartered College of Teaching (developed in England in 2016) https://chartered. college (replaced the General Teaching Council for England (GTCE), closed by the UK government in 2011; http://webarchive.nationalarchives.gov.uk/20111213132132/http:/www.gtce.org.uk

Northern Ireland - www.gtcni.org.uk/

Scotland - www.gtcs.org.uk/home/home.aspx

Wales - The Education Workforce Council (EWC) http://www.ewc.wales/site/index.php/en/(replaced the General Teaching Council for Wales (GTCW) which was reconfigured and renamed to become the EWC on 1st April 2015).

Subject associations

Council for Subject Associations

The following associations are members of the UK Council for Subject Associations which acts as a voice for subjects for government and for the press and the public. www.subjectassociations.org.uk

Association membership keeps you up-to-date through giving you access to specialist education conferences, workshops, professional development sessions and publications. Many associations have international links that aid knowledge flow from country to country.

See the Council for Subject Associations website for live links and further information. All the URLs here were checked in July 2018.

Art and Design	
National Society for Education in Art and Design (NSEAD)	www.nsead.org
Assessment	
The Association for Achievement and Improvement through Assessment (AAIA)	www.aaia.org.uk

Citizenship	
Association for Citizenship Teaching (ACT)	www.teachingcitizenship.org.uk
Computing and Information Technology	
Technology, Pedagogy and Education Association (previously Information Technology in Teacher Education (ITTE))	www.itte.org.uk
Computing At School (CAS)	www.computingatschool.org.uk
Dance	
One Dance UK	www.onedanceuk.org
Design and Technology	
The Design and Technology Association	www.data.org.uk
Drama	
National Drama (ND)	www.nationaldrama.co.uk
English	
The English Association (EA)	www.le.ac.uk/engassoc
National Association for the Teaching of English (NATE)	www.nate.org.uk/
United Kingdom Literacy Association (UKLA)	www.ukla.org
Geography	
The Geographical Association (GA)	www.geography.org.uk
Royal Geographical Society with IBG (RGS)	www.rgs.org
History	
The Historical Association (HA)	history.org.uk
Languages	
Association for Language Learning (ALL)	www.all-languages.org.uk
National Association for Language Development in the Curriculum (NALDIC)	www.naldic.org.uk
Mathematics	
Joint Mathematical Council of the United Kingdom	www.jmc.org.uk
Media	
Media Education Association (MEA)	www.themea.org.uk
Music	
Incorporated Society of Musicians	www.ism.org
UK Association for Music Education – Music Mark	www.musicmark.org.uk
Physical Education	
Association for Physical Education (afPE)	www.afpe.org.uk

PSHE	
PSHE Association	www.pshe-association.org.uk
Religious Education	
National Association of Teachers of Religious Education (NATRE)	www.natre.org.uk
Science	
Association for Science Education (ASE)	www.ase.org.uk
Special Educational Needs	
NASEN	www.nasen.org.uk
Professional Association of Teachers of Students with Specific Learning Difficulties (Patoss)	www.patoss-dyslexia.org

Appendix 3

Useful websites

Providers of web resources for teachers do so for a range of purposes. Some sites are professional such as subject associations sharing knowledge between professionals, others explicitly support government policy so advice may be changed or withdrawn on ideological grounds, and others are designed to sell you products. The list below includes websites from:

- Professional Associations, Teaching Councils and Unions (see also Appendix 2);
- Charities and University Research Centres and social enterprises;
- Government-funded organisations;
- Private companies.

For the most part, we have excluded websites apparently linked with just one individual. Exceptions are where the individuals have clearly researched and published widely in the area.

There are formal and informal networks on various social media sites including: Facebook, LinkedIn and Twitter.

You are advised to check the reliability of any advice – on the internet or in print. For teaching to be an evidence-informed profession, teachers need to know the strength of evidence for any pedagogical intervention. By strength of evidence we mean:

- Methods and ethics: Has the advice been gathered by ethical (see the BERA ethical code www.bera.ac.uk) and reliable research methods (See Unit 5.4 in *LTT8*, 2019 and Patterson's MESHGuides – http://www.meshguides.org). Usual research instruments are interviews, questionnaires, documentary analysis and observation, but there is a huge variation of options within each instrument.
- Independence: Were the researchers independent? Who funded the research? Were researchers free to publish adverse findings?
- Quality assurance: Has the advice been independently peer reviewed? Peer review, by an independent panel of educators, is the normal form of quality assurance used

for professional association and professional journal sites. Materials from other sites may or may not be peer reviewed.

- Sample: What is the size and type of the sample used to provide the evidence? What confidence does this give you in the results?
- Transferability: How transferable is the advice likely to be? How similar is the research context to your context? This is not at all to say you reject research and evidence from contexts different to your own but just that you need to bring your professional judgement to bear in applying the findings. Teachers in many countries face similar challenges in maximising the learning of young people and there is a lot to learn from solutions elsewhere.

> All websites listed here were accessed in July 2018.
> Further information is given only where it is not obvious what the website offers.
> The list starts with generic websites followed by a list of sites grouped alphabetically by theme, e.g. Behaviour, Neuroscience, Subject Associations, Unions etc.

Generic Websites (covering a wide range of areas):

- British Education Research Tool in Education (BERTIE): www.bathspa.ac.uk/static/bertie/bertie.html
- British Educational Research Association (https://www.bera.ac.uk). Repository of British Education Research Association conferences research papers: www.bera.ac.uk
- Ed Talks: www.edtalks.org
- Education Endowment Foundation: see EEF
- Education Evidence Portal: www.eep.ac.uk (This is a search tool for specific sites but has not been updated since the 2012 decisions of the UK coalition government to close online services for teachers in England. It is useful for historical documents.)
- Education-line: www.leeds.ac.uk/bei/COLN/COLN_default.html
- EEF (Education Endowment Foundation): https://educationendowmentfoundation.org.uk
- ERIC (USA Government Education Resources Information Center): http://eric.ed.gov
- European SchoolNet: www.eun.org
- Evidence for Policy and Practice Information Centre: https://eppi.ioe.ac.uk/cms; This has a list of systematic reviews of practice in education.
- Khan Academy – teaching videos: www.khanacademy.org
- MESHGuides (Mapping Education Specialist knowHow): www.meshguides.org
- National STEM Centre: www.stem.org.uk/resources
- Open University, Open Learn: www.open.edu/openlearnworks/course/view.php?id=1490%3F
- Seneca Learning (www.senecalearning.com) free homework and revision platform
- Stanford University Teaching Commons – Resources tab: https://teachingcommons.stanford.edu
- Teacher Education Observatory: http://teachereducationobservatory.org
- TED-Ed Lessons Worth Sharing: http://ed.ted.com

- Times Educational Supplement: www.tes.co.uk
- You Tube: Teaching Channel and Teachers: www.youtube.com/user/teachers and www.youtube.com/user/TeachingChannel

UK Government:

- England: Department for Education: www.education.gov.uk and inspection: Office for Standards in Education, Children's Services and Skills (Ofsted): www.ofsted.gov.uk
- Northern Ireland: Department of Education Northern Ireland: www.deni.gov.uk and inspection: The Education and Training Inspectorate Northern Ireland: www.etini.gov.uk/index/inspection-reports.htm
- Scotland: Education Scotland: www.educationscotland.gov.uk/index.asp and The Scottish Government: www.gov.scot/Topics/Statistics/Browse/School-Education
- Wales: Welsh Government: http://gov.wales/topics/educationandskills/%20?lang=en and inspection: Estyn – the office of Her Majesty's Inspectorate for Education and Training in Wales: www.estyn.gov.uk

Additional websites by theme:

A

- Assessment for learning: see specialist MESHGuides: www.meshguides.org and, for example, Wiliam, D.: www.dylanwiliam.org/Dylan_Wiliams_website/Welcome.html
- Autism: National Autistic Society: www.nas.org.uk

B

Behaviour:
See DFE advice:

- (January 2016) Behaviour and discipline in schools Advice for headteachers and school staff: www.gov.uk/government/publications/behaviour-and-discipline-in-schools
- (February 2014) Screening, searching and confiscation: www.gov.uk/government/publications/searching-screening-and-confiscation
- (April 2012) www.gov.uk/government/publications/behaviour-and-discipline-in-schools
- (July 2013) Behaviour checklist: www.gov.uk/government/publications/behaviour-and-discipline-in-schools
- (July 2013) Guidance for governing bodies: www.gov.uk/government/publications/behaviour-and-discipline-in-schools-guidance-for-governing-bodies
- (July 2013) Use of reasonable force: www.gov.uk/government/publications/use-of-reasonable-force-in-schools

- (August 2013) Preventing and Tackling Bullying: www.gov.uk/government/publications/preventing-and-tackling-bullying
- (September 2014) www.gov.uk/government/policies/improving-behaviour-and-attendance-in-schools

C

Citizenship:

- British Humanist Association: www.humanism.org.uk/education/education-policy
- Citizenship Foundation: www.citizenshipfoundation.org.uk
- CitizED subject resource bank: www.citized.info. Accessed 9 April 2015.
- Jubilee Centre for Character and Virtues: www.jubileecentre.ac.uk

Code of practice for teaching – see Teaching Councils
Curriculum – National requirements:

- England:www.gov.uk/government/publications/national-curriculum-in-england-framework-for-key-stages-1-to-4/the-national-curriculum-in-england-framework-for-key-stages-1-to-4
- Northern Ireland: www.nicurriculum.org.uk
- Scotland: www.educationscotland.gov.uk/learningandteaching/thecurriculum/whatiscurriculumforexcellence
- Wales: http://wales.gov.uk/topics/educationandskills/schoolshome/curriculuminwales/arevisedcurriculumforwales/?lang=en

D

Deaf and Hearing Impaired:

- National Deaf Children's Society: www.ndcs.org.uk
- BATOD Foundation: www.batodfoundation.org.uk

Dialogic teaching:

- Alexander, R. (2015): www.robinalexander.org.uk/dialogic-teaching
- University of Cambridge: www.educ.cam.ac.uk/research/projects/dialogic/whatis.html

E

English as an additional language:

- Flynn, N, Pim, C. and Coles, S. (2015) *Teaching English as an Additional Language MESHGuide*, University of Winchester, UK: https://www.meshguides.org/guides/node/112

- Equality and Human Rights Commission (EHRC): www.equalityhumanrights.com
- Joseph Rowntree Foundation (focus: poverty and injustice): www.jrf.org.uk

Ethics:

- Professional – see Teaching Councils
- Research – see BERA

Europe: European Schoolnet (EUN): www.eun.org

G

Gifted and Talented:

- National Association for Able Children in Education: www.nace.co.uk

H

Handwriting:

- National Handwriting Association: www.nha-handwriting.org.uk

Health:

- British Nutrition Foundation: www.nutrition.org.uk
- Food Standards Agency: www.eatwell.gov.uk
- NICE (National Institute for Health and Care Excellence): www.nice.org.uk/guidance

I

- Intelligence: Gardner, H. http://howardgardner.com/multiple-intelligences

L

Lesson Study:

- Dudley, P.: http://lessonstudy.co.uk/about-us-pete-dudley

Learning theories – see the specialist sites in this list:

- Claxton, G. (2015) *Building Learning Power*: www.buildinglearningpower.co.uk

M

MESHGuides:

- www.meshguides.org – research summaries to support evidence-informed teaching.

N

Names (remembering):

- Buzan: www.open.edu/openlearn/body-mind/psychology/buzan-on-how-remember-names-and-faces
- TeacherVision: https://www.teachervision.com/teaching-strategies/getting-know-your-students

- National Qualifications Framework (NQF): www.gov.uk/what-different-qualification-levels-mean

Neuroscience:

- Blakemore, S.: www.ted.com/talks/sarah_jayne_blakemore_the_mysterious_workings_of_the_adolescent_brain?language=en
- Centre for Neuroscience in Education led by Professor Usha Goswami: www.cne.psychol.cam.ac.uk/people/ucg10@cam.ac.uk
- Neuroscience for Kids: http://faculty.washington.edu/chudler/neurok.html
- Royal Society: http://royalsociety.org/policy/projects/brain-waves/education-lifelong-learning
- The Brain from Top to Bottom: http://thebrain.mcgill.ca
- The International Mind, Brain and Education Society: www.imbes.org

P

- Philosophy: Philosophy of Education, www.philosophy-of-education.org/resources/students/video-listing.html

Projects:

- Collaborative projects across Europe – E-twinning: www.etwinning.net/en/pub/index.htm
- WebQuests UK: www.webquestuk.org.uk

R

Risk:

- CLEAPSS: www.cleapss.org.uk/attachments/article/0/L196.pdf?Secondary/Science/Guides
- Eaton Vale Schools Activity Centre: www.eatonvale.co.uk/schools/riskassessments.aspx
- Health and Safety Executive: www.hse.gov.uk/risk/classroom-checklist.htm

Research methods/research ethics:

- British Educational Research Association (BERA): www.bera.ac.uk
- Patterson, E. (2016a) *Research Methods 1: How to Get Started on a Literature Review MESHGuide*, University of Winchester, UK: www.meshguides.org
- Patterson, E. (2016b) *Research Methods 2: Developing Your Research Design MESHGuide*, University of Winchester, UK: www.meshguides.org
- Patterson, E. (2016c) *Research Methods 3: Considering Ethics in Your Research MESHGuide*, University of Winchester, UK: www.meshguides.org

S

- Safer Internet Day: www.saferinternetday.org
- SEND: see also deaf, dyslexia: NASEN (National Association for Special Educational Needs): www.nasen.org.uk and www.nasen.org.uk/onlinesendcpd
- Blamires, M. and others (2014) *Special Educational Needs and Disability: Enabling Pupil Participation MESHGuide*: www.meshguides.org/category/special-needs-2/enabling-pupil-participation-special-needs-2
- The Professional Association of Teachers of Students with Specific Learning Difficulties (PATOSS): www.patoss-dyslexia.org
  Royal National Institute for the Blind: www.rnib.org.uk
- Subject Associations - are represented by the Council for Subject Associations: www.subjectassociation.org.uk

T

Teacher Support Network:

- www.teachersupport.info (24-hour confidential counselling)

Teacher Standards:

- England: https://assets.publishing.service.gov.uk/government/uploads/system/uploads/attachment_data/file/665520/Teachers__Standards.pdf; www.legislation.gov.uk/uksi/2003/1662/schedule/2/made
- Northern Ireland: www.deni.gov.uk/index/school-staff/teachers-teachinginnorthernireland_pg.htm
- Scotland: www.gtcs.org.uk/standards
- Wales: http://gov.wales/topics/educationandskills/publications/circulars/becomingateacher/?lang=en

Thinking - See also Dialogic teaching:

- Education Scotland (2015) *Skills in Practice: Thinking Skills*: www.educationscotland.gov.uk/resources/s/skillsinpracticethinkingskills/knowing.asp

- University of Cambridge. Thinking Together: https://thinkingtogether.educ.cam.ac.uk
- University of Cambridge/Professor Neil Mercer (2015) Thinking together: http://thinkingtogether.educ.cam.ac.uk/resources
- Transitions: www.dundee.ac.uk/eswce/research/resources

U

- UK Council for Child Internet Safety (UKCCIS): www.gov.uk/government/groups/uk-council-for-child-internet-safety-ukccis

Unions:

- Irish National Teachers' Organisation, Northern Ireland: www.into.ie/NI
- National Association of Schoolmasters/Union of Women Teachers, England, Wales, Scotland and Northern Ireland: NASUWT www.nasuwt.org.uk
- National Education Union: https://neu.org.uk/best-atl-and-nut
- Scottish Secondary Teachers' Association, Scotland: www.ssta.org.uk
- The Educational Institute of Scotland (EIS): www.eis.org.uk
- Ulster Teachers Union, Northern Ireland: www.utu.edu
- Voice, previously the Professional Association of Teachers, England, Wales and Northern Ireland: www.voicetheunion.org.uk

REFERENCES

Abbiati, G., Azzolini, D., Piazzalunga, D., Rettore, E. and Schizzerotto, A. (2018) *MENTEP Evaluation Report, Results of the Field Trials: The Impact of the Technology-Enhanced Self-Assessment Tool (TET-SAT)*, Brussels: European Schoolnet.

ACARA (Australian Curriculum, Assessment and Reporting Authority) (2016) *Australian Curriculum*. Available from: www.australiancurriculum.edu.au/f-10-curriculum/general-capabilities/literacy/ (accessed 12 November 2018).

Adair, J. (1997) *Leadership Skills*, London: Institute of Personnel and Development.

Ainscow, M., Dyson, A. and Hopwood, L. (2016a) Pressures on school standards are fuelling a rise in pupil segregation, TeachWire. Available from: www.teachwire.net/news/pressures-on-school-standards-are-fuelling-a-rise-in-pupil-segregation

Ainscow, M., Dyson, A., Hopwood, L. and Thomson, S. (2016b) *Primary Schools Responding to Diversity: Barriers and Possibilities*, York: Cambridge Primary Review Trust.

Alboraz, A., Pearson, D., Farrell, P. and Howes, A. (2009) *The Impact of Adult Support Staff on Pupils and Mainstream Schools*, London: University of London Institute of Education. Available from: http://eppi.ioe.ac.uk/cms/Portals/0/PDF%20reviews%20and%20summaries/Support%20 staff%20Rpt.pdf?ver=2009-05-05-165528-197 (accessed 23 September 2018).

Alexander, R. (2004) *Towards Dialogic Teaching: Rethinking Classroom Talk*, Cambridge: Dialogos.

Alexander, R. J. (2005) *Towards Dialogic Teaching: Rethinking Classroom Talk*. Dialogues: York.

Alexander, R. J. (2015) www.robinalexander.org.uk/dialogic-teaching.

Anderson, L.W. and Krathwohl, D. (eds.) (2001) *A Taxonomy for Learning Teaching and Assessing: A Revision of Bloom's Taxonomy of Educational Objectives*, New York: Longman.

Anstey, M. and Bull, G. (2018a) *Foundations of Multiliteracies: Reading, Writing and Talking in the 21st Century*, Abingdon: Routledge.

Anstey, M. and Bull, G. (2018b) *Elaborating Multiliteracies Through Multimodal Texts: Changing Classroom Practices and Developing Teacher Pedagogies*, Abingdon: Routledge.

Avramidis, E. and Norwich, B. (2002) 'Teachers' attitudes towards integration/inclusion: A review of the literature', *European Journal of Special Needs Education*, 17(2), 129–147.

Baglieri, S. and Shapiro, A. (2017) *Disability Studies and the Inclusive Classroom: Critical Practices for Embracing Diversity in Education*, Abingdon: Routledge.

Baggaley, J. (2018) quoted in Government takes 'major step' towards better PSHE for all. Available from: www.pshe-association.org.uk/news/government-takes-'major-step'-towards-better-pshe (accessed 18 August 2019).

Ball, S. (2008) 'Performativity, privatisation, professionals and the state'. In: B. Cunningham (ed.) *Exploring Professionalism*, London: Bedford Way Papers.

Ball, S. (2018) 'The tragedy of state education in England: Reluctance, compromise and muddle – a system in disarray. Sir John Cass Foundation Lecture 7 March 2018', *Journal of the British Academy*, 6, 207–238.

Bandura, A. (1982) 'Self-efficacy mechanism in human agency', *American Psychologist*, 37, 122–47.

Barnes, C. (2012) 'The social model of disability: Valuable or irrelevant?' In: N. Watson, A. Roulstone and C. Thomas (eds.) *The Routledge Handbook of Disability Studies*, Abingdon: Routledge, pp. 12–29.

Barnes, D. (1976) *From Communication to Curriculum*, Harmondsworth: Penguin.

Barnes, D. and Todd, F. (1977) *Communication and Learning in Small Groups*, Abingdon: Routledge.

Barnette, J., Orletsky, S. and Sattes, B. (1994) Evaluation of teacher classroom questioning behaviours. Paper presented at the *Third Annual National Evaluation Institute Field Symposium*, Gatlinburg.

Barrow, R. (1984) *Giving Teaching Back to Teachers*, Brighton: Wheatsheaf.

Bates, B. (2017) *A Quick Guide to Special Needs and Disabilities*, London: Sage Publications.

Battersby, J. (2006) 'Learning about teaching: Learning from experience'. In: J. Battersby and J. Gordon (eds.), *Preparing to Teach*, London: Routledge.

Beacco, J., Flemming, M., Goullier, F., Thurmann, E. and Vollmer, H. (2015) *The Language Dimension in all Subjects: A Handbook for Curriculum Development in Teacher Training*. Language Policy Unit, Directorate of Democratic Citizenship and Participation, Council of Europe. Available from: www.ecml.at/coe-docs/language-dimensions-subjects-EN.pdf (accessed 14 November 2018).

Beadle, P. (2010) *How to Teach*, Carmarthen: Crown House.

Bellou, I., Papachristos, N.M. and Mikropoulos, T.A. (2018) 'Digital learning technologies in chemistry education: A review'. In: D. Sampsom, D. Ifenthaler, J.M. Spector, and P. Isaias (eds.), *Digital Technologies: Sustainable Innovations for Improving Teaching and Learning*. Cham, Switzerland: Springer, (pp. 57–80)

Bennett, T. (2017) 'Running a room: How routines and responses are the key to better behaviour', Lecture, University College London Institute of Education, 8 February.

Bennett-Worth, S.L. (n.d.) *The Digital Performer*. Available from: https://thedigitalperformer.co.uk/a-z-of-digital-technology-for-performing-arts/ (accessed 12 November 2018).

BERA (British Educational Research Association) (2018) *Ethical Guidelines for Educational Research*, London: BERA. Available from: www.bera.ac.uk/researchers-resources/publications/ethical-guidelines-for-educational-research-2018 (accessed 18 August 2019).

BERA-RSA (British Educational Research Association-Royal Society of Arts) (2014a) *Research and the Teaching Profession: Building the Capacity for a Self-Improving Education System*, London: BERA. Available from: www.bera.ac.uk/wp-content/uploads/2013/12/BERA-RSA-Research-Teaching-Profession-FULL-REPORT-for-web.pdf?noredirect=1 (accessed 18 August 2019).

BERA-RSA (British Educational Research Association-Royal Society of Arts) (2014b) *The Role of Research in Teacher Education: Reviewing the Evidence, Interim Report for the BERA-RSA Inquiry*, London: BERA. Available from: www.bera.ac.uk/wp-content/uploads/2014/02/BERA-RSA-Interim-Report.pdf?noredirect=1

Bennett, T. (2017) *Creating a Culture: How School Leaders Can Optimise Behaviour*, London: DfE. Available from: www.gov.uk/government/publications/behaviour-in-schools (accessed 25 November 2018).

Berrington, A., Roberts, S. and Tammes, P. (2016) 'Educational aspirations among UK Young Teenagers: Exploring the role of gender, class and ethnicity', *British Educational Research Journal*, 42(5), 729-756.

Biesta, G. (2009) 'Good education in an age of measurement: On the need to reconnect with the question of purpose in education', *Educational Assessment, Evaluation and Accountability*, 21(1), 33-46.

Biggs, J. and Collis, K. (1982) *Evaluating the Quality of Learning the SOLO Taxonomy*, New York: Academic Press.

Black, P., Harrison, C., Lee, C., Marshall, B. and William, D. (2003) *Assessment for Learning: Putting It into Practice*, Maidenhead: Open University Press.

Black, P., Harrison, C., Lee, C., Marshall, B. and William, D. (2004) 'Working inside the black box: Assessment for learning in the classroom', *Phi Delta Kappan*, 86(1), 9-21.

Blanchard, K., Fowler, S. and Hawkins, L. (2018) *Self-Leadership and the One Minute Manager, Gain the Mindset and Skillset for Getting What You Need to Succeed*, London: Thorsons.

Blatchford, P., Bassett, P., Brown, P., Martin, C., Russell, A. and Webster, R. (2009) *Deployment and Impact of Support Staff (DISS) Project. Research Brief*, London: Institute of Education, University of London. Available from: www.maximisingtas.co.uk (accessed 21 September 2018).

Blatchford, P., Russell, A. and Webster, R. (2012) *Reassessing the Impact of Teaching Assistants*, Abingdon: Routledge.

Bleiklie, I. (2006) 'Policy regimes and policy making'. In: M. Kogan, M. Bauer, I. Bleiklie and M. Henkel (eds.) *Transforming Higher Education: A Comparative Study*, 2nd edn, Dordrecht, the Netherlands: Springer, pp. 39–68. (Available as an e-book from the University of Liverpool Library.)

Bloom, B.S., Englehart, M.D., Furst, E.J., Hill, W.H. and Krathwohl, D.R. (eds.) (1956) *Taxonomy of Educational Objectives: The Classification of Educational Goals–Handbook I: Cognitive Domain*, New York: David McKay.

Bolton, G. (2010) *Reflective Practice*, London: Sage.

Bonell, C., Humphrey, N., Fletcher, A., Moore, L., Anderson, R. and Campbell, R. (2014) 'Why schools should promote students' health and wellbeing', *British Medical Journal*, 348, g3078.

Booth, N. (2019) 'In-school summative and minute-by-minute formative assessment in the classroom', In: S. Capel, M. Leask and S. Younie (eds.) *Learning to Teach in the Secondary School: A Companion to School Experience*, 8th edn, Abingdon: Routledge, pp. 411–425.

Booth, T., Ainscow, M., Black-Hawkins, K., Vaughan, M. and Shaw, L. (2002) *Index for Inclusion*, Bristol: Centre for Studies on Inclusive Education.

Bourdieu, P. (1973) *Cultural Reproduction and Social Reproduction in Knowledge, Education and Cultural Change*, London: Tavistock.

Bradshaw, P. and Younie, S. (2018) 'Understanding online ethics and digital identity'. In: S. Younie and P. Bradshaw (eds.) *Debates in Computing and ICT Education*, Abingdon: Routledge.

Brooks, B., Gilbuena, D., Krause, S. and Koretsky, M. (2014) 'Using word clouds for fast, formative assessment of students' short written responses', *Chemical Engineering Education*, 48(4), 190–198.

Brooker, P. (2017) *Re-Imagining Learning. How Can Ofsted and Its Framework Help to Re-Imagine Learning so That the Curriculum Gives all Pupils Opportunities to Succeed?* Presentation by Ofsted at Headteacher Conference, Bedford.

Bruner, J.S. (1960) *The Process of Education*, Boston, MA: Harvard University Press.

Bruner, J.S. (1966) *Toward a Theory of Instruction*, Cambridge, MA: Harvard University Press.

Bryant, P. and Nunes, T. (2004) 'Morphology and spelling'. In: T. Nunes and P. Bryant (eds.) *Handbook of Children's Literacy*, Dordrecht: Springer.

Burke, R.J. and Cooper, C.L. (eds.) (2006) *Inspiring Leaders*, London: Routledge.

Burn, K. (2007) 'Professional knowledge and identity in a contested discipline: Challenges for student teachers and teacher educators', *Oxford Review of Education*, 33(4), 445–467.

Burnage, S. (2017) 'Leading a support staff team', *SecEd*, 05 July. Available from: www.sec-ed.co.uk/best-practice/leading-a-support-staff-team/ (accessed 22 September 2018).

Busby, E. (2017) *Exclusive: Justine Greening Confirms 90 Percent EBacc Target to be Pushed Back*. Available from: www.tes.com/news/school-news/breaking-news/exclusive-justine-greening-confirms-90-cent-ebacc-target-be-pushed (accessed 26 September 2017).

Bush, T., Abbot, I., Glover, D. and Smith, R. (2012) *Establishing and Developing Highly Performing Leadership Teams*, Nottingham: National College for School Leadership. Available from: www.stjosephrc.co.uk/school/images/TeachersAsLearners/establishing-and-developing-high-performing-leadership-teams.pdf (accessed 2 September 2018).

Busher, H. and Harris, A. (1999) 'Leadership of school subject areas: Tensions and dimensions of managing in the middle', *School Leadership and Management*, 19(3), 305–317.

Butt, G. and Lance, A. (2009) ''I am not the teacher!' Some effects of remodelling the roles of teaching assistants in English primary schools', *Education 3–13: International Journal of Primary, Elementary and Early Years Education*, 37(3), 219–231. Available from: www.tandfonline.com/doi/abs/10.1080/03004270802349430 (accessed 4 April 2013).

Byrne, R. (2013) *Free Technology for Teachers: Kahoot!–Create Quizzes and Surveys Your Students Can Answer on any Device*. Available from: www.freetech4teachers.com/2013/11/kahoot-create-quizzes-and-surveysyour.html (accessed 18 August 2019).

Cameron, E. and Green, M. (2012) *Making Sense of Change Management: A Complete Guide to the Models, Tools and Techniques of Oranizational Change*, 3rd edn, London: Kogan.

Capel, S., Leask, M. and Younie, S. (eds.) (2019) *Learning to Teach in the Secondary School: A Companion to School Experience*, 8th edn, Abingdon: Routledge.

Capel, S., Leask, M. and Turner, T. (eds.) (2010) *Readings for Learning to Teach in the Secondary School: A Companion to M Level Study*, Abingdon: Routledge.

Carnell, E. and Lodge, C. (2002a) 'Support for students' learning: What the form tutor can do', *Pastoral Care in Education*, 20(4), 12-20.

Carnell, E. and Lodge, C. (2002b) *Supporting Effective Learning*, London: Paul Chapman Publishing.

Carpenter, B., Ashdown, R. and Bovair, K. (eds.) (2017) *Enabling Access: Effective Teaching and Learning for Pupils with Learning Difficulties*, Abingdon: Routledge.

Carter, A. (2015) *Carter Review of Initial Teacher Training (ITT)*. Available from: https://assets. publishing.service.gov.uk/government/uploads/system/uploads/attachment_data/ file/399957/Carter_Review.pdf (accessed 18 August 2019).

Casel (the Collaborative for Academic, Social and Emotional Learning) (2016) *Casel Website for Acdemic, Social and Emotional Learning*. Available from: www.casel.org/ (accessed 24 November 2018).

Caslin, M. (2014) 'Behaviour, emotion and social attitudes: The education of "challenging" pupils'. In: D. Bolt (ed.) *Changing Social Attitudes Toward Disability: Perspectives from Historical Cultural, and Educational Studies*, Abingdon: Routledge.

Cazden, C. (2001) *Classroom Discourse: The Language of Teaching and Learning*, Portsmouth: Greenwood Press.

CBI (Confederation of British Industry) and Pearson Education (2016) *The Right Combination: The CBI/Pearson Education and Skills Survey 2016*, London: CBI.

Chatzitheochari, S., Parsons, S. and Platt, L. (2014) 'Bullying experiences among disabled children and young people in England: Evidence from two longitudinal studies', Department of Quantitative Social Science Working Paper No. 14-11, London: Institute of Education.

Cherniss, C. (2006) 'Leadership and emotional intelligence'. In: R.J. Burke and C.L. Cooper (eds.) *Inspiring Leaders*, London: Routledge, pp. 132-148.

Childs, A., Burn, K. and McNicholl, J. (2013) 'What influences the learning cultures of subject departments in secondary schools? A study of four subject departments in England', *Teacher Development*, 17(1), 35-54.

Chopra, R. and Uitto, D. (2015) 'Programming and planning within a multi-faceted classroom'. In: D. Chambers (ed.) *Working with Teaching Assistants and Other Support Staff for Inclusive Education* (International Perspectives on Inclusive Education, Volume 4), Bingley: Emerald Group Publishing Ltd, pp. 3-25. Available from: http://dx.doi.org/10.1108/S1479-363620150000004001 (accessed 28 September 2017).

Church, A. (2001) *Bloom's Digital Taxonomy*. Available from: http://burtonslifelearning.pbworks. com/f/BloomDigitalTaxonomy2001.pdf (accessed 16 November 2018).

Claxton, G. (2002) *Building Learning Power: Helping Young People Become Better Learners*, Bristol: TOL.

Cohen, L., Manion, L. and Morrison, K. (2017) *Research Methods in Education*, 8th edn, London: Routledge.

Coleman, J.C. (2011) *The Nature of Adolescence*, 4th edn, Abingdon: Routledge.

Cook, V., Major, L., Hennessy, S., with Ahmed, Calcagni and others (2018) *MESHGUIDE: Classroom Dialogue and Learning Cambridge Educational Dialogue Research Group (CEDiR)*. Available from: www.meshagain.meshguides.org (accessed 18 August 2019).

Coskeran, S. (2013) 'Effective teacher mentoring', *SecEd*, 3 October. Available from: www.sec-ed. co.uk/best-practice/effective-teacher-mentoring (accessed 24 November 2017).

Cowley, S. (2002) 'Nothing beats the sound of silence', *Times Educational Supplement*, 22 November. Available from: www.tes.com/news/nothing-beats-sound-silence (accessed 22 August 2019).

Cox, B. (1991) *Cox on Cox: An English Curriculum for the 1900s*, London: Hodder and Stoughton.

Creative Education (2015) 'Delegation: 7 Ways outstanding school leaders get it right', *Creative Education Blog*, 11 May 2015. Available from: www.creativeeducation.co.uk/blog/delegation-for-success/ (accessed 2 December 2018).

Cremin, H., Thomas, G., Vincett, K. (2005) 'Working with teaching assistants: Three models evaluated', *Research Papers in Education*, 20(4), 413-432. doi: 10.1080/02671520500335881.

Cresswell, J.W. (2018) *Educational Research: Planning, Conducting and Evaluating Qualitative Research*, 6th edn, London: Pearson.

Cross, J. (2014) 'Introduction to Kahoot for your classroom assessments'. Available from: www. youtube.com/watch?v=PYfoRRtLXys (accessed 18 August 2019).

Cuerden, J. (2018) 'Mentoring the newly qualified teacher'. In: T. Wright (ed.) *How to Be a Brilliant Mentor: Developing Outstanding Teachers*, 2nd edn, Abingdon: Routledge, pp. 147-161.

Cultural Learning Alliance (2017) *GCSE Results Announced Today See a Continuing Free Fall in Arts Subject Entries.* Available from: https://culturallearningalliance.org.uk/gcse-results-announced-today-see-a-continuing-free-fall-in-arts-subject-entries/ (accessed 18 August 2019).

Cych, L., Williams, L. and Younie, S. (2018) 'Using Web 2.0 technologies to enhance learning and teaching'. In: S. Younie and P. Bradshaw (eds.), *Debates in Computing and ICT Education*, Abingdon: Routledge.

Danielson, C. (2007) 'Teachers as leaders: The many faces of leadership', *Educational Leadership*, 65(1), 14–19.

Day, C., Edwards, A., Griffiths, A. and Gu, Q. (2011) 'Beyond survival – Teachers and Reslience'. In: *Key Messages from an ESRC-Funded Seminar Series*, Notttingham, University of Nottingham.

DCFS (2008) *Byron Review: Safer Children in a Digital World*, Nottingham: DCSF Publications.

DCFS (2010) *Do We Have Safer Children in a Digital World? A Review of the Progress since the 2008 Byron Review*, Nottingham: DCSF Publications.

DCSF (Department for Children, Schools and Families) (2010) *Salt Review: Independent Review of Teacher Supply for Pupils with Severe, Profound and Multiple Learning Difficulties (SLD and PMLD)*, Nottingham: DCSF Publications.

de Boer, A., Pijl, S. and Minnaert, A. (2010) 'Regular primary schoolteachers' attitudes, towards inclusive education: A review of the literature', *International Journal of Inclusive Education*, 15(3), 331–353.

Dellos, R. (2015) 'Kahoot! A digital game resource for learning', *International Journal of Instructional Technology and Distance Learning*, 12(4), 49–52.

DES (Department of Education and Science) (1975) A Language for Life, *The Committee of Enquiry Chaired by Sir Alan Bullock*, London: HMSO.

DES (Department of Education and Science) (1988) *The National Curriculum Framework for England and Wales*, London: HMSO.

Dewhirst, S., Pickett, K., Speller, V., Shepherd, J., Byrne, J., Almond, P., Grace, M., Hartwell, D. and Roderick, P. (2014) 'Are trainee teachers being adequately prepared to promote the health and well-being of school children? A survey of current practice', *Journal of Public Health*, 36(3), 467–475. doi: 10.1093/pubmed/fdt103.

DfE (Department for Education) (1994) *Code of Practice on the Identification and Assessment of Special Educational Needs*, London: DFE.

DfE (Department for Education) (2010) *The Importance of Teaching: The Schools' White Paper*, Norwich: The Stationary Office. Available from: www.gov.uk/government/publications/the-importance-of-teaching-the-schools-white-paper-2010 (accessed 27 November 2018).

DfE (Department for Education) (2011) *Teachers' Standards. Guidance for School Leaders, School Staff and Governing Bodies*, London: DfE. Available from: www.gov.uk/government/publications/teachers-standards (accessed 23 November 2018).

DfE (Department for Education) (2012a) *The Impact of Pupil Behaviour and Wellbeing on Educational Outcomes*, London: DfE.

DfE (Department for Education) (2012) *Pupil Behaviour in Schools in England: RR* 218, London: DfE.

DfE (Department for Education) (2013a) *English Programmes of Study: Key Stages 1 and 2 National Curriculum in England.* Available from: https://assets.publishing.service.gov.uk/government/uploads/system/uploads/attachment_data/file/335186/PRIMARY_national_curriculum_-_English_220714.pdf (accessed 1 November 2018).

DfE (Department for Education) (2013b) *English Programmes of Study: Key Stage 3 National Curriculum in England.* Available from: https://assets.publishing.service.gov.uk/government/uploads/system/uploads/attachment_data/file/244215/SECONDARY_national_curriculum_-_English2.pdf (accessed 1 November 2018).

DfE (Department for Education) (2013c) *National Curriculum: Secondary Curriculum.* Available from: www.gov.uk/government/publications/national-curriculum-in-england-secondary-curriculum (accessed 10 May 2018).

DfE (Department for Education) (2013d) *Reforming the Accountability System for Secondary Schools*, London: Crown Copyright. Available from: www.gov.uk/government/speeches/reforming-the-accountability-system-for-secondary-schools (accessed 18 August 2019).

DfE (Department of Education) (2013e) *Reforming the Accountability System for Secondary Schools: Government Response to the February to May 2013 Consultation on Secondary School Accountability*, London: Crown Copyright.

DfE (Department for Education) (2014a) *National Curriculum in England: Framework for Key Stages 1–4*, Norwich: The Stationary Office. Available from: www.gov.uk/government/publications/national-curriculum-in-england-framework-for-key-stages-1-to-4/the-national-curriculum-in-england-framework-for-key-stages-1-to-4 (accessed 27 November 2018).

DfE (Department of Education) (2014b) *Secondary Accountability Measures (Including Progress 8 and Attainment 8)*, Norwich: The Stationary Office. Available from: www.gov.uk/government/publications/progress-8-school-performance-measure (accessed 27 November 2018).

DfE (Department for Education) (2014c) *National Curriculum in England: Mathematics Programme of Study*. Available from: www.gov.uk/government/publications/national-curriculum-in-england-mathematics-programmes-of-study/national-curriculum-in-england-mathematics-programmes-of-study (accessed 24 November 2018).

DfE (Department for Education) (2014d) *The National Curriculum in England: Key Stages 3 and 4 Framework Document*, London: Crown Copyright. Available from: www.gov.uk/government/publications/national-curriculum-in-england-secondary-curriculum (accessed 24 November 2018).

DfE (Department for Education) (2015a) *Personal, Social, Health and Economic Education: A Review of Impact and Effective Practice*, London: DfE.

DfE (Department of Education) (2015b) *Progress 8 Measure in 2016 and 2017: Guide for Maintained Secondary Schools, Academies and Free Schools*, London: Crown Copyright.

DfE (Department for Education) (2015c) *The Final Report of the Commission on Assessment without Levels*, London: Department for Education. Available from: www.gov.uk/government/uploads/system/uploads/attachment_data/file/483058/Commission_on_Assessment_Without_Levels_-_report.pdf (accessed 1 December 2018).

DfE (Department for Education) (2015d) *Government Response to the Workload Challenge*, London: DfE. Available from: https://assets.publishing.service.gov.uk/government/uploads/system/uploads/attachment_data/file/415874/Government_Response_to_the_Workload_Challenge.pdf (accessed 1 December 2018).

DfE (Department for Education) (2016a) *National Statistics: School Workforce in England: November 2016*. Available from: https://assets.publishing.service.gov.uk/government/uploads/system/uploads/attachment_data/file/620825/SFR25_2017_MainText.pdf (accessed 24 November 2018).

DfE (Department for Education) (2016b) *Mental Health and Behaviour in Schools: Departmental Advice for School Staff*. Available from: https://assets.publishing.service.gov.uk/government/uploads/system/uploads/attachment_data/file/508847/Mental_Health_and_Behaviour_-_advice_for_Schools_160316.pdf (accessed 01 October 2018).

DfE (Department of Education) (2016c) *Progress 8 Measure in 2016, 2017 and 2018: Guide for Maintained Secondary Schools, Academies and Free Schools*, London: Crown Copyright. Available from: https://dera.ioe.ac.uk/27619/1/Progress_8_school_performance_measure_13_Oct_update.pdf (accessed 18 August 2019).

DfE (Department for Education) (2016d) *Progress 8. How Progress 8 and Attainment 8 Measures Are Calculated*. Available from: www.gov.uk/government/uploads/system/uploads/attachment_data/file/561021/Progress_8_and_Attainment_8_how:measures_are_calculated.pdf (accessed 2 January 2018).

DfE (Department for Education) (2017a) *Special Education Needs in England-January 2017*, SFR 37/2017. Available from: https://assets.publishing.service.gov.uk/government/uploads/system/uploads/attachment_data/file/633031/SFR37_2017_Main_Text.pdf (accessed 18 August 2019).

DfE (Department of Education) (2017b) *Policy Paper English Baccalaureate EBacc*. Available from: www.gov.uk/government/publications/english-baccalaureate-ebacc/english-baccalaureate-ebacc. (accessed 18 August 2019).

DfE (Department for Education) (2017c) *National Professional Qualifications: Frameworks*, London: DfE. Available from: www.gov.uk/government/publications/national-professional-qualifications-frameworks (accessed 17 October 2018).

DfE (Department for Education) (2018a) *Reducing Teacher Workload*. Available from: www.gov.uk/government/publications/reducing-teachers-workload/reducing-teachers-workload (accessed 1 December 2018).

DfE (Department of Education) (2018b) *Workload Reduction Toolkit*, Norwich: The Stationary Office. Available from: www.gov.uk/government/collections/workload-reduction-toolkit (accessed 27 November 2018).

DfE (Department for Education) (2018c) *Keeping Children Safe in Education: Statutory Guidance for Schools and Colleges.* Available from: https://assets.publishing.service.gov.uk/government/uploads/system/uploads/attachment_data/file/741314/Keeping_Children_Safe_in_Education__3_September_2018_14.09.18.pdf (accessed 01 November 2018).

DfE (Department for Education) (2018d) *Essential Digital Skills Framework,* London: Department for Education. Available from: www.gov.uk/government/publications/essential-digital-skills-framework/essential-digital-skills-framework (accessed 18 August 2019).

DfE and DoH (Department for Education and Department of Health) (2015) *Special Educational Needs and Disability Code of Practice: 0 to 25 years: Statutory Guidance for Organisations which Work with and Support Children and Young People who have Special Educational Needs or Disabilities,* London: Department for Education and Department of Health. Available from: www.gov.uk/government/publications/send-code-of-practice-0-to-25 (accessed 18 October 2018).

DfES (Department for Education and Skills) (2001b) *Special Educational Needs Code of Practice,* London: DfES.

DfES (Department for Education and Skills) (2002) *Transition from Year 6 to Year 7; Units of Work.* London: DfES.

DfES (Department for Education and Skills) (2003a) *Raising Standards and Tackling Workload: A National Agreement,* London: DfES, 0172/2003.

DfES (Department for Education and Skills) (2003b) *Developing Children's Social, Emotional and Behavioural Skills: Guidance,* London: DfES.

DfES (Department for Education and Skills) (2004) *Creating Conditions for Learning, Unit 20, Classroom Management,* London: DfES.

DfES (Department for Education and Skills) (2006) *Learning Outside the Classroom Manifesto,* London: DfES. Available from: www.lotc.org.uk/wp-content/uploads/2011/03/G1.-LOtC-Manifesto.pdf (accessed 25 November 2018).

Dix, P. (2010) 'Behaviour problem: The kids are running riot', *Times Educational Supplement,* 5 April. Available from: www.tes.com/news/behaviour-problem-kids-are-running-riot (accessed 22 August 2019).

Dix, P. (2012) 'Starting out on the right foot'. *Times Educational Supplement,* 7 September, 8–9. Available from: www.tes.com/news/starting-right-foot (accessed 22 August 2019).

Dix, P. (2017) *When the Adults Change, Everything Changes,* Carmarthen, UK: Independent Thinking Press.

DoH (Department of Health) (2009) *Healthy Child Programme from 5 to 19 Years,* London: Department of Health. Available from: https://assets.publishing.service.gov.uk/government/uploads/system/uploads/attachment_data/file/492086/HCP_5_to_19.pdf (accessed 01 November 2018).

Dreyfus, H.L. and Dreyfus, S.E. (1986) *Mind over Machine: The Power of Human Intuition and Expertise in the Age of the Computer,* Oxford: Basil Blackwell.

Dweck, C. (2000) *Self-Theories: Their Role in Motivation, Personality and Development,* Philadelphia, PA: Psychology Press.

Dweck, C. (2017) *Mindset: Changing the Way You Think to Fulfil Your Potential,* 6th edn, New York: Robinson.

Durrant, J. and Holden, G. (2006) *Teachers Leading Change: Doing Research for School Improvement,* London: Paul Chapman Publishing.

Edmondson, A. (2008) 'The competitive imperative of learning', *Harvard Business Review,* 86(7–8), 60–67.

Edmondson, A.C. and Lei, Z. (2014) 'Psychological safety: The history, renaissance and future of an interpersonal construct', *Annual Review of Organizational Psychology and Organizational Behavior,* 1(1), 23–43.

EEF (Education Endowment Framework) (2018) *Digital Technology.* Available from: https://educationendowmentfoundation.org.uk/evidence-summaries/teaching-learning-toolkit/digital-technology/ (accessed 17 November 2018).

EEF (Education Endowment Framework) (2018) *Projects and Evaluation.* Available from: https://educationendowmentfoundation.org.uk/projects-and-evaluation/ (accessed 24 August 2019).

Eiraldi, R.B., Mazzuca, L.B., Clarke, A.T. and Power, T.J. (2006) 'Service utilization among ethnic minority children with ADHD: A model of help-seeking behavior', *Administration and Policy in Mental Health and Mental Health Services Research,* 33(5), 607–622.

Elliott, J. (1991) *Action Research for Educational Change*, London: McGraw-Hill.

Elliott, J.G. (2007) *Keynote Address, Behaviour for Learning Conference*, University of Warwick, 24 May.

Elliott, J.G. (2009) 'The nature of teacher authority and teacher expertise', *Support for Learning*, 24(4), 197-203.

Erlam, G., Smythe, L. and Wright-St Clair, W. (2017) 'Simulation is not a pedagogy', *Open Journal of Nursing*, 7, 779-787.

Evangelou, M., Taggart, B., Sylva, K., Melhuish, E., Sammons, P. and Siraj-Blatchford, I. (2008) (eds.) *What Makes a Successful Transition from Primary to Secondary School?* London: DCSF.

Fairbrother, R. (1975) 'The reliability of teachers' judgements of the abilities tested by multiple choice items', *Educational Research*, 17(3), 202-210.

Faupel, A. (ed.) (2003) *Emotional Literacy: Assessment and Intervention: Ages 11 to 16*, London: nferNelson.

Fautley, M. (2009) 'Assessment for learning in music'. In: J. Evans and C. Philpott (eds.) *A Practical Guide to Teaching Music in the Secondary School*, Abingdon: Routledge, pp. 63-72.

Fautley, M. and Kinsella, V. (2015) 'Bloom's Taxonomy and higher order thinking'. In: N. Economidou Stavrou and M. Stakelum (eds.) *Every Learner Counts: Democracy and Inclusion in Music Education*. Volume 4 of European Perspectives on Music Education. Innsbruck, Austria: Helbling Verlag, (pp. 111-123).

Fautley, M. and Savage, J. (2008) *Assessment for Learning and Teaching in Secondary Schools*, Exeter: Learning Matters.

Fenwick, A.J.J., Minty, S. and Priestley, M. (2013) 'Swimming against the tide: A case study of an integrated social studies department', *Curriculum Journal*, 24(3), 454-474.

Findon, M. and Johnston-Wilder, S. (2019) 'Developing your resilience: Managing stress, workload and time'. In: S. Capel, M. Leask and S. Younie (eds.) *Learning to Teach in the Secondary School: A Companion to School Experience*, 8th edn, Abingdon: Routledge, pp .43-59.

Flanders, N. (1970) 'Analysing teacher behaviour as part of the teaching-learning process'. *Educational Leadership*. Available from: https://pdfs.semanticscholar.org/d144/08462d090a 88a1eaac38df9e92f09aa2938f.pdf (accessed 18 August 2019).

Fletcher, S. (1997) 'ITE and form tutoring: A question of responsibility?', *Mentoring and Tutoring: Partnership in Learning*, 4(3), 45-51.

Flores, M.A. and Day, C. (2006) 'Contexts which shape and reshape new teachers' identities: A multi-perspective study', *Teaching and Teacher Education*, 22(2), 219-232.

Freebody, P. and Luke, A. (1990) 'Literacies programs: Debates and demands in cultural context', *Prospect: Australian Journal of TESOL*, 5(7), 7-16.

Freidson, E. (2001) *Professionalism: The Third Logic*, Cambridge: Polity Press.

Friend, L. (2017) 'IRE and content area literacies: A critical analysis of classroom discourse', *Australian Journal of Language and Literacy*, 40(2), 124-134.

Furlong, J. and Whitty, G. (2017) *Knowledge and the Study of Education*, Oxford: Symposium Books.

Galton, M., Morrison, I. and Pell, T. (2003) 'Transfer and transition in English schools: Reviewing the evidence', *International Journal of Educational Research*, 33(4), 341-363.

Gambling Commission (2017) *Young People and Gambling Report*. Available from: http://live-gamblecom.cloud.contensis.com/PDF/survey-data/Young-People-and-Gambling-2017-Report.pdf (accessed 3 May 2018).

Gardner, P. (2002) *Strategies and Resources for Teaching and Learning in Inclusive Classrooms*, London: David Fulton Publishers.

Gardner, P. (2014) 'Becoming a teacher of writing: Primary student teachers reviewing their relationship with writing'. *English in Education*, 48(2), 128-148.

Garner, P. (2016) 'Managing classroom behaviour: Adopting a positive approach'. In: S. Capel, M. Leask and S. Younie (eds.) *Learning to Teach in the Secondary School: A Companion to School Experience*, 7th edn, Abingdon: Routledge, pp. 180-199.

Garner, P. (2019) 'Managing classroom behaviour: Adopting a positive approach', in S. Capel, M. Leask and S. Younie (eds.) *Learning to Teach in the Secondary School: A Companion to School Experience*, 8th edn, Abingdon: Routledge, pp.164-183.

Garnett, J. (2013) 'Beyond a constructivist curriculum: A critique of competing paradigms in music education'. *British Journal of Music Education*, 30(2), 161-175.

Gateshead Council (2009) *Understanding and Managing Change*. Available from: www.gateshead.gov.uk/DocumentLibrary/council/pois/managingreactionstochange.pdf (accessed 25 May 2017).

Ghaye, T. (2011) *Teaching and Learning through Reflective Practice: A Practical Guide for Positive Action*, 2nd edn, New York: Routledge.

Gibbs, G. (1988) *Learning by Doing: A Guide to Teaching and Learning Methods*, Oxford: Oxford Polytechnic, Further Education Unit.

Gill, N.S. (2018) *Greek and Latin Roots*, ThoughtCo. Available from: www.thoughtco.com/greeklatin-roots-stems-prefixes-affixes-4070803 (accessed 14 November 2018). Group work/DARTs

Gill, R. (2011) *Theory and Practice of Leadership*, 2nd edn, London: Sage.

Giroux, H.A. (2001) *Theory and Resistance in Education: Towards a Pedagogy for the Opposition*, Santa Barbara, CA: Greenwood Publishing Group.

Glazzard, J. (2013) 'A critical interrogation of the contemporary discourses associated with inclusive education in England', *Journal of Research in Special Educational Needs*, 13(3), 182–188.

Goldsmith, H. (2018) 'How to develop impactful CPD for support staff', *Times Educational Supplement*, January 2018. Available from: www.tes.com/news/how-develop-impactful-cpd-support-staff (accessed 25 October 2018).

Goleman, D. (1996) *Emotional Intelligence. Why It Can Matter More than IQ*, London: Bloomsbury.

Goleman, D. (1998) 'What makes a leader?', *Harvard Business Review*, 76(6), 92–102.

Goleman, D. (2000) 'Leadership that gets results', *Harvard Business Review*, 78(2), 78–90.

Goleman, D. (2011) *Leadership: The Power of Emotional Intelligence*, Northampton: More Than Sound.

Goleman, D., Boyatzis, R. and McKee, A. (2013) *Primal Leadership: Unleashing the Power of Emotional Intelligence*, Boston, MA: Harvard Business School Press.

Goodley, D. and Runswick-Cole, K. (2016) 'Becoming dishuman: Thinking about the human through dis/ability', *Discourse: Studies in the Cultural Politics of Education*, 37(1), 1–15. doi: 10.1080/01596306.2014.930021.

Gough, P. and Tunmer, W. (1986) 'Decoding, reading and reading disability', *Remedial and Special Education*, 7(1), 6–10.

Gov.uk (1993) *Education Act 1993*, London: HMSO. Available from: www.legislation.gov.uk/ukpga/1993/35/pdfs/ukpga_19930035_en.pdf (accessed 1 December 2018).

Gov.uk (2018) *Education for a Connected World*. Available from: www.gov.uk/government/publications/education-for-a-connected-world (accessed 12 August 2019).

Graves, S. and Williams, K. (2017) 'Investigating the role of the HLTA in supporting learning in English schools', *Cambridge Journal of Education*, 47(2), 265–276. doi:10.1080/0305764X.2016.1157138.

Gray, C. (2000) *The New Social Story Book*, Arlington, TX: Future Horizon, Inc.

Greening, J. (2016) *Written Ministerial Statement by Education Secretary Justine Greening on Primary Education*. Available from: www.gov.uk/government/speeches/primary-education (accessed 21 August 2018).

GTCS (General Teaching Council Scotland) (n.d.a) *Professional Guidance on the Use of Electronic Communication and Social Media*. Available from: www.gtcs.org.uk/web/FILES/teacher-regulation/professional-guidance-ecomms-social-media.pdf (accessed 18 August 2019).

GTCS (General Teaching Council for Scotland) (n.d.b) *Standards for Registration*. Available from: www.gtcs.org.uk/professional-standards/engaging-with-the-standards/overview-of-the-standards.aspx (accessed 1 December 2018).

Gu, Q. and Day, C. (2013) 'Challenges to teacher resilience: Conditions count', *British Educational Research Journal*, 39, 22–44. doi: 10.1080/01411926.2011.623152.

Gunter, H.M. (2001) *Leaders and Leadership in Education*, London: SAGE.

Guzdial, M. (2016) *Five Principles for Programming Languages for Learners*, New York: Association of Computer Machinery.

Haigh, G. (2005) 'Who's afraid of the big school?', *Times Educational Supplement*, June 3, p. 20.

Hall, F., Hindmarch, D., Hoy, D. and Machin, L. (2015) *Supporting Teaching and Learning*, Northwich: Critical Publishing Limited.

Halliday, M. (1978) *Language as a Social Semiotic: The Social Interpretation of Language and Meaning*, London: Edward Arnold.

Hannay, L.M. and Ross, J.A. (1999) 'Department heads as middle managers? Questioning the black box', *School Leadership and Management: Formerly School Organisation*, 19(3), 345-358.

Hardman, F., Abd-Kadir, J. and Smith, F. (2008) 'Pedagogical renewal: Improving the quality of classroom integration in Nigerian primary schools', *International Journal of Education Studies*, 28(1), 55-69.

Hargreaves, A. (1994) *Changing Teachers, Changing Times: Teachers' Work and Culture in the Postmodern Age*, London: Cassell.

Harris, A. and Lambert, L. (2003) *Building Leadership Capacity for School Improvement*, Maidenhead: Open University Press.

Haydn, T. (2012) *Managing Pupil Behaviour: Improving the Classroom Atmosphere*, Abingdon: Routledge.

Haydn, T. (2015) 'Working to improve classroom climate using a ten point scale and focusing on the development of the classroom management skills of individual teachers', *Creative Education*, 6(22), 2351-2360.

Haydn, T. (2019) *Managing Pupil Behaviour*. Available from: https://terryhaydn.co.uk/managing-pupil-behaviour/ (accessed 18 August 2019).

Haydon, G. and Heilbronn, R. (2016a) 'Aims of education'. In: S. Capel, M. Leask and S. Younie (eds.) *Learning to Teach in the Secondary School: A Companion to School Experience*, 7th edn, Abingdon: Routledge, pp. 489-500.

Haydon, G. and Heilbronn, R. (2016b) 'The school curriculum'. In: S. Capel, M. Leask and S. Younie (eds.) *Learning to Teach in the Secondary School: A Companion to School Experience*, 7th edn, Abingdon: Routledge, pp. 501-512.

Heilbronn, R. (2004) 'The pastoral role: Tutoring and personal, social and health education'. In: S. Capel, R. Heilbronn, M. Leask, and T. Turner (eds.) *Starting to Teach in the Secondary School: A Companion for the Newly Qualified Teacher*, 2nd edn, Abingdon: RoutlegdeFalmer, pp. 45-59.

Heilbron, R., Orchard, J. and Haydon, G. (2019) 'Aims of education'. In: S. Capel, M. Leask and S. Younie (eds.) *Learning to Teach in the Secondary School: A Companion to School Experience*, 8th edn, Abingdon: Routledge, pp. 258-272.

Henderson, R. and Exeley, B. (2019) 'Thinking about planning for literacies learning'. In: R. Henderson (ed.) *Teaching Literacies: Pedagogies and Diversity*, Docklands, VIC: Oxford University Press.

Higgins, S., Katsipataki, M., Coleman, R., Henderson, P., Major, L.E., Coe, R. and Mason, D. (2015) *The Sutton Trust-Education Endowment Foundation Teaching and Learning Toolkit*, London: Education Endowment Foundation.

Hinshaw, S. (1994) *Attention Deficit Disorder and Hyperactivity in Children*, Thousand Oaks, CA: Sage.

Hmelo-Silver, C.E. (2006) 'Design principles for scaffolding technology-based inquiry'. In: A. M. O'Donnell, C. E. Hmelo-Silver, and G. Erkens (eds.) *Collaborative Reasoning, Learning and Technology*. Mahwah, NJ: Erlbaum, (pp. 147-170).

HM Government (2017) Internet Safety Strategy – Green Paper, Crown Copyright.

HM Government (2018) Government Response to the Internet Safety Strategy Green Paper, Crown Copyright.

HM Government (2019) The Online Harms White Paper. Available from: https://www.gov.uk/government/consultations/online-harms-white-paper (accessed 18 August 2019).

HNAP (Higher Level Teaching Assistant National Assessment Partnership) (2018) *Gaining Higher Level Teaching Assistant Status Preparation for Assessment Handbook*. Available from: www.hltanorth.com/wp-content/uploads/2018/08/Provider-and-Candidate-Handbook-Revised-July-18.pdf (accessed 23 September 2018).

Hobson, A.J. and Malderez, A. (2013) 'Judgementoring and other threats to realizing the potential of school-based mentoring in teacher education', *International Journal of Mentoring and Coaching in Education*, 2(2), 89-108.

Hodgen, J. and Webb, M. (2008) 'Questioning and dialogue'. In: S. Swaffield (ed.) *Unlocking Assessment: Understanding for Reflection and Application*, Abingdon: Routledge.

Hook, P, Booth, N., Price, A. and Fobister, L. (2019) *SOLO Taxonomy in Music Education: Growing High Quality Musicians Through a Reflective Learning Environment*, New Zealand: Essential Resources Educational Publishers Limited

Hook, P. and Mills, J. (2011) *SOLO Taxonomy: A Guide for Schools. Book 1. A Common Language of Learning*, New Zealand: Essential Resources Educational Publishers.

Hoover, W. and Gough, P. (1990) 'The simple view of reading', *Reading and Writing: An Interdisciplinary Journal*, 2(2), 127-160.

Hordern, J. (2015) 'Bernstein's sociology of knowledge and education(al) studies'. In: J. Furlong and G. Whitty (eds.) *Knowledge and the Study of Education*, Oxford: Symposium Books.

Hornberger, N. (ed.) (2008) *The Encyclopaedia of Language and Education*, Switzerland: Springer. Available from: https://link.springer.com/referenceworkentry/10.1007/978-0-387-30424-3_84 (accessed 14 November 2018).

Hughes, S. (2018) 'Mentoring and coaching: The helping relationship'. In: T. Wright (ed.) *How to Be a Brilliant Mentor: Developing Outstanding Teachers*, 2nd edn, Abingdon: Routledge, pp. 120-135.

ICO (2018) *Guide to the General Data Protection Regulation*, Wilmslow: Information Commissioner's Office. Available from: www.gov.uk/government/publications/guide-to-the-general-data-protection-regulation.

IAEEA (International Association for the Evaluation of Educational Achievement) (n.d.) *Trends in International Mathematics and Science Study (TIMSS)*. Available from: www.iea.nl/timss (accessed 1 December 2018).

Independent Teacher Workload Review Group (2016) *Eliminating Unnecessary Workload Around Marking*, London: Crown Copyright. Available from: https://assets.publishing.service.gov.uk/government/uploads/system/uploads/attachment_data/file/511256/Eliminating-unnecessary-workload-around-marking.pdf (accessed 24 November 2018).

Irvine, P.A. and Brundrett, M. (2017) 'Negotiating the next step: The part that experience plays with middle leaders' development as they move into their new role', *Educational Management Administration and Leadership*, 20(10), 1-17.

Jackson, A. and Burch, J. (2016) 'School Direct, a policy for initial teacher training in England: Plotting a principled pedagogical path through a changing landscape', *Professional Development in Education*, 42(4), 511-526.

Jenkins, A. and Ueno, A. (2017) 'Classroom disciplinary climate in secondary schools in England: What is the real picture?', *British Journal of Educational Research*, 43(1), 124-150.

Jindal-Snape, D. and Miller, D. (2008) 'A challenge of living? Understanding the psycho-social processes of the child during primary-secondary transition through resilience and self-esteem theories', *Educational Psychology Review*, 20(3), 217-236.

Jindal-Snape, J. (2019) 'Primary-secondary transitions'. In: S. Capel, M. Leask and S. Younie (eds.) *Learning to Teach in the Secondary School: A Companion to School Experience*, 8th edn, Abingdon: Routledge, pp. 184-197.

JISC (2018) *Digital Capability Framework*. Available from: http://jiscdesignstudio.pbworks.com/w/page/60225593/Developing%20digital%20literacies%20in%20the%20curriculum (accessed 18 August 2019).

Johns, K. (2015) 'Engaging and assessing students with technology: A review of Kahoot!', *Delta Kappa Gamma Bulletin*, 81(4), 89.

Jones, S., Myhill, D. and Bailey, T. (2013) 'Grammar for writing? An investigation of the effects of contextualised grammar teaching on students' writing', *Reading and Writing*, 26(8), 1241-1263.

Kafai, Y., Bruke, Q. and Resnick, M. (2014) *Connected Code: Why Children Need to Learn Programming*, Boston, MA: MIT Press.

Kalantzis, M., Cope, B., Chan, E. and Dalley-Trim, L. (2016) *Literacies*, 2nd edn, Port Melbourne, VIC: Cambridge University Press.

Keay, J. (2009) 'Being influenced or being an influence: New teachers' induction experiences', *European Physical Education Review*, 15(2), 225-247.

Keay, J. (2019) 'Developing further as a teacher'. In: S. Capel, M. Leask and S. Younie (eds.) *Learning to Teach in the Secondary School: A Companion to School Experience*, 8th edn, Abingdon: Routledge, pp. 497-510.

Knapp, P. (1992) *Resource Book for Genre and Grammar*, Parammatta: Metropolitan West Literacy and Learning Program, NSW Department of School Education.

Knapp, P. and Watkins, M. (2005) *Genre, Text, Grammar: Technologies for Teaching and Assessing Writing*, Sydney, NSW: University of New South Wales Press.

Ko, J., Hallinger, P. and Walker, A. (2015) 'Exploring whole school versus subject department improvement in Hong Kong secondary schools', *School Effectiveness and School Improvement*, 26(2), 215–239.

Kucharski, A.J., Wenham, C., Brownlee, P., Racon, L., Widmer, N., Eames, K.T.D. and Conlan, A.J.K. (15 July 2018) 'Structure and consistency of self-reported social contact networks in British secondary schools', *PLOS ONE*, 13(7), e0200090. Available from: https://journals.plos.org/plosone/article?id=10.1371/journal.pone.0200090 (accessed 24 November 2018).

Laluvein, J. (2010) 'School inclusion and the "community of practice"', *International Journal of Inclusive Education*, 14(1), 35–48.

Lange, J. and Burroughs-Lange, S. (2017) *Learning to Be a Teacher*, London: Sage Publications.

Laurillard, D. (2012) *Teaching as a Design Science: Building Pedagogical Patterns for Learning and Technology*, Abingdon: Routledge.

Lave, J. and Wenger, E. (1991) *Situated Learning: Legitimate Peripheral Participation*, 1st edn, Cambridge: Cambridge University Press.

Lawton, D. (1975) *Class, Culture and the Curriculum*, London: Routledge.

Leask, M. (2019) 'And Finally'. In: S. Capel, M. Leask, and S. Younie (eds.) *Learning to Teach in the Secondary School: A Companion to School Experience*, 8th edn, Abingdon: Routledge, pp. 541–544.

Lechtenberger, D., Barnard-Brak, L., Sokolosky, S. and McCrary, D. (2012) 'Using wraparound to support students with developmental disabilities in higher education', *College Student Journal*, 46, 856–866.

Lemov, D. (2015) *Teach Like a Champion 2.0*, San Francisco, CA: Jossey-Bass.

Lemov, D. (2017) 'Managing behaviour is all in the eyebrow', *Times Educational Supplement*, 5 May, pp. 24–25.

Liasidou, A. (2012) *Inclusive Education, Politics and Policymaking*, London: Continuum.

Lindsay, S., Proulx, M., Thomson, N. and Scott, H. (2013) 'Educators' challenges of including children with Autism Spectrum Disorder in mainstream classrooms', *International Journal of Disability, Development and Education*, 60(4), 347–362. doi: 10.1080/1034912X.2013.846470.

Liu, J. and Le, T. (2011) 'A case study on college English classroom discourse', *International Journal of Interdisciplinary Research*, 2, 1–10.

LKMCo (2018) Schools and youth mental health: A briefing on current challenges and ways forward. Available from: www.lkmco.org/wp-content/uploads/2018/06/Schools-and-Youth-Mental-Health.-Menzies-et-al.-2018.pdf (accessed 18 August 2019).

Long, R. (2017) *Personal, Social, Health and Economic Education in Schools (England)*, Briefing Paper, House of Commons Library Number 07303, 2 March 2017. Available from: http://dera.ioe.ac.uk/28815/1/CBP-7303.pdf (accessed 14 May 2018).

Long, R. and Bolton, P. (2017) Briefing Paper Number 06045 English Baccalaureate, House of Commons Library. Available from: https://beta.parliament.uk/search?q=Briefing+Paper+Number+06045+English+Baccalaureate (accessed 25 November 2018).

Lucey, H. and Reay, D. (2000) 'Identities in transition: Anxiety and excitement in the move to secondary school', *Oxford Review of Education*, 26(2), 191–205.

Lunzer, E. and Gardner, K. (eds.) (1979) *The Effective Uses of Reading*, London: Heinemann.

Lyle, S. (2008) 'Learners' collaborative talk'. In: N.H. Hornberger (ed.) *Encyclopedia of Language and Education*, Boston, MA: Springer.

Marcus, A.S., Stoddard, J.D. and Woodward, W.W. (2017) *Teaching History with Museums: Strategies for K-12 Social Studies*, Abingdon: Routledge.

Marland, M. and Rogers, R. (2004) *How to Be a Successful Form Tutor*, London: Continuum.

Martin, J.R. and Rothery, J. (1993) 'Grammar – Making meaning in writing'. In: B. Cope and M. Kalantzis (eds.) *The Powers of Literacy – A Genre Approach to Teaching Literacy*, London: Falmer Press.

Marzano, R. (1991) 'Language, the language arts and thinking'. In: J. Flood, D. Lapp and J. Squire (eds.) *Handbook of Research on Teaching the English Language Arts*, New York: Macmillan.

Matthews, B. (2004) 'Promoting emotional literacy, equity and interest in KS3 science lessons for 11-14 year olds; the "Improving Science and Emotional Development" project', *International Journal of Science Education*, 26(3), 281–308.

Matthews, B. (2006) *Engaging Education: Developing Emotional Literacy, Equity and Co-Education*, Buckingham: McGraw-Hill/Open University Press.

Matthews, L. (2007) 'Can the process of transition for incoming secondary pupils be supported through a creative art project?', *The International Journal of Art and Design Education*, 26(3), 336-344.

Maynard, T. and Furlong, J. (1995) *Mentoring Student Teachers: The Growth of Professional Knowledge*, London: Routledge.

McEwan, E.K. (2008) *The Reading Puzzle: Word Analysis*, Thousand Oaks, CA: Corwin Press. Available from: www.readingrockets.org/article/root-words-roots-and-affixes (accessed 14 November 2018).

McLaughlin, C. (2019) 'External assessment and examinations'. In: S. Capel, M. Leask and S. Younie (eds.) *Learning to Teach in the Secondary School: A Companion to School Experience*, 8th edn, Abingdon: Routledge, pp. 426-438.

McLaughlin, C. and Byers, R. (2001) *Personal and Social Development for All*, London: David Fulton Publishers.

McNaught, C. and Lam, P. (2010) 'Using Wordle as a supplementary research tool', *The Qualitative Report*, 15(3), 630-643.

McNicholl, J., Childs, A. and Burn, K. (2013) 'School subject departments as sites for science teachers learning pedagogical content knowledge', *Teacher Development*, 17(2), 155-175.

McWhirter, J., Boddington, N. and Barksfield, J. (2017) *Understanding Personal, Social, Health and Economic Education in Secondary Schools*, London: Sage.

Measor, L. and Woods, P. (1984) *Changing Schools*, Milton Keynes: Open University Press.

Meiers, M. (2010) 'Language in the mathematics classroom', *The Digest*, NSWIT. Available from: www.nswteachers.nsw.edu.au (accessed 14 November 2018).

Mercer, N. (2000) *Words and Minds: How We Use Language to Think Together*, Abingdon: Routledge.

Mercer, N. (2004) 'Sociocultural discourse analysis: Analysing classroom talk as a mode of thinking', *Journal of Applied Linguistics*, 1(2), 137-168.

Mercer, N. (2015) *Group talk - Benefits for Science Teaching*. Available from: http://oer.educ.cam.ac.uk/wiki/The_educational_value_of_dialogic_talk_in_whole-class_dialogue (accessed 19 August 2017).

Mercer, N. and Dawes, L. (2008) 'The value of exploratory talk'. In: N. Mercer and S. Hodgkinson (eds.) *Exploring Talk in School*, London: Sage.

Mercer, N. and Hodgkinson, S. (eds.) (2008) *Exploring Talk in School*, London: Sage.

Mercer, N. and Littleton, K. (2007) *Dialogue and the Development of Children's Thinking: A Sociocultural Approach*, Abingdon: Routledge.

Merriman, J. (2005) *A History of Modern Europe, from the French Revolution to the Present, Volume 2*, 2nd edn, New York: Norton and Company.

Miller, A. (2014) 'Twelve ideas for teaching with QR codes', *Edutopia (George Lucas Educational Foundation)*. Available from: www.edutopia.org/blog/QR-codes-teaching-andrew-miller (accessed 18 August 2019).

Mintz, J. and Wyse, D. (2015) 'Inclusive pedagogy and knowledge in special education: Addressing the tension', *International Journal of Inclusive Education*, 19(11), 1161-1171. doi: 10.1080/13603116.2015.1044203.

MITA (Maximising the Practice of Teaching Assistants) (2018) www.maximisingtas.co.uk/

Montgomery, A. and Mirenda, P. (2014) 'Teachers' self-efficacy, sentiments, attitudes and concerns about the inclusion of students with developmental disabilities', *Exceptionality Education International*, 24(1), 18-32.

Moore, B. and Stanley, T. (2010) *Critical Thinking and Formative Assessments*, Larchmont, NY: Eye on Education.

Moore, D.A., Gwernan-Jones, R., Richardson, M., Racey, D., Rogers, M., Stein, K., Thompson-Coon, J., Ford, T.J. and Garside, R. (2016) 'The experiences of and attitudes toward non-pharmacological interventions for attention-deficit/hyperactivity disorder used in school settings: A systematic review and synthesis of qualitative research', *Emotional and Behavioural Difficulties*, 21(1), 61-82. doi: 10.1080/13632752.2016.1139296.

Morgan, B. and Ashbaker, B. (2011) 'TAs join the team: UK expands role of teaching assistants in the classroom', *Journal of Staff Development*, 32(3), 38-41. Available from: www.learningforward.org (accessed 22 September 2018).

Morrison, B.B., Margulieux, L.E. and Guzdial, M. (2015) 'Subgoals, context and worked examples in learning computing problem solving', *International Conference on International Computing Education Research (ICER '15)*, July 09-13, 2015, ACM, pp. 21-29.

Morrison, L. and Matthews, B. (2006) 'How pupils can be helped to develop socially and emotionally in science lessons', *Pastoral Care in Education*, 24(1), 10–19.

Mulholland, M. and O'Connor, U. (2016) 'Collaborative classroom practice for inclusion: Perspectives of classroom teachers and learning support/resource teachers', *International Journal of Inclusive Education*, 20(10), 1070–1083. doi: 10.1080/13603116.2016.1145266.

Myers, B.A., Hudson, S.E. and Pausch, R. (2000) 'Past, present and future of user interface software tools', *ACM Transactions on Computer-Human Interaction*, 7(1), 3–28.

Naido, J. and Wills, J. (2016) *Foundations for Health Promotion*, 4th edn, London: Bailliere Tindall.

NAHT (National Association of Head Teachers) (2016) *The NAHT School Recruitment Survey 2016*, West Sussex: NAHT Edge. Available from: file:///C:/Users/rache/Downloads/NAHT%20 recruitment%20survey%202016%20%20(2).pdf (accessed 2 September 2018).

National Numeracy (2017) *What Is Numeracy?* Available from: www.nationalnumeracy.org.uk/what-numeracy (accessed 25 November 2018).

NCFE (2015a) '*SecEd* guide to progress 8', *SecEd*, January 2015. Available from: www.sec-ed.co.uk/best-practice/seced-guide-to-progress-8 (accessed 1 December 2018).

NCFE (2015b) *Guide to Essential Middle Leadership Skill*. ACSL. Available from: www.sec-ed.co.uk/best-practice/guide-to-essential-middle-leadership-skills/ (accessed 2 September 2018).

NCTL (National College For Teaching and Leadership) (2016) *Newly Qualified Teachers: Annual Survey 2016*, London: Crown. Available from: https://assets.publishing.service.gov.uk/government/uploads/system/uploads/attachment_data/file/570147/NQT2016_National_Survey_FINAL.pdf (accessed 24 November 2018).

Newby, P. (2014) *Research Methods for Education*, 2nd edn, Harlow: Pearson Education Ltd.

Nolan, J.F. (2007) 'Five basic principles to facilitate change in schools', *Catalysts of Change*, 35(1), 3–9.

Norris, S.P. and Phillips, L.M. (2003) 'How literacy in its fundamental sense is central to scientific literacy', *Science Education*, 87(2), 224–240.

Norwich, B. (2013) *Addressing Tensions and Dilemmas in Inclusive Education*, Abingdon: Routledge.

OECD (Organisation for Economic Cooperation and Development) (2009) *Programme for International Student Assessment (PISA) Results: What Students Know and Can Do*, Paris: OECD.

Ofqual (The Office of Qualifications and Examinations Regulation) (2016) *Marking Consistency Metrics*. Available from: https://assets.publishing.service.gov.uk/government/uploads/system/uploads/attachment_data/file/681625/Marking_consistency_metrics_-_November_2016.pdf (accessed 18 August 2019).

Ofsted (Office for Standards in Education, Children's Services and Skills) (2008) *Learning Outside the Classroom. How far Should You Go? Reference no. 070219*, London: Crown Copyright. Available from: www.lotc.org.uk/wp-content/uploads/2010/12/Ofsted-Report-Oct-2008.pdf (accessed 24 November 2018).

Ofsted (Office for Standards in Education, Children's Services and Skills) (2012a) *School Inspection Handbook: Handbook for Inspecting Schools in England under Section 5 of the Education Act 2005 (as Amended) from September 2012*, Manchester: Ofsted/UK Government.

Ofsted (Office for Standards in Education, Children's Services and Skills) (2012b) *Pupil Behaviour in Schools in England*, London: DfE.

Ofsted (Office for Standards in Education, Children's Services and Skills) (2013a) *Personal, Social, Health and Economic (PSHE) Education Survey Visits: Generic Grade Descriptors and Supplementary Subject Specific Guidance for Inspectors on Making Judgements during Visits to Schools*. Available from: www.pshe-association.org.uk/uploads/media/17/7604.pdf (accessed 1 December 2018).

Ofsted (Office for Standards in Education, Children's Services and Skills) (2013b) *Not Yet Good Enough: Personal, Social, Health and Economic Education in Schools (Personal, Social and Health Education in English Schools in 2012)*, Manchester: Ofsted. Available from: www.gov.uk/government/publications/not-yet-good-enough-personal-social-health-and-economic-education (accessed 1 December 2018).

Ofsted (Office for Standards in Education, Children's Services and Skills) (2014) *Below the Radar: Low-level Disruption in Classrooms*, London: Ofsted. Available from: www.gov.uk/government/publications/below-the-radar-low-level-disruption-in-the-countrys-classrooms (accessed 24 November 2018).

Ofsted (Office for Standards in Education, Children's Services and Skills) (2015) *Key Stage 3: The Wasted Years?*, Manchester: Ofsted.

Ohan, J.L., Visser, T.A.W., Strain, M.C. and Allen, L. (2011) 'Teachers' and education students' perceptions of and reactions to children with and without the diagnostic label "ADHD"', *Journal of School Psychology*, 49(1), 81–105.

Ojino, R. and Mich, L., 2018. 'Mobile applications in university education: Ehe case of Kenya', *Journal of e-Learning and Knowledge Society*, 14(1), 111–125.

Oliver, M. (1996) *Understanding Disability: From Theory to Practice*, Basingstoke: Macmillan.

Packer, N. (2017) 'SEN: Effective partnerships with teaching assistants', *SecEd*, 11 October. Available from: www.sec-ed.co.uk/best-practice/sen-effective-partnerships-with-teaching-assistants/ (accessed 24 November, 2018).

Padget, S. (ed.) (2013) *Creativity and Critical Thinking*, Abingdon: Routledge.

Papert, S. (1980) *Mindstorms: Children, Computers and Powerful Ideas*, New York: Basic Book.

Parker, R. (1985) 'The "Language Across the Curriculum Movement": A brief overview and bibliography', *College Composition and Communication*, 3(2), 173–177. Available from: www.jstor.org/stable/pdf/357438.pdf (accessed 12 November 2018).

Paton, G. (2014) *Ofsted Penalising Schools Over 'Chalk and Talk' Teaching*. Available from: http://www.telegraph.co.uk/education/educaationnews/10973572/Ofsted-penalising-schools-over-chalk-and-talk-teaching.html (accessed 19 August 2017).

Patrick, F., Elliott, D., Hulme, M. and McPhee, A. (2010) 'The importance of collegiality and reciprocal learning in the professional development of beginner teachers', *Journal of Education for Teaching*, 36(3), 277–289.

Patterson, E.W. (2016a) *Research Methods 1: Doing a Literature Review: How to Find and Make Sense of Published Research*, MESHGuide, University of Winchester, UK. Available from: http://www.meshguides.org/guides/node/406 (accessed 18 August 2019).

Patterson, E.W. (2016b) *Research Methods 2: Developing Your Research Design*, MESHGuide, University of Winchester, UK. Available from: http://www.meshguides.org/guides/node/483?n=438 (accessed 18 August 2019).

Patterson, E.W. (2016c) *Research Methods 3: Considering Ethics in Your Research*, MESHGuide, University of Winchester. Available from: http://www.meshguides.org/guides/node/592?n=519 (accessed 18 August 2019).

Pay, B. (2016) 'Pupil-pupil talk: Does the "Thinking Together Programme" enhance pupil-pupil talk within the classroom?', *The STEP Journal*, 3(2), 14–23.

Peacey, N. (2019) 'An introduction to inclusion, special educational needs and disability'. In: S. Capel, M. Leask and S. Younie (eds.) *Learning to Teach in the Secondary School: A Companion to School Experience*, 8th edn, Abingdon, UK: Routledge, pp. 273–290.

Pearcy, M. (2016) 'A Wordle to the wise: Using "word clouds" meaningfully in the classroom', *Social Studies Research and Practice*, 11(2), 96–110.

Pedder, D. and Opfer, V.D. (2011) 'Are we realising the full potential of teachers' professional learning in schools in England? Policy issues and recommendations from a national study'. *Professional Development in Education*, 37(5), 741–758.

Pierce, K. and Gilles, C. (2008) 'From exploratory talk to critical conversations'. In: N. Mercer and S. Hodgkinson (eds.) *Exploring Talk in School*, London: Sage.

Plump, C.M. and Larosa, J. (2017) 'Using Kahoot! in the classroom to create engagement and active learning: A game-based technology solution for elearning novices', *Management Teaching Review*, 2(2), 151–158.

Pollard, A. (ed.) (2010) *Professionalism and Pedagogy: A Contemporary Opportunity. A Commentary by TLRP and GTCE*, London: TLRP. Available from: http://reflectiveteaching.co.uk/media/profandped.pdf (accessed 18 August 2019).

Pont, B., Nusche, D. and Moorman, H. (2008) *Improving School Leadership, Volume 1: Policy and Practice*, Paris: OECD. Available from: www.oecd.org/edu/school/44374889.pdf (accessed 2 September 2018).

Poulou, M. and Norwich, B. (2000) 'Teachers' perceptions of students with emotional and behavioural difficulties: Severity and prevalence', *European Journal of Special Needs Education*, 15(2), 171–187.

Pring, R. (2004) *Philosophy of Education: Aims, Theory, Common Sense and Research*, London: Continuum.

Pring, R., Hayward, G., Hodgson, J., Johnson, J., Keep, E., Oancea, A., Rees, G., Spours, K. and Wilde, S. (2009) *Education for All. The Future of Education and Training for 14-19 Year Olds*, Abingdon: Routledge.

PSHE (Personal, Social and Health Education) Association (2012) *Handling Sensitive or Controversial Issues*. Available from: www.pshe-association.org.uk/curriculum-and-resources/resources/handling-sensitive-or-controversial-issues-through (accessed 17 July 2018).

PSHE Association (2017) *PSHE Education Programme of Study, Key Stages 1-5*. Available from: https://www.pshe-association.org.uk/system/files/PSHE%20Education%20Programme%20of%20Study%20%28Key%20stage%201-5%29%20Jan%202017_2.pdf (accessed 18 August 2019).

PSHE Association (n.d.) *The 10 Principles of PSHE Education*. Available from: www.pshe-association.org.uk/curriculum-and-resources/resources/ten-principles-effective-pshe-education (accessed 20 November 2018).

Public Health England (2014) *The Link between Pupil Health and Wellbeing and Attainment: A Briefing for Head Teachers, Governors and Staff in Education Settings*, London: PSHE Association. Available from: www.gov.uk/government/publications/the-link-between-pupil-health-and-wellbeing-and-attainment (accessed 1 December 2018).

Public Health England (2017) *Children and Young People*. Available from: www.gov.uk/government/publications/better-mental-health-jsna-toolkit/5-children-and-young-people (accessed August 2019).

Puentedura, R. (2006) *Transformation, Technology and Education*. Available from: http://hippasus.com/resources/tte/ (accessed 24 November 2018).

Puentedura, R. (2014a) *Building Transformation: An Introduction to the SAMR Model*. Available from: www.hippasus.com/rrpweblog/archives/2014/08/22/BuildingTransformation_AnIntroductionToSAMR.pdf (accessed 24 November 2018).

Puentedura, R. (2014b) *Learning, Technology and the SAMR Model: Goals, Processes and Practice*. Available from: http://hippasus.com/blog/archives/127 (accessed 24 November 2018).

Pulsford, M.J. (2019) '"I could have been the caretaker in a suit": Men as primary school SENCos in an era of change', *Education 3-13: International Journal of Primary, Elementary and Early Years Education*, http://dx.doi.org/10.1080/03004279.2019.1659386.

Punch, K. and Oancea, A.E. (2014) *Introduction to Research Methods in Education*, 2nd edn, London: Sage.

Purdy, N. (ed.) (2013) *Pastoral Care 11-16: A Critical Introduction*, London: Bloomsbury Academic.

Puttick, S. (2016) 'An analysis of individual and departmental geographical stories and their role in sustaining teachers', *International Research in Geographical and Environmental Education*, 25(2), 134-150.

Puttick, S. (2017) '"You'll see that everywhere": Institutional isomorphism in secondary school subject departments', *School Leadership and Management*, 37(1-2), 61-79.

Puttick, S. (2018) 'Student teachers' positionalities as knowers within school subject departments', *British Educational Research Journal*, 44(1), 25-42.

Putwain, D. (2008) 'Examination stress and exam anxiety', *The Psychologist*, 21(12), 1026-1029.

Ranaldi, F. (2010) *Using Digital Resources across the Curriculum in Schools*, Glasgow: Scottish Qualifications Authority.

Redecker, C. (2017) *European Framework for the Digital Competence of Educators: DigCompEdu*, Luxembourg: Publications Office of the European Union.

Rees, D. and Porter, C. (2015) *Skills of Management and Leadership: Managing People in Organizations*, London: Palgrave.

Resnick, M., Myers, B., Nakakoji, K., Shneiderman, B., Pausch, R., Selker, T., and Eisenberg, M. (2005). *Design Principles for Tools to Support Creative Thinking*. National Science Foundation Workshop on Creativity Support Tools. Washington, DC.

Reynolds, D. (1999) 'It's the classroom, stupid', *Times Educational Supplement*, May 28, p. 13.

Rice, F., Frederickson, N., Shelton, K., McManus, C., Riglin, L. and Ng-Knight, T. (2008) *Identifying Factors that Predict Successful and Difficult Transitions to Secondary School*. Available from: www.nuffieldfoundation.org/sites/default/files/files/STARS_report.pdf (accessed 25 November 2018).

Richards, J. (2017) *The Government Is not Investing Enough in Teaching Assistants or Giving them the Recognition They Deserve*. Available from: www.tes.com/news/government-not-investing-enough-teaching-assistants-or-giving-them-recognition-they-deserve (accessed 16 October 2018).

Rizvi, S. and Limbrick, P. (2015) 'Provision for learners with SLD/PMLD from ethnic minority families'. In: P. Lacey, R. Ashdown, P. Jones, H. Lawson and M. Pipe (eds.) *Routledge Companion to Severe, Profound and Multiple Learning Difficulties*, Abingdon: Routledge.

Roberts, J. and Simpson, K. (2016) 'A review of research into stakeholder perspectives on inclusion of students with autism in mainstream schools', *International Journal of Inclusive Education*, 20(10), 1084–1096.

Robinson, J. (2015) 'Data analysis in participatory research with adults with Asperger's syndrome'. In: L. Hardwick, R. Smith and A. Worsley (eds.) *Innovation in Social Work Research: Using Methods Creatively*, London: Jessica Kingsley.

Robinson, J. (2017) 'Notions of support challenged by participatory research with adults with Asperger's syndrome', *Groupwork*, 26(22), 51–73.

Rodriguez, P., Nussbaum, M. and Dombrovskaia, L. (2012) 'ICT for education: A conceptual framework for the sustainable adoption of technology-enhanced learning environments in schools', *Technology, Pedagogy and Education*, 21(3), 291–315.

Roegman, R., Pratt, S., Goodwin, A. and Akin, S. (2017) 'Curriculum, social justice and inquiry in the field: Investigating retention in an urban teacher residency', *Action in Teacher Education*, 39(4), 432–452. doi: 10.1080/01626620.2017.1300956.

Rogers, W. (2011) *You Know the Fair Rule*, 3rd edn, Victoria: ACER Press.

Rogers, E.M. (1962) *Diffusion of Innovation*, New York: Free Press of Glencoe.

Roosevelt, F.D. (1933) First Inaugural Address (excerpts). Saturday, March 4.

Rosenblatt, L. (1978) *The Reader, the Text, the Poem: The Transactional Theory of the Literary Work*, Carbondale, IL: Southern Illinois University Press.

Rosenthal, R. and Jacobson, L. (1968) *Pygmalion in the Classroom: Teacher Expectation and Pupils' Intellectual Development*, New York: Holt, Rinehart and Winston.

Ross, A. (2000) *Curriculum: Construction and Critique*, London: Falmer Press.

Ruohotie-Lyhty, M. (2013) 'Struggling for a professional identity: Two newly qualified language teachers' identity narratives during the first years at work', *Teaching and Teacher Education*, 30, 120–129.

Russell, A., Webster, R. and Blatchford, P. (2016) *Maximising the Impact of Teaching Assistants: Guidance for School Leaders and Teachers*, 2nd edn, Abingdon: Routledge.

Sadler, R. (1989) 'Formative assessment and the design of instructional systems', *Instructional Science*, 18(2), 119–144.

Sakellariadis, A.I. (2007) *Voices of Inclusion: Perspectives of Mainstream Primary School Staff Working with Disabled Children*, PhD thesis, University of Bristol.

Sameshima, P. (2008) 'Letters to a new teacher: A curriculum of embodied aesthetic awareness', *Teacher Education Quarterly*, Spring, 29–44.

Schleppergrell, M.J., Greer, S. and Taylor, S. (2008) 'Literacy in history: Language and meaning', *Australian Journal of Language and Literacy*, 31(2), 174–187.

Schön, D. (1983) *The Reflective Practitioner: How Professionals Think in Action*, New York: Basic Books.

Schrag, F. (1989) 'Are there levels of thinking?', *Teachers College Record*, 90(4), 529–533.

Scottish Government (2010) *Supporting Children's Learning: Code of Practice*, Edinburgh: The Scottish Government.

Scriven, A. (2010) *Promoting Health – A Practical Guide*, 6th edn, London: Baillirère Tindall.

Sedgewick, F. (2012) *Learning Outside the Primary Classroom*, Abingdon: Routledge.

Serafini, F. (2012) 'Expanding the four resources model: Reading visual and multimodal texts', *Pedagogies: An International Journal*, 7(2), 150–164.

Shaffer, D.W. and Resnick, M. (1999) '"Thick" authenticity: New media and authentic learning', *Journal of Interactive Learning Research*, 10(2), 195–216.

Shakespeare, T. (2008) 'Debating disability', *Journal of Medical Ethics*, 34(1), 11–14.

Sharples, J., Webster, R. and Blatchford, P. (2015) *Making Best Use of Teaching Assistants: Guidance Report*, London: Education Endowment Foundation.

Shaw, M. (2019) 'Active learning'. In: S. Capel, M. Leask and S. Younie (eds.) *Learning to Teach in the Secondary School: A Companion to School Experience*, 8th edn, Abingdon: Routledge, pp. 308–329.

Shively, J. (2015) 'Constructivism in music education', *Arts Education Policy Review*, 116, 128–136.

Shulman, L.S. (1987) 'Knowledge and teaching: Foundations of the new reform', *Harvard Educational Review*, 57(1), 1–22.

Sinclair, J. and Coulthard, R. (1975) *Towards an Analysis of Discourse: English Used by Teachers and Pupils*, Oxford: Oxford University Press.

Sirna, K., Tinning, R. and Rossi, T. (2008) 'The social tasks of learning to become a physical education teacher: Considering the HPE subject department as a community of practice', *Sport, Education and Society*, 13(3), 285–300.

Siskin, L.S. (1994) *Realms of Knowledge: Academic Departments in Secondary Schools*, London: The Falmer Press.

Slee, R. (2010) 'Revisiting the politics of special educational needs and disability studies in education with Len Barton', *British Journal of Sociology of Education*, 31(5), 561–573.

Smith, J.F. and Skrbis, Z. (2017) 'A social inequality of motivation? The relationship between beliefs about academic success and young people's educational attainment', *British Educational Research Journal*, 43(3), 441–466.

Solar, M., Sabattin, J. and Parada, V. (2013) 'A maturity model for assessing the use of ICT in school education', *Journal of Educational Technology and Society*, 16(1), 206–218.

Sostrin, J. (2017) 'To be a great leader, you have to learn how to delegate well', *Harvard Business Review*. Available from: https://hbr.org/2017/10/to-be-a-great-leader-you-have-to-learn-how-to-delegate-well (accessed 17 October 2018).

Spielman, A. (2018) *HMCI Commentary: Curriculum and the New Education Inspection Framework*. Ofsted. Available from: www.gov.uk/government/speeches/hmci-commentary-curriculum-and-the-new-education-inspection-framework (accessed 16 August 2019).

Spruce, G. (2001) 'Music assessment and the hegemony of musical heritage'. In: C. Philpott and C. Plummeridge (Eds.) *Issues in Music Teaching*. London, UK: Routledge Falmer, (pp. 118–130).

Stenhouse, L. (1975) *An Introduction to Curriculum Research and Development*, Oxford: Heinemann.

Strand, S. (2016) 'Do some schools narrow the gap? Differential school effectiveness revisited', *Review of Education*, 4(2), 107–144.

SWGfL (SOUTH WEST GRID for Learning) (2015) *Digital Literacy and Citizenship from SWGfL*. Available from: https://digital-literacy.org.uk (accessed 23 August 2019).

Tainio, L. and Laine, A. (2015) 'Emotion work and affective stance in the mathematics classroom: The case of IRE sequences in Finnish classroom interaction', *Educational Studies in Mathematics*, 89, 67–87.

Talboys, G.R. (2010) *Using Museums as an Educational Resource: An Introductory Handbook for Students and Teachers*, 2nd edn, Farnham: Ashgate Publishing.

Taylor, C. (2011) *Getting the Simple Things Right: Charlie Taylor's Behaviour Checklists*, London: DfE. Available from: http://media.education.gov.uk/assets/files/pdf/c/charlie%20taylor%20checklist.pdf (accessed 5 January 2018).

TDA (Training and Development Agency) (2008) *National Occupational Standards for Supporting Teaching and Learning in Schools*, London: Education Endowment Foundation.

TDA (Training and Development Agency for Schools) (2011) *Staff Structure (Primary)*, London: TDA.

Thomas, G. and Loxley, A. (2007) *Deconstructing Special Education and Constructing Education*, 2nd edn, Maidenhead: Open University Press.

Thorley, C. (2016) *Education, Education, Mental Health: Supporting Secondary Schools to Play a Central Role in Early Intervention Mental Health Services*. IPPR. Available from: www.ippr.org/publications/education-education-mental-health (accessed 18 August 2019).

Titchmarsh, A. (2019) 'Pupil grouping, progression and differentiation'. In: S. Capel, M. Leask and S. Younie (eds.) *Learning to Teach in the Secondary School: A Companion to School Experience*, 8th edn, Abingdon: Routledge, pp. 201–216.

Trussler, S. and Robinson, D. (2015) *Inclusive Practice in the Primary School: A Guide for Teachers*, London: Sage.

Turner, C. (2017) 'Stop expelling troublesome pupils to boost league table performance, Chief Inspector says', *Daily Telegraph*, 10 December.

Tutt, R. and Williams, P. (2015) *The SEND Code of Practice 0–25 Years: Policy, Provision and Practice*, London: SAGE.

Twiselton, S. 2004, 'The role of teacher identities in learning to teach primary literacy', *Educational Review*, 56(2), 157–164.

UK Parliament (2002) *Education Act*, London: The Stationary Office. Available from: www.legislation.gov.uk/ukpga/2002/32/pdfs/ukpga_20020032_en.pdf (accessed 1 November 2018).

UK Parliament (2004) *Children Act, Chapter 31*, London: The Stationary Office. Available from: www.legislation.gov.uk/ukpga/2004/31 (accessed 25 November 2018).

UK Parliament (2006) *Education and Inspections Act*, London: The Stationary Office. Available from: www.legislation.gov.uk/ukpga/2006/40/pdfs/ukpga_20060040_en.pdf (accessed 1 November 2018).

UK Parliament (2010) *Academies Act*, London: The Stationary Office. Available from: www.legislation.gov.uk/ukpga/2010/32/pdfs/ukpga_20100032_en.pdf (accessed 1 November 2018).

Ulvik, M. and Langørgen, K. (2012) 'What can experienced teachers learn from newcomers? NQTs as a resource in schools', *Teachers and Teaching: Theory and Practice*, 18(1), 43–57.

Underwood, J. and Dillon, G. (2011) 'Chasing dreams and recognising realities: Teachers' responses to ICT', *Technology, Pedagogy and Education*, 20(3), 317–330.

UNESCO (United Nations Education, Scientific and Cultural Organisation) (1994) *The Salamanca Statement and Framework for Action on Special Needs Education. Adopted by the World Conference on Special Needs Education: Access and Equity*, Paris: UNESCO.

UNESCO (United Nations Education, Scientific and Cultural Organisation) (2011) *UNESCO ICT Competency Framework for Teachers*, Paris: UNESCO.

UNESCO (The United Nations Educational, Scientific and Cultural Organization) (2015) *Sustainable Development Goal 4 and Its Targets*. Available from: https://en.unesco.org/gem-report/sdg-goal-4 (accessed 18 August 2019).

UNESCO (United Nations Education, Scientific and Cultural Organisation) (2018a) *Guidelines: Designing Inclusive Digital Solutions and Developing Digital Skills*, Paris: UNESCO.

UNESCO (United Nations Education, Scientific and Cultural Organisation) (2018b) *A Landscape Review: Digital Literacies for Low-Skilled and Low-Literacy People*, Paris: UNESCO.

UNISON (2013) *The Evident Value of Teaching Assistants: Report of a UNISON Survey: January 2013*. Available from: www.wiltslt.co.uk/index.php/our-services/closing-the-gap/closing-the-gap-useful-information/teaching-assistants?download=518:the-evident-value-of-tas-research (accessed 22 September 2018).

UNISON, NAHT (National Association of Head Teachers), NET (National Education Trust), MPTA (Mazimising the Practice of Teaching Assistants), MITA (Maximising the Impact of Teaching Assistants) and RTSA (2016) *Professional Standards for Teaching Assistants. Advice for Headteachers, Teachers, Teaching Assistants, Governing Boards and Employers*. Available from: http://maximisingtas.co.uk/assets/content/ta-standards-final-june2016-1.pdf (accessed 18 August 2019).

van den Akker, J. (1998) 'The science curriculum: Between ideals and outcomes', *International Handbook of Science Education*, 42(4), 421–447.

Vollmer, H.J. (2006) 'Language across the curriculum'. In: *Intergovernmental Conference – Languages of Schooling: Towards a Framework for Europe*, Strasbourg, 16–18 October 2006. Available from: https://rm.coe.int/16805c7464 (accessed 12 November 2018).

Vygotsky, L. (1978) *Mind in Society*, Cambridge: Harvard University Press.

Wade, S. and Moje, E. (2000) 'The role of tests in classroom learning'. In: M. Kamil, P. Mosenthal, P. Pearson and R. Barr (eds.) *Handbook of Reading Research: Volume 3*, Mahwah, NJ: LEA.

Warhurst, C., Nickson, D., Commander, J. and Gilbert, K. (2014) '"Role stretch": Assessing the blurring of teaching and non-teaching in the classroom assistant role in Scotland', *British Educational Research Journal*, 40(1), 170–186. doi: 10.1002/berj.3036.

Wastiau, P., Blamire, R., Kearney, C., Quittre, V., Van De Gaer, E. and Monseur, C. (2013) 'The use of ICT in education: A survey of schools in Europe', *European Journal of Education*, 48(1), 11–27.

Watkins, C., Carnell, E. and Lodge, C. (2007) *Effective Learning and Classrooms*, London: Sage Publications.

Weale, S. (2017) 'Primary school children lose marks in Sats tests for misshapen commas', *The Guardian*, 10 July. Available from: www.theguardian.com/education/2017/jul/10/primary-school-children-lose-marks-in-sats-tests-for-mis-shaped-commas (accessed August 2019).

Wearmouth, J. (2017) *Special Educational Needs and Disabilities in Schools: A Critical Introduction*, London: Bloomsbury Publishing.

Webster, R. (2017) 'The five steps teaching assistants must follow to increase student independence', *Times Educational Supplement*, 26 March 2017. Available from: www.tes.com/news/five-steps-teaching-assistants-must-follow-increase-student-independence.

Webster, R. and Blatchford, P. (2013) *Making a Statement (MAST) Report*. Available from: www.maximisingtas.co.uk (accessed 22 September 2018).

Webster, R. and Blatchford, P. (2015) 'Worlds apart? The nature and quality of the educational experiences of pupils with a statement for special educational needs in mainstream primary schools', *British Educational Research Journal*, 41(2), 324-342. doi: 10.1002/berj.3144.

Webster, R. and Blatchford, P. (2017) *The Special Needs in Secondary Education (SENSE) Study: Executive Summary*, London: University of London Institute of Education. Available from: www.maximisingtas.co.uk (accessed 22 September 2018).

Wedell, K. (2008) 'Inclusion: Confusion about inclusion: Patching up or system change?', *British Journal of Special Education*, 35(3), 127-135.

Wegerif, R. and Dawes, L. (2004) *Thinking and Learning with ICT: Raising Achievement in Primary Classrooms*, London: Routledge.

Weintrop, D. and Wilensky, U. (2015) 'Using commutative assessments to compare conceptual understanding in blocks-based and text-based programs'. In: *Eleventh Annual International Conference on International Computing Education Research (ICER '15)*, 09-13 July 2015, ACM, pp. 101-110.

Welsh Government (2017) *Digital Competence Framework*, Cardiff: Welsh Government.

Wenger, E. (1998) *Communities of Practice: Learning, Meaning and Identity*, New York: Cambridge University Press.

West, P., Sweeting, H. and Young, R. (2010) 'Transition matters: Pupils' experiences of the primary-secondary school transition in the West of Scotland and consequences for well-being and attainment', *Research Papers in Education*, 25(1), 21-50.

Westerhof, G.J. and Keyes, C.L.M. (2010) 'Mental illness and mental health: The two continua model across the lifespan', *Journal of Adult Development*, 17(2), 110-119.

White, J. (2007) 'What schools are for and why', *Impact*, 14(14), pp. vi-51.

Wiles, R., Heath, S., Crow, G. and Charles, V. (2005) *Informed Consent in Social Research: A Literature Review*, NCRM Methods Review Papers, NCRM/001. Available from: http://eprints.ncrm.ac.uk/85/1/MethodsReviewPaperNCRM-001.pdf.

Wiliam, D. (2000) 'Integrating summative and formative functions of assessment', *Keynote Address to the European Association for Educational Assessment*, Prague.

Wiliam, D. (2011) *Embedded Formative Assessment*, Bloomington, IN: Solution-Tree.

Wiliam, D. (2013) *Principled Curriculum Design*, London: SSAT (The Schools Network) Limited. Available from: https://webcontent.ssatuk.co.uk/wp-content/uploads/2013/09/Dylan-Wiliam-Principled-curriculum-design-chapter-1.pdf (accessed 24 November 2018).

Wiliam, D. (2014) *Redesigning Schooling: Principled Assessment Design*, SSAT (The Schools Network). Available on the SSAT website.

Williamson, B. (2017) 'Coding for what? Lessons from computing in the curriculum', *NAACE Advancing Education Journal*. Available from: https://mirandanet.ac.uk/blog/2017/09/02/coding-lessons-computing-curriculum/ (accessed 24 November 2018).

Wilshaw, M. (2014) Quoted in R. Adams 'Headteachers too soft on unruly pupils, says Ofsted chief Sir Michael Wilshaw', *The Guardian*, 25 September. Available from: https://www.theguardian.com/education/2014/sep/25/headteachers-too-soft-unruly-pupils-ofsted-chief-sir-michael-wilshaw (accessed 18 August 2019).

Winch, C. (2010) 'Theory, underpinning knowledge and practice'. In: C. Winch (ed.) *Dimensions of Expertise: A Conceptual Exploration of Vocational Knowledge*, London: Continuum.

Wubbels, T. (2011) 'An international perspective on classroom management: What should prospective teachers learn?', *Teaching Education*, 22(2), 113-131.

Wyse, D., Baumfield, V.M., Egan, D., Hayward, L., Hulme, M. and Gallagher, C. (2013) *Creating the Curriculum*, Abingdon: Routledge.

YMCA (2016) *Eudaimonia: How Do Humans Flourish? A Research Report into the Impact of Lifestyle Factors on People's Wellbeing Found That Financial Confidence Was the Factor That Has the Most Impact on Wellbeing*, London: YMCA.

Young, M. (2009) 'What are schools for?' In: H. Daniels, D. Lauder and J. Porter (eds.) *Knowledge, Values and Educational Policy: A Critical Perspective*, Abingdon: Routledge, pp. 10-18.

Zack, V. and Graves, B. (2001) 'Making mathematical meaning through dialogue: "Once you think of it, the Z minus three seems pretty weird"', *Educational Studies in Mathematics*, 46(1/3), 229-271.

Zagona, A.L., Kurth, J.A. and MacFarland, S.Z.C. (2017) 'Teachers' views of their preparation for inclusive education and collaboration', *Teacher Education and Special Education*, 40(3), 163-178. doi: 10.1177/0888406417692969.

Zeedyk, S., Gallacher, J., Henderson, M., Hope, G., Husband, B. and Lindsay, K. (2003) 'Negotiating the transition from primary to secondary school. Perceptions of pupils, parents and teachers', *School Psychology International*, 24(1), 67-79.

Zwozdiak-Myers, P. and Capel, S. (2019) 'Communicating with pupils'. In: S. Capel, M. Leask and S. Younie (eds.) *Learning to Teach in the Secondary School: A Companion to School Experience*, 8th edn, Abingdon: Routledge, pp. 123-141.

AUTHOR INDEX

SUBJECT INDEX